T0138634

The Real-Time Enterprise

OTHER AUERBACH PUBLICATIONS

The Real-Time Enterprise

Dimitris N. Chorafas

AUERBACH PUBLICATIONS

A CRC Press Company

Boca Raton   London   New York   Washington, D.C.

Library of Congress Cataloging-in-Publication Data

Chorafas, Dimitris N.
    The real-time enterprise / Dimitris N. Chorafas.
    p. cm.
    Includes bibliographical references and index.
    ISBN 0-8493-2777-6 (alk. paper)
    1. Real-time data processing — Management. 2. Business — Data
processing — Management. 3. Information technology — Management.
4. Real-time control. 5. Business enterprises — Technological
innovations I. Title.

HF5548.3.C46 2004
658'.05—dc22   2004053127

Visit the Auerbach Publications Web site at www.auerbach-publications.com

© 2005 by CRC Press
Auerbach is an imprint of CRC Press

No claim to original U.S. Government works
International Standard Book Number 0-8493-2777-6
Library of Congress Card Number 2004053127
Printed in the United States of America 1 2 3 4 5 6 7 8 9 0
Printed on acid-free paper

CONTENTS

PREFACE

The rapid advancement of technology has brought up the issue of *cultural change*. Only people with conceptual skills and companies with superior organization can readily capitalize on the sophisticated information systems currently at our disposal and be able to use them to gain competitive advantages. This is the general background of this book on *The Real-Time Enterprise*.

The text has been designed both for professionals and for the academic market, particularly seniors and graduate students in colleges and universities. A major part of the contents is based on an extensive research project done by the author in 2003 in the United States, United Kingdom, and continental Europe.

In regard to the professional market, the book addresses all levels of management as well as practitioners in information technology. It is for anyone with responsibility for planning, developing, applying, and delivering advanced information systems: chief information officers, systems architects, system designers, management services directors — and end users.

The central theme of this text is the changing role of technology and the ongoing transition taking place in business, industry, and the economy at large. To master this transition, we must learn how to organize the future to compete with the present. This brings under perspective three issues central to any successful financial and industrial enterprise:

- *Seeing the future*, a concept that in times of rapid change distinguishes successful companies from those that encounter problems
- *Gaining technological leadership*, along with the ability to understand the changes needed, inspire people, and provide a sound basis for planning and control
- *Capitalizing on in-house experience and skills*, through straight through processing, reality online, knowledge management, a corporate memory facility, client mirror, and overall real-time solutions

The text brings the reader's attention to the fact that critical to good management is the identification of cost and return derived from the implementation of new technology. Help can be found by asking critical questions: What sort of conditions may the twenty-first century technology bring for which a company must be prepared? Are there real benefits? What is the best way to achieve them?

The most critical questions address themselves to executives and technologists who approve, evaluate, or make proposals for the justification of investments in information technology. This means people concerned with preparation, implementation, and control of IT budgets; establishment of programs; control of projects; and responsibilities for day-to-day and longer-term management of technology.

Through a practical, documented approach based on case studies, personal experience, and interviews with experts, 17 chapters analyze the forward-looking implementation of IT in an enterprise. They do so by focusing on the many opportunities that exist through better organization for *improving* a company's efficiency while *reducing* its operating costs.

The case studies describe, in realistic terms, how to select the level of technology and to evaluate its return. Emphasis is placed on management's wish to estimate the most likely benefits to be derived from the huge amount of money spend on computers, communications, software, and personnel. Practical cases have been particularly chosen to provide insight and foresight on the fact that in the twenty-first century the most profitable use of technology is to serve in real-time customer requirements, and to improve our knowledge of the market and of *our* business partners. The epoch in which technology was employed as a means of automating data processing, substituting clerical work, and (hopefully) reducing paperwork is resolutely past.

The book is divided into four parts. Part One documents the reason why advanced information technology is a moving target and why companies that want to reach it set priorities and move quickly. An example is provided by the concept of the real-time enterprise and the implementation of superior organization by top-tier financial institutions and industrial firms. This is the theme of Chapter 1.

Chapter 2 explains why technological advances may never become meaningful to companies spending money on them unless their practical application fits into and promotes the goals established by the company's strategic plan. The use of technology to reach specific objectives is not only the best approach through which to examine current trends in information technology — it is the only one, as Chapter 3 suggests. Chapter 4 further promotes this concept by explaining why the use of *high technology* is a matter of business survival, not of scientific curiosity.

Part Two covers some of the most recent developments in information technology and its implementation. Using practical examples, Chapter 5 provides a definition of straight through processing (STP) as well as examples on its contribution to transaction handling. Chapter 6 addresses the ever-important issue of data capture at point of origin, using the modern paradigm of reality online.

The next two chapters provide the reader with the latest developments in executive information systems (EIS) and client information systems (CIS). Chapter 7 provides practical examples on EIS from business and industry, including the notion of corporate memory facility. Chapter 8 introduces the reader to new concepts like the virtual double; it also explains the importance of customer mirror.

Part Three is dedicated to case studies with real-time enterprises. Each of its four chapters addresses a specific applications area: Chapter 9, real-time applications including the use of knowledge engineering among the most advanced credit institutions; Chapter 10, real-time treasury operations; Chapter 11, real-time solutions for more effective risk management; and Chapter 12, the implementation of real-time approaches to replace office automation.

Advanced applications, like those covered by the first 12 chapters of this book, pose significant prerequisites, the theme of Part Four. Chapter 13 outlines the characteristics of a business architecture that helps in providing real-time support; as well as the transition to this architecture. Because data quality is a most critical problem to every organization, Chapter 14 concentrates on prerequisites for data quality and online data mining.

The subject of Chapter 15 is a case study–based approach to how financial institutions use and misuse the Internet. Lessons learned from current applications on the Internet are then employed as the background for efficient end-to-end solutions and for obtaining better deliverables. This is done within the content of an Internet ecosystem in Chapter 16.

Last but not least, attention is paid to business continuity, the aftermath of operational risk, contingency planning, and damage control. These four themes to which Chapter 17 addresses itself are the *alter ego* of the real-time enterprise.

* * *

This is a basic text on goals, tools, and perspectives regarding the deployment of strategic information technology. It covers both guidelines and advanced applications in a presentation enriched with practical examples and with a number of comprehensive case studies. The aim is to provide a much-needed upgrade of knowledge and skills for professionals and for technologists seeking solutions beyond the confines of the more traditional-type IT implementations.

* * *

I am indebted to a long list of knowledgeable people and organizations for their contribution to the research that made this book possible, as well as to several senior executives and experts for contributing not only their experience but also constructive criticism during the preparation of the manuscript.

Let me take this opportunity to thank John Wyzalek for suggesting this project and seeing it all the way to publication, and Sally Wade and Lynn Goeller for the editing work. To Eva-Maria Binder goes the credit for compiling the research results, typing the text, and preparing the camera-ready artwork and index.

Dr. Dimitris N. Chorafas

ACKNOWLEDGMENTS

(Countries are listed in alphabetical order)
The following organizations, through their senior executives and system specialists, participated in the recent research projects that led to the contents of this book and its documentation.

Austria

National Bank of Austria
Dr. Martin Ohms, Finance Market
   Analysis Department
Vienna

Association of Austrian Banks and Bankers
Dr. Fritz Diwok, Secretary General
Vienna

Bank Austria
Dr. Peter Fischer, Senior General
   Manager, Treasury Division
Peter Gabriel, Deputy General
   Manager, Trading
Vienna

Die Erste (First Austrian Bank)
Franz Reif, Head of Group Risk
   Control
Vienna

Creditanstalt
Dr. Wolfgang Lichtl, Market Risk
   Management
Vienna

Wiener Betriebs and Baugesellschaft mbH
Dr. Josef Fritz, General Manager
Vienna

France

Banque de France
Pierre Jaillet, Director, Monetary
   Studies and Statistics
Yvan Oronnal, Manager, Monetary
   Analyses and Statistics
G. Tournemire, Analyst, Monetary
   Studies
Paris

Secretariat Général de la Commission Bancaire — Banque de France
Didier Peny, Director, Control of
   Big Banks and International
   Banks
F. Visnowsky, Manager of International Affairs, Supervisory Policy
   and Research Division
Benjamin Sahel, Market Risk
   Control
Paris

Ministry of Finance and the Economy, Conseil National de la Comptabilité
Alain Le Bars, Director International
   Relations and Cooperation
Paris

Germany

Deutsche Bundesbank
Hans-Dietrich Peters, Director
Hans Werner Voth, Director
Dr. Frank Heid, Banking and
  Financial Supervision Department
Frankfurt am Main

Federal Banking Supervisory Office
Hans-Joachim Dohr, Director Dept. I
Jochen Kayser, Risk Model Exami-
  nation
Ludger Hanenberg, Internal Controls
Berlin

European Central Bank
Mauro Grande, Director
Frankfurt am Main

Deutsches Aktieninstitut
Dr. Rüdiger Von Rosen, President
Frankfurt am Main

Commerzbank
Peter Bürger, Senior Vice President,
  Strategy and Controlling
Markus Rumpel, Senior Vice Presi-
  dent, Credit Risk Management
Frankfurt am Main

Deutsche Bank
Prof. Manfred Timmermann, Head
  of Controlling
Rainer Rauleder, Global Head
  Capital Management
Hans Voit, Head of Process Manage-
  ment, Controlling Department
Frankfurt am Main

Dresdner Bank
Oliver Ewald, Head of Strategic Risk
  & Treasury Control
Dr. Marita Balks, Investment Bank,
  Risk Control
Dr. Hermann Haaf, Mathematical
  Models for Risk Control
Claas Carsten Kohl, Financial
  Engineer
Frankfurt am Main

Volkswagen Foundation
Katja Ebeling, Office of the General
  Secretary
Hanover

Herbert Quandt Foundation
Dr. Kai Schellhorn, Member of the
  Board
Munich

*GMD First — Research Institute for
Computer Architecture, Software
Technology and Graphics*
Prof. Dr. Ing. Wolfgang K. Giloi,
  General Manager
Berlin

Hungary

*Hungarian Banking and Capital
Market Supervision*
Dr. Janos Kun, Head, Department of
  Regulation and Analyses
Dr. Erika Voros, Senior Economist,
  Department of Regulation and
  Analyses
Dr. Géza Nyiry, Head, Section of
  Information Audit
Budapest

Hungarian Academy of Sciences
Prof. Tibor Vamos, Chairman,
  Computer and Automation
  Research Institute
Budapest

Iceland

The National Bank of Iceland Ltd
Gunnar T. Andersen, Managing
  Director, International Banking &
  Treasury
Reykjavik

India

i-flex
H. S. Rajashekar, Principal
  Consultant, Risk Management
Bangalore

Italy

Banca d'Italia
Eugene Gaiotti, Research Department, Monetary and Financial Division
Ing. Dario Focarelli, Research Department
Rome

Istituto Bancario San Paolo di Torino
Dr. Paolo Chiulenti, Director of Budgeting
Roberto Costa, Director of Private Banking
Pino Ravelli, Director Bergamo Region
Bergamo

Luxembourg

Banque Générale de Luxembourg
Prof. Yves Wagner, Director of Asset and Risk Management
Hans Jörg Paris, International Risk Manager
Luxembourg

Clearstream
André Lussi, President and CEO
Luxembourg

The Netherlands

ABN Amro
Jos Weileman, Senior VP Group Risk Management
Amsterdam

Poland

Securities and Exchange Commission
Beata Stelmach, Secretary of the Commission
Warsaw

Sweden

The Royal Swedish Academy of Sciences
Dr. Solgerd Bjorn-Rasmussen, Head Information Department

Dr. Olof Tanberg, Foreign Secretary
Stockholm

Skandinaviska Enskilda Banken
Bernt Gyllenswärd, Head of Group Audit
Stockholm

Irdem AB
Gian Medri, Former Director of Research at Nordbanken
Sollentuna

Switzerland

Swiss National Bank
Dr. Werner Hermann, Head of International Monetary Relations
Dr. Bertrand Rime, Vice President, Representative to the Basle Committee
Prof. Urs Birchler, Director, Advisor on Systemic Stability
Zurich

Federal Banking Commission
Dr. Susanne Brandenberger, Risk Management
Renate Lischer, Representative to Risk Management Subgroup, Basle Committee
Bern

Bank for International Settlements
Mr. Claude Sivy, Head of Internal Audit
Stephen Senior, Member of the Secretariat, Basle Committee on Banking Supervision
Hirotaka Hideshima, Member of the Secretariat, Basle Committee on Banking Supervision
Herbie Poenisch, Senior Economist, Monetary and Economic Department
Ingo Fender, Committee on the Global Financial System
Basle

Crédit Suisse
Dr. Harry Stordel, Director, Group
  Risk Management
Christian A. Walter, Vice President,
  Risk Management
Ahmad Abu El-Aat, Managing
  Director, Head of IT Office
Dr. Burkhard P. Varnholt, Managing
  Director, Global Research
Zurich

Bank Leu AG
Dr. Urs Morgenthaler, Member of
  Management, Director of Risk
  Control
Zurich

*Bank J. Vontobel and Vontobel
Holding*
Heinz Frauchiger, Chief, Internal
  Audit Department
Zurich

United Bank of Switzerland
Dr. Heinrich Steinmann, Member of
  the Executive Board (Retired)
Zurich

UBS Financial Services Group
Dr. Per-Göran Persson, Executive
  Director, Group Strategic Analysis
George Pastrana, Executive, Eco-
  nomic Capital Allocation
Zurich

University of Fribourg
Prof. Dr. Jürgen Kohlas
Prof. Dr. Andreas Meier
Fribourg

Swiss Re
Dr. Thomas Hess, Head of Economic
  Research & Consulting
Zürich

United Kingdom
Bank of England
Richard Britton, Director, Complex
  Groups Division, CGD Policy
  Department

Ian M. Michael, Senior Manager,
  Financial Industry and Regulation
  Division
London

Financial Services Authority (FSA)
Lieselotte Burgdorf-Cook, Interna-
  tional Relations
London

British Bankers Association
Paul Chisnall, Assistant Director
London

Accounting Standards Board
A.V.C. Cook, Technical Director
Sandra Thompson, Project Director
London

Barclays Bank Plc
Brandon Davies, Treasurer, Global
  Corporate Banking
Tim Thompson, Head of Economic
  Capital
Julian Knight, Manager, Group Risk
  Analysis and Policy
Alan Brown, Director, Group Risk
London

Citigroup
Dr. David Lawrence, European
  Head of Risk Methodologies and
  Analytics
London

Rabobank Nederland
Eugen Buck, Managing Director,
  Senior Project Manager Economic
  Capital
London

*Abbey National Treasury Services
plc*
John Hasson, Director of Informa-
  tion Technology & Treasury
  Operations
London

ABN-AMRO Investment Bank N.V.
David Woods, Chief Operations
  Officer, Global Equity Directorate

Annette C. Austin, Head of Operational
Risk Management Wholesale Client
London

Bankgesellschaft Berlin
Stephen F. Myers, Head of Market Risk
London

Standard & Poor's
David T. Beers, Managing Director,
Sovereign & International Public
Finance Ratings
Barbara Ridpath, Managing Director,
Chief Credit Officer, Europe
Walter Pompliano, Director, Finan-
cial Institutions Group, Financial
Services Ratings
London

Moody's Investor Services
Samuel S. Theodore, Managing
Director, European Banks
David Frohriep, Communications
Manager, Europe
London

Moody's KMV
Alastair Graham, Senior Vice
President, Director of Global
Training
Lynn Valkenaar, Project Manager, KMV
Lars Hunsche, Manager
London

Fitch Ratings
Charles Prescott, Group Managing
Director
David Andrews, Managing Director,
Financial Institutions
Travor Pitman, Managing Director,
Corporations
Richard Fox, Director, International
Public Finance
London

A.M. Best Europe
Jose Sanchez-Crespo, General
Manager
Mark Colman, Financial Analyst
London

Merrill Lynch International
Bart Dowling, Director, Global
Asset Allocation
Elena Dimova, Vice President,
Equity Sales
Erik Banks, Managing Director of
Risk Management
London

The Auditing Practices Board
Jonathan E.C. Grant, Technical
Director
Steve Leonard, Internal Controls
Project Manager
London

*International Accounting Standards
Committee*
Ms. Liesel Knorr, Technical Director
London

MeesPierson ICS
Arjan P. Verkerk, Director, Market Risk
London

Charles Schwab
Dan Hattrup, International Invest-
ment Specialist
London

Charity Commission
Susan Polak
Mike McKillop
J. Chauhan
London

The Wellcome Trust
Clare Matterson, Member of the Ex-
ecutive Board and Head of Policy
London

*Association of Charitable
Foundations*
Nigel Suederer, Chief Executive
London

IBM United Kingdom
Derek Duerden, Technical Strategy,
EMEA Banking Finance & Securi-
ties Business
London

City University Business School
Professor Elias Dinenis, Head,
   Department of Investment, Risk
   Management & Insurance
Prof. Dr. John Hadnioannides,
   Department of Finance
London

TT International
Timothy A. Tacchi, Co-Chief
   Executive Officer
Henry Bedford, Co-Chief Executive
   Officer
Robin A.E. Hunt
London

*Alternative Investment Management
Association (AIMA)*
Emma Mugridge, Director
London

Ernst & Young
Pierre-Yves Maurois, Senior Man-
   ager, Risk Management and
   Regulatory Services
London

Brit Syndicates Limited at Lloyd's
Peter Chrismas, Hull Underwriter
Anthony Forsyth, Marine Underwriter
London

Trema UK Ltd
Dr. Vincent Kilcoyne, Business
   Architecture
London

STP Information Systems
Graeme Austin, Managing Director
London

United States

*Federal Reserve System, Board of
Governors*
David L. Robinson, Deputy Director,
   Chief Federal Reserve Examiner
Alan H. Osterholm, CIA, CISA,
   Manager, Financial Examinations
   Section

Paul W. Bettge, Assistant Director,
   Division of Reserve Bank Operations
Gregory E. Eller, Supervisory
   Financial Analyst, Banking
Gregory L. Evans, Manager, Finan-
   cial Accounting
Martha Stallard, Financial Account-
   ing, Reserve Bank Operations
Washington, District of Columbia

Federal Reserve Bank of Boston
William McDonough, Executive
   Vice President
James T. Nolan, Assistant Vice
   President
Boston, Massachusetts

*Federal Reserve Bank of San
Francisco*
Nigel R. Ogilvie, CFA, Supervising
   Financial Analyst, Emerging Issues
San Francisco, California

*Seattle Branch, Federal Reserve
Bank of San Francisco*
Jimmy F. Kamada, Assistant Vice
   President
Gale P. Ansell, Assistant Vice
   President, Business Development
Seattle, Washington

*Office of the Comptroller of the
Currency (OCC)*
Bill Morris, National Bank Exam-
   iner/Policy Analyst, Core Policy
   Development Division
Gene Green, Deputy Chief Accountant,
   Office of the Chief Accountant
Washington, District of Columbia

*Federal Deposit Insurance
Corporation (FDIC)*
Curtis Wong, Capital Markets,
   Examination Support
Tanya Smith, Examination Special-
   ist, International Branch
Doris L. Marsh, Examination
   Specialist, Policy Branch
Washington, District of Columbia

Office of Thrift Supervision (OTS)
Timothy J. Stier, Chief Accountant
Washington, District of Columbia

Securities and Exchange Commission, Washington, D.C.
Robert Uhl, Professional Accounting Fellow
Pascal Desroches, Professional Accounting Fellow
John W. Albert, Associate Chief Accountant
Scott Baylsess, Associate Chief Accountant
Washington, District of Columbia

Securities and Exchange Commission, New York
Robert A. Solazzo, Associate Regional Director
New York, New York

Securities and Exchange Commission, Boston
Edward A. Ryan, Jr., Assistant District Administrator (Regulations)
Boston, Massachusetts

Microsoft
Dr. Gordon Bell, Senior Researcher
San Francisco, California

American Bankers Association
Dr. James Chessen, Chief Economist
Mr. Douglas Johnson, Senior Policy Analyst
Washington, District of Columbia

International Monetary Fund
Alain Coune, Assistant Director, Office of Internal Audit and Inspection
Washington, District of Columbia

Financial Accounting Standards Board
Halsey G. Bullen, Project Manager
Jeannot Blanchet, Project Manager
Teri L. List, Practice Fellow
Norwalk, Connecticut

Henry Kaufman & Company
Dr. Henry Kaufman
New York, New York

Soros Fund Management
George Soros, Chairman
New York, New York

Carnegie Corporation of New York
Armanda Famiglietti, Associate Corporate Secretary, Director of Grants Management
New York, New York

Alfred P. Sloan Foundation
Stewart F. Campbell, Financial Vice President and Secretary
New York, New York

Rockefeller Brothers Fund
Benjamin R. Shute, Jr., Secretary
New York, New York

The Foundation Center
New York, New York

Citibank
Daniel Schutzer, Vice President, Director of Advanced Technology
New York, New York

Swiss Re
David S. Laster, PhD, Senior Economist
New York, New York

Prudential-Bache Securities
Bella Loykhter, Senior Vice President, Information Technology
Kenneth Musco, First Vice President and Director, Management Internal Control
Neil S. Lerner, Vice President, Management Internal Control
New York, New York

Merrill Lynch
John J. Fosina, Director, Planning and Analysis
Paul J. Fitzsimmons, Senior Vice President, District Trust Manager

David E. Radcliffe, Senior Vice President, National Manager Philanthropic Consulting
New York, New York

Permal Asset Management
Isaac R. Souede, President and CEO
New York, New York

HSBC Republic
Susan G. Pearce, Senior Vice President
Philip A. Salazar, Executive Director
New York, New York

International Swaps and Derivatives Association (ISDA)
Susan Hinko, Director of Policy
New York, New York

Standard & Poor's
Clifford Griep, Managing Director
Mary Peloquin-Dodd, Director, Public Finance Ratings
New York, New York

Moody's KMV
Askish Das, Analyst
Michele Freed, Analyst
San Francisco, California

Moody's KMV
Marc Bramer, Vice President, Strategic Clients
South Bend, Indiana

State Street Bank and Trust
James J. Barr, Executive Vice President, U.S. Financial Assets Services
Boston, Massachusetts

MBIA Insurance Corporation
John B. Caouett, Vice Chairman
Armonk, New York

Global Association of Risk Professionals (GARP)
Lev Borodovski, Executive Director, GARP, and Director of Risk Management, Credit Suisse First Boston (CSFB), New York

Yong Li, Director of Education, GARP, and Vice President, Lehman Brothers, New York
Dr. Frank Leiber, Research Director, and Assistant Director of Computational Finance, Cornell University, Theory Center, New York
Roy Nawal, Director of Risk Forums, GARP
Thornwood, New York

Group of Thirty
John Walsh, Director
Washington, District of Columbia

Broadcom Corporation
Dr. Henry Samueli, Co-Chairman of the Board, Chief Technical Officer
Irvine, California

Edward Jones
Ann Ficken, Director, Internal Audit
Maryland Heights, Missouri

Teachers Insurance and Annuity Association/College Retirement Equities Fund (TIAA/CREF)
John W. Sullivan, Senior Institutional Trust Consultant
Charles S. Dvorkin, Vice President and Chief Technology Officer
Harry D. Perrin, Assistant Vice President, Information Technology
Patty Steinbach, Investment Advisor
Tim Prosser, Lawyer
New York, New York

Sterling Foundation Management
Dr. Roger D. Silk, Principal
Sherman Oaks, California

Grenzebach Glier & Associates, Inc.
John J. Glier, President and Chief Executive Officer
Chicago, Illinois

Massachusetts Institute of Technology
Peggy Carney, Administrator, Graduate Office

Michael Coen, PhD Candidate, ARPA Intelligent Environment Project Cambridge, Massachusetts

New York University, Stern School of Business
Edward I. Altman, Professor of Finance and Vice Director, NYU Salomon Center
New York, New York

Henry Samueli School of Engineering and Applied Science, University of California, Los Angeles
Dean A.R. Frank Wazzan, School of Engineering and Applied Science
Prof. Stephen E. Jacobson, Dean of Student Affairs
Dr. Les Lackman, Mechanical and Aerospace Engineering Department
Prof. Richard Muntz, Chair, Computer Science Department
Prof. Dr. Leonard Kleinrock, Telecommunications and Networks
Prof. Chih-Ming Ho, PhD, Ben Rich-Lockheed Martin Professor, Mechanical and Aerospace Engineering Department
Dr. Gang Chen, Mechanical and Aerospace Engineering Department
Prof. Harold G. Monbouquette, PhD, Chemical Engineering Department
Prof. Jack W. Judy, Electrical Engineering Department
Abeer Alwan, Bioengineering
Prof. Greg Pottie, Electrical Engineering Department
Prof. Lieven Vanderberghe, Electrical Engineering Department

Anderson Graduate School of Management, University of California, Los Angeles
Prof. John Mamer, Former Dean
Prof. Bruce Miller

Roundtable Discussion on Engineering and Management Curriculum (October 2, 2000)
Dr. Henry Borenstein, Honeywell
Dr. F. Issacci, Honeywell
Dr. Ray Haynes, TRW
Dr. Richard Croxall, TRW
Dr. Steven Bouley, Boeing
Dr. Derek Cheung, Rockwell
Los Angeles, California

University of Maryland
Prof. Howard Frank, Dean, The Robert H. Smith School of Business
Prof. Lemma W. Senbert, Chair, Finance Department
Prof. Haluk Unal, Associate Professor of Finance
College Park, Maryland

Gartner Group
David C. Furlonger, Vice President & Research Director, Gartner Financial Services
Raleigh, North Carolina

Accenture
Stanton J. Taylor, Partner
Dr. Andrew E. Fano, Associate Partner
Dr. Cem Batdar, Analyst
Kishire S. Swaminathan, Analyst
Chicago, Illinois

1

ADVANCED
INFORMATION
TECHNOLOGY
IS A
MOVING TARGET

1

TECHNOLOGY AND THE REAL-TIME ENTERPRISE

1.1   INTRODUCTION

In an October 2003 lecture, Roger W. Ferguson, Jr., vice chairman of the Federal Reserve, remarked that technological change has played an important role in improving risk measurement at financial institutions. This may be one reason why banks have weathered the 2000 to 2003 economic downturn. Ferguson also emphasized the role of technology in breaking down traditional distinctions between commercial banking, investment banking, and insurance — to the point that the Gramm–Leach–Bliley Act can be thought of as a response to technological change.

Phil Condit, the CEO of Boeing, says it is the way that information technology (IT) has changed business processes that is reaping rewards for manufacturers today. His company's new aircraft could not have been developed so quickly without the benefit of investment in up-to-date IT — which means that parts for the plane can be produced more accurately right from the start, eliminating the need for expensive rework, as well as for tools on the assembly floor to hold parts in position while fitters trim to get everything to match.[1]

This is by no means the first time technological change has attracted the attention of people responsible for the evolution of an industry or its regulation. The results of technology become embedded in the design, production, distribution, and consumption of goods, which inspires the work of engineers, economists, salespeople, and public administrators. However, not all of their proposals materialize.

As an example of predictions that have not come true, Ferguson mentioned a forecast of several decades ago that technological change would end the use of paper checks and make the brick-and-mortar branches of commercial banks obsolete. As we know, the paper check is still very much in use and the number of brick-and-mortar branches did not appreciably change.

Other things, however, did develop as predicted, for example, the change in work habits made possible through technology. An interesting case is that of time transformation from clock time "t" to what is called at various places *business time, activity time, or intrinsic time.* It may sound paradoxical, but five minutes of business activity in New York is not equal to five minutes in Tokyo, Istanbul, or Lagos.

Istanbul's *Daily News* had this to say when comparing business time in Turkey and in Japan:

> Time is moving faster in Japan. Japan and Turkey occupy the opposite ends of Asia . . . (Business time differences are important because) globalization is knocking on our door . . . Developing and developed countries have become neighbors in more than just the geographical sense . . .[2]

As Marcel Proust said, "The days may be equal for a clock, but they are not for a person."

In New York and in Tokyo time moves faster because business activity is more intense. In Istanbul and in Lagos, by contrast, it moves slower due to the inverse reasons. Figure 1.1 provides an example of what this means in business terms. The *real-time enterprise* is an agent of this change in speed of financial and industrial activity. Another agent is the environment in which business time transformation takes place and its aftereffects. Companies that work through low technology in a high-tech business environment get obliterated. Companies able to implement high technology in an otherwise lower-technology business landscape move ahead of the curve.

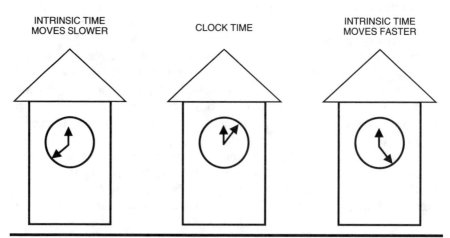

Figure 1.1   Intrinsic Time Can be Shorter or Much Longer than Clock Time

In the term "real-time enterprise," *real-time* means that transactions are executed by straight through processing (see Chapter 5); information is captured at point of origin through reality online (see Chapter 6); and databases are updated continuously, shared, and mined (see Chapter 14) in ways that makes their content more meaningful and more actionable.

The result gives information technology (IT) the potential for real impact, for instance, making it feasible to significantly improve the use of physical assets, and thus of operations and running a business far more efficiently than would otherwise be possible.

Is this sounding *déjà vu*? It might be. However, we are at a turning point of using technology in business — a point at which advanced holistic solutions count much more than advances in devices. To continue delivering results, holistic solutions require postmortems. Samuel Johnson (1709–1784) once said:

> I know not anything more pleasant, or more instructive, than to compare experience with expectation, or to register from time to time the difference between idea and reality. It is by this kind of observation that we grow daily less liable to be disappointed.

1.2 FORESIGHT, INSIGHT, AND COMPETITIVE ADVANTAGES

In October 2003, a number of scientists and engineers gathered in Oxford for the first International Workshop on Complex Agent-Based Dynamic Networks. Several papers presented sought to explain the world's behavior through the use of *agents*, mobile knowledge artifacts that serve their masters but also may act in a self-interested manner in their dealings with other agents inside a network.[3]

One of the papers highlighted the ability of this arrangement to mimic almost *any interactive system*, from a stockmarket to a business supply chain. The discussion that followed, however, brought attention to the fact that, while the underlying concept is interesting, there are many unknowns and a long list of challenges in understanding agent interactions and setting up agent-based environments.

Not the least of the challenges is that of clearly defining what individual agents, particularly those able to learn from their actions, want to achieve. This reservation seems reasonable enough, and there is no difficulty in accepting it. But at the same time, it is just as true that the challenge being described is much more general, because it is faced by every enterprise with or without the use of agents. First and foremost, this is a management challenge.

Another issue brought into perspective at the conference is that simplifications do not always help and lack of constraints may lead to excesses. Some other findings, too, were interesting, for example, that the market is less efficient than people think — partly because of parasitic strategies, which try to game the system.

One of the agent-based models was designed to study the behavior of individual market makers in attempting to find the true value of an asset. In the simulation, a market value was assigned arbitrarily and was not told to the agents; they had to work it out. The simulated trading environment had to arrive at an approximation of fair value. It did so by using a zero-profit strategy, and implying restrictions on the prices that a market maker sets for buying and selling shares.

Market makers could make a profit by selling for slightly more and buying for slightly less than the formula dictated. When the experimenter simulated a market using this approximation, results matched the statistics of real-world markets. The concept behind the test engine reflected the fact that usually market makers behave instinctively and have difficulty explaining exactly how they set prices. This experience has the three characteristics implicitly presented in the Introduction:

- Online connectivity
- Real-time response
- In-context performance

All three are pillars of market behavior. It is the connectivity, real-time response, and in-context performance among market players — not one company alone — that sets the clock in motion. Nobody can tell exactly who builds up the momentum, though the market manages to unmistakably identify those companies that have a price advantage or disadvantage.

The results of the Oxford conference are so interesting because they provide evidence that, contrary to past notions about paperwork reduction and the like (which never really materialized), the main object of computing is foresight, insight, analysis, and design. It is not the automation of numerical calculation or of office functions. Though these aims, too, could be achieved at least part of the time, they constitute secondary issues to the survival of the fittest.

1.2.1 Real-Time Information's Cornerstones to Adaptation and Survival

In 1851, Charles Darwin published *Survival of the Fittest*, which concluded that only those able to adapt to the environment will survive. Two decades down the line, in 1872, Darwin improved upon his theory, and what he then said about survival can be applied to market economies because the market resembles a biological system. But there are also differences, particularly in the domain of intrinsic time. Nature is evolution in action. Such evolution, however, takes millions of years to materialize. By contrast, a modern economy evolves not in millions of years but in years, or months, or even weeks, with information and technology acting as accelerators.

The clock, not the steam engine, is the key machine of the modern industrial age. The computer is the extension of the clock. The orderly, punctual life that first took place in monasteries is native neither to nature nor to mankind, though by now western countries are thoroughly regimented by the clock: "Time is money."

Value creation, however, has prerequisites. It requires organization, technology, and skills — in short, persons and entities ahead of the others in terms of their competitiveness. On a level playing field, real-time information provides a cutting edge to companies in developing and marketing products and services. They are ahead of the curve because they have better information than do their competitors.

The trouble in many large enterprises is that endusers feel disenfranchised from their information technology systems, and even more so by the poorly planned covergence of telecommunications, databases, computing, and other business processes being supported. Old standards can no more satisfy:

■ Fast developing user requirements
■ Compliance to new regulatory rules

Today, global network management has much to do with what is going on at customer premises, and it is *not* just a matter of getting bandwidth across. Network monitoring and management should gauge service levels as endusers perceive them. This means that IT specialists should have a clearer understanding of business processes than ever before — and they should rethink the way they provide backup and recovery, as well as the way they support business continuity as the tragic events of September 11, 2001, documented.

1.2.2 Assisted by Experimentation, Analysis, and Design, An Enterprise May Reinvent Itself and Survive

To create a competitive advantage for itself, in a market economy a company has to be identified as a leader in a chosen field. This helps to establish and maintain a temporary monopoly that is renewable through innovation.

An example of gaining competitive advantages through information technology is presented in Figure 1.2, which traces more than a century in usage and misusage of IT. The careful reader will notice the reasons that divide, and are projected to continue dividing, winners and losers.

To be competitive and to sustain its competitiveness, a company must steadily evaluate itself, its clients, its products, its services, and its competitors. This is the role of executive information systems (see Chapter 7) and of

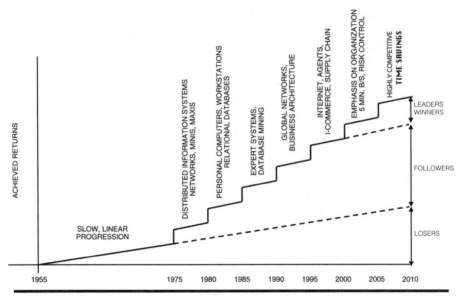

Figure 1.2 Quantum Jumps in Benefits Distinguish Winners

client information systems (see Chapter 8). It should do so against the market forces and its challengers in terms of costs, innovation, value differentiation, and the effectiveness of delivery channels.

Flexibility and profitability count a great deal. The same is true of cash flow and profits; as well as, most evidently, of accountability for results. Another "must" is steady vigilance, which is one of the benefits of real-time response. It is crucial because competitive advantages are quickly consumed by the action and reaction of competitors. Successful companies appreciate that to survive they have to reinvent themselves. To survive and prosper, companies must:

■ Rapidly renew their products.
■ Take products apart and redesign them.
■ Cut their processes and reassemble them.
■ Put their competitive advantages together again in a different way.

A certain sense of stability in this rapid transition is provided by the underlying business architecture (see Chapter 13), whereas the sustenance of a fast pace in product innovation is only possible by means of advanced technology — including increasingly intelligent systems. Technology, however, is not a goal but a means. A different way of making this statement is that world-class technology is absolutely necessary but in itself is not enough. We must create value in order to benefit from the law of survival of the fittest.

1.3   REINVENTING THE FUNCTIONS OF MANAGEMENT

The coordination of human effort is the essence of all group activities. The basic component of a coordinated effort is *management* — the process of getting things done through people. Although the Industrial Revolution of the nineteenth century is often regarded as a significant social and technical event, its most important impact has been the structuring of the functions of management and the processing of capitalism.

When we are dealing with capitalism, we confront an evolutionary process that is organizational and technological. The development of new products and the opening up of new markets are activities of industrial mutation that revolutionize the economic structure from within by destroying the old state of affairs and creating anew that which has its own prerequisites in terms of operations adaptation and renewal.

The development of a coherent organizational theory of Darwinian evolution built from the underlying mechanisms of mutation and selection is far from complete. But there is plenty of evidence that the six functions of management, shown in Figure 1.3, are changing in function of time and of tools available to accomplish them. They are changing because they are influenced by the challenges management must confront and the means that become available for their execution. Real-time information is one of them.

An organizational theory is composed of principles that explain relationships and facts. An organizational theory is evolutionary. *If* principles are basic truths that explain certain phenomena, as indeed they are, *then* there can be no inconsistency between theory and practice. When the fundamental facts change, the theory, too, has to change to reflect the new reality. The *theory of management* rests on this premise.

One of the reasons why the theory of management changes is that the technology which we use, in order to extend our reach, evolves. It is not always the best technology that wins; it is the best approach in using available technology. Technology acts as a catalyst in improving performance and in changing our environment to one in which there is more give and take within the company itself and between the company and its market.

For instance, one of the important management tools, especially now in the post-Enron era, is internal and external auditing — and, with it, internal control.[4] To be rigorous and independent in its management control functions, the board requires vast improvements, auditing theory and practice, which in turn call for better use of information technology. A focused auditing goal cannot be met through the gradual, slow-moving approach endemic in most companies.

"The greatness of any enterprise," says C. Northcote Parkinson, "depends upon leadership and leadership implies movement."[5] As far as planning, operating, and control activities are concerned, the modern company is

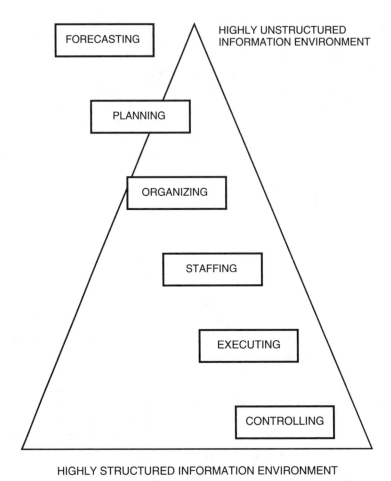

FORECASTING

HIGHLY UNSTRUCTURED
INFORMATION ENVIRONMENT

PLANNING

ORGANIZING

STAFFING

EXECUTING

CONTROLLING

HIGHLY STRUCTURED INFORMATION ENVIRONMENT

Figure 1.3   The Real-Time Enterprise Helps to Recast the Functions of Management

information in motion. Lack of information that is actual and accurate means mental stagnation, poor management, and bleak financial results.

Goldman Sachs puts senior managers to the test. As a fund manager, the company estimates that nearly one-quarter of Britain's top 100 companies are run by managers who are either poor or very poor performance wise. Goldman has also rated one in six of the best-known cross-border European companies as poorly managed.[6] Corporate scandals and bankruptcies have led to growing unease about the worth of chief executive officers (CEOs), prompting closer scrutiny by investors. The rankings allow Goldman Sachs to rate a company's leadership on:

- Competence
- Integrity
- Board structure
- Commitment to shareholders

The rating system uses a management quality score (MQS) together with a business quality score (BQS) to reach an overall judgment of a company. Goldman Sachs awards points on one-to-five scale, with one representing the superior mark and five the inferior. The lowest rating means that management may be placing their own interests above those of their shareholders and has a record of making bad deals that could have been driven by factors other than those that preserve the company's assets and shareholders' interest.

About a quarter of companies in the FTSE 100 (index for the London Stock Exchange) scored either four or five, and in continental Europe 36 known companies received a score of four or five in Goldman's classification. These results raised questions about top executives' spiraling pay. At FTSE 100 companies, for example, executives enjoyed an average salary rise of 9.7 percent during 2001 over the previous year. Other cash elements of their earnings rose by an average of nearly 11 percent — although management skill and performance have been found to be nearly dismal.

Real-time information technology will *not* make a good manager out of a bad manager, but lack of it may well turn a good manager into a bad one. Lack of timely information limits one's vision over the area of competition, because ignorance is added to other negative human traits like indifference and inertia. This has disastrous effects in an era of globalization, when corporate governance becomes so much more complex in topology and product channels, as Figure 1.4 indicates.

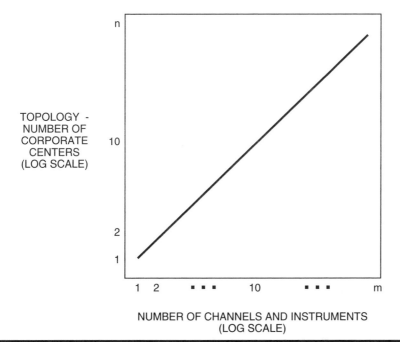

Figure 1.4   Corporate Governance Becomes More Complex with Globalization

Goldman Sachs is not the only entity interested in management quality and performance. Independent rating agencies, like Standard & Poor's (S&P) and Moody's Investors Service, are always alert to the quality of management and the way in which senior executives perform their duties. Although sound capitalization is necessary, it is not sufficient for a high credit rating. "We look at capital but also beyond capital," said Walter Pompliano of Standards & Poor's, for instance, "management decisions, management actions, and corporate outlook."

Other rating criteria that have a good deal to do with quality of management are risk appetite, risk control, access to funding, diversification, and change in risk profile. Any one of these factors going berserk would not allow high credit rating. Notice, however, that the two most important elements behind these factors are management skill and timely information — which speaks volumes about the competitive advantages of the real-time enterprise.

An important dimension of the real-time enterprise is interactive reporting to top management on risk exposure. The chief risk officer (CRO) should regularly check with the chief executive officer on risk control methods and tools being used. Both should come under rigorous examination. The more dynamic the economy in which we live, the more we need to ensure that nothing that is important in corporate governance drops into the cracks of the system.

1.3.1 The Law of Unwanted Consequences: E-mail and IM

Unwanted consequences, e-mail, and Instant Messaging (IM) traffic are a case in point. Few people truly appreciate that the use of technology has a downside, as it often takes some time to reveal itself. An excellent example is provided by e-mails and IM traffic which, in the early years of the twenty-first century, have become cornerstone to many investigations and lawsuits.

It is estimated, in the short span of a few years, up to 20 percent of U.S. employers have had staff e-mail and IM exchanges subpoenaed in the course of a lawsuit or regulatory probe. Based on the responses of 840 companies, a 2004 study commissioned by the American Management Association and ePolicy Institute, documents a significant increase in the use of electronic communications in court, and as part of investigations by regulators, such as the Securities and Exchange Commission (SEC).

This number of companies served with subpoenas for electronic support information in 2003 is 50 percent higher than the 2002 numbers; and the 2002 statistics had shown a 50 percent increase over those of 2001. Also, 12 percent of respondents to the AMA/ePolicy study said they have fought workplase lawsuits triggered by staff e-mails.

That is the quantitative side of the issue. From a qualitative viewpoint e-mail exchanges have played a crucial role in a number of recnt court cases including the prosecution of Frank Quattrone, the former star technology investment banker at Credit Suisse First Boston, and Henry Blodget, Merrill Lynch's Internet analyst.

Both the quantitative numbers and qualitative aftermath can be expected to increase because the Sarbanes-Oxley Act on corporate governance and other legislation aimed at improving business ethics, mandated companies to archive copies of all electronic communications and to produce them on request. Yet, inspite of legal risks and penalties for noncompliance, the AMA/ePolicy Institute survey found most employers are still ill prepared to manage their e-mails and IMs.

According to the same findings, only 20 percent have adopted a policy governing e-mail and IM use and content. This has led to abuses. The survey revealed that 90 percent of respondents spend up to 90 minutes each day on IM. Another 10 percent of staff spend more than half the working day on e-mail, with the large majority engaged in personal correspondence. The business community's failure to retain e-mail and IM according to new regulations, and to establish written retention and deletion policies, is most surprising. As the survey documents only 30 percent have an e-mail retention policy, and only 6 percent of organizations archive potentially significant IM.[7]

The AMA/ePolicy survey concludes that in 2003 there has been a practically insignificant improvement over similar figures, reported in previous years. There is as well a failure on the part of employers to educate staff about policies and procedures relating to modern communications media. For instance, discriminating between business records, that must be retained and insignificant messages that may be deleted. Company regulations should not be looking to the past, but to the future.

1.4 KNOWLEDGE NAVIGATION AND THE REAL-TIME ENTERPRISE

From product innovation and market leadership to risk control, *knowledge* is the added value to timely and accurate information. Therefore, prior to examining how the real-time enterprise enhances managerial knowledge, it is appropriate to briefly look into what knowledge is and what can be achieved through knowledge navigation.

Knowledge can be *articulate* and *tacit*. Articulate describes formal knowledge usually acquired through long years of training. In the first four decades after World War II, articulate knowledge was in great demand. In the 1950s, for example, a PhD had a virtual license to print money. That is no longer true. Comparatively speaking, the value of *articulate knowledge* is going down, whereas the value of *tacit knowledge* is going up.

Underpinning the growing importance of tacit knowledge is the fact that although formal training continues to be vital, direct, hands-on experience has gained the upper ground. This includes not "any" experience, of course, but one that is polyvalent, is renewable, and helps to create a flexible, adaptable personality. I emphasize polyvalence because sometimes twenty years of experience is one year's experience repeated twenty times.

Tacit describes the knowledge that cannot easily be articulated because it reflects judgment based on such polyvalent and renewal experience, which may take into account hundreds of variables to reach a factual decision. Moreover, a factual decision will require streams of fresh information to assist the decision maker in updating the value of the variables and analyzing the correlations that may exist between them.

Like virtue, tacit knowledge cannot be taught. Up to a point, it might be transferred by osmosis, by observing the master and learning along the way. How well this transfer mechanism will work depends a great deal on human interaction — a process significantly assisted through knowledge navigation. The sense of knowledge navigation is provision of a facility to combine information from different sources that have not yet been integrated and to discover probable links, leading to prompts, alerts, or alarms — and to effective action.

Prominent among the many reasons for our failure to channel our tremendous accumulation of knowledge and resources has been our inability to coordinate people so that individual objectives can be translated into group attainments. Coordination requires *connectivity*, now provided by the Internet (see Chapters 15 and 16), *interactive access* to databases and knowledge bases (see Chapter 14), and *economic objectives* that can lead to action.

It is appropriate to notice that connectivity, interactive access, and economic objectives are critical in making knowledge navigation an integrative project whose effectiveness can be judged by whether it assists in better business visibility and helps in the evolution of events expected to happen sometime in the future — in terms of products, markets, and customer relationships, as shown in the upper half of Figure 1.5. Information, most of it in real-time, is necessary along a polyvalent frame of reference, shown in the second half of the same figure. To a significant extent, it is because of knowledge navigation that the real-time enterprise substitutes "economy of access" to "economy of scale" and is able to value-differentiate itself against its competitors.

According to the Gartner Group, one of the better known U.S. consultancies, these characteristics of the real-time enterprise are the new criteria of business success. In the modern economy, winners do things much faster with better information than do their competitors. The constraint is what *our* information technology can reach and what are its deliverables.

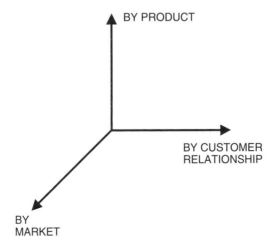

BY PRODUCT

BY CUSTOMER
RELATIONSHIP

BY
MARKET

REAL-TIME INFORMATION MUST BE PROVIDED IN A
MULTIDIMENSIONAL FRAME OF REFERENCE

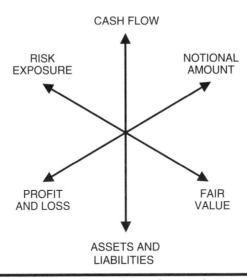

CASH FLOW

RISK
EXPOSURE

NOTIONAL
AMOUNT

PROFIT
AND LOSS

FAIR
VALUE

ASSETS AND
LIABILITIES

**Figure 1.5   Management Must Be Informed in Real-Time about Operations
Anywhere in the World**

In the old business environment, big companies could master the market
better than small ones. This has been the principle of economy of scale,
but it is no longer at the top of the list. In 2003, a Gartner survey asked 120
CEOs to name their primary focus. Above all came the answer *direct client
access*, which, to a significant extent, defines one of the basic values of the
new economy. In the economy of access core competencies must be

subservient to business strategy and resources must be aligned to serve core competencies in the best possible way.

This brings into perspective the reasons why knowledge navigation is a competitive advantage. What is surprising is that few companies capitalize on their resources to take advantage of the economy of access. As a recent survey has found, 60 percent of companies have no link between their strategy and the way they run their IT. This hinders them, because next to economy of access, in the list of twenty-first-century priorities are other deliverables such as risk-based pricing for all products, particularly the financial, and the ability to produce a virtual balance sheet within a few minutes after it is required.

Companies gain a market edge through the able use of technological advances, which makes it feasible to effectively apply their internal intelligence and skill in the management of their business. Other examples of technological advancements are straight through processing (STP, see Chapter 5), reality online (see Chapter 6), corporate memory facility (CMF, see Chapter 7), and the virtual double (VD, see Chapter 8).[8]

In this book, a chapter is devoted to each of the subjects introduced in the preceding paragraph, but a brief description at this point helps in positioning them. *Straight through processing* is mainly concerned with online execution of transactions. *Reality online* addresses the use of a system of sensors that provides timely and precise data capture at point of origin. A *corporate memory facility* is the repository of all management decisions. The *virtual double* is the databased and data-mined image of a real entity.

All of these facilities can be seen as successive layers of an information pyramid, with knowledge navigation at the top. This is shown in Figure 1.6. Each of these layers has a *function*, which refers to the staff responsible for carrying out specific activities and responsibilities. The layer's name is not intended to denote any particular organizational structure.

Under this perspective, the layered structure in Figure 1.6 is characterized by a holistic approach with an eye for latent connections. The real-time enterprise incorporates all information to act upon. Latent connections enhance the ability to do quick but well-documented inferences, enhancing foresight and insight, as discussed earlier.

1.5 PAST BREAKTHROUGHS, ADVANCED KNOWLEDGE, AND EFFICIENCY

Since the invention of money thousands of years ago, financial intermediaries with more timely and more accurate information have been taking advantage of lenders and borrowers with more limited or obsolete information resources. To amplify the Introduction, the financial services industry has made major strides in analytical evaluation and prognostication of the likely outcome of current events.

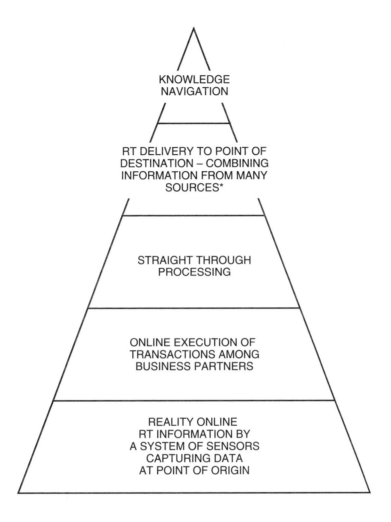

Figure 1.6 Knowledge Navigation, STP, and Reality Online in the Real-Time Enterprise

Connectivity, data mining, and models have been at the foundation of this approach. This essentially means that to survive as profitable entities, banks have to capture the *information advantage*. Real-time information permeates people, markets, products, and activities that dominate the financial system.

Advanced business knowledge is acquired by means of a combination of laboratory research and practical experience, the tacit knowledge discussed earlier. Its antithesis is a hodge-podge of guesswork and often biased opinion, checked only here and there by sporadic statistics. Advanced knowledge in a business environment contrasts, as well, to slow-going scholarly investigators because, although both are underpinned by scientific analysis, advanced business knowledge has no time for purely theoretical diatribes.

For instance, to better the knowledge and promote understanding between different professions, the Deutsche Aktiengesellschaft (an institution established to promote private ownership of equities) brings together people from German federal courts and from small companies to discuss the law and its practicality in day-to-day business.

"The judges must know how companies are organized and how they operate," said Rüdiger von Rosen, the CEO of Deutsche Aktiengesellschaft. "In Germany the new accounting rules, regulations and laws are a headache for the small to medium companies." The aim of getting rid of such headaches led to the process of organizing and providing a platform of exchanges in tacit knowledge and permitting people from different professions to know each other and to communicate on problems important to them all.

Behind this example, as well as in the background of advanced business knowledge, lies the idea of *efficiency*, a notion drawn from physics that helps in supplying a rationale for the use of expertise and of superior organization. The evolution of organizational principles is of great interest to the real-time enterprise since future competition will depend far more on quality of management and organizational planning characterized by flexibility, continuity, and precision in control than on advances or even breakthroughs at device level.

The concept of management efficiency is by no means new. In industrial history, it acquired a meaning at the end of the nineteenth century when the newly discovered laws of thermodynamics were used to analyze the input/output energy of the steam engine. Thanks to mechanical engineers, efficiency attainted quantitative precision and began to be applied to the industrial workplace.

As the nineteenth century turned into the twentieth, Frederick Winslow Taylor toiled to uncover the "scientific principles" of managerial efficiency at the production floor. He reached his end when he developed the methodology of time studies, carefully observing (watch in hand) what the workmen were doing, to make the workers' labor more rational and more productive.

Taylor addressed himself primarily to *skills*. He wrote about the "law of heavy laboring" and the science of shoveling, in the belief that every act of every worker could be reduced to a mechanical principle and made more efficient. This production floor work was preceded, in the mid-nineteenth century, by that of Henri Fayol, who was the first on record to address the notions of authority, responsibility, discipline, and unity of command.

Fayol has demonstrated that sound management is not the manipulation of funds nor is it going ahead day by day in a routine way. To prove this, he tried to find explanations for the job or jobs that management should perform. In the process, Fayol set up the essentials for establishing and maintaining intersecting relationships on a properly run basis, providing a process of self-adjustment but also promoting the hierarchical channel and the notion of span of control.

These concepts largely contradict one another — the more intermediate the steps of a hierarchy are, the shorter is the *span of control* — the latter meaning the number of managers reporting to a superior at the next organizational level. A short span of control means *managerial fat*, which loads the balance sheet of a company on the wrong side.

To avoid the affect of centrifugal forces, information-poor industrial enterprises have many intermediate organizational levels. By contrast, real-time enterprises use timely data streams and knowledge artifacts to do away with medium management layers, reducing overhead and greatly improving efficiency.

In the aftermath of contributions by H. Fayol, F. W. Taylor, H. L. Gantt (who invented the planning chart of the same name), F. B. and L. M. Gilbreth (who contributed the motion study), and other industrial engineers, principles of *scientific management* were developed, often rooted in observation and experiment and motivated by the search for general laws that paralleled the laws of nature. One of the convictions of these pioneers in the art of management was that science could foster harmony and cooperation in the workplace and could do so with it greater efficiency. In hindsight, the second of these two hypotheses has been better sustained than the first.

Indeed, the term "scientific management" and the tools it brought along were still prevalent in the immediate post-World War II years. Today, it has faded away, substituted by emphasis on tools such as decision support systems, simulation, management information systems, timesharing, real-time, expert systems, agents — and the experimental approach based on the seminal work of Claude Bernard, a medical doctor who first developed the notion of experimental medicine.

All this is highly relevant to the evolution of the real-time enterprise because information technology is common ground to the concepts and tools of the last four decades, briefly mentioned in the preceding paragraph. All of the pioneers and their methods contributed to the fact that the late twentieth century and early years of the twenty-first have focused not on skills but on executive knowledge, with a "try anything" philosophy at center stage.

The online, ad hoc availability of fairly accurate information has seen to it that tier-one management now prefers talk and debate to printed reports and long memorandums. Another characteristic of our time is that top-tier management knows how to use a circle of experts that may be wide and informal but also fairly well documented, having done their homework through analysis and experimentation.

As far as efficiency is concerned, the principle behind oral debate is that talk keeps ideas from being prematurely fixed. Although a sense of the meeting filters through, the executive's attention may move to the next intellectual puzzle promoted by availability of real-time information. The philosophy behind this action plan allows persons to respond to a problem, whereas feedback channels are kept open to provide for timely and rigorous postmortems.

Within this changing landscape of management planning and control, the real-time enterprise sets the stage for greater efficiency by making the decision maker a "ganglion for reception, expression, transmission, combination, and realization," as H. G. Wells said of Franklin Delano Roosevelt. Like Roosevelt, first-class executives are delighted in playing their advisers off against each other, using their disputes as a means of screening and developing policy ideas and, at the same time, retaining control of what truly matters: the power to decide.

This power to decide is second nature to successful executives, but the majority of average managers fail to realize that it requires an experimental impulse that has something to do with science, even if it is motivated by the exigencies of taking action. It has to do with science because efficiency requires fact-finding without interminable deliberation that inhibits action until all evidence is in hand. The lack of evidence is made up for by testing methods.

1.6 NOTES

1. *The Economist*, November 15, 2003.
2. *Daily News*, November 20, 2003.
3. D.N. Chorafas, *Agent Technology Handbook,* McGraw-Hill, New York, 1998.
4. D.N. Chorafas, *Reliable Financial Reporting and Internal Control: A Global Implementation Guide,* John Wiley, New York, 2000.
5. C. Northcote Parkinson, *Left Luggage, from Marx to Wilson,* John Murray, London, 1967.
6. *Financial Times*, November 18, 2002.
7. *Financial Times*, July 15, 2004.
8. D.N. Chorafas, *Corporate Accountability, with Case Studies in Finance,* Macmillan/Palgrave, London, 2005.

2

STRATEGIC PLANNING, TECHNOLOGY, AND ORGANIZATION

2.1 INTRODUCTION

In today's fast-paced business environment, opportunities can appear and disappear in an instant. Therefore, companies must be able not only to plan for their survival in a factual and documented manner but also to control the execution of their plans in accordance with their boards' strategic directives. A plan-versus-realities comparison must be properly laid out, tested, and kept up to date.

Technology can help in this mission. Chapter 1 raised the issue that technology should be developed within the guidelines of a strategic plan and that technology should work for, not against, it. This means that having the latest information instantly available and continuously updated is only half the challenge.

Strategies are not formulated in a vacuum and not often made unilaterally by the manager of strategic planning. Strategic plans are undertaken, and policies formulated, with the realization that they must be adjusted in accordance with the reactions of competitors, customers, suppliers, employees, and others inside and outside the enterprise.

Strategy is a master plan positioning the company against its corporate opponents. As such, it should be elaborated by the board, the CEO, and senior management; it should include goals, timetables, resources (human and financial), and deliverables. Subservient to it is the *technological plan*.

The person responsible for working out the details of the technological plan is the chief technology officer (CTO). Such details include architectural standards, solutions analysis, platform choices to be made, software policies, priorities, reliability to be assured, transition procedure to be followed, business continuity (see Chapter 17), cost and return, resource analysis, and implementation milestones to keep ahead of competition.

Time and again, experience has demonstrated that real power is flowing to firms with a strategic plan for IT investments. Technology no longer sells itself simply by being new or because other companies use it. Sam Palmisano, IBM's CEO, has put his engineers to work on a formal model of connectivity between:

■ A firm's strategy
■ Its operations
■ Its underlying IT infrastructure

The aim is to build a model so sophisticated that as strategy changes at the top, new systems configurations develop automatically for IT operations.[1] In the background of this move lies the fact that there seems to be no breath-taking new technological advances (see Chapters 3 and 4). Competitive advantages come from better ways to make IT work.

Reaching Palmisano's goals means turning whatever is known today of system design on its head. An observer of the transformation expected to be taking place within the next few years will feel akin to Jonathan Swift's Gulliver who thought the professors, or *projectors* as he called them, were out of their senses when he visited the Grand Academy of Lagado on the Isle of Balnibarbi. The many improbable schemes like constructing houses from the roof down and training pigs to plow with their snouts amused Gulliver. In a similar manner, automatic system reconfigurations will most probably amuse old EDPers (adherents to the culture of electronic data processing). Bold and inventive approaches, which are urgently necessary, might remain incomprehensive to old hands, who will be hinting to fundamental deficiencies in the new ideas.

New system configurations that might be adaptable automatically as strategy changes at the top will be primarily applied to augment enterprise integration solutions. Efficient connectivity requires steady vigilance in reconfiguring enterprise information channels, including engineering designs, production facilities, sales figures, customer information, supply chain data, presenting new patterns in a practical format. Such information can then be shared among internal users and with trusted external partners.

2.2 A LONG, HARD LOOK INTO THE FUTURE

To keep pace with the rapidly changing business environment and to further develop the existing information systems, senior management must pay full attention to employee skills prior to committing financial resources. Concentrating more on equipment than on employee know-how has many downsides. Infrastructural support decays when we just throw money at a problem — no matter how much money we may be throwing, for example, at new investments that fail to fully account for the strategic choices made at board level. Placing too much emphasis on hardware and software at the detriment of organizational studies is a wrong policy.

Failure to take the proverbial long, hard look is wrong approach. As *The Economist* aptly remarked, "What if tech's next big thing turns out not to be a technology at all but a better way to make it work?"[2] This better way is, for any practical purpose, the real-time enterprise. Looking ahead into the twenty-first century, we should appreciate that technology is not just an IT operation. It is a fundamental force driving a company's growth and survival. It is an integral part of the strategic business plan.

Technology choices must definitely respond to the company's strategic objectives, with a consistent effort made to expand the often-narrow area of IT expertise as new challenges develop and job responsibilities change. In the better-managed consultancies, the computer people become instant experts in a new business field when necessary.

The steady evolution of one's expertise, in order to remain competitive, has become the basic requirement of any professional, whether, systems analyst, financial expert, scientist, or engineer. Anyone who has been out of school for at least five years has already started to become obsolete, because he is bound to work with instruments and systems that were not even conceptualized at graduation time.

Professional survival requires learning details of new business, both through lifelong learning and by means of hands-on experience through job rotation. Moreover, since many current and future challenges can be faced only through analytics, the increasingly more sophisticated information needs of managers and professionals must be satisfied on a priority basis. This is not yet the general case. Figure 2.1 dramatizes the misallocation of IT investments in two ways:

- *First, by personnel cost.* Information technology expenditures have been classically misplaced because only 7 percent to 20 percent is allocated to people, who, in the company's budget, account for about 66 percent of salaries and wages. This is return on investment (ROI) turned on its head.
- *Second, by requirements for improved functionality.* Technology requirements for an executive information system (EIS) are outlined in Chapter 7 and for a client information system (CIS) in Chapter 8.

Coupled with fast time-to-market demands, first-class technological solutions require focused attention on information support of the company's professionals, enhanced by intensive life-long education, to keep everyone abreast of the latest knowledge as well as of new methods and techniques.

Lifelong learning is a steady personal challenge. The overriding requirement is to amplify the professional's vision — a notion that is inherently

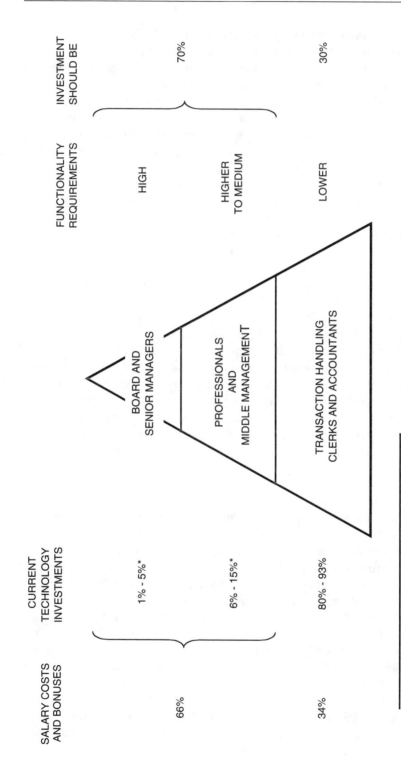

Figure 2.1   The Allocation of IT Investment to Organizational Levels Has Never Been Rational

elusive yet grounded in knowledge, experience, and information as well as the ability to cope with the latest market moves.

Facing the action by our competitors, particularly the new and most aggressive ones, requires much more than a classical response. There is always a new challenge. An example is the *Internet giveaway* policy that started with the Netscape browser. The premise is that companies that give a product away will get paid in a nontraditional way later on.

What Netscape did, to come up from under, was to offer its browser as bait to potential customers. There have been some examples before Netscape that deviated from the classical pay-as-you go and outright buy models, one of them being to offer a line of services targeted to the original product that makes money even if the basic product is sold at below cost. Gillette, for example, more or less gave away its razor but made money on the blades.

Other mechanisms for generating profits out of being seemingly generous with the original product are various sorts of service agreements, maintenance fees, and upgrade fees. All of them bet on income from the steady flow of features, old and new. Cellular phone companies sometimes give away the handset in return for a steady stream of service revenue.

Because the giveaway strategy comes under many guises, well-managed companies concentrate on the product's lifecycle rather than the single sales event. The nearly zero cost to the user is a one-off happening. In Netscape's case, once the buyer was going to pay for some features of the browser, he was going to pay for the attachments and upgrades, too. Such strategies succeed or fail depending on whether or not the producer is able to target the market and continue adding value, whereas competitors do not undercut the producer's plans to make money from add-on offers.

Zero pricing might seem simple enough. But it is a strategy that requires both vision and steady follow-up. Both must be supported by effective connectivity with business partners and by monitoring competitors' moves and reactions. Short of a long, hard look at connectivity, the company with zero pricing strategy may turn belly up.

Technology could help to put vision to practical use by blending imagination with reality, helping in follow-ups connected to innovation, and making it possible to be in charge of change. This is one of the major challenges in designing and implementing an executive information system. It is also an example of prerequisites that exist in today's IT environment, even if these are rarely fulfilled. In spite of 50 years of computer availability, on average only 10 percent of information necessary to run an enterprise is in databases.

The rest still finds itself in paper archives, save some minor part that is microfilms and other standalone supports. A counterpart of this statistic is that 90 percent of all printed paper in an organization is for internal consumption. As long as this policy of 10 percent of databased information and 90 percent of printed paper archives continues, the real-time enterprise is just fiction.

Change in paper-bound policies is a must, and the good news is that, at least as far as future information is concerned, change may come in spite of organizational inertia, as we are moving away from the *data-centric* world that characterized the last three decades. The new paradigm is *message-centric*.

The emergence of the Internet ecosystem (see Chapter 16), which provides a communication standard for applications, opens up the possibility of incorporating different streams of multimedia across enterprise boundaries. Part of this flow will be data from the physical world coming in from sensors (see Chapter 6), including the ability to create new types of displays at the user's request, in order to bring into perspective an event or juncture that calls for action.

This promises to revolutionize business-to-business (B2B) communications, whose growth is projected to overtake by a significant margin Internet commerce as we know it today. Figure 2.2 brings to the reader's attention this bifurcation in market impact. The prompt to action will be messages that span, or exist, outside users' requests. Because such models will be exposing too many specifics of one's work to the environment, they will not only call for more rigorous security solutions than ever before but will also require a much better system of identification organization.

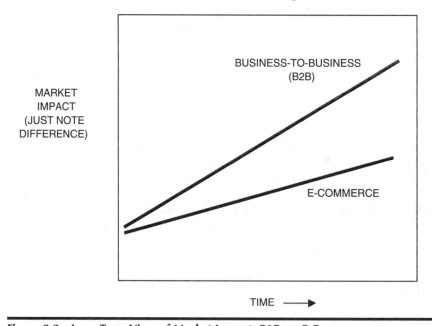

Figure 2.2 Long-Term View of Market Impact: B2B vs. E-Commerce

2.3 ORGANIZATION, IDENTIFICATION, AND FAST DELIVERABLES

The long, hard look into the future of technology's successful implementation brought into perspective the evolution toward a message-centered world. Like any other development, this too has prerequisites that will be better appreciated if we keep in mind that every decade over the last 50 years had its own characteristic technology. The transition has been from emphasis on computation in the 1950s and 1960s to information in the 1970s, knowledge in the 1980s, communications in the 1990s, and organization and identification in the first decade of the twenty-first century.[3]

A world of system-to-system message exchange and of increased business-to-business automation must necessarily be based on sound organizational principles that transcend the former boundaries of "this" or "that" industrial entity. *If* online B2B solutions are our strategy, *then* we must provide a taxonomical classification that makes possible the coordination of the overall cross-product data and message exchange. Classification is needed in order to:

- Define and manage standards for product, partner, and market information
- Analyze each business case, business partner strategy, and transaction fallout
- Optimize production chores, inventory levels, product routing, delivery approaches, and, above all, profit and loss accounts

Taxonomical classification is at the roots of a sound organization. The principle is that most problems of management, human and material factors, cannot be solved by a single answer. The principles of organization are guidelines. Solutions must be derived through experimentation. Scientific work always requires the duality of classification and identification.

Within this context of a dynamic and flexible organization, *define, analyze,* and *optimize* are keywords — all the way from product innovation to market leadership and cost control (see Chapter 17). Whether we talk of products, market relationships, or the technology that we use, costs always matter — but for almost 50 years IT escaped cost scrutiny. This has tremendously changed since the 2000 market downturn. Today, for almost any project, there is an unprecedented level of scrutiny, including the questions:

- How will it benefit the company?
- What are the deliverables on which management should count?
- Can we leave some of the secondary issues out and cut the budget?

One way to look at how organizational issues and return-on-investment considerations have changed is to remember that these questions were not asked a few years ago. By contrast, today budget approval depends on the answers given to the above queries and on the documentation being provided, as well. Cost control is, an integral part of better organization.

Efficient organization, rigorous classification, and unambiguous identification help in getting results when committing resources and funds as well as when monitoring progress and judging whether or not there is value realization. A similar statement is valid about assuming synergies delivered across business units and with partner companies. Furthermore, a well-done classification of all objects handled through computers permits a company to:

- Develop valid organizational models
- Properly design workstreams and supporting information
- Define in an accurate manner business and technical requirements
- Identify people and processes responsible for rollout in each business transaction
- Manage inventories in a way that saves money and increases customer satisfaction.

Here is a practical example of what can be achieved in terms of system solutions through a rigorous process of classification and identification. This case study comes from Osram, the global lamp company. The mission has been to build a new information system that enables very efficient product management, from engineering design to production, marketing, and after-sales service.[4]

The company's old identification system mixed product identification and classification into one 24-digit-long code. As a result, it was prone to errors. Because of this, a parallel code system was developed along classification lines, covering all of the company's products. Identification followed the classification results, producing a short code with parity. The parallel approach provided a unique and unambiguous frame of reference.

Prior to the results obtained by means of a thorough classification, senior management had a rather hazy idea of the company's product line. Marketing thought it was selling some 15,000 products, but some in the division periodically expressed doubt that these products were really different from one another in terms of technical specifications or characteristics made to improve sales appeal.

Indeed, the introduction of the classification system permitted streamlining of the product line, and this was greeted as a major achievement by management. The marketing people applied the unique classification and identification solution with the help of system specialists, and they established that the truly different products the company was selling were not 15,000 but 7,400.

It was found that with the old product numbering system, some of the products in the line used as many as thirty-five different codes to identify and sell the same product. Another even more serious mistake was that up to five diverse products were coded with the same number. Things like that happen quite often in industry, and it takes time and effort to correct the situation.

Quite importantly, the rigorous classification helped to clarify a key subject that, for years, had eluded the accountants: how much profit or loss had each product brought to the company? Once a unique and reliable identification system was implemented, it was possible to answer this question in a documented way. It was then found that of the resulting 7,400 distinct products:

■ 2,500 were mass-produced items that made good money, to cover the losses of the others and leave a profit
■ 850 articles were manufactured on demand and, therefore, followed a different procedure in P&L calculation
■ 370 products just broke even, although several had a good market perspective or were necessary for the company to sustain a complete product line
■ By contrast, 2,640 products lost money (some heavily) and were unnecessary to sustain the company's image as a universal lamp producer

Classification helps in mapping a decision and action space into the configuration of an information environment, whose dimensions correspond to a class in taxonomical organization. Without a classification background, the process of configuring an information space will be unstructured and unduly complex because there are a great number of choices available in each dimension that might look relevant to a given process.

Notice that structuring is in no way synonymous to inflexibility. The system has to be flexible from the end user's viewpoint. The characteristic of a dynamic configuration is that of being able to interpret data based on the user's intended purposes. Structure is being promoted as a design characteristic, which makes the system dependable in its functions.

In an information environment where superior organization prevails, agents will provide the interface between professionals and technological resources, as suggested in Figure 2.3. This example comes from an application that cut across divisional lines to interactively provide a profit-and-loss (P&L) analysis.

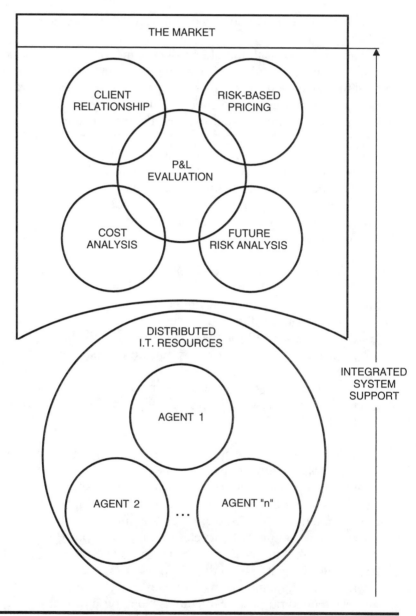

Figure 2.3   An Interactive Risk-Based Pricing Solution for a Derivative Financial Instruments and Other Banking Products

As far as future applications are concerned, the emphasis on organization and identification (including taxonomical classification) will lead to rather significant changes in system design. Several practical examples, presented in the eight chapters of Part Two and Part Three, document that leading companies are already working to thoroughly restructure their information technology.

Moving away from legacy solutions, adopting a flexible business architecture (see Chapter 13), and using visual programming languages at end user level will change the deliverables of modern information systems, putting a premium on short development cycles. The more efficient work will be done through small but expert teams, addressing well-defined, contained projects.

Tier 1 organizations appreciate the advantages obtained through fast deliverables. The practice of long development time followed by outmoded data processing may result in a system solution that no longer meets practical requirements. In my research, I have found this to be true for 80 percent of ongoing data processing projects.

A different way of making this statement is that the real-time enterprise should work in real-enough time in product development, innovation, and software support. Innovation in both industrial and financial products is not feasible without new software. Many programming products at the competitive edge have to be custom made; software development cycles must be measured in hours, days, or (at maximum) weeks, not years.

Since the 1990s, the financial industry has held a most competitive organizational philosophy to tap the full potential of the market. New financial products that are not endowed with custom-made software for both business opportunity analysis and risk control are either stillborn, highly risky, or both. Because an integral part of the new landscape is an accurate calculation of risk and reward, fast software deliverables are a necessity.

2.4 COORDINATION THROUGH MANAGEMENT BY OBJECTIVES

The creation of an efficient management planning and control mechanism provides both the means and the spirit for compliance to the strategic plan as well as coordination and supervision throughout the organization. Compliance and effective coordination should be the rule both for business unit to business unit and in regard to functional areas. A basic ingredient of a sustainable solution is the policy of management by objectives (MBO).

What are the prerequisites? First and foremost is the existence of an MBO policy decision by the board, followed by the definition of specific goals that promote the strategic plan. Because the attainment of objectives within a given timetable must be controlled, these objectives should be clearly stated in quantitative and qualitative terms. The following rules help in dimensioning the objectives so that they

■ Must be achievable through planned effort
■ Fall within strategic guidelines

- Directly relate to the problem at hand
- Represent a decision, not an alternative
- Be feasible and acceptable in relation to their cost
- Be compatible with other objectives, providing a unified basis for planning

Certain objectives may be achievable but irrelevant to the company's strategic plan. When this happens, they are not qualified for an MBO solution. We should manage by objectives that are sound, not based on hype. A now-classical case is that of overbuilding telecom channel capacity during the late 1990s.

According to a study by Merrill Lynch, the average transport network is used at just 6.6 percent of capacity. In terms of potential long-distance capacity, only 1 to 2 percent is in use. By contrast, local and regional land-based networks in operation are running at 35 percent of capacity; moreover, this market is better off because it grows at 85 percent per year. Companies must reflect on these statistics. *If* the utilization of only 2 percent of installed capacity was part of the strategic plan, *then* the strategy itself was a failure. *If* such overbuilding has been done outside the strategic plan, *then* the fault is at the execution side and MBO could have provided urgently needed means of management control.

In this specific case, it was the strategies of telecommunications companies that had run wild. For instance, eggheads had decreed that Internet traffic would grow exponentially. In reality, Internet traffic doubles every year, which is impressive but short of projections. Therefore, it will take time to make installed long-distance capacity break even — particularly so as, in the meantime, the industry has engaged in price wars.

Apart from being realistic, objectives must be measurable, concrete, and fitting a policy of management control. An effective MBO implementation requires much more in terms of organizational practice and senior management support than the mere task of setting of objectives. An integral part of meeting goals after they have been spelled out is to allocate resources and to establish schedules that make explicit the execution timeframe and its business time requirements (see Chapter 1).

Though many people pay lip service to managing by objectives, few really feel comfortable with it. The more enthusiastic are the innovators who are after measurable results as well as people who desire to gain status. Both with MBO and with real-time solutions, status is an important motivation for adoption of either and both processes, all the way to deliverables.

A sound approach to the evaluation of results obtained through management by objectives is in terms of what it provides by way of strategy-and-technology coordination: Does it guide IT investments toward supporting rather than contradicting strategic moves? Are the objectives being set making *our* company an innovator, early adopter, late adopter, or laggard in terms of new technology? Similar questions can be posed in regard to *our* company's level of organization.

An integral part of MBO is to identify activities needed to accomplish an objective — those that are critical, mapping the status and highlighting those issues that require greater attention, as well as, analyzing failures in meeting objectives and finding out the reasons. Some of the basic principles to be observed in an organizational sense are:

- Objectives must be meaningful, precise, and tangible
- Provide a workable plan by establishing realistic target dates
- Offer benchmarks for the measurement of progress toward their attainment

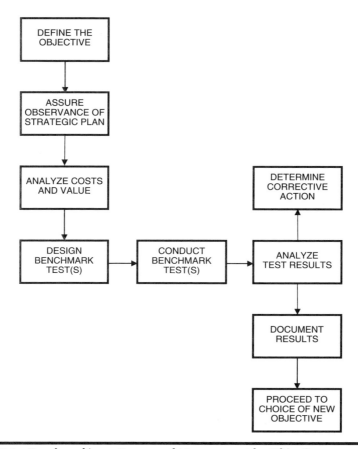

Figure 2.4   Benchmarking a Process of Management by Objectives

An example of a benchmark process designed along this line of reference is given in Figure 2.4. Factual and documented evaluation of meeting successive objectives can help in *strategic innovation*. It also assists in following and achieving identified opportunities. Because results must be properly documented, strategic reviews should concentrate on performance in terms of quality of results and observance of timetables.

Objectives that are in clear terms, stated with comprehensive terminology and suitable explanatory information, offer great advantages to management. Among the benefits are the simplification of the process of supervision, better understanding of the goals of strengthening communication, and what management gains in terms of personal development.

All these are characteristics of a superior organization. Companies that want objectives to be clearly understood put them in writing and phrase them in a way of ensuring consistency of directives. But regardless of who actually writes the objective(s), a number of difficulties may be encountered in their development and preparation. Many managers are articulate, but few of them are accustomed to clarifying their concepts or ideas and expressing them in terminology that can be easily understood.

One of the downsides of a corporatewide MBO process is that objectives may not be consistent with each other. Many executives have found that when they formulate objectives, they fail to look at the whole firm focusing instead on a business unit of a product line, for which they frame an individual directive. This stand-alone approach can lead to contradictions characteristic of poor management.

Also, at least at times, objectives may not be consistent with some of the company's long-standing directives. Objectives need to be tested on whether they integrate into the strategic plan and policy statements of the company. Moreover, objectives must be consistent with laws and regulations. They must also account for internal and external constraints unless their goal is to change the current environment or the way of doing things, e.g., turning away from electronic data processing and toward

- Exponential technology
- Sophisticated software solutions
- Rapid, competitive developments
- Increasing-return economics

This brings into perspective prerequisites. *If* the objective is to change the way information technology is run, *then* the first milestone is cultural change. This is a strategic issue because companies that do not take seriously the need to steadily adapt to business evolution and reinvent themselves do not survive. This has always been true, but it has intensified since the 1990s. Look at the roster of the 100 largest U.S. companies at the beginning of the 1990s; only 16 are still in existence.

2.5 STRATEGIC PLANS SHOULD ACCOUNT FOR NEW TECHNOLOGY'S IMPACT

The relation between strategic planning and technology works both ways. As the preceding sections emphasized, IT investments and developments should be preceded by organizational studies, and they should be made within the framework of the company's strategic plan. At the same time, the strategic plan must be sensitive to new technological advances and organizational solutions because they make possible decisions and actions that were not feasible until recently.

As shown in Chapter 3, developments at the device level are not coming at the same pace as they were. The law of the photon did not hold the same promises as Moore's law; information technology is a long way from exhausting its potential. Many analysts expect to see a powerful new economic engine emerge that uses new solutions allied to a service-oriented form of business architecture and software support.

Tomorrow's advanced IT approaches will be supercharged with tools from knowledge engineering and focused at the end user, both at home and in the office. With this transition in process, fierce competition will characterize the service industry, which means that a company's market position is always at risk. An company's ability to maintain its current market share will depend upon its ingenuity to:

- Satisfy customer requirements
- Enhance existing products
- Develop and introduce new products
- Achieve market acceptance of such products

Knowledge management is in high demand in an environment that expects near miracles from system integration, including the ability to significantly improve connectivity with business partners and to provide the backbone of the real-time enterprise. For instance, in regard to both straight through processing (see Chapter 5) and reality online (see Chapter 6), a great deal of new technology's impact depends on how well system integration has been done.

Historically, system integrators made their money from complexity. In a way, the more complex the project, the more money they could charge. Today, however, system integrators are no longer promoting time and materials contracts. Instead, they go for very tight fixed-price projects that need superior tools in order to succeed and make a profit for the consultancy.

A successful system integration project needs classification and organization. Both are required for streamlining and integrating product lines, in a way akin to what Alfred Sloan did in the 1920s with General Motors. Sloan saw to it that different products — shown in Figure 2.5 as P1 to P5 —

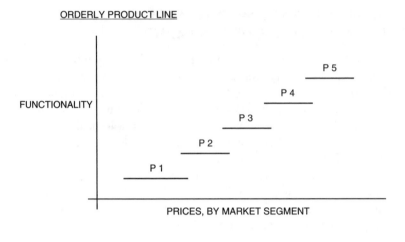

ORDERLY PRODUCT LINE

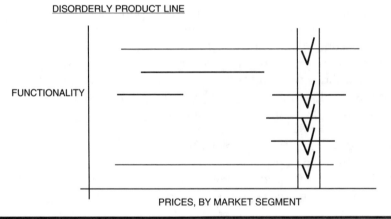

DISORDERLY PRODUCT LINE

Figure 2.5   Product and Market Orientation Requires an Orderly Approach with Risk-Based Pricing in the Background

should only partly overlap each other in terms of cost and functionality. Wild overlaps in a disorderly manner are not attractive to a sophisticated market and make the mission of managing them much more complex and uncertain.

Superficially, the preceding two paragraphs on systems-and-product line integration may seem to address two different issues. A closer look, however, reveals that this is not at all true. Most often, IT systems and subsystems stand alone, in the sense that they lack integration, because they have been designed in a way heterogeneous to that of other subsystems. For instance, they were projected to help in handling products of a particular division rather than take an integrative approach to the company's product line.

When this is the case, product-line streamlining and IT-oriented integration correlate, as the one assists the other in reaching its goal. It is always helpful to keep in mind that an organization is efficient if its actions are effective with the minimum unsought consequences or costs. Moreover, senior management can more successfully identify new product opportunities using technology (see Chapter 4). *If* new products are not brought to the market in a timely and cost-efficient manner, *then* the company's business growth will suffer and demand for its products and services will collapse.

IBM went through this vicious cycle in the late 1980s by forgetting the basic principle that products die. Development work associated to product lifecycle falls into a number of essential phases. Researchers typically conceive of or envision a product that addresses a critical customer need or is able to generate new customer interest. Manufacturing engineers develop processes that observe the product's intended functionality, outgoing quality, and target cost. They test to validate that the product is produced according to design specifications.

All this requires first-class information technology support. If the product is technical, sales engineers should be manning the marketing effort, assisted through knowledge engineering, as Digital Equipment used to do with XSEL and XCON (respectively, expert salesman and expert configurer). The sales engineers must assure not only that the product they sell attracts the customer's attention but also that its applications make the market tick. Then comes after-sales service, from purchase to disposal. The more technologically intense and the more sophisticated the product, the more it requires the services of first-class information technology through its lifecycle.

To my experience, streamlining of the product line and information technology integration are also of significant help in pricing. Orderly, rational pricing must not only reflect risk and return but also make extensive use of sophisticated IT support. This has not escaped the attention of well-managed companies. In a 2000 Conference Board (the U.S. think tank) survey of 200 executives at 158 large multinationals, 80 percent said they had knowledge management projects in the works, and many had already instituted a chief knowledge officer function.

Not only companies but also governments look to positive fallout from technology. Projects aimed to promote high technology in the early 1980s, like MCC in the United States, Alvey in the United Kingdom, and Esprit in the European Union brought new concepts in evaluating the aftermath of investments in IT. A metric established in the mid-1990s to gauge investments in information technology is the percent of gross national product (GNP).

In Group of Ten (G-10) countries, information technology today represents nearly 20 percent of GNP. In less than two decades, this share will be closer to 50 percent. (The G-10 today includes the United States, Canada, England, Germany, France, Italy, Japan, Belgium, Holland, Luxembourg, Sweden, and Switzerland.)

In fact, if growth rather than share of GNP is used as the criterion, this 50 percent mark has already been reached. In the United States, information technology represents 50 percent of annual growth. No company can leave such statistics out of its strategic plan and still hope to survive in a market that is more competitive than ever.

2.6 NOTES

1. economist.com (accessed June 19, 2003).
2. economist.com/business (accessed June 20, 2003).
3. D.N. Chorafas, *Integrating ERP, CRM, Supply Chain Management and Smart Materials*, Auerbach, New York, 2001.
4. D.N. Chorafas, *Integrating ERP, CRM, Supply Chain Management and Smart Materials*, Auerbach, New York, 2001.

3

NEW TRENDS
IN INFORMATION
TECHNOLOGY

3.1 INTRODUCTION

The evolution of information technology over the last six decades can be best appreciated if we step back and briefly review four epochs: The take-off, IBM's high time, "Wintel"'s rise to power, and the latest, which we may call the Internet ecosystem, not just for lack of a better label but also for fundamental reasons (as we will see in Section 2).

The take-off epoch lasted from 1947 to 1965. For all practical purposes, the computer industry was born in 1947 with the Eckert-Mauchly computer company, which a few years later was bought by Remington and renamed Univac. Eckert-Mauchly's company produced the first commercially available engine; others followed. At least seventeen companies participated during that period. They were (in alphabetical order) Bendix, Bull, Burroughs, Control Data, English Electric, Fujitsu, General Electric, Hitachi, Honeywell, IBM, ICL, NCR, NEC, Philco, RCA, Siemens, and Univac.

Computer history books write that perhaps the most common characteristic of all the competitors has been the fact that they have tried to overtake one another by producing increasingly fast engines. Though the speed of these primitive, bulky computers was no match to that of microprocessors of three decades later, the concept of *faster* computation acted as a spearhead in opening the market.

IBM mastered the 1965 to 1983 timeframe; therefore, the second epoch is named for that company. This period is characterized by the belief that a single-platform architecture, particularly suitable to centralized data processing, is good for all kinds of computing. The alter ego of this notion has been that of an operating system (OS), which becomes heavier and heavier and consumes an inordinate amount of processing cycles.

The standard that has been imitated by many competitors — most particularly the Japanese, in the early 1970s, with "System M" — became IBM's System/360 line with OS/360, a hierarchical database management system (DBMS) and teleprocessing routine (TPR) that used Cobol as the programming language. Bulky compilers and different utilities that required large quantities of code to accomplish even the simplest tasks proved to be a poor technological basis.

Contrary to the take-off period in which (with minor exceptions like Bendix) computer manufacturers exhibited monolithic products, the 1960s and 1970s saw several innovations in computer design. In the decade of 1965 to 1975 , a new goal created much interest — minicomputers, which can be briefly phrased as smaller and smaller engines. Minicomputers made feasible distributed data processing, which challenged the centralized basis on which IBM's dominance rested. The design characteristic of the decade 1975 to 1985 was the personal computer (PC), and the industry motto became cheaper and cheaper devices. This is where "Wintel" came in. "Wintel"'s epoch lasted from 1983 to 2000. It was so named after Windows, Microsoft's operating system, and Intel, whose microprocessors acquired universal fame. Wintel established a hardware/software architecture that became a de facto standard. Over the years, Intel's commodity processors evolved from the early 1970s days of 4004 to 8008, 8080, X86, and the Pentium line.

The hallmark of this period is devices that steadily became smaller and cheaper, but not necessarily newer and newer, as some people have predicted. This same epoch has been characterized by two parallel developments: that of supercomputers and that of the increasing implementation of artificial intelligence (AI), first in the form of expert systems and then as mobile agents.[1]

The Internet ecosystem epoch is post-2000 (more on this concept in Section 2). Its most important contribution is the process of effective connectivity through any-to-any and end-to-end networking (see Chapter 16), enabling a nearly unlimited number of contributors. During this epoch, the dominant suppliers are operators providing high-quality solution selling; consultancies able to assist customers in dealing with complex problems; and vendors of intelligent systems and components, competing on the provision of trustworthy solutions that are low cost and characterized by short time to delivery.

Some people, and evidently some companies, deliberately choose to live with old technology and believe that high technology is bleeding edge. That is the wrong concept. Although new technology has unknowns, staying put in the past is an antithetical position in a fast-moving IT environment. The best way to describe the continuing use of old IT is as a case of *consistent inconsistency*.

3.2 A CONCEPT OF THE INTERNET ECOSYSTEM

Why should the fourth epoch be labeled the Internet ecosystem? The easy answer is: Why not? A label must be simple and catchy. This one satisfies both requirements. A more basic reason, however, is that the new epoch seems to satisfy the most fundamental characteristics of an ecosystem, which are seamless connectivity and interdependence of its components. The intelligent, broadband Internet would go beyond the any-to-any and end-to-end connectivity, using novel ways to carry out the functions of which it is capable. In this particular evolution, a great deal can be learned from ecology, the study of the environment, and the way a natural ecosystem works as well as from the integrative forces whose presence affects every part of the environment — and every party.

What are the basic components of a natural ecosystem? In addition to the biblical air, water, fire, earth, and sun worship (of monotheistic religions), there are the plants, animals (and their impact), wind, weather, pollution, purification processes, death, birth, and regeneration. Practically all of these ecosystem characteristics have subclassifications. For instance humans impact the ecosystem individually, through companies, and through society as a whole. Actions of an *anthropogenic* origin affect both the natural ecosystem and manmade ecosystem (like the Internet). The latter is composed largely by manmade notions of connectivity and of links, nodes, workstations, servers, databases, software, and people working on or through these devices. The links may be fixed (terrestrial) or mobile (radio). The networks may be local area, metropolitan, or long haul. The software may be dumb, smart, or intelligent — and the same is true of the people, who may be end users or IT experts.

Switzerland's Federal Technical University (Ecole Polytechnique Fédérale de Lausanne, EPFL) has an advanced information technology project exploring the applicability of bio-inspired approaches to the development of self-organizing, evolving, adaptive, and autonomous IT technologies. According to EPFL, these may meet requirements of next-generation information systems, such as diversity, scalability, robustness, and resilience. Bio ADT's aim is to become a base on which to build a networked symbiotic environment for the twenty-first century. *If* we accept the principle that a natural ecosystem is an ecological community and that its environment functions as a unit, *then* we have to admit that that is precisely what the Internet ecosystem does, albeit at a logical frame of reference including people, companies, and the other proactive components.

Some of the components of the Internet ecosystem are conceptual constructs; others are physical. Both have some sort of formal identity, and they interact among themselves because of the relationships they share.

Links, nodes, and servers are at a lower level of the Internet ecosystem food chain. Higher up are applications, and still higher is the object of such applications, i.e., the management of money.

The Internet ecosystem's sophistication is constantly evolving. Under past practices, the users of Internet commerce typically had to find, compile, and analyze their own product information and vendor lists to come to purchasing conclusions. A similar approach has been used with Internet banking. This, however, changed as a new class of *mediated agents* emerged to do most of the work for buyers and sellers, from finding product sources and assessing vendor reputation to the negotiation of pricing and contractual conditions.

Benefits to buyers from the evolution of the Internet ecosystem include more personalized services, faster search, lower costs, better prices, and purchase decisions involving a greater variety of goods. Sellers benefit from increased efficiency, larger market reach, better sales growth, and an improved understanding of:

- Who their customers are
- What they are buying
- What makes them tick

As the Internet ecosystem evolves, software agents automate many of the steps needed for I-commerce transactions. Experts project that, through agents, consumers and vendors will be able to use wireless communications technologies, bringing transactions to the level of hand-held devices while at the same time increasing their pallet of options.

An important reference for Internet banking is that agent-mediated commerce boosts attention to buyer behavior connected to product identification, brokering, and negotiation (for more on I-banking, see Chapter 15). Significant improvements in online dealing are possible by mining customer databases (see Chapter 14) on behalf of designers and marketers to find product characteristics sustained by market and buyer patterns, leading to the anticipation of needs.

Within the perspective of an Internet ecosystem, whether we talk of financial or physical goods, the goal of measuring consumer preference through agents is to qualify and quantify the processes that go into a person's decision to choose or buy something. Being able to understand what motivates a consumer (or company buyer) permits optimization the tradeoffs between:

- The likelihood of purchase
- The cost of production and distribution

Ramifications abound. In the realms of engineering design, Web-based virtual prototyping enables acquisition-specific consumer information quickly and inexpensively. As a result, interactivity sustained by the Internet can lead manufacturers to a new level in product development, becoming known as *user design.*

Interactive Internet solutions put clients at the core of the decision process. This is important because product development is changing very rapidly; therefore companies that can use predefinable development and production processes have a competitive advantage. A growing number of experts now consider product development speed cutting-edge technology.

The sense of these references is that if we are going to lead and win, we have to compete by developing business processes and associated commercializing technology more and more, but with due regard to costs and quality. Let us not forget that product development has become a cross-functional, companywide process in which specifications flow from the front end, where product technology and value chain roadmaps are defined. Then products are handled in accounting terms by the back office as financial settlement follows the product delivery pipeline.

In this Internet ecosystem model, the virtual or physical product is designed, produced, tested, and readied for the market in record time. Because an ecosystem cares for its own efficiency, there is a parallel development of new products and processes, including balancing acts to ensure adequate performance, low cost, high quality, and the creation of new features — all to the beat of *business time* (see Chapter 1), which should command the product consistency and the architectural solution to be chosen (see Chapter 13).

Other concepts of the Internet ecosystem are still evolving. One of them is *meaning,* or the significance of information to system components that process it. Another is the degrees of freedom that should exist in a given situation to choose among signals, symbols, messages, or patterns. Still another is the level of intelligence the Internet ecosystem and its components should possess. Even partial ignorance precludes communication, making connectivity impossible.

3.3   TRENDS IN NETWORKED SOPHISTICATED APPLICATIONS

The Introduction to this book makes reference to faster and faster, smaller and smaller, cheaper and cheaper, newer and newer trends. These continue to be design characteristics of computer hardware, but they are no more *the* competitive advantages they used to be. As Chapter 2 brought to the reader's attention, IT's next big accomplishment is not going to be in classical technology but, rather, a much better way to make technology work through ingenious organization.

If one thing is to be retained from my July 2002 meeting with Dr. Gordon Bell, Microsoft's senior scientist, it is his statement that "the technology which will have a major effect on the economy for some time is simply not there. This can be seen from projects in the labs." By contrast, companies have a great deal of work to do in:

■ Prearchitecturing their applications
■ Developing new, competitive, intelligence-enriched, trustworthy solutions

Though both corporate laboratories and university research centers are currently working on new technologies, particularly around processes of microminaturization (see sections 5 and 6) and of biocomputers, their broader practical applications are a decade or so away. Nearer to implementation are engineering hybrids, particularly connecting those to sensing technologies (see Chapter 4), which, however, do not constitute a holistic solution.

Dr. Bell's thesis has been that, given where we are in computer technology, we can do nearly everything that is currently required for business reasons, for instance, establishing a real-time basis for tracking transactions and risks (more on this Chapter 5 on STP). The keyword is advanced organization. Figure 3.1 brings to the reader's attention what should be the focus of modern, competitive organization-and-IT studies.

The infrastructure of solutions along this frame of reference is real-time networking, data mining, and computing, with round-the-clock sophisticated application, interactive access to enhance connectivity, online support to endusers, and educational services. Superior organizations must:

■ Attack cost and complexity
■ Accelerate delivery
■ Provide for mobility in usage commensurate with security

As we will see in subsequent chapters, there are several prerequisites in addressing the company's own (and its customers') strategic business challenges and information requirements in an innovative way. A holistic advanced solution, be built by one company alone. It requires a robust partner community, including independent software vendors, system integrators, original equipment manufacturers (OEM), and resellers able to add value to systems and services, extending their reach and the expertise of system designers. Moreover, developing and deploying holistic IT solutions over the network requires a steadily upkept infrastructure that is:

■ Enterprise ready
■ Economically compelling
■ Of high reliability
■ Ahead of the curve

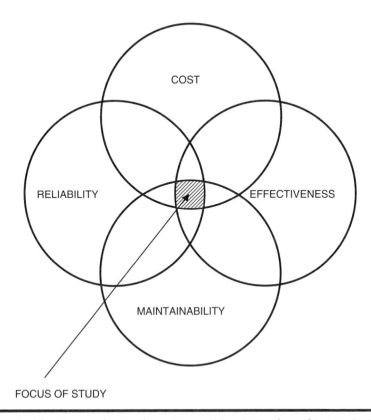

Figure 3.1   The Focus of a Modern, Competitive IT Study and Its Basic Design Parameters

As the service economy gains momentum, a dependable advanced network of this type will be ringing all Group of Ten countries, in a way similar to what railroads did in the late nineteenth century, to serve an economy based on physical goods. Nineteenth-century networks are evidently no match for twenty-first-century requirements, in which logical goods hold the upper ground. In fact, statistics from the Association of American Railroads, Department of Commerce, and Bureau of the Census show that, as the new economy supercedes the old, the U.S. railroad system is in full decline. Figure 3.2 dramatizes this development.

To be effective in terms of providing competitive solutions to the user organization and its clients, such networks must be characterized by 24-hour operations at 99.99 percent level of dependability or better. This statement is synonymous with saying that they must sustain the real-time enterprise for all its dealings. Take the banking industry as an example. In the context of 24-hour financial operations, round-the-clock trading is important because it brings the bank back to its main role of a financial intermediary.

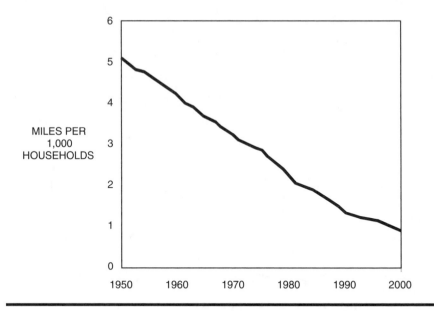

Figure 3.2   During the Last 50 Years, Railroad Mileage Has Been in Steady Decline

This can be achieved by institutions that control the art of highly reliable financial networking at affordable cost and are ready to act as system operators for their business partners at any time, anywhere in the world.

Evidently, 24-hour networking poses challenges beyond technology's own level. The two greatest challenges are cultural and organizational. Both cultural change and organizational ingenuity are indispensable in making advanced technology work in a competitive way, helping *our* company to be ahead of its competitors.

Within an any-to-any nonstop environment, the proprietary knowledge-enriched software to provide content on these networks must be job specific. For instance, no matter how sophisticated the overall programming support may be, software for 24-hour trading would not serve 24-hour retail banking because these are basically different activities. Twenty-four-hour trading on an institutional level usually involves fewer transactions, each of major amount and of significant exposure in terms of credit risk and market risk (see Chapter 11). Commercial 24-hour banking is typically retail oriented, with many transactions of smaller amounts and with credit risk often covered by insurance (as in the case of credit cards and ATM networks).

Other design criteria are the effective, seamless integration of solutions that are already in place. For instance, one of the leading financial entities set itself a goal to make feasible that worldwide trading and account management be done from *one virtual book*, in *one virtual place*. Still another worthy goal is the personalization of deliverables. As we will see in greater detail in subsequent chapters, in finance, the challenge and the trend are to identify:

- *Risk*, per instrument, counterparty, transaction, desk, and trader
- *Cost*, per unit of production and distribution
- *Customer* relationship P&L (profit and loss) through customer mirror (see Chapter 8)

Moreover, the regulators now require that banks report on *recognized* but *not realized* gains and losses (STRGL). This can be done through real-time updates of exposure assumed by counterparty, instrument, trader, and desk anywhere in the world. It is therefore important to distinguish 24-hour trading from the more general banking operations that have been classically addressed.

Seen from the perspective of the Internet ecosystem whose concept we examined in Section 2, 24-hour trading stands higher in the ecosystem's food chain than general banking chores of the demand deposit accounts type. Investments in securities, too, are higher up in the food chain. We will take a closer look at them in Chapter 15.

3.4 BACK TO BASICS

If the better way to make technology work is to apply return on investment (ROI) criteria in budgeting information technology expenses, *then* companies have a great interest in instituting a policy of restructuring and revamping. This means taking a critical look at the organization as a whole and turning systems and procedures on their heads — which can only be done by going back to basics.

The trading example we considered in Section 3 in connection to real-time banking and the Internet ecosystem can help as the background. An able solution to 24-hour trading necessarily focuses on all of the means by which a portfolio of securities (or other assets) is traded internationally 24 hours a day. This provides a holistic view. By contrast, the more traditional global trading represents the involvement of a number of different business units in transactions that are not necessarily done in a networking sense.

Whether or not the bank's branches work as a network is important inasmuch as optimization depends on the ability of integrating the bank's multinational branches and their transactions. Traders in these branches should work with their colleagues as a network rather than stand-alone. *If* traders in each location care only for the profit and loss (P&L) of their desk, putting the institution's global profits on the backburner, *then* there is no global trading environment to optimize. In this case:

- "Basics" is organization and structure
- Behind organizational decisions stands the board's strategy

Back to basics essentially means fundamental organizational work that addresses structural and procedural aspects for greater efficiency. Solutions have to be dynamic because the background of competition changes due to globalization, technology, and steady innovation, as well as because financial supply chain integration has become a must while at the same time:

- Core values have taken the high ground
- High-performance applications have become a focal point
- There is a shift to message-based integration beyond e-mail

The need for message-based integration has led to the development of messaging architectures and of tools for handling them. Their goal is to integrate activities based on more sophisticated protocols than are currently available. With message-based integration comes media convergence. Media convergence is a better term than multimedia support because it identifies the process of merging bit streams belonging to different media. Convergence of voice, data, graphics, and video necessitates faster traffic technology, involving solutions that increase the bandwidth of existing networks and allow sharing bit streams among mobile devices and local, metropolitan, and wide area networks. There are other prerequisites, for example, the seamless integration shown in Figure 3.3.

It is appropriate to keep in mind that seamless integration and easy access to reasons become a necessity now more than ever before, as with terabit-per-second (TBS) capacity we talk about 10^3 to 10^5 more connectivity than we now have. At the same time, for network management purposes and other overhead, we must differentiate between

- Raw bandwidth
- Useful bandwidth

This, too, is a back-to-basics proposition as far as network design is concerned. Moreover, to better appreciate the trend toward media convergence, we have to realize that even telephone calls are changing, converting to digital streams for transmission across fast networks. An example is the digital subscribe line (DSL). Along this frame of reference, although the applications we are aiming at grow increasingly complex, digital data is evolving into the common language for all communications.

To face the challenge posed by this process, R&D labs work to bring together technologies that, when aggregated, make media convergence

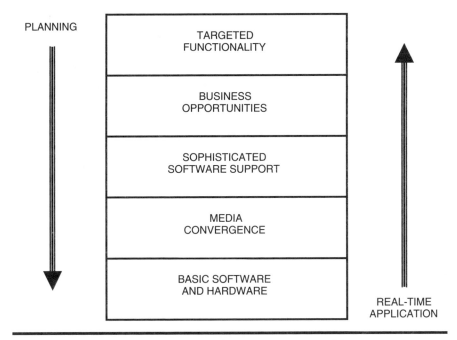

PLANNING

TARGETED
FUNCTIONALITY

BUSINESS
OPPORTUNITIES

SOPHISTICATED
SOFTWARE SUPPORT

MEDIA
CONVERGENCE

BASIC SOFTWARE
AND HARDWARE

REAL-TIME
APPLICATION

Figure 3.3   The Planning and Usage of a New Business Architecture Must Focus on Five Areas

possible. The markets addressed by these developments represent various facets of the bigger broadband picture, including data streams ranging from optical networks to third-generation (3G) wireless connectivity and other types of two-way interactive communications — which is also a back-to-basics proposition, because our whole frame of reference might change in the next few years.

As I had the opportunity to point out in a book on enterprise architecture,[2] we might be approaching the limits of Moore's law, which has led designers and applications engineers by the hand for three decades. Moore's Law has been correctly predicting that densities of transistor technology would at least double every 18 months. This "law" was coined by Intel's founder Gordon Moore, who in essence described a physical phenomenon with significant financial aftermath. Product innovations such as denser memories or faster microprocessors have been typically designed and sold at high initial prices. But as demand for them zoomed and the volume of production increased, yields also increased, the amortization of equipment became smaller for each unit, and unit costs sharply decreased.

The cheaper it is to manufacture a part over time, and the greater the competition is, the lower the price the manufacturer can charge. Market elasticity causes volume to go up even more. At some point, new design rules are developed to increase the packing density and the die size shrinks. This is beneficial to the yield, thereby making the part even cheaper to produce.

The reason some experts think this process might be approaching its end is that there surely exist physical limits. New strategies must be found, and transitional plans must be made to take advantage of such strategies. As we will see in section 5, microminiaturization will be playing a key role in this transition, including novel ways to integrate sensors and smart materials.

Promotors of real-time sensor networks point to the growing use of radio-frequency identity (RFID) tags, as evidence that embedding tiny wireless devices in everyday items makes commercial sense. These RFID tags are the size of a small grain, do not contain a battery, and are "woken up" by a pulse of radio energy.

Such energy is absorbed and used to power up a small chip transmitting a response that is usually an identification (ID) number. Also known as low frequency ID (LFID), as of 2004 such tags are employed by retailers like Wal-Mart and Tesco for inventory control. Indeed, mid-March 2004 Wal-Mart required its top 100 suppliers to acquire and employ LFID tags by January 2005. The company believes that their use will significantly improve inventory management. A person today deals with, on average 100 bar codes per day.

The guiding light in the design and implementation of new departures will necessarily be organization and targeting. Microminiaturization alone will not carry the day all alone. Keep this in mind when we talk of the evolution of information technology and its applications in the coming years.

3.5 MINIATURIZATION AND SENSING TECHNOLOGY

There are many different ways we can look at maturization and its aftereffect, from radically revamping an existing technology, making it more popular and more cost effective, to providing the possibility for new solutions that constitute a major innovation or an altogether novel product offered at an affordable price.

As the evolution of integrated circuits documents, miniaturization steadily progresses at higher and higher densities. Industry experts believe that by the end of this decade, electronics, computing, and their hybrids will be contributing some $300 billion per year to the total market revenues for nanotechnology-enabled products and services. According to other estimates, sensing technology, too, will grow by leaps and bounds.

Sensing technology has been around since the mid-nineteenth century, when cameras fastened to balloons took pictures of topographical mapping. Another example is radio frequency identification devices, which, though they have become more sophisticated over time, are still relatively simple, consisting of a tiny transceivers surrounded by fine antennae. A new product along that frame of reference is the *smart tag*,[3] which can be as small as a match head with antenna but which is capable of transmitting the product's unique identification (ID) code to the appropriate receiver (see also Section 6).

The integration of miniaturization and sensing technology has significantly enlarged the implementation landscape of computing devices. It has also widened the range of machines and devices directly benefiting from technological advances. Computer experts see no visible end (yet) to this process.

As Figure 3.4 demonstrates, at the high end of the application, an aggregate of small computing devices is a supercomputer. The first of its kind has been the Connection Machine of the late 1980s, a hypercube that gave thousands of MIPS power at a fraction of the cost of what was then the Cray-type monolithic supercomputer. Among other users, Dow Jones em-

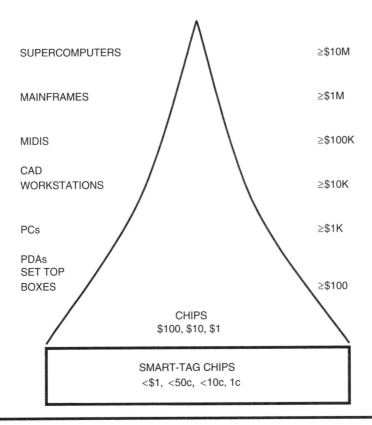

Figure 3.4   The New Pyramid of Computing at the Beginning of the Twenty-First Century

ployed two Connection Machines to run its public database — the largest in the world — substituting a group of mainframes.[4]

More recently, a compact supercomputer that could provide the model for high-performance systems in the years ahead has been built by the Research and Development in Advanced Network Technology (RADIANT) group at Los Alamos National Laboratory. Known as *Green Destiny*, this machine has been built from hundreds of blade servers, compact servers stripped to their most basic components. The system consumes far less power, requires less maintenance, and is more cost effective than typical supercomputers.

Moreover, unlike many such systems that use specialized components and fill an entire building, Green Destiny fits 240 blade servers into a server rack that would fit inside most closets. It also requires no active cooling because of its substantial difference in heat dissipation,[5] as contrasted to other more classical engines.

What is new in these examples is the significant expansion of IT capabilities through miniaturized products, in a range that goes from a ten-cent smart tag to a $10 million supercomputer. This range is shown in Figure 3.4. Smart tags are not the only application with low-cost devices near the bottom of this pyramid. Smart dust (introduced in Section 6) and reality online implementations (explained in Chapter 6) are other examples.

When looking at the impressive pyramid of computing devices shown in Figure 3.4, Green Destiny falls midrange in that scale. Below the level, a smaller version of the engine called Metablade has been up and running since 2001, costing about $33,000 to buy and operate for four years. This compares favorably to $120,000 for a comparable Pentium 4–based workstation and $93,000 for a Pentium 3–based workstation.

The reader should retain from these references the principle that each time we truly cut down the cost, we increase the user population in a significant way. This is valid of all devices, including hybrids. Among them are microelectromechanical systems (MEMs), which combine tiny sensors with actuators that are capable of assessing situations for which they have been designed and of taking appropriate action.

MEMs' advent is a breakthrough of miniaturization and sensing technology. They are constructed of silicon elements and can be currently produced on the micro scale. Research laboratories are also developing ever-smaller and more powerful devices at the nanometer scale — one-billionth of a meter. Of course, size alone is not the ultimate goal. The new products' objective is the combination of small size and self-contained power (the theme of Section 6 on *smart dust*). Their applications landscape respond, to real-time prerogatives, they are holistic, and they help to open new perspectives in R&D.

Nanotechnology is one of the most important current trends in IT. Its impact will be felt throughout the industry, from faster chips and better optical switches to denser storage drives and a myriad of other devices. At the core is the growing synergy of nanotechnology with electronics and mechanical engineering. R&D is now targeting nanoscale dimensions up to 50,000 times thinner than a strand of hair, allied with attributes of:

- Flexibility
- Resilience
- Strength
- High thermal and electrical conductivity

Nanotechnology solutions are expected to support electronics, fiber optics, avionics, and telecoms and to impact many other industries — all the way to lubricants and coatings. One of the interesting developments is that of transistors built from carbon nanotubes, capable of outperforming silicon transistors. In the background of this research is the forecast that silicon-based technology's potential for smaller and faster chips will reach a limit by the middle of the next decade.

Improved connectivity is in the background of work done in many laboratories. Since the current and future environments are communications intense, nanometer-scale antennae, for example, attract considerable interest. Implementationwise, nanoscale antennas can significantly augment the accuracy of medical diagnostic imaging and devices detecting chemical and biological agents.

Moreover, with the data storage sector moving toward the superparamagnetic threshold, there is growing demand for nanotechnology breakthroughs such as organic films, in which data is written, stored, and read in collections of molecules within low-cost films. Microelectromechanical systems will be used to perform the reading into and writing from this new type of storage.

In terms of power supply, as Section 4 indicated, there is no way of bypassing it. On the other hand, it is projected that the use of nanobatteries will improve the capabilities of portable electronics. Nano-sized particles are set to boost power storage, since lithium ions will have a smaller distance to travel during diffusion. These microbatteries will also be used in powering tiny pumps or presses in MEMs and other devices expected to integrate into the manmade ecosystem.

3.5.1 Smart Dust Protocols and Smart Fluids

The Insitute of Electrical and Electronics Engineers (IEEE) has recently drawn up a standard communication protocol, called 802.15.4, for these tiny devices comming under the collective title of smart dust. The ZigBee Alliance, an industry group, hopes its ZigBee standards will popularize 802.15.4 in the same way that the Wi-Fi Alliance popularized another IEEE standard, 802.11, known as Wi-Fi.

Critics, however, point out that these two issues should not be confused. They are quoting experts who believe that Wi-Fi is a creature of regulation, having in its origin more lawyers than engineers. Behind this lies the fact that, by all likelihood, Wi-Fi would not have existed without a decision taken in 1985 by the Federal Communications Commission (FCC) to open several bands of wireless spectrum, allowing them to be used without the need for government licensing.

In essence, the FCC took chunks of spectrum from the industrial scientific, and medical bands at 900 MHz and 2.4 GHz, already allocated to equipment that used radio-frequency energy for purposes other than communications, and opened them up to communications outfits — with the condition that any devices using these bands would have to steer around interference from other equipment.

Many people now think that the allocation of an appropriate band and associated FCC ruling is urgent and should be settled before a boom in smart dust applications brings the whole process out of regulatory control. Let's remember that such sensors can be installed quickly and easily, since they use self-configuring wireless links, and they can have their own internal power supply.

Moreover, there is a growing body of opinion that smart dust should be looked at as an evolutionary process; and silicon is not the only means. Other devices may be able to include shape-memory alloys, which change shape according to temperature, and piezoelectric materials that mechanically deform when an electric field is applied.

Materials mentioned in the preceding paragraphs are said to be smart because they can be used to sense and respond to the environment. Smart materials are not limited to solids. Liquids can be smart too, finding their way into all sorts of devices, from cars to digital cameras. This has brought to the foreground a new term: *smart fluid*, generally applied to fluids whose properties can be changed by the application of an electrical or magnetic field.

Not only are these different supports in full evolution, but also the applications domains themselves are changing. One of the most ambitious experiments on smart dust is that involving an 885-foot oil tanker, *Loch Rannocj*, operated by BP. This tanker has been outfitted with 160 sensors that measure things like vibrations in the ship's pumps, compressors, and engines and pass on their readings by using wireless links. BP wants to test the robustness of sensor networks for wider use, and obtain documentation on whether or not the smart dust network can help to predict equipment failures.

The company is also considering using smart dust-type sensors in some 40 other projects. One of them aims to bind together sensors networks to bridge the gap between more classical information systems and the real world.[7] BP has also put sensors in its trucks to monitor and measure their routes, as well as obtain information on driver behavior. Those in favor say such sensors are needed for safety reasons. Those against consider them an invasion of privacy.

3.6 WHAT CAN BE EXPECTED FROM SMART DUST?

With the possible exception of military applications, today the term *smart dust* is an exaggeration because most devices are matchbox size; tough research projects focus on packages measuring about 12 cubic millimeters. Still, in that small size they contain a clock, digital controller, a couple of sensors, analog-to-digital converter, optical receiver and transmitter, and power supply. In terms of current applications, the term smart dust is mainly applied to devices that are cheap but able to communicate with each other through intelligent wireless sensors. Typically, such devices form autonomous networks that can monitor:

- Presence of people
- Volume of passing traffic
- Local temperature
- Extent of explosion or earthquake

Kris Pister, who did the original research at University of California, Berkeley, coined the term *mote* to describe these small intelligent devices. The mote term has since passed into computer-speak to mean a wireless sensor. In structural terms, these devices feature onboard:

- A microprocessor
- Light sensor
- Bidirectional radio

At laboratory level, motes are much smaller than the dimensions given in the opening paragraph of this section. Those rolling out of the research labs at University of California, Berkeley, are as small as a grain of rice. Berkeley scientists are working to trim smart dust to 1 to 2 cubic millimeters, with more built-in capabilities — eventually down to head-of-a-pin size. Basic reasons for interest in this and similar research projects are that such devices will be:

- Fairly inexpensive
- Far smarter than earlier forms of sensor technology
- Able to be deployed in different environments forming intelligent networks

Smart dust devices will be able to identify an object, give contextual information about its location and status, and provide a track regarding its past and present operating conditions. This, too, is an example of the evolving Internet ecosystem. Most importantly, smart sensors will not operate in isolation but, rather, will work in tandem, using wired and wireless capabilities as well as Web services. As Chapter 6 will explain, reality online applications require devices capable of organizing themselves into communications networks and transmitting rich data streams in execution of operational objectives.

The smart devices at Berkeley have their own operating system that runs on as little as 8 kilobytes. Known as *TinyOS*, it benefits from a large open-source community continuing its development. Part of the TinyOS job is to manage the hardware resources, including various sensors, radio link to other motes, and power supply. It has to do this while consuming relatively little power.

The same motes can be reprogrammed for different tasks, with reprogramming done in wireless mode. Established connectivity permits design of the program on a PC and transmission to the nearest mote. The smart device reprograms itself and then sends the new instructions to the other motes in the network until the whole population is ready to perform the new task.

Power supply is a challenge. The projection is that future versions of smart sensors will be able to do away with batteries, gaining power from their surroundings and establishing a network of silent, little-seen sentinels that record and transmit information about their environment.

The existence of smart sensors and their potential led several experts to suggest that by the end of this decade most data traffic will not be between human beings but between intelligent components. By all likelihood, this timescale is an exaggeration, but it is no less true that the *sensor revolution* has its beginnings in two forms, and both have good potential:

■ Wholesalers and retailers are experimenting with the simple smart tag providing radio frequency ID (RFID), mentioned in Section 5.6 An example of the merchandizing operation is that of RFID-tagged goods, with each item promptly identifying itself and all of them joining with databased information and computing facilities to create an up-to-date inventory.

■ Control engineers experiment with motes and their ability to create their own network within the manmade ecosystem. For instance, Honeywell sells smart sensors to supermarkets for monitoring energy use in refrigeration units. In terms of military applications, rumors have it that very small smart devices scattered in the environment and able to communicate have been used in Afghanistan and Iraq. The hypothesis is that eventually they may be everywhere, for instance, scattered in forests to detect a starting fire.

In a similar way, microsensors scattered over a farmer's field might note when individual plants need water and eventually turn on localized irrigation units to meet irrigation requirements. Also, smart equipment could anticipate a coming breakdown, generate a maintenance call, or shut down equipment to prevent a failure.

Embedding intelligent sensors in equipment and in materials will be instrumental in changing the way day-to-day maintenance is done. The usual way of servicing mechanical and electric equipment is after being in use for a given number of hours, which reflects the expected point of failure. Mean time between failures (MTBF), however, varies. By consequence, production or transport equipment is taken offline for maintenance before it is actually needed or after a severe failure. Smart technology can make it possible to monitor the true reliability condition of equipment and anticipate failure, rescheduling maintenance on an as-needed basis.

As an example, Amskan, an Australian engineering services company, uses currently available sensors to monitor railcar axle boxes for heat buildup. Sensing stations positioned along the tracks detect when there is excess heat, which is an indicator of imminent bearing failure. The computer matches the reading with a specific railcar and notifies maintenance of the need for service.

These are the positive views of work on smart materials. But there exists contrarian thinking based on the fact that the development and implementation of solutions suggested by the foregoing paragraphs are taking a large amount of time and money. Adverse reactions point out that much is claimed about the benefits of smart materials but little has been shown (so far) by way of solutions. Prices for these smart materials are higher than they were expected to be, and nobody yet has answered the question "What's the value?"

The truth most probably lies between these two positions. Breakthroughs will come when people and businesses see deliverables and they believe that very practical results can be obtained at affordable cost.

The message the reader should retain from these references is that as new trends come onstream, the way we do our work changes. Here we no longer talk of stepwise improvements but of innovations that could bring a totally new look at the way we perform our functions, as Figure 3.5 shows. Some of the new developments may be controversial in a social sense. For example, governments plan to integrate smart dust into passports, and banks are studying its integration into passbooks. The aftermath will have an impact on personal privacy.

It is said that the European Central Bank (ECB) looks at embedding smart dust into the euro by the end of this decade. While the control of fraud and forgery is the main objective, other applications of smart dust may be to detect money hidden away in mattresses.

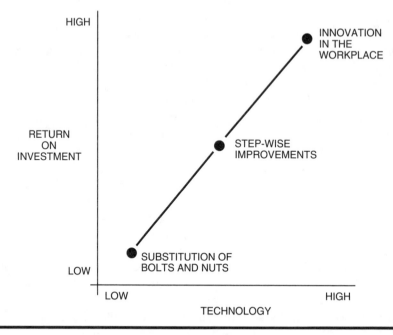

Figure 3.5   Innovation in the Workplace Means a Totally New Look at the Way We Work

These diminutive sensors already are stirring up fears of personal intrusion. Billions of tiny tags could track movements of individuals. Privacy concerns will grow as sensors make their way into payment systems, are placed inside other products as ID devices, and are used for other missions. Science and technology, however, are not known to relinquish their ground. Eventually, people learn to live in the new environment.

3.7   NOTES

1. D.N. Chorafas, *Knowledge Engineering,* Van Nostrand Reinhold, New York, 1990; and D.N. Chorafas and Heinrich Steinmann, *Expert Systems in Banking,* Macmillan, London, 1991.
2. D.N. Chorafas, *Enterprise Architecture and New Generation Information Systems,* St. Lucie Press/CRC, Boca Raton, Florida.
3. D.N. Chorafas, *Integrating ERP, CRM, Supply Chain Management and Smart Materials,* Auerbach, New York, 2001.
4. D.N. Chorafas and H. Steinmann, *Supercomputers,* McGraw-Hill, New York, 1990.
5. *Communications of the ACM,* August 2002, Vol. 45, No. 8.
6. D.N. Chorafas, *Integrating ERP, CRM, Supply Chain Management and Smart Materials,* Auerbach, New York, 2001.
7. *The Economist,* June 12, 2004.

4

WHAT IS MEANT
BY HIGH TECH?

4.1 INTRODUCTION

To a significant extent, the adoption of high technology is a matter of
corporate culture, and the same is true of low technology — except that
the latter culture is much more widespread. The proof is that in Group Ten
countries today, the majority of banks and of insurance companies are
currently devoting about 80 percent to 90 percent of their IT budgets to
maintenance of existing legacy systems, leaving only a small part of their
funding for new investments, including high tech. Many of these institutions cannot even answer the questions:

- What kind of differentiating technology could you invest in if your IT
  maintenance costs were reduced by 20, 30, 40, or 50 percent?
- How would you allocate your human and financial resources if your
  IT costs were variable and based on factual and documented use?

Whether through more imaginative applications, through better utilization of existing assets, through more self-management features, or based
on actual demand for information services (see Chapters 5 to 11), the policy
of well-managed banks is to spend less on routine IT and more on high-
technology, sophisticated applications designed to supply them with a competitive edge. Today, to a very substantial extent, it is clear that the emerging technology will be. What is still a puzzle is how companies with
routine-type IT thinking would change their culture without leadership at
the board and CEO levels.

The first three chapters of this volume have identified several of high-
tech's aspects: connectivity, the Internet ecosystem, straight through processing, reality online, interactive visualization, and, of course, fully real-time
solutions. Being "a little bit real-time" is like saying "a little bit pregnant."
It's not workable.

The results of high-tech implementation must be visible. Senior management should not let routine operations hide competitive advantages that can be realized through the implementation of newer technology. During the Battle of England, in World War II, the British were far ahead of Germans in information technology, which gave them an edge in winning the war. As a German commander relayed it:

> Sometimes when our pilots engaged in battle they were under dated instructions, old by a couple of hours. By contrast, the English received their instructions by radio, even during combat.[1]

In banking, as well as in any other business, low technology is the equivalent of peaceful sell-out, leading to loss of assets. Margaret Thatcher describes the loss of the HMS *Sheffield* as the result of a number of mishaps and mistakes, one-channel technology being major among them:

> The *Sheffield* was a relatively old ship with outdated radar: It was transmitting via satellite to London moments before the missile struck, interfering with its capacity to detect the attack sufficiently in advance to throw up chaff as a decoy.[2]

Many large institutions are currently spending $1 billion a year on low technology. This money goes down the drain for the privilege of being hit by the next Exocet (we will see some practical examples). By contrast, those credit institutions and other companies who are in the high-tech camp concentrate on the management of change and on value differentiation rather than simply throwing money at the problem.

The management of change is not linear because companies are made of people and, like people, they find it difficult to change their old habits. This is particularly true when companies have a technology-illiterate board and mediocre executives who cannot appreciate that the marks of good management are

- *Alertness* to the process of change
- *Evaluation* of its direction and impact
- *Response* through long-term policy measures

The shift from the short-term view to a long–term one is a must for high-tech implementation. It also brings with it the need for new concepts. This applies to every major activity in society. For example, to be ahead of the curve and also increase the visibility of research results, universities now enter into joint ventures with industry in biotechnology, computers, communications, and other domains in which emphasis is placed on R&D and creative thinking.

4.2 USING HIGH TECHNOLOGY FOR BUSINESS SURVIVAL

A manager's most important survival skill is his ability to *anticipate* change, identify and exploit new business opportunities, and also control the risk associated to them. If one is able to figure out what changes are in store in the marketplace, he or she gains extraordinary leverage against competition. That is what the use of high technology is all about. What did we learn from more than 50 years of computers and communications experience in banking?

A. Able application of information systems is a matter of culture, not of machines.

B. We get little from our investment unless we have clear goals and are able to effectively use technology to reach them.

C. If we want to be one of the first into a new territory, we cannot wait for large amounts of evidence. We have to take some risks in judging what is ahead.

Without insight and foresight, enriched by the proper know-how and the will to use it, results will be minimal because the course that we follow is nothing more than the beaten path almost everybody else takes. Superior know-how should be applied to the job. It should not be left as a theory, and it is not true that experts know best.

In the mid-1980s, when personal computers (PCs) were the "in" thing, a 13-year-old boy sued the State of Massachusetts because labor laws did not allow him to work in a computer store although he was a PC genius. The judge ordered a test, and the test showed that the 13-year-old knew more about PCs than 95 percent of the computer experts who participated in the test.

If today money is thrown at IT problems and the results leave so much to be desired, this is dut to two reasons that have been reinforcing one another: (1) Companies have failed to steadily train their IT experts through lifelong learning of *new* technology and (2) the computer experts themselves have become virtually unionized by clustering together around the *status quo* rather than moving out of it to conquer new territory.

This is the thinking that led to the dreadful statistics on the use of IT investments that we saw in the Introduction. Table 4.1 presents additional evidence on the status quo and its negative deliverables. This information has been the result of an IT audit of a major financial institution that spends large sums every year on computers and communications and employs a

Table 4.1 The Missing Technology for Controlling Risk at a Major Financial Institution

	Currently Is	It Should Be
Interest rate risk	Partially RT*	RS**
Global market risk	Batch	RS
Position risk	Batch	RS
Credit risk	Batch	RT
Investment policy risk	Batch	RT
Event risk	Nothing	RT
Sales conditions risk	Limits only	RS
Transaction processing risk	Nothing	RT***
Funds transfer risk	Nothing	RT
Settlement risk	Batch	RS

* Real-time (RT)
**Real-space (RS)
*** Specifically, straight through processing (STP)

small army of 2,500 computer experts; yet its information system is in shambles.

- Of eleven major applications domains that have to do with risk management, only two are partly on real-time.
- The other nine are either batch — which means too little, too late to control exposure — and there is no IT support for them whatsoever.

Every one of these core procedures should have been working in real-time, and the majority should have handled management information requirements in *real-space,* meaning the ability to process and report at a moment's notice, providing worldwide risk information about:

- Any instrument
- Any counterparty
- Any transaction
- Any operation, anywhere in the global landscape

This flexible, instantaneous, results-oriented approach contrasts with the status quo and its substandard deliverables. Dominated by mainframes and the dumb, 30-year-old Cobol programs, legacy "solutions" still work batch. By sticking to old technology, thorny issues brought up by real-time, data mining, secure remote data access, and network latency (among others) are bypassed at great detriment to the company.

A similar statement about leaving challenging problems on the back burner can be made about the reliability of the system as well as of the need to satisfy other requirements, for instance, tuning in new real-time users to more sophisticated applications without performance degradation and without expensive architectural redesigns.

The shortcomings of legacy-type applications cannot be overcome through a spotty implementation of high tech. A 2002 research confirms that IT specialists would have to work both harder and in a more imaginative manner than ever before. This study by the Gartner Group found that IT departments should expect workloads to increase by about 50 percent between 2002 and 2006[3] while the required sophistication of applications also grows.

Parallel to this, the *Chicago Tribune* reports that as a survey of 1,400 chief information officers (CIOs) across the United States has shown, only 15 percent intended to add staff, whereas 4 percent may reduce staff even if the workload increases. The same survey also found that the safest IT jobs are those whose work history has demonstrated contributions to the bottom line—which can best be obtained through high tech.

A good way of looking at the results of these studies and surveys is that during the economic downturn that followed the technology bubble of the late 1990s, something rather radical has happened. For companies to squeeze out a profit, they have had to implement strategies that anticipate where the greatest challenges are likely to occur and what they are likely to be, strategies that would enable a company to take advantage of new realities and convert the status quo into opportunity for change.

4.2.1 Failures in IT Applications Can Be Costly. A Case Study with AT&T Wireless

As 2003 came to a close, AT&T Wireless found out the hard way how costly executed software upgrades can be. What was supposed to be a weekend project turned into six-weeks of disaster recovery. The snafu concerned the increase in the capacity of the company's customer relationship management (CRM) software. The way it has been reported, this CRM upgrade cost AT&T Wireless well over $100 million. Three quarters of this amount represented customer credits, overtime wages, and reseller commissions.

Another huge cost was an 82 percent drop in net customer additions during the fourth quarter of 2003. "(The IT problems) affected our customer growth and probably cost us several hundred thousand net adds," said AT&T Wireless chairman and CEO John Zeglis.[4] Adding just 128,000 customers to its base of 22 million in the fourth quarter of 2003, the company suffered an 81.8 percent year-on-year drop in net adds.

Compounding the damage, the CRM failure greatly affected the carrier's sales capacity. "We lost sales in our own channels when representatives had limited access to the system in November (2003)," added Zeglis.

Indirect sales, which generally account for 40 percent of total sales, were hit hard, because the IT problem soured relations with the company's resellers, and forced management to increase dealer commissions, reportedly by up to 50 percent.

AT&T Wireless (which has since been sold to Cingular) estimated the cost of these higher commissions at $16 million. To appreciate the extent of the damage created by the IT applications failure to the company's customer base, the reader should know that this CRM implementation was central to AT&T Wireless' plans to migrate its roughly 20 million TDMA customers over the GSM. The software problems meant that sales personnel were often unable to enter new customers into the system, and call center employees had no way to either access or account for existing GSM customer records.

Management's failure goes beyond the IT snafu because the timing of the migration itself was risky, coming just before the Christmas sales period. Those who made this decision believed the cut-over would be a matter of just a few days, and chose to switch over just after the third quarter 2003 financial results were announced and before the holiday selling season began.

Some analysts estimated that the net loss to shareholders from this CRM application breakdown amounted to 3 cents a share. Growth was halted when system unavailability blocked new customer activations. This, along with $25 million worth of credits given to complaining customers, saw to it that average revenues per user (ARPU) for AT&T Wireless has been down to an all-time low of $58.70 — bad news for AT&T, but an excellent case study on how deeply IT impacts a company's operations, and how much a failure in critical subsystems, like CRM, can hit an entity's profitability.

4.3 EXTENDING THE CURRENT TECHNOLOGY'S FRONTIER

The need to cut costs, including IT costs, led companies to more fully use their existing technology. Internet usage became the backbone of many enterprises, large and small, bringing along with it a sense of results to be obtained through real-time. Several companies found their solution by using productivity-enhancing IT to trim jobs and outsource production. But only a few, those best managed, took a holistic view of requirements and means.

Those who did take the proverbial long, hard look at their business's future, have found that because high tech is so dependent on senior management's far-sighted decisions and on system design culture, the needed background is not too different than that characterizing design, production, and marketing of other advanced products, e.g., avionics. An advanced technological product must be designed to:

■ Fit different markets through customization
■ Be flexible to satisfy a variety of applications
■ Be able to develop into a coherent product line
■ Use in large part standard component parts

■ Minimize maintenance requirements

As Figure 4.1 shows, a good example of the implementation of the above five principles is the flexibility provided by the Boeing 707. A bad example is the monolithic Concorde, the Anglo-French supersonic white elephant of the 1960s, which consumed an inordinate amount of money in R&D (and in subsequent air transport operations) but boxed itself into one version: It could not become bigger, nor could it become smaller. Monolithic products do not succeed, nor do they recover their development cost. By contrast, product continuity:

■ Spreads the R&D investments
■ Permits a better market focus
■ Brings benefits of a mass effect
■ Protects the flanks against competition

At the time they debuted, both the 707 and Concorde were been high-tech aircraft. As supersonic transport, the Concorde's hardware was more advanced than the 707. Boeing held the upper hand in system design that delivered the first integrative commercial product line and that line contained many competitive advantages. To apply this concept to a banking environment, for instance, high-tech IT must steadily care through connectivity for:

A GOOD EXAMPLE IS THE FLEXIBILITY PROVIDED BY THE BOEING

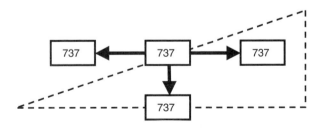

A BAD EXAMPLE IS THE MONOLITHIC CONCORDE

Figure 4.1 Flexibility in Design Does Ensure Market Success, But Don't Bet on It as Being the Only Factor

- Customer care
- Regulatory compliance
- Core value creation
- Leveraging of existing channels
- Security and disaster recovery
- Further cost containment

These are the areas that today attract significant investments in information technology. Although they take the longer-term view, well-managed companies always pay particular attention to short-term tangible returns from their projects. This is compatible with high-tech orientation. IT projects can become low technology by the time deliverables arrive.

Advanced treasury management systems are examples of projects that should definitely fall in this rapid delivery category. This is achievable, provided that home-grown software is out and a top-tier package is implemented at the base (see Chapter 10) while value differentiation is done through proprietary knowledge engineering artifacts. Real-time treasury management is an application that stands relatively high in the Internet ecosystem food chain (see Chapter 3).

Connectivity and competitiveness correlate. The way an economist looks at Wal-Mart's business success is that the efficiency of its IT systems and the cheapness of its nonunionized labor force ($8 to $10 an hour compared with $17 or more for midsized players such as Albertsons, Ahold, Safeway, and Kroger) give it a massive advantage. The merchandiser's competitiveness has a favorable aftereffect on the customer's purse. For example, Wal-Mart sells Colgate toothpaste for an average of 63 percent off its competitors' prices, Tropicana orange juice for 58 percent off, and Kellogg's Corn Flakes for 56 percent off.[5]

Other high-tech implementation examples, but of a different type, include multimedia-based real-time connectivity in groupware for complex design projects shared between engineering labs, distributed computing based on mobile code and mobile agent technologies, and the development of context-aware smart environments. Virtual company solutions are still another worthy reference (see Section 6).

Approaches along this line must address the increasingly complex requirements posed by building and managing sophisticated distributed applications in a way capable of supporting integration of smart components with systemwide services. The way to bet is that the evolving application environments will be spanning multiple autonomous administrative domains, which further complicates the prerequisite organizational study. To succeed, high-tech solutions must be supported by:

- Business architecture
- New programming styles

- Database semantics
- Interactive user interfaces

Successful systems of this type are knowledge based. It is important to investigate a priori their requirements, starting with the query: "What is knowledge?" This is not written in a general sense, but in the particular implementation domain of the study to be done. Associated with that question are others, such as:

- How should knowledge be acquired?
- How should knowledge be represented?
- How should it be managed?
- Where and how should it be stored, physically, and logically?
- How should it be retrieved and processed?
- How should we define basic operations on knowledge?

While answers to these queries must be domain specific, there exist general issues to be addressed networkwide. For instance, which definition of data view should be allowed? Another example is the targeted quality-of-service (QOS), which includes not only quality per se but also reliability, availability, real-time guarantees, security, and synchronization of data streams in delivery.

To a significant extent, quality of service is a knowledge-engineering challenge, because under a high-tech definition QOS requires mechanisms based on meta-level approaches. Knowledge assimilation, knowledge accommodation, and knowledge equilibration engines are also necessary. These are challenges that top-tier companies addressed by in the 1980s. However, for the majority of companies these are still alien thoughts because they have been living for too long in a low-tech environment.

4.4   MANAGING INFORMATION AS A PRODUCT

The 1995 bankruptcy of Barings, the venerable British merchant bank, is an example of what happens to an institution when its internal control is weak, and information is neither timely, accurate, nor comprehensive. In many institutions information on exposure is arrived at partly by guesswork and partly based on what branch managers, traders, or loan officers report over the phone to their bosses, while senior management:

- Pays only scant attention to critical risk elements and
- Lets too much exposure escape control, which damages the company beyond repair

Retrograde, and therefore weak, information technology makes an institution highly vulnerable to adversity (see Chapter 11). It can also decimate its client base. A bank's more important clients are typically those most advanced in their financial and technical weaponry, who know how to capitalize on opportunities presented by the deregulated global financial market and arbitrage the risks they are taking. Both risks and opportunities matter, and it takes technology leadership to keep exposure under lock and key.

Being ahead of the curve does not mean just getting information. Risk information must be focused, and it must also be fine grain. As Figure 4.2 shows, the difference between fine-grain and coarse-grain information can be up to six orders of magnitude, yet the latter is what (unwisely) a great number of companies offer to themselves—in spite of the inordinate amount of money that they spend on IT.

I have found in my professional life that it is not enough to have the best hardware and software money can buy. High-tech equipment can be effaced by a low-tech level of implementation. There are myriad examples to prove this point. Every IT application that does not observe the principles of any-to-any connectivity, seamless access, and real-time processing is misapplying the resources at its disposal. The benefits from its deliverables do not correspond to the incurred costs. However, it is not possible to deliver a high-tech solution by using low-technology hardware, software, and programming languages. Fine-grain data streams, interactive multimedia software, and subsecond response to ad hoc requirements will not be delivered through mainframes, Cobol programming, hierarchical DBMS, and retrograde networks.

Information has to be managed like a product offered to the market with good likelihood for success. If it is not the result of careful research and development to make it appealing both in functionality and in appearance, and if it is not the result of very competitive pricing, it will not sell. Yet, for the most part, in business and industry today information is not properly managed:

■ It is available in overabundance or not at all
■ It is seldom timely and complete
■ It is provided at a cost that cannot be determined

Today's approach to information management is based on yesterday's concepts and means. The image of what can be done with present-day technologies dates back to three or four decades ago. The result is reflected in Figure 4.3, of which is based on a research project targeting management information for right-functioning of an enterprise, with criteria of response time and analytical capability. Neither test gave commendable results.

A couple of other examples are given in Table 4.2. Both compare what can be achieved through new versus old technology. The first case com-

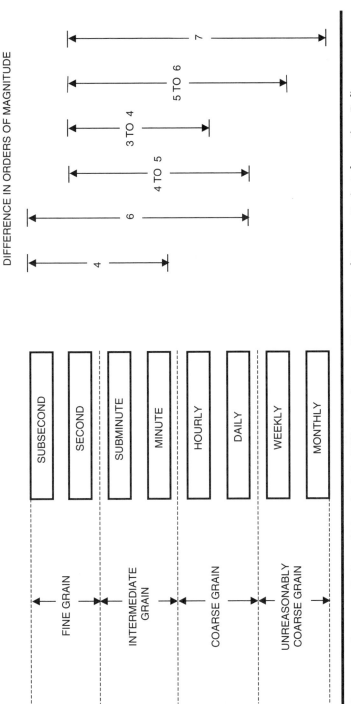

Figure 4.2. There Are Orders of Magnitude in Difference between Fine Grain and Coarse Grain Information Delivery

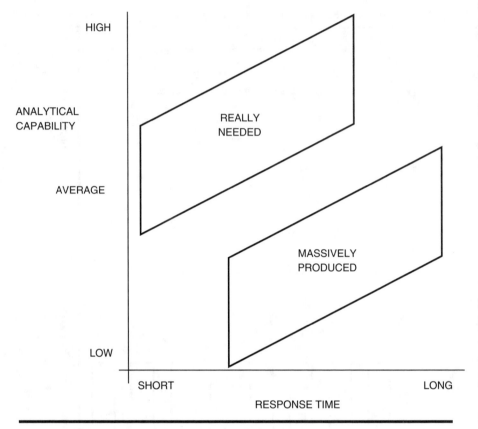

Figure 4.3. Management Information Needed to Do Business versus Data That Is Massively Produced

pares Nordbanken, a Swedish commercial bank that nearly went bankrupt in the early 1990s and was salvaged by taxpayers' money to Securum. Securum is a Swedish financial company set up to manage the bad loans, real estate, and other holdings of Nordbanken with the objective of avoiding a fire sale.

The Swedish government's decision to proceed through a new institution in salvaging the majority of money in bad loans and unwise investments by state-owned Nordbanken included the provision that Securum had to be a self-standing independent entity with its own IT. Securum's information technology became operational in a matter of a few months, thereby developing high-tech applications from scratch. Nordbanken had taken three to five years to deliver a new credit risk management program. Using prototyping and visual programming, Securum did the same in a matter of weeks.

The second case in Table 4.2 compares Securum to Deutsche Bank. In the background is the Jürgen Schneider scam. Schneider was a real estate

Table 4.2 Two Examples of Old versus New Technology in Managing Loans

Example No. 1: Nordbanken vs. Securum

Nordbanken	Securum
Mainframes	Client-server
Everything centralized	Fully distributed
Largely batch	Everything integrative
IMS	Relational DBMS
Cobol	C, prototyping
3 to 5 years to deliverables	Weeks to months in deliverables

Example No. 2: Deutsche Bank vs. Securum

Deutsche Bank	Securum
Paid for 20,000 m² instead of 9,000 m² that were built .	Interactive 3-D follow-up on real estate loans
Gave loans for work done at 90% although it was done at 40%	Immediate correlation of progress report with accounting and loans

magnate who managed to get financing for buildings he never finished and covered m² of construction that never existed. There is no evidence the large German bank had the technology to follow up in real-time the progress of work done by this or any other real estate developers before advancing money. If this were the case, Deutsche Bank would not have lost a rumored DM 5 billion ($2.5 billion) with Schneider. Through high tech, small Securum was able to closely track the work of developers prior to making advances.

Another example of how much more accurate is the work accomplished through high technology than by legacy approaches comes from year 2000 (Y2K) compliance. The statistics in Table 4.3 originate from a 1999 study based on a statistically valid sample of companies, some of which used mainframes and others client-servers. The message is so clear that it hardly needs explaining. These statistics are based on inventories of 10 million to 30 million lines of code, depending on the bank, on average, little less than 40 percent was bought software.

Managing information as a product is, first of all, a matter of policy established by the board and the CEO, but it is only one feature system design. Under the right policy, the search for appropriate solutions must go all the way from system analysis and prototyping to the choice of most appropriate programming languages to serve the applications environment. Table 4.4 presents two examples:

Table 4.3 Inventory of Applications Regarding the Year 2000 Problem (Average Percent Figures Based on a Research Sample)

	Mainframes	Client Servers
In-house Developments		
Compliant	32%	73%
Non-compliant, to be corrected	58%	7%
To be eliminated	9%	20%
Bought Software		
Compliant	0%	85%
Non-compliant, to be corrected	80%	7%
To be eliminated	20%	8%

■ A study made by U.S. government–sponsored Microelectronics and Computer Development Corporation (MCC) on lines of code and consumed machine power
■ A study done by IBM that focused on broad areas of programming activity and that, in a way, complements MCC's findings.

Based on a sample of 60 U.S. companies, MCC found that (in general) about 80 percent of the code consumed just 2 percent of machine cycles. This should definitely be left at prototyping language level. By contrast, 2 percent of the code used 50 percent of installed machine power. These programs should be in assembler or, even better, in machine language. The distribution of the balance of percent code/percent cycles was specific to the company.

Table 4.4 Prototyping versus Programming and Compiling

Example No. 1: An MCC Study		
Machine Power	*Lines of Code*	
2%	80%	Prototyping
50%	2%	HLL Programming
48%	18%	Variable by company
Example No. 2: An IBM Study		
Percent of Programming Effort		
40%	Interactive queries, mainly end user	
40%	Database management	
20%	Data processing	

IBM's study was done at about the same time (early 1980s). Its contribution has been that it classified the inventory of applications routines by broader class of programming effort. It is interesting that interactive queries and database management took the lion's share of the code. I bring these studies to the reader's attention as the lessons learned from them are fundamental to any company that aims to manage information as a product.

Optimizing the programming effort in function of direct labor invested in analysis/coding/testing and consumed machine power kills two birds with one well-placed stone. It looks at information as a product that, like any other product or service, must be designed in a cost-effective way in order to be successful, and it capitalizes on the evolution of technology to bend the cost curve, since the cost of MIPS steadily shrinks while the cost of human effort involved in programming steadily increases over time.

Both the MCC and IBM studies reflected the critical requirements of their time. Today, similar studies should evidently account, as well, for other factors characterizing the current computational and communications environment. For instance, any advanced system solution should:

■ Follow dynamic design paradigms
■ Make use of mobility mechanisms
■ Address networked applications

Designers are required to rethink executable parts of programs, including flow of computation, distributed data spaces, and dynamic code execution. The advantage of managing mobile code through agents is that it makes feasible mobility of knowledge, which may be weak or strong.

Different types of weak mobility are characterized by the nature of code, direction in which it moves, synchronization, and time of execution. The code itself may be stand-alone or dependent on another part, executed immediately or deferred. This kind of mobility may be synchronous or asynchronous.

For their part, within the grand design of the computational environment, available resources can be transferable or nontransferable (static). Transferability needs to be defined as to its desirability in particular situations. In that sense, transferable resources can be free to move or fixed.

For instance, if the executing unit moves to a new computational environment the resource can be moved with the executing unit if it is transferable and free. Alternatively, in the case that the resource can not be reallocated in the new environment, a network reference mechanism must be set up. Its existence implies that the data space is effectively distributed over the network, but resources may be bound by value to the executing environment.

Code mobility versus its absence, transferable versus nontransferable resources, and synchronous versus asynchronous operations are characteristics that did not catch the designer's eye two decades ago and, therefore, are not reflected in the MCC and IBM studies briefly described in the preceding paragraphs. Today, however, they constitute important design parameters in any-to-any connectivity, and they should be accounted for when managing information as a product.

4.5 R&D IS AN INTEGRAL PART OF HIGH-TECH IMPLEMENTATION

What is available today in design is just a forerunner of things to come. The future applications, system solutions, languages, and other wares either are laboratory projects or await their time to go into R&D. Any self-respecting enterprise must have a budget for research and development in IT; for many companies success in research and development means survival. Here is how Steve Ballmer, Microsoft's CEO, expressed his thoughts:

> R&D is a large number for us. The critical issue for us is: Do we have the right product? Are we in the market at the right time? Do we have the innovation? I will trade off a number of things on the cost side to make sure that we have that . . . (and) it helps to not only be in the maelstrom of activity, it helps to be close to the biggest market in the world. You've got to try things out on customers.[6]

Product development projects must be focused. They should have a sponsor, and they must have observed timetables for deliverables. Take the global electronics industry as an example. For the first time, it has to face the conventional reality that research and development budgets are attracting the scrutinizing gaze of accountants and of auditors. For a long time, R&D was the protected element of a company's financial planning. More money for research was virtually an automatic upgrade decision of management.

This is no longer the case. R&D projects are closely scrutinized. But if we want to manage information as a product, there should always be research and development financing aiming at developing tomorrow's applications, as today's top-of-the-line IT becomes rather common place and it no longer offers competitive advantages.

An example is MIT's Oxygen Project, which targets a 300 percent improvement in personal productivity. Its core system is composed of three parts: intelligent room (E21), handheld devices (H21), and embedded devices and wireless communications (N21). Among Oxygen's major goals are:

- Location of resources by intent, a totally new goal in computing
- Nomadic software that can be updated on the fly
- Ambient interfaces permitting objects to preserve their physical existence
- Person-centric security, rather than device centric
- Cross-network integration: local, buildingwide, terrestrial, satellite

This project uses a number of agents (knowledge artifacts) to sustain the intelligent environment.[7] The project's intelligent room records both events and nonevents through its scatterbrain agents. The agents ponder such questions as why people make certain decisions in certain types of situations and why people do not make something when they are expected to.

Each of the scatterbrain agents is responsible for a different room function. The speech agent interfaces with the speech recognition subsystem. Other agents capture gesture and context. Most importantly, this interactive intelligent environment operates without a central controller. Therefore, it is robust. Dependability is one of the key design criteria in handling information as a product.

Ringcam, by Microsoft, has similarities to the intelligent room. It is a video-teleconferencing technology based on a device that looks like a small table lamp, with five cameras circling the top and eight tiny microphones around the base. This gives a 360-degree view of a room. Knowledge-enriched software matches the audio and visual feeds. People tapping into the meeting from elsewhere automatically see the person who is talking in a window of their computer screen.

It is not sure whether Microsoft benefited from MIT's precompetitive research, which it cosponsors, or made its own development — though its Ringcam looks like a localized scaled-down version of the Oxygen Project. What is sure is that it can benefit MIT's intelligent environment, which provides the prototype of trustworthy, real-time intelligent systems that will most likely characterize the next 20 years.

To a large extent, the MIT Oxygen Project currently addresses lower-level sensor technology, not a systemwide middleware solution. This might have been influenced by the fact that real-time new sensor technology is currently in high esteem, as we have already seen in Chapter 3 and will examine in an implementations-oriented sense in Chapter 6 in connection to reality online.

The project's critics say that its design is largely influenced by military command and control considerations, not by the requirements of manufacturing or financial systems. I would not particularly worry about this argument: many projects that start through military sponsorship find very fertile applications in business and industry.

Countries that do not have a huge military budget engage in other fields of research. For instance, in November 2003, in Switzerland, the explorer

Bertrand Piccard embarked on an ambitious round-the-world flight in solar aircraft. The project was cosponsored by the Swiss Federal Institute of Technology in Lausanne (EPFL).

Piccard's airplane achieved an altitude of 10,000 meters using only renewable forms of energy and remained airborne without generating polluting emissions. This project aimed to honor the great firsts and record-breaking flights that punctuated the history of twentieth-century aviation. It was also expected to produce new light materials, batteries, motors, and expert systems that would promote the competitiveness of Swiss industry and to draw attention to the need for essential changes to ensure future energy resources and the ecological balance of the earth.

Other projects, too, focus on similar goals. An article in *The Economist* stated, "For smaller aircraft, an emerging green alternative is lightweight fuel cells for use in micro-jets. The technology looks as though it could power planes with around 20 passengers. (In 2004) a 1,000 lb (450 kg) battery-powered plane being developed by Advanced Technology Products of Worcester, Massachusetts, should have its first flight."[8]

The Swiss and the U.S. efforts may well be the tip of the iceberg for future sustainable development in air travel. One of the major constraints with deliverables of advanced projects is that people are not appropriately trained to appreciate the importance of resource preservation and use high tech to such an end. Working on such imaginative projects is significantly helped if system solutions are learned as a generic aspect of sustainable industrial, financial, and cultural life — not as a stagnant subject reserved to the system specialist.

4.6 HIGH TECHNOLOGY AND THE VIRTUAL COMPANY

Since the mid-1990s an interesting concept in business and industry has been the *virtual corporation*, in which a company has a core of managers and professionals but, to a great degree, the majority of employees are contingent: temporary, part-time, or short-term contractors. This is an evolving model of corporate services, with job security being more and more dependent on technological know-how and the ability to produce results.

A virtual company is a temporary consortium of independent member companies coming together to quickly exploit fast-changing local, national, or worldwide business opportunities. Companies cooperating in a virtual enterprise share costs, skills, and core competition that collectively enable them to access markets and provide world-class solutions that their members could not deliver individually.

These are the basic concepts on which a virtual organization rests. Virtuality is characterized by the usage of complementary resources existing in cooperating firms. Such resources are left in place, but they are integrated to support a particular product effort for as long as this is viable.

In principle, resources are selectively allocated to the virtual company if they can be more profitably utilized there than in the home company. To be effective, virtual companies must be supported by virtual office systems based on agents that help expand the boundaries of an organization. The goals of intelligence-enriched system solutions are:

- Speeding of business processes to facilitate commerce
- Supporting online interactions with a broader business range than is possible under traditional approaches

In a dynamic market, intra- and intercompany resource availability can change from minute to minute. Advantages accrue to parties able to rapidly arbitrage resource availabilities. Virtual organizations use smart software to supplement their cognitive capabilities, thus providing themselves with an advantage, given tight time constraints and finite resources.

A common ground is provided by a set of principles for metamanaging activities concerning the virtual enterprise, whether these are industrial or financial. Typically, such activities are undertaken by virtual teams, or groups of individuals that collectively possess specific skills.

- Metamanagement makes goals explicit
- Substitutes for the central role played by a classical company's hierarchy

High-tech-supported connectivity provides the virtual company's infrastructure and also lowers the cost of switching among real companies to create a new virtual company. An example of an approach enacting such a switch is the *Virtual Lab Notebook* (VILAN), which utilizes proactive software agents grouped into two types:

- Data source wrapper agents, encapsulating various heterogeneous data sources
- Broker agents, intermediating requests from users through knowledge about, and transactions with, data source agents

The wrapper makes it possible for one agent to communicate on some higher level with other agents while still being able to fully exploit domain-specific software. The broker finds information that could enable answering of user requests, accommodating single-occurrence demands and recurring behavioral objectives.

A good way to look at virtual companies is as federated entities, working as if they were federated independent business units of a corporation. The Japanese conglomerates are an example. *Federalism* is not just another word for decentralization.

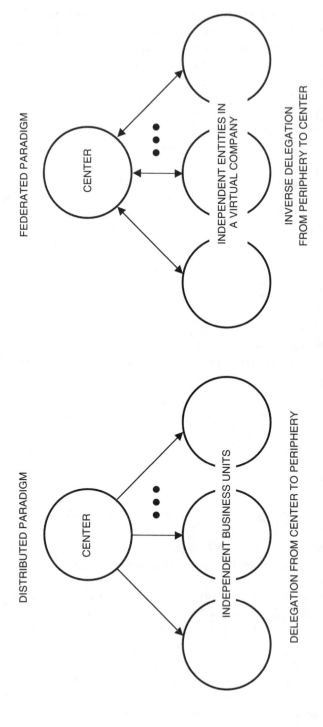

Figure 4.4. There Is an Essential Difference between Decentralization and Federation of Independent Entities

■ Decentralization implies that the center delegates certain tasks or duties to the outlying units, while remaining in overall control; the center does the delegating, initiating, and directing.

■ In federalism, the center's powers are given to it by the outlying groups, in a form of reverse delegation. The center coordinates, advises, influences, suggests, and even controls — but it does not order.

This difference is shown in Figure 4.4, which documents that the two modes, federation and decentralization, are totally distinct, with federation being a structural response to bringing together diverse entities and jurisdictions to pursue common goals, while these entities retain their independence. The Basel Committee on Banking Supervision provides an example of federation.

Real-time any-to-any connectivity, reality online, straight through processing, and the Internet ecosystem are concepts that integrate well with federated solutions. Always, however, remember the principle that real-time information can be adequately conveyed, perceived, and acted upon, when there are well-trained receivers. Organizations are made of people, and if the people do not know how or do not want to do what the federation — or virtual corporation — implies, the result will be somewhere between chaos and uncertainty.

4.7 NOTES

1. Leonard Mosley, "The Battle of England," Time-Life, 1979.
2. Margaret Thatcher, *The Downing Street Years*, HarperCollins, London, 1993.
3. Communications of the ACM, February 2003, Vol. 45, No. 2.
4. Total Telecom, March 2004.
5. *The Economist*, December 13, 2003.
6. *Business Week*, December 1, 2003.
7. D.N. Chorafas, *Agent Technology Handbook*, McGraw-Hill, New York, 1998.
8. *The Economist*, December 13, 2003.

II

STRAIGHT THROUGH PROCESSING, REALITY ONLINE, AND KNOWLEDGE MANAGEMENT

5

STRAIGHT THROUGH PROCESSING

5.1 INTRODUCTION

The concept underpinning straight through processing (STP) has been embedded in many applications linking business partners. Historical reference suggests that a more generalized interest in implementing STP started around 1997. The Swift organization says it invented the term in connection with front-desk/back-office integration; however, there is no clear evidence of this, though it might be possible. The "STP Newsletter," which was issued that same year, helped in popularizing the term.

A critical question used in information technology is: What about the substance? This is particularly true when it is not easy to present in one short sentence the basic notions behind a new term because the experts cannot agree on a single definition. This is the case with straight through processing.

With Graeme Austin, the managing director of STP Information Systems and of *STP Magazine*,[1] we started looking for a comprehensive definition of STP by going back to basics. "The core," Austin said, "is seamless internal processing. Something similar to SWIFT, but oriented to transactions." A subject on which we were in agreement is that STP makes sense only in connection to real-time operations. That definition has been enlarged to include messages and decision-making processes.

The above definition may not apply to e-mail, however. This may seem contradictory. The reason for this reservation is that whether or not electronic mail should be included, depends on how automated the analysis of its content is. Austin also made a distinction between:

- *Internal STP,* for instance, a seamless front-desk/back-office connection assisted by intranets
- *External STP,* which interconnects business partners and may be served through proprietary networks, or extranets

External STP may be inbound if it receives input from clients and suppliers and outbound if it forwards an input to the systems of our company's counterparties. Figure 5.1 presents, in a nutshell, the STP relationship to business partners served by an any-to-any network, whether Internet or extranet. As far as the interests of parties to this solution are concerned, a top priority is the ability to execute transactions, share knowledge, and link value chains.

Within this STP definition and approach, the seamless real-time access is assured through other software like ERP (see section 5), CRM, just-in-time (JIT) solutions, and fast flow replenishment (FFR). Modern treasury packages (see Chapter 10), sales order handlers, and execution reports can be also part of STP execution. Also, there is need for supporting online facilities, an example being seamless database mining.

Straight through processing is an internal online passthrough process with automatic external connections to other internal online passthroughs belonging to counterparties. The broader integration of the aforementioned services gives muscle to STP, even if its comprehensive definition is still wanting. As one of the lecturers in a recent event said, It has not been possible to get agreement in a committee meeting on STP's definition about what STP *is*. Other experts suggested that neither is there an agreement on how fast STP could be implemented.

It does not take ages to put an STP solution in practice. Dell and Nasdaq provide an example on how quickly this can be accomplished. This case study was conducted in late October 1997, when the economic crisis in Asia and other reasons sparked stockmarket activity that sent trading volumes

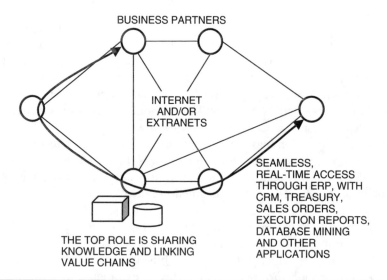

Figure 5.1 Straight Through Processing on an Any-to-Any Network

to a record high. In one day, Nasdaq received 20 million hits at its Internet trading site nasdaq.com.

Nasdaq urgently needed additional services to handle this large increase. At its request, Dell built and shipped eight custom-configured, fully tested server systems in just 36 hours. Three days later, Nasdaq was effectively using the servers to conduct its online business through state-of-the-art technology. From request to full-scale implementation, it took exactly 4½ days.

Rapid implementation has evident advantages: being a leader in the supply chain, sustaining or increasing the profit margins, accelerating the cash flow, and, above all, improving the level of confidence the market has in the organization. Critical to a sound solution is the reliability of the infrastructure, which consists of basic facilities, services, equipment, software, and supporting installations needed for the functioning of STP. The reliability of a real-time infrastructure must be at least 99.99 percent, and, as we will see, STP should work in real-time.

5.2 A PRACTICAL EXAMPLE WITH STP: CONTINUOUS LINK SETTLEMENT

Clearing payments and settlements are processes indivisible from banking and from business activities at large. This requires much manual intervention, high costs, and a fair amount of operational risk, including legal risk. All three issues suggest that real-time straight through processing can contribute to better management control and therefore present significant advantages, provided the necessary conditions are fulfilled (see Sections 3 and 4).

Since there is no general agreement on the definition of straight through processing, the best way to demonstrate what this term really means and what it can contribute in information handling is through a practical example. The case study in the section is the Continuous Linked Settlement (CLS) solution, designed fo handling foreign exchange (FX, forex) transactions and the elimination of associated settlement risk.

The solution, which has been adopted for CLS and should be representative of STP approaches, is based on delivery versus payment (DVP) methodology, with settlements done by book-to-book transfer. If a trade cannot be settled, the settlement is returned. In every user organization, a decision tree at the front desk helps in determining which trades are eligible for CLS and the system provides for protection of principal amount.

Among the advantages of the method are one global standard for payment processing, with core payment kernel applicable for all types of FX payments, central bank reporting included. This solution fulfills security and reliability requirements, as should always be the case with a global cash management system. The implementation perspective is shown in Figure 5.2.

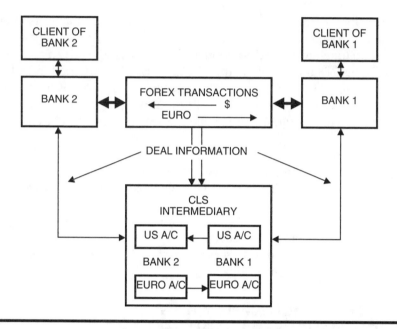

Figure 5.2   Forex Transactions under Continuously Linked Settlements

- The CLS solution meets regulatory concerns for FX market stability and FX market integrity.
- As a private sector initiative, CLS helps to mitigate forex settlement risk and regulatory capital charges.

At his lecture at the Trema World Forum,[2] Wayne W. Ferguson of Deutsche Bank emphasized that client benefits of CLS include foreign exchange trading proper, liquidity management, and a simplification of other associated operations. In his opinion the client of CLS benefits from:

- Reduction of forex settlement risk
- Less use of credit lines due to multilateral netting
- Decreased exposure to daily settlement limit
- A certain potential for two-tier marketplace

The aftermath of multilateral netting is that of a lower number of payments to be effected, a lower amount of receivables to be reconciled, and a reduced interest expense for compensation. Beyond this are liquidity enhancements, with liquidity management improved because cash flows become predictable. There is less use of liquidity considerations due to the aforementioned multilateral netting. An added advantage is that treasurers are automatically advised of actual funding needs (see also Chapter 10).

Apart from other critical issues of concern to the treasury, liquidity management is important in execution of transactions because it poses both financial and technological prerequisites, like seamless real-time access to databases, to avoid delays in seeing money transfers through. (These and many other subjects connected to liquidity fall outside the scope of this book.)[3]

It is also appropriate to note the cost associated with liquidity. So far, in the majority of cases, liquidity in the sense of interbank credit has been provided free of charge. Central banks now say that this cannot continue. The free lunch has ended. Hence, informing the treasurer about funding needs is very important, since banks participating in a real-time 24-hour settlement system need to ensure that there are adequate funds in their accounts.

A better control of operational risk is another advantage derived from continuous link settlement. Every transaction carries with it a certain cost due to op risk, and this increases as international payments go beyond what national regulations imply. We cannot hope to achieve the closer integration required by 24-hour-per-day real-time settlements while standards of operational risk management are low. Precisely for this reason, the new capital adequacy framework (Basel II) by the Basel Committee on Banking Supervision addresses operational risk control.[4]

Requirements for secure paperless settlements are pressing. Financial markets, and especially securities and foreign exchange markets, have much at stake because they deal with such large volume. Among other reasons why operational risk can be subject to more efficient control with CLS is the reduction in number of payments and number of receivables as well as the greater automation of the transaction.

A similar statement is valid in regard to straight through processing and the fact that it contributes to the reconciliation process. With trades settled individually through CLS, the sender's trade references are included on Web information and end-of-day statements. The sender's original information is carried on any subsequent amends or cancellations. What in CLS jargon is called "marching criteria" includes critical information such as:

- Sender bank ID code
- Receiver bank ID code
- Value date
- Currency bought
- Amount bought
- Currency sold
- Amount sold

Forex trades are submitted through existing SWIFT protocols, and status of trade is advised by SWIFT-Net with point-to-point communication. These choices have been deliberate for cost effectiveness reasons. CLS uses existing systems to reduce implementation cost and employs SWIFT to keep in control item level; and employs net funding of pays to reduce the number of executions (see also Section 6).

5.3 CONTINUITIES AND DISCONTINUITIES IN STP IMPLEMENTATION

In terms of the implementation of straight through processing, the good news is that this is no monolithic process; it can come by subsystem. However, as it has been stated in the STP definition and will be further explained in Section 4, there is no real systemwide solution, in STP terms, until all subsystems are in place and they work as an aggregate in real-time.

This statement is valid both for internal straight through processing, done under the company's own authority, and for external STP, which extends to the business partners. True, parts of the latter are conditioned by the technology of counterparties who may not have in place real-time solutions. When this happens:

- The part of STP that is under authority of the company may rest on the principles characterizing the real-time enterprise.
- By contrast, the whole STP solution, affecting the operations of our company, might be on a two-speed pattern, as shown in Figure 5.3.

I contend that a non-real-time STP is nothing more than smoke and mirrors. Graeme Austin stated that "70 percent STP is no solution worth talking about," but he quickly added, "I don't believe STP should be exclusive. Most companies have pockets of STP in parts of their applications, though not necessarily a system solution."

On that particular account, opinions among experts differ most significantly. Information technology solutions closely emulate the convoy principle in World War II: the slowest vehicle sets the pace. Having an approach that uses 50 percent real-time and 50 percent batch is like the sausages manufacturer who was selling his produce as 50–50 horse and rabbit — to the proportion of one horse and one rabbit. Batch plays the horse's role.

Let me repeat this statement to ensure it is well understood. The problem with pockets of STP, although the rest still works batch, in the convoy allegory is that the slowest ship that set the convoy's speed made the whole convoy vulnerable to German submarines. Quite similarly, with information technology batch programs still in the system, it makes the system work backwards, as if they were all batch. This is a medieval approach to IT problems.

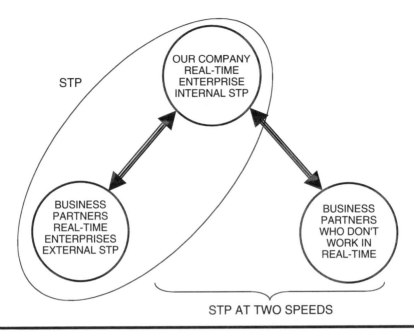

Figure 5.3 Business Partner Solutions May Be 2-Speed, Depending on the Level of Technology of the Other Companies

As Chapters 3 and 4 have explained, pockets of batch processing see to it that real-time's competitive advantage evaporates. Austin took this issue stoically: "That's the way it works." Should it? "No," he said, "but in a world where the broker is inhibited by his clients, that's the IT result one obtains." The batch issue aside, also working against STP is backward technology like incompatible databases and heterogeneous data formats.

In a recent survey by the Gartner Group, companies were found to have up to 60 different incompatible databases and a multiplicity of messaging standards. It is indeed surprising that companies do not wish to understand the discontinuities existing in their technology or the lack of return on investment, and their persistence in using legacy approaches cuts the branch on which they are sitting. Moreover, many companies have the wrong belief that *if* they increase their level of automation, *then* they will reduce their costs significantly.

That is unsubstantiated thinking. The headcount is not being taken care of by "more automation," because the people working for the organization reposition themselves. As a result, costs might actually increase. In banking this is often the case. Given that banking is generally overmanned in spite of the glorious pronouncement by this or that institution that it is trimming overhead, quite often the overhead survives unscathed.

Weeding out discontinuities in IT, reengineering, and cutting organizational fat correlate and produce results if, and only if, the board and the CEO ask for concrete evidence about what has been attained. Reengineering means several things, some of them expected to be done simultaneously and with resolve, e.g., focusing on core business, restructuring, downsizing, demolishing and rebuilding, zero-budgeting, and thoroughly revamping information technology and infrastructure

This is the way to make STP work. In fact, implementing straight through processing assists in making a thorough system analysis to weed out pockets of batch processing. Reengineering done with resolve can provide a fully online business rule definition and the competitive advantages resulting from it, thereby helping to reduce infrastructural overhead, shrink the time to implementation by promoting concrete goals, and attain a shorter timeframe to realize cost benefits.

As with every information technology project, when we set *a priori* a concrete goal with STP, we usually obtain increased control over development and implementation (see also Chapter 2). Never forget that high overhead and inadequate information technology solutions are prime reasons why administrative costs account for an estimated 15 percent to 25 percent of total spending in business activities. Because much of this organizational fat is at the nodes of transaction handling, STP represents a good way to trim costs on trivial and administrative duties, transforming current practices. But the solution has to be 100 percent real-time.

The reader should appreciate that significant economies can be obtained even from one single application that interfaces seamlessly to others. This is not true when the interfacing involves plenty of inefficiencies. STP should be characterized by a streamlined environment, providing reliable information to participants, and serving the whole chain of business partners.

As my research documents, what has just been stated is the goal of the best-managed organizations, and it is reachable. However, the solutions that are chosen should not be half-baked, and they should not promote the status quo over reengineering and greater efficiency.

If a company does not have internal resources for implementing straight through processing in an integrative way, it should address itself to reputable consultancies. During our August 2003 meeting at Accenture's Research Laboratories in Chicago, Stanton Taylor, an Accenture partner, defined as follows the basic building blocks of an STP solution designed to sustain continuity within an environment that includes equities, forex, and other financial instruments:

- *Building Block 1:* Leveraging the new messaging standards
- *Building Block 2:* Transforming the delivery of reference data
- *Building Block 3:* Reengineering corporate actions and their supports
- *Building Block 4:* Automating the front-to-back process flow

The careful reader will observe that building blocks 1 to 4 are general and can fit practically any real-time STP implementation, particularly one designed for transaction handling with business partners. By contrast, other building blocks may be special to a particular application. For instance, with reference to one of the implementations done by Accenture, Taylor mentioned:

- *Building Block 5:* Accessing emerging markets
- *Building Block 6:* Managing change in established markets

Depending on the specific implementation environment, straight through processing may call for other criteria linking transaction processing to research, development, sales, trading, payments and settlements, custody, legal risk management, and so on. It will also be wise to add to the basic building blocks of STP (1 to 4 in this example) internal control and regulatory compliance. To a substantial extent, both should be handled online.

5.4 EXCEPTION HANDLING AND STRAIGHT THROUGH PROCESSING

Outside CLS, which is an international example, more success stories on STP have thus far come from the United States rather than from Europe, most probably because of a cultural reason. In the United States, information technology integration is considered to involve both an internal and an external perspective, the latter bringing business partners all the way into the picture. By contrast, most companies in Europe consider IT integration as a primarily internal problem, which limits both implementation perspective and return on investment.

Moreover, American companies seem to be more appreciative of the fact that a basic STP solution can be enriched with add-ons leading to value differentiation. An example of a competitive edge solution is the use of knowledge artifacts to automatically manage exception processing, compared to a more elementary approach that spots but does not manage exceptions.

Knowledge engineering plays a role in defining the level of STP. Sophisticated straight through processing would use agents to inform their master about successfully processed trades. An argument I heard from IT people thinking along old EDP lines is that it is not part of STP to say if transactions have or have not gone through. Such an argument is evidently wrong.

It takes intelligence-enriched facilities to handle exceptions by computers. An example is the policy followed by AT&T when it ran its successful credit card operation. "We track everything that moves and everything that *does not move,*" said AT&T's director of marketing in a meeting we had in

London some years ago, when the AT&T credit card services were up and coming. This was done through intelligent artifacts capable of spotting and managing exceptions.

Exceptions are best managed in real-time. One of the questions I posed to Graeme Austin was whether STP is synonymous with the *real-time enterprise*. There was a bifurcation in his answer. "Theoretically 'yes,' but practically 'no,'" Austin replied, making the point that it is better to think of STP as a hands-free operation done online in real-time from front data capture to data delivery.

Given the level of technology currently characterizing most firms, STP would not have many adherents. Austin pressed the point that a commendable way to look at STP is as a culture, not as software. Austin added that an STP solution must be supported by a framework to describe how organization and IT contribute to online seamless handling of transactions. Hence, these are three basic issues:

■ Cultural change
■ Design of a framework
■ Knowledge-based handling of exceptions

These three bulleted points show that STP solutions have to be holistic; otherwise, there is no effective straight through processing implementation. Not only does the STP solution have to be end to end (see Chapter 16), without discontinuities, but also attention should be paid to technical problems and complexities associated to multisite STP implementations, where, for instance, at each site there are different choices leading to heterogeneous supports. Some of the complexities in STP in implementation come from the generalized nature of the off-the-shelf applications and the tendency to personalize the software to procedures of the user organization.

The principle with packages is that user organizations should not alter the bought software. This principle, however, is rarely observed. Even in the same user organization the different IT sites put their figures in the code, with the result that maintenance becomes much more complicated and costly and the performance of the system at another site is affected in a negative way.

User organizations, therefore, are well advised to plan multisite straight through processing applications very thoroughly and to weed out deviations before committing themselves to an STP solution.

Technical issues altering the pace or extent of an STP implementation range from heterogeneous platforms and OS/DBMS at user organization premises to failure at keeping the distributed system updated to the same release. Even if, at the beginning, problems of heterogeneity of platforms are temporarily solved, they can resurface as different business units make changes at their end or, alternatively, perceive migrations to a new release as difficult, time consuming, and costly.

One of the reasons why migration between successive releases of software has proved to be a challenge is that the newer version is a finer grid through which errors in the new routines do not pass but went undetected in previous versions. This is reasonable because one of the aims of new releases is that of improving business processes. Indeed, user organizations continuously pressure software vendors in adding more functionality and improving the efficiency of their programming products.

The evolution of straight through processing solutions is also influenced by the fact that changing market conditions shift the focus of programming products toward more sophisticated approaches that may be beyond the culture and skills of the user entity. An aftermath of end-to-end STP applications is that some of the company's business partners may not be able to proceed with updates the moment a new version becomes available. This is the World War II convoy principle of which we have been talking, and it is a practical issue because both business processes and technology change very fast.

Because of the reasons this section has described, requirements relating to flexibility of implementation of straight through processing dictate that the end-to-end application should benefit from a conceptual model covering all business partner connections. Rigid phase-by-phase implementation can be counterproductive. Flexible targeting concepts fit well with both customization techniques and new releases, keeping in mind that many business functions integrating into STP have to be executed:

- Simultaneously
- Interactively
- In real-time

Business experts and systems staff should work in close collaboration, addressing all types of implementation issues both within the firm and between companies linked through STP. The use of modeling tools can help the development process, and the same is true of a corporate memory facility (CMF, see Chapter 7) storing the results of:

- Discussions
- Decisions
- Pending issues
- Functional definitions

A factual and documented approach enables better collaboration both at the business end and at the technical end. It also provides a good linkage to further upgrades that become prominent as a significant number of STP application users gain experience with the system and start to like its deliverables.

5.5 CONNECTING STP TO ENTERPRISE RESOURCES PLANNING

Straight through processing will not operate stand-alone. As Sections 3 and 4 brought to the reader's attention, it has to link in an effective manner to other procedures that are both internal to the enterprises and external, connecting to clients, suppliers, and other business partners. A good example of a procedure STP should connect to is enterprise resource planning (ERP). Here are some basic facts:

1. Like STP, ERP maps processes, not functions.
2. ERP can help in reengineering the supply chain (see Section 3).
3. Pass-through by ERP processes strengthens business partner relations.
4. Commodity ERP software helps to integrate many formerly discrete island processes.
5. As with STP, the able use of commodity ERP software requires a great deal of preparatory work.

One of the advantages of a proper linkage that has been designed and implemented between STP and ERP is that the resulting system can provide the platform for new applications like the virtual customer initiative (see Chapter 8). To appreciate other pluses to be gained through a seamless STP-ERP connectivity, it is proper to get insight into enterprise resource planning.

The term is used as a collective reference to various suites of business software able to support an internal and external information structure. Its objective is to help in the control production (from scheduling to in-process execution), inventory management, purchasing, just-in-time manufacturing, order tracking, and financials associated with these processes.

Given this polyvalence of functions addressed by ERP, it is reasonable to think that many different routines have integrated into it. One of them is manufacturing resource planning programs that primarily addressed internal or local functions like in-plant production management. ERP distinguishes itself by providing an effective business partner connection, because both the company and its business partners share common data and cover end-to-end operations in real-time.

With both STP and ERP, there is a learning curve for all users, but contrary to STP, which primarily concerns itself with transactions, ERP takes charge of activities, eventually leading to a transaction. For instance, it takes in the latest orders and planning forecasts from the assembly lines, calculates minimum component stock to meet production targets, and sends order plans to suppliers.

To execute these functions in an able manner, enterprise resource planning interfaces with other programs to monitor order execution against plans, adjust component stocks, and help in managing a number of variants. None of these references is part of STP functions, whose contribution comes right after production and inventory chores have taken place and therefore the transaction, so to speak, matures.

One of the interesting applications of ERP in a cross-company sense comes from Cisco, which is known to have gained both competitive advantages and a significant amount of money in annual cost savings by moving most of its supply chain operations to the Web. The company's customers can configure products and place orders entirely over the Internet.

At the root of this application are improvements in customer service, making it easier for clients to interact with the manufacturer. One of the important gains is that the majority of orders received by Cisco are shipped without any intervention by its employees. Also, the company's management is able to scale its operations without having to proportionately increase the number of required people.

Cisco's suppliers access the company's enterprise resource planning system to see product demand and product planning on a real-time basis. This makes feasible efficiency processes such as dynamic replenishment, enabling the company and its suppliers to reduce inventories without compromising production processes or product availability.

It is appropriate to notice that deliverables are not obtained just by using this or that programming product or method, no matter how advanced it is. It takes much effort and dedication to get commendable results. Lack of proper preparation and lightly done assumptions give the process or method a bad name. In the opinion of Hubert d'Hondt,[5] there is a certain amount of hype around enterprise resource planning. He looks at it through what he calls the four myths:

■ *Myth 1: ERP is the enterprise information system.* As d'Hondt points out, ERP does a good job in production, procurement, sales, and accounting, and might help in human resources. However, it is not adequate for other basic functions in a holistic enterprise information system.
■ *Myth 2: ERP means no interfaces.* This is patently wrong, because the typical company's IT is a costly patchwork of programming routines that are rather difficult to manage and integrate. Interfaces are always necessary. Every software vendor, and quite often every site and function, has its own standards that must be interfaced with one another.

- *Myth 3: ERP is a project.* Right? Wrong. ERP is no project with a starting and ending date. In fact, ERP is a process; it is not a project at all. D'Hondt calls ERP an "infrastructure in progress."
- *Myth 4: ERP is flexible.* It is an old but misplaced belief that off-the-shelf packages are flexible and easily customizable. Any customization requires costly code changes and often extensions. Both are time-consuming and messy.

As d'Hondt says, many people, including IT experts, confuse flexibility, i.e., the ability to evolve from one way of working to another, with versatility, which he defines as the ability to pick functions supported by programming products in a library. Such confusions did not start yesterday. Some of them are as old as IT.

Moreover, it should be evident that a real-time system solution addresses online both sides of the supply chain — clients and suppliers. It requires a transaction execution and payments counterpart that also works in real-time. This is the role played by straight through processing applications, as we saw in Section 2, with the example on continuous link settlement.

5.6   COST AND BENEFIT WITH STRAIGHT THROUGH PROCESSING

Section 5 looked at STP and ERP as processes providing the ability to handle online in real-time (respectively) business transactions, sales orders, and order queries. This is done without manual intervention from order origination to transaction and settlement, thereby improving efficiency and reducing operational risk.

Given this implementation perspective, both STP and ERP should be seen as agents for business enablement and as a means of significant cost and risk reduction. Neither is constrained within the walls of a given company. Both reach out to clients and suppliers, enhancing an entity's market infrastructure. This, however, does not mean that there are no wrong beliefs associated with STP. One incorrect idea is that *if* we increase our level of automation, *then* we will automatically reduce our costs.

That is unsubstantiated, because as we have already discussed, people reposition themselves. Therefore, costs might go up not as a result of STP but in the aftermath of people's gaining the system. The careful reader will recall that in banking this often the case, because banking is overmanned. Any way one looks at this issue, there is no way to assure STP will save money in terms of headcount. The real savings will come from:

- Real-time customer service
- Better liquidity management
- Control over operational risks

Apart from the nature and most likely the origin of cost savings, there are other misunderstandings. In my research I have found that many firms are worried about costs associated with the introduction of real-time STP — hence the half-baked approaches they are choosing — but very few have a clear cost-and-reward plan regarding IT implementation at large, let alone specific processes like ERP and STP.

The problem is one of overall IT mismanagement, rather this or that application specifics. This being said, it is absolutely correct that the board and the CEO are right to be concerned about return on investment (ROI) with STP. Costs matter. If we spend money on a certain process or procedure, we would like to know what we earn in return. "Very few people have been able to measure ROI with STP," said Graeme Austin. To do so will require something many companies lack: well-established goals and rigorous metrics on cost effectiveness.

General statements like "the higher the level of STP, the greater the ROI" have no value whatsoever. In fact, to assure STP will save money, a company must have in place a tough cost control culture, including standard costs.[6] More often than not, this is missing, though the major recession of 2000–2003 has done wonders in cost consciousness.

It may be ironic to say so, but it is to the credit of the 2000–2003 recession that in the last few years several companies have started to account for cost benefit from IT at large and, most specifically, in connection to transaction management — hence, STP. With time, it could be expected that there is keener interest in measuring ROI from infrastructural improvements.

Some of the companies participating in the research that led to this book believe that benefits from infrastructural improvements will be more in the line of business-to-business (B2B) transactions than plain Internet commerce. In Chapter 2, Figure 2.2 has made this point through trend lines that will likely develop, giving B2B the upper ground.

This reference to an increasingly B2B oriented implementation of STP might be extended to cover all sorts of payments systems provided attention is paid to the missing link: the need to automate security measures to the level of processing at 99.99 percent dependability, which is at the core of any successful payment system. High security brings business confidence, and business confidence is critical to obtaining tangible financial benefits with external STP. Another must is the ability to deliver at the sell side along two dimensions:

■ Gaining existing clients comfortable with real-time operations
■ Obtaining new clients that are technologically advanced and *want* online links.

Both bullets help in documenting arguments advanced by some companies, e.g., "We are 70 percent STP compatible" as absurd. With systems solutions, as with laws, one is either 100 percent compatible or not at all. It is not possible to observe the rules of a new technology only a little or even by majority. In fact, doing so during any time period outside a rapid transition is counterproductive.

Certain companies have been fulfilling the STP preconditions and requirements more than others. Toyota is an example of a successful STP implementor. Cisco and Wal-Mart are two U.S. examples of profitable end-to-end STP applications. Allied Carpets is an example from the United Kingdom.

Some companies choose to wait to implement real-time STP until costs go down. This is an excuse for doing nothing. Costs will never go down of their own accord. Others look at STP as a way of primarily swamping operational risk costs. As we have already seen, this is more realistic, but it cannot be, and should not be, the one and only goal.

STP could help in heading off some aspects of operational risk, not just because it looks at the business world as a system but also because it automates data capture at point of origin all the way to data delivery at point of destination. It is precisely this online real-time procedure that helps to control operational risk connected to data streams and involves a great deal of office operations (see Chapter 12).

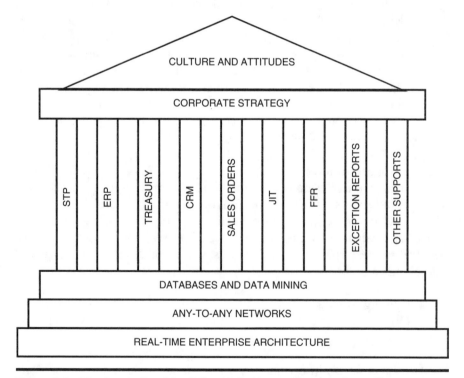

Figure 5.4 The Acropolis of Real-Time Solutions and Some of Its Pillars

To help in integrating the notions this chapter has brought to the reader's attention, see Figure 5.4. At the top is culture, including systems culture, and the attitude taken by designers and users. Into this same framework comes the way people and companies develop a methodology and employ the software available to them. In the foundation are networks and databases. One of the pillars of this whole structure is STP, but it will not hold the ceiling without the contribution of the other pillars.

5.7 NOTES

1. *STP Magazine,* available at www.stpzone.com
2. July 4–5, 2003, Grimaldi Forum Monte Carlo, Monaco.
3. D.N. Chorafas, *Liabilities, Liquidity and Cash Management. Balancing Financial Risk,* Wiley, New York, 2002.
4. D.N. Chorafas, *Operational Risk Control with Basel II. Basic Principles and Capital Requirements,* Butterworths-Heinemann, London and Boston, 2004.
5. Hubert d'Hondt, Information Technology and Logistics, in *The Essentials of Logistics and Management,* eds. Francis-Luc Perret and Corynne Jaffreux, EPFL Press, Lausanne, 2002.
6. D.N. Chorafas, *Bank Profitability,* Butterworth, London, 1989.

6

REALITY ONLINE
AS AN INTEGRATIVE
SOLUTION[1]

6.1 INTRODUCTION

Reality online is a term denoting a solution integrating a system of networked sensors. The term finds its origin at Chicago-based Accenture Technology Labs. The principle is that a single intelligent sensor means very little in terms of contribution to end results. The aggregate of deployed smart sensors is everything, provided it works in real-time. Intelligent sensor networks will be more effective when they address implementation areas currently characterized by opacity of information. Critical queries are:

- What needs to be sensed?
- What can be sensed, and how?
- How can a system of sensors provide information that increases process visibility?

Current technology makes feasible the application of smart sensor approaches in the physical world. Procter & Gamble, Gillette, Honeywell, and many other companies offer excellent examples in this domain. By contrast, the general state of the art in sensors provides little leverage for visibility into applications in the virtual world of finance and banking, but this too might change sometime in the future (see Chapter 3).

In the physical world, where today's applications of networked intelligent sensors primarily focus, reality online stands for system solutions characterized by convergence of a number of technologies. Most are characterized by miniaturized components that have both intelligence and communications abilities, working together to gather and deploy large amounts of information and to enable reality itself to be captured online.

Implementationwise, the concepts underpinning reality online have evolved over the past few years. As new experience is gained, the original approaches have been modified by feedback from business executives with whom implementers discuss their ideas and obtain results.

In the background of a reality online solution lies the fact that, even if it takes considerable time to reach larger-scale implementation, with advancements in broadband technology, in another 10 or 15 years practically everything may be interconnected. The question is not whether a wider application of networks of online smart sensors will see the light but when.

Indeed, some experts believe that the reach and impact of Internet-commerce and business-to-business applications (see Chapters 15 and 16) will continue to be rather limited until they include online data capture from the real world of tangible bodies and physical assets, because that is where:

■ Opportunities come about
■ Business gets done
■ Costs are incurred

Reality online goes well beyond the idea of virtual reality, which is basically a computer-generated world. Not only new technologies but also rigorous systems studies are necessary to analyze, reflect, and enhance information derived from the physical world of business, including the way companies make, distribute, sell, and service their products. In a manner fairly similar to what has been stated in Chapter 5 about STP and ERP, information pertaining to the physical world must be captured in context and in real-time.

The output of reality online is the business system's input, whereas STP and ERP are outputs of the production and distribution subsystems of an entity. Contrary to policies of the last dozen years, when most companies were wrestling with the problems of generating content and designing interfaces and online input at point of origin took a back seat, input at point of origin has now become central to modern system solutions. The priorities have changed in the twenty-first century.

6.2 SYSTEM DESIGN FOR REALITY ONLINE

Let's start with the following scenario which stands a good chance of seeing the light sometime in the future. Every physical entity is endowed with intelligence, is networked, and has a virtual double (VD).[2] Accenture gets credit for this term, which means mapping into computer memory all of the characteristics of a given object. Doing so in a way that is consistent and complete provides for easy retrieval and enhances connectivity among real objects and their mapping into computer systems (their doubles).

The virtual double is a logical entity, named this way because its information elements are doubling those of the physical entity to which it corresponds. The databased VD has plenty of information elements corresponding to the physical entity, for instance, a product's dynamic pricing, clients to which it appeals, and delivery schedules.

Action and response between the virtual double and the information entity to which it corresponds, including its sensors, are in real-time. As everything is connected, data comes directly from objects and the environment, not from classical IT input — with its delays, mistakes, and operational risks. In this environment action/response time is nearly zero. Real-time connectivity has a favorable impact on competitiveness and on business practices.

Combining the virtual double and its information with real-time, online computing helps in dealing with business partners beyond the frame of reference discussed in Chapter 5 in connection with straight through processing and enterprise resource planning. For instance, it assists in prescreening business relations, therefore concentrating on partners (clients and suppliers) whose VD history shows they can be trusted. As a result, collaboration between people and companies regarding commercial activities into which they engage may no longer be done through obsolete criteria derived from static data but, rather, by means of updated and accurate information contributed online by intelligent communicating objects.

This is what reality online is all about, and such a solution can have great impact in many sectors of industry, as the following examples contributed by Stanton J. Taylor document.

Take, as an example, the case of networked sensors scattered over acres of ground for tracking wildlife roaming a vast landscape, detecting forest fires when they start, or receiving input from soldiers maneuvering over rugged terrain. In each case, the networked sensors constitute a data collection grid that can be programmed to automatically provide, at point of origin, up-to-the-minute information needed to meet specific objectives.

During our meeting, Taylor mentioned the case of a Mexican cement manufacturer who uses reality online to optimize its plants and fleet, thereby transforming its classical delivery approach into an interactive service business. Rather than rigidly scheduling the fleet of cement delivery trucks to meet incoming orders, this entity manages deliveries dynamically. Each truck is equipped with a computer and a satellite GPS transmitter. Such connectivity gives a central dispatcher a continuously updated picture of the truck's location.

Capitalizing on the online touch, incoming order flow, and databased information, the system is sustaining a virtual double of the vehicle. When an order comes in, the dispatcher can send the nearest truck to the delivery point while continuing to monitor weather, traffic, and inventory levels at the order site.

The company's production plants, too, are linked through satellite communications and, therefore, they can dynamically adjust production schedules as far as cement-manufacturing technology allows. For their part, the company's customers gain the flexibility to upgrade their order up to the minute of delivery. To increase customer satisfaction, the company has reduced through technology its delivery window from 3 hours to 20 minutes and now boasts an on-time performance of better than 98 percent, which is met with 35 percent fewer trucks than before this system was implemented.

Along a similar frame of reference, Stan Taylor suggests that networked intelligent sensors could be incorporated into places where we live and work, all the way into something as basic and intimate as our clothing. It is expected that eventually such networks of smart sensors will make it possible to micromanage an individual's surrounding temperature and humidity for better comfort.

An imaginative application that I heard at the aforementioned meeting would practically do away with legacy computer input. This could be achieved through sensors attached to a person's fingertips, allowing a user to interact with a computer by virtual typing instead of the classical physical keyboard. Freedom from physical keying-in has been a yet-unrealized data-processing goal for four decades.

The next example is even more imaginative. If my understanding is right, Accenture Technology Labs has a Reality Instant Messaging prototype that capitalizes on interactivity not simply with reality itself but also with other people about that reality. Through this, an individual alone anywhere in the world can be part of a virtual group, able to work online with colleagues on a project. This individual's view is personalized, but the viewing experience itself is groupwide.

By means of Reality Instant Messaging, agents look after the coupling of engineering design and execution reality. This pattern may be to the digital world what person-to-person meetings and cooperation are to the real world. To better appreciate the further-out impact, should this become true reality, according to records of the last couple of decades of the twentieth century and of the early years of the twenty-first, living alone is what we increasingly do with the help of technology. But technology may also help to reintegrate social goals (see Section 6).

This Accenture Technology Labs reference can be brought a step further by considering strategies in adding value for Internet marketing, ameliorating price competition, and using virtual doubles to incorporate consumer preferences and establish user trust. Design challenges connected to such a procedure revolve around how to go about designing a virtual personal shopping adviser.

In an Internet business environment, data streams from point-of-origin input, captured through smart sensors, can help companies to adjust their supply chain strategies and assess strengths and weaknesses. A further extension is what MIT calls an "*atomic* electronic commerce business model." Mining databases enriched with point-of-origin information (see Chapter 14) could help in answering questions such as: Which part of our I-business should we migrate to a new model? How well can our client base support more sophisticated supply chain dynamics?

Factual and documented answers to these and similar queries may help senior management in repositioning the firm against market forces, leveraging internal capabilities, and applying reality online principles in a very fast clockspeed environment (see Chapter 1 on business time and Chapter 16 on Internet time).

Models exploring virtual double information can prove of assistance in investigating how supply structure dynamics vary in different parts of the chain and how supply structures are affected by speed of change in a given industry. Research at MIT suggests the wisdom of examining supply chain design in a double-helix product architecture, including clockspeed amplification in speed-up effect and volatility amplification in the bullwhip effect.

Other issues to be researched by capitalizing on timely and accurate data captured at point of origin impact upon research, development, and design for greater customer satisfaction and competitiveness. How should a company focus its product and process technology to remain viable in the future? Is the option most attracting us able to position our company for future growth? Ensure timely development of state-of-the-art solutions? Allow us to survive the shorter product life cycles and heightened customer expectations?

The way some of the experts look at most probable fallouts from system design capitalizing on reality online is that it might be revolutionizing engineering and marketing in a way similar to what state-of-the-art ERP has done to manufacturing and logistics. More precisely, it may be instrumental in integrating Internet time thinking into supply management decisions and assisting to identify the right moves for a specific customer-and-product orientation as well as to develop a particular commercial model. A practical example is given in Section 3.

6.3 REALITY ONLINE AND SMART CARS

The examples presented in this section are at a different end of the implementation of technology than those in Section 2. Their objective is to demonstrate that activities profiting from high tech are not just one track, to prove that what at a certain time seems to be a far-out, even unlikely, objective can become reality some years down the line.

This is the case of projections made in the motor vehicle business in 1998 and realization attained in the following years up to 2004. I chose this industry as an example because one of the sectors where sensors, computing devices, and connectivity solutions find themselves embedded into classical products is automobiles. IT powerhouses such as Microsoft, Intel, IBM, Sun Microsystems, and auto industry suppliers like Delphi and Visteon are making contributions in this area.

For instance, sophisticated forward-looking sensing systems are currently being developed to extend actuators immediately prior to impact and therefore improve safety. It is projected that future cars would have bumpers that extend forward to absorb impact or just to improve the aerodynamics, using both pneumatic and hydraulic actuators.

Other research centers in the automotive industry are working on developments that target rear-pointing radar systems. An example is a transparent spoiler made up as an array of thin prisms, technically described as a Fresnel device. Looking at the spoiler through the rear view mirror gives a virtual view of what is happening immediately behind a car. Seeing right behind the car alerts drivers to obstacles near the ground and makes reversing into a traffic lane or parking space much easier.

It is also possible to use the Fresnel lens spoiler as a message display board. This and several other examples document what can be currently brought into automobile design through sensors and in-car personal communications capabilities. Services include:

- Internet access
- Voice mail and e-mail
- Infrared data links
- Messaging
- Navigational assistance

Note that these examples are not at high-tech level like the discussion on reality online in Section 2, but they do constitute advances in the state of the art. What the reader should retain from these references is that the auto industry is laboring to put to work an enabling technology that has a long way to go. Voice-activated controls, heads-up displays, and satellite communications are other examples.

To gauge the pace of such advances, it is proper to recall that only a short time ago in-car mobile phone and fax were state-of-the-art applications. But enlightened spirits foresaw that more was coming. In a conference held in Monte Carlo in 2000, Michael Bloomberg, then CEO of Bloomberg, projected that in the not-too-distant future, General Motors would ship more computer power than IBM.[3] This may well become true. A couple of years earlier, in the 1998 SAE Congress in Detroit, Delphi showed two demonstration vehicles. One was a joint venture with Saab designed to exhibit state-of-the-art systems that have already gone into production. The other, a Chevrolet

Blazer, was a fully networked vehicle with intelligent sensors, reflecting developments in the future.

The Saab Personal Productivity Vehicle exploited an auto PC using the Microsoft Windows CE operating system. Developed at the Delphi Delco subsidiary in Sweden, it integrated AM/FM receivers, CD-ROM, serial port interface, universal serial bus, compact flash expansion slot, and high-resolution 256 x 63 display. The steering wheel controls had been endowed with interactive speech technology to respond to driver commands, and speech synthesis was employed to communicate text information. Through speech recognition, a driver could send e-mail, obtain turn-by-turn directions through a global positioning system (GPS), ask for traffic and weather conditions, and locate the exact address of his destination.

Such solutions were high tech in 1998, but today they are already in use, even if limited to the more expensive motor vehicle models. Most likely, in the future advanced versions of the examples I have given will be employed to enable auto manufacturers, as well as various OEM suppliers, to get real insights into:

- When, where, and how various customers drive
- What features they prefer to use
- How different parts of the vehicle perform over time

Take as another example the case of a cellular modem connection that summons roadside assistance and receives Internet information. An infrared data link allows data to be transferred from handheld devices over radio to nodes, then distributed from network nodes via optical fiber, passive star, and opto-electronic devices. This, too, is one of the applications that, in the short span of six years, has become common. What about the more futuristic exhibit of the 1998 SAE event?

Delphi's Network Vehicle demonstrated connectivity of new wireless computers to mobile applications, with Java-based technology used for real-time data streaming over a wireless network. This approach enabled more complex features to be incorporated into the car: electronic distribution of memos, setting work schedules, and listening to and dictating responses to faxes or e-mails. Solutions also featured individual passenger terminals interacting over the Internet.

Visteon brought to the market a high-tech solution, demonstrated in the same SAE Congress. Called Information, Communication, Entertainment, Safety and Security (ICES), it used Microsoft's AutoPC operating system with Intel microprocessors. (A prototype, dealer-installed version of ICES had been piloted in 1998.)

Visteon's speaker-independent voice-activated control system recognizes natural speech patterns and performs across a range of voices, languages, and dialects. Incorporated into this solution is the remote emergency satellite cellular unit (RESCU), considered to be the first factory-installed system to combine GPS technology and cellular phone network, to help drivers in distress. Significant advantages of this approach enable car owners to customize systems and to add more features simply by installing new software.

What Delco and Visteon demonstrated in 1988 have since entered the mainstream. These features have common points with what Accenture said in 2003 in connection to networks of smart sensors (see Section 2). For instance, the consultancy made reference to tracking done by both passive technology, such as image processing, and active technology, such as global positioning system (GPS) transmissions or multicamera triangulation. Both help to create a virtual double of an event and all of its participants, even in motion. In addition, the recorded pattern is updated within preestablished time limits that are not far from real-time.

As we push further out the frontiers of knowledge, the line between physical reality and the virtual world might well disappear. We are not yet there, and some of the examples we saw in Section 2 are much further out than the 1998 SAE exhibits were at their time. But the important reference is the trend that timescales change. In the early 1960s, a Delphi method opinion analysis among experts placed the man-on-the-moon landing in the 1990s, but it happened in 1969.[4]

6.4 SYSTEM INTEGRATION BY THE SWISS CUSTOMS AUTHORITY: A CASE STUDY

From where may come the delays in the implementation of the further-out vision of reality online? One answer is the economy. In the financial and economic lows of the first four years of the twenty-first century, companies are not coming up with budgets to invest in new and unproven technology. But economic cycles have ups and downs, and the market's mood changes.

More by way of impedance to near-global implementation of new technology is the lack of system integration in a complex environment. For starters, system integration should take place not at one but at several different reference levels. One of them is architectural and therefore conceptual. Another is functional and works at the actor's level. A third is procedural, including the interfaces to other functions and leading all the way to the end-user level. We will see a case study with a highway toll-collection system in Switzerland in this section.

It would be superfluous to add that platforms, operating systems, database management systems, transaction-processing routines, integrated software, and programming languages all play a crucial role in providing effective system integration. Cornerstone to a successful solution is the skill of the project manager, who must account both for end users and for what is available at state of the art.

Effective links are most critical because system integration must take place within a vast and growing array of data communications protocols and gateways, account for requirements for multimedia channel integration, and consider the existence of heterogeneous central and distributed computer resources, including data warehouses. Moreover, this maze of incompatible components must be transparent to the end user, who should be able to look at reality online solutions as intelligent machines, resembling a sort of extension of the human mind.

Besides taking care of past failures and facing up to new challenges (and what I said so far is only a partial list), the system integrator is confronted with a pace of work so dense, as well as with component parts and functions so interrelated, that minor oversights can turn back the clock. Take as an example road tolling, which uses sensor technology.

To a significant extent, how automated tolling systems are built depends on how the engineers see the world around them and their mission in it. Is the system they built supposed to charge for access to a city center, such as London, all roads in a country, or a selected turnpike network? Moreover, is industrial policy an issue? London's congestion-charging system was built quickly in 2002 and the city's transport agency opted for proven technology and the use of video cameras.

The European Commission has proposed mandating a toll-collection system throughout the European Union (EU). In 2003, Germany implemented a system of sorts and the result has been a snafu (see Section 5). Switzerland has also introduced a road-tolling system for heavy vehicles, calculating fees according to distance traveled. This has been fairly successful. Its basic component is an onboard unit (OBU) that combines a:

■ GPS receiver
■ Microwave receiver
■ Odometer data
■ Smart cards

The fact that system design incorporated everything necessary into OBU, including the GPS antenna, reduced installation cost. On the other hand, it created a problem of efficient isolation from high-frequency noise of the truck's digital subsystems. (More on this in Section 5.)

The Swiss road tolling design for trucks uses satillite links and is more complex than the London solution, but it does not incorporate the most advanced technology either — though it delivers commendable results, monitoring and charging transport companies between Euro 0.11 ($0.13) and Euro 0.45 ($0.54) per kilometer.

The Swiss Customs Authority required installation of OBUs in every Swiss truck during 2000. More than 80,000 onboard units have been manufactured, and some 60,000 Swiss trucks, as well as an increasing number of foreign trucks that regularly pass through Switzerland, now carry these devices. The network link is GPS.[5]

As the vehicle begins to move, the GPS receiver automatically identifies the road on which the vehicle is traveling. The onboard unit uses the truck's characteristic information, and number of kilometers driven, to calculate the toll. The wireless communications link transmits the distances traveled by each vehicle for toll handling. I am not privy to the exact system design, but it would seem that it more or less follows the block diagram in Figure 6.1.

Several key decisions have shaped the *a priori* system integration procedures, device specifications, and subsequent design of an OBU with multifunctional capabilities. Known as the distance-related heavy vehicle fee (DRHVF), the adopted solution calls for toll-fee calculation based on the total number of kilometers driven in Switzerland, the registered net weight of the truck, and the truck's pollutant Euro-class category.

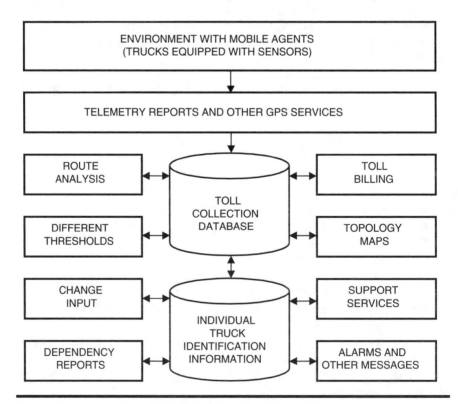

Figure 6.1 An Integrated Toll Collection Management System

Reportedly, the complexity of the solution has been increased by the need to account for payment of vehicle tax for travel over the entire Swiss road network, not just the motorways. In addition to the distance-related toll, there is a fixed fee for the Alps transit passages.

To get the best of the whole sensor system in terms of functionality, power requirements, and space, the analysts developed a mixed-signal, application-specific integrated circuit that combines analog and digital parts. The result has been a reasonably efficient approach capable of detecting driving status and vehicle speed.

The system solution required incorporation of a dedicated short-range communication 5.8-Ghz microwave link for possible interoperability with other existing and forthcoming applications. Another necessity has been foolproofing the OBU, including the case of manipulation or fraud. The adopted solution also includes an optical display, visible from outside the truck, for reasons of enforcement.

One of the challenges in the design has been storage, particularly in regard to distinguishing for toll-calculating purposes the distance driven within and outside Switzerland. This necessitated an approach to border recognition, and it resulted in further storage requirements. To deliver a compact system, the designers brought initial storage needs of about 2 MB down to 30 KB, and then to 7 KB.

An advancement in border control design has been the two border lines contained in the OBU, producing a corridor zone from 100 meters to 2 kilometers in width. With a single border line, there can be only in or out status. The corridor makes feasible additional functionality. The cross-border algorithm also presented problems. The designers tried both simple and complex formulas. Searching through algorithms developed for computer games, they found useful input that permitted increased calculation time.

With information from sensors well secured, as well as the communications, storage, and algorithmic challenges solved, the designers applied their skills to what Section 2 called the virtual double, which replicates in the database all the important information about a given object. Data mining has been able to provide all relevant information about status and operations characterizing truck traffic in Switzerland, down to the individual unit: the single truck.

In conclusion, as high technology advances and system integration challenges are solved, sophisticated methods of detection, data capture, and analysis become possible in real-time. Such solutions will eventually become easier, cost less, and be done more quickly and more accurately. Study of the virtual double of objects will, in all likelihood, permit instant and certain knowledge of operations, observance of rules, effect of performance specifications, and work histories. We will talk more about these issues in Chapters 7 to 12.

6.5 PREREQUISITES FOR AND PAYOFFS FROM SYSTEM INTEGRATION

The case study in Section 4 was used to demonstrate that system integration requires a concept, appropriate definition of objectives, ingenious system design, thorough component evaluation (and, if necessary, redesign), and implementation that provides flexibility for renewal and expansion. The real payoff does not come from each unit taken individually on a standalone basis but from:

- Linking a series of components in a network
- Allowing information to flow freely in many forms
- Exploiting this information as it becomes available to reach desired objectives

The methodology for system design shown in Figure 6.2 is following a double track: process goal(s) and network structure. These are leading, respectively, to activity analysis and performance analysis. Such approach is consistent with the definition of system design, which integrates polyvalent functions into a working aggregate. The members of this aggregate can be either loosely or tightly coupled, but the architectural solution must be both effective and cost efficient, with:

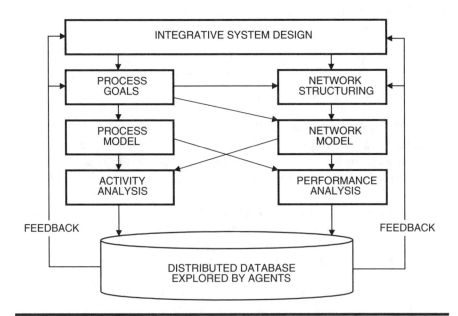

Figure 6.2 Interactive Approach to System Design Assisted by Data Mining and Agents

- Low overhead
- Improved mirroring capabilities
- Minimum instructions required for passthrough from one subsystem to another

To assure fault-detection capabilities, hardware and software in each attached device should be checked for all types of errors, proceeding with error correction or closing itself down once a fault is discovered that it cannot handle. Integrity is the degree to which the system tolerates faults and resulting errors that, when processed by resident software, will produce system failures. Therefore, design prerequisites are:

- Confinement, detection, and diagnosis
- Fault tolerance through isolation of errors
- Prevention of further damage through appropriate control
- Recovery restoring a stable, consistent system state
- Effective restart of normal operations after recovery

By accommodating a multiplicity of independent operating processors (including smart sensors), this approach provides the opportunity for flexible design, affordable cost, and timely delivery while ensuring systemwide error detection, diagnosis, and recovery. The result is a much greater dependability over centralized procedures. The Swiss mobile distance–related heavy vehicle system we have examined in Section 4 provides an example.

As a distributed environment, the Swiss case study documented that an ingenious design permits management of data streams at the granular level. It also opens up a new perspective in defining and delivering information services. Stanton J. Taylor mentioned a different example that follows similar architectural guidelines: package deliveries. In Accenture's Dynamic Delivery prototype, data required for delivery is organized around the customer, and the service draws on a range of technologies:

- Intelligent agents and global positioning system capabilities track the customer's whereabouts
- Through wireless services, the customer is notified of an imminent delivery
- The driver is given access (with permission) to the customer's personal calendar
- Signature payment and signature release are electronically enabled, when necessary

In these and many other cases, service breakthroughs happen as it becomes possible to reach anyone, anywhere, at any time, as well as to see and understand the context of their reality at that moment. Such reality includes where a person is, what he is doing, and how people are moving and responding to inputs.

Some experts look at integrative approaches (like the aforementioned examples) as gateways to personalization of services that use the latest advances in technology combining them with an ingenious knowledge-enriched system design. The hallmark of distinction in reaching objectives is simplicity, integration, and completeness of the solution.

Simplicity comprises ease of learning and ease of use. Its level is heavily affected by the way we proceed with integration, which refers to ensuring that the many different components work in unison, ease of moving between the various functions of a product, and the making of different components to appear similar to the user. The best way to describe completeness is through the characteristics of a mathematical system whose rules must be complementary but not contradictory.

Successful integrative efforts usually observe the aforementioned prerequisites, and when they do so, they can have a far-reaching commercial aftermath. Sometimes, however, results do not go according to plan. Section 4 made reference to an April 2003 proposal by the European Commission for a pan-European Union toll collection system to become cross-border by 2008, the same year Galileo comes online. If successful, this network would most likely accelerate adoption and implementation of GPS and Galileo functionality on millions of land vehicles. The Euroland's parliaments will be quick to tax the consumer for the use of roads that have been, thus far, toll free.

A major test has been Germany's automatic autoban toll-collection system for truckers. Known as Toll Collect, it was supposed to be the most advanced, but it failed to work as expected. Critics say the German government wanted to help DaimlerChrysler and Deutsche Telekom, Toll Collect's main shareholders, to develop a exportable technology. The third partner has been Cofiroute, the French motorway operator. They set out to build a theoretically ambitious approach that determined much of the system's architecture, but they ended up with a practical snafu, a bruised face, and a hole in the pocket.

Budgeted at $7.7 billion, Toll Collect has not been as successful as its more economical Swiss counterpart. Like the Swiss, the German toll-collection system used GPS-equipped onboard units to measure truck movements along roads, but other components were different. DaimlerChrysler, Deutsche Telekom, and Cofiroute was supposed to offer the service in 2003. They did keep the deadline, but the system's operation led to chaos and total paralysis of the German autobahnen.

On February 19, 2004, a day after the DaimlerChyrsler board announced it would extend Jürgen Schrempp's contract as chief executive, Schrempp ran into a storm of questions over his company's role in the botched highway toll-collection system. Appearing at a DaimlerChrysler's news conference in Sindelfingen, near Stuttgart, Daimler's CEO admitted the company had stumbled on the project. The German government angrily canceled the project mid-February 2004, after the aforementioned technical breakdown.

The failed system, which is still in development with a vague delivery date in early 2005, was supposed to set the *standard* for Europe and the world. Instead, it became a humiliating symbol to the members of its Consortium, and an indicator of the decline of German engineering — with the German government threatening to hold DaimlerChrysler and its partner, Deutsche Telekom, liable for damages in excess of Euro 6.5 billion ($7.8 billion). The companies have already paid Euro 250,000 ($300,000) a day in fines, a penalty scheduled to increase to Euro 500,000 a day.[6]

Both positive and negative examples must be considered when planning for new departures in system design. More or less, we have the technology today to embed sensors that can monitor their hosts' status second by second, or millimeter by millimeter, detecting and reporting changes in the hosts' condition as well as prodding for corrective action. The challenge is to make the integrated system work in a way that people and companies cannot really imagine life without it.

6.6   LIKELY SOCIAL IMPACT OF REALITY ONLINE

Good news first, reality online may reintroduce a sense of communal living in cyberspace. This will be a U-turn from the trend in the physical world in which we now perform all alone things that once were a group activity. The growing tendency to live alone is exemplified by statistics. Taking a sample from Scandinavia, 66 percent of households in Stockholm, 63 percent in Oslo, and 59 percent in Helsinki are single households.

In a way, this is a return to tribalization, in which the tribe is the single person networked through his connectivity in the Internet ecosystem with other single persons. This can have tremendous implications on society — from family life to education, jobs, and politics — because it is making the world very different from the one that we know or that ever existed.

Technology is not the only motor behind the transformation. Another crucial factor is job mobility and globalization of labor. About 66 percent of people in Silicon Valley were not born in the United States; they migrated to the mecca of technology through a process of self-selection. At the same time, they lost the roots they had for generations, and this has a psychologically destabilizing effect.

It may sound curious, but a third critical factor for the ongoing abstraction from physical objects to logical objects and their connectivity is what can be called institutional limitation. The simplest way to express it is that the difference in species disappears. For instance, one often cannot tell the difference between cars today, and the same is happening in architectural design.

Take education as another example. There are some 560 MBA programs in Europe. This number is expected to increase by 200 in the coming years. They advertise very similar programs, appeal to the same population, and lack any sign of distinction to make them unique.

Still another critical variable in the transformation in which we are spectators rather than agents is the growing level of transparency characterizing an open society. Little by little, it infiltrates every area, from political manipulations to business scandals.[7] Organizations tend to become open systems. The boundaries between what is confidential and what is public knowledge become blurred. The result is that, in an open society, being average means being nobody. Therefore, it is a bad idea. To escape from averages, people alter their behavior in ways that create new risks.

What I just stated about averages is compounded by the fact that the criteria for analysts of what is acceptable and unacceptable behavior are changing. Such criteria define the difference between the past and the new reality. It is in this light that the examples in this chapter, as well as possible future developments, should be viewed.

The bad news is that Big Brother may be just around the corner. In Britain, politicians ready themselves to vote for a GPS-based system now being tested in one of the country's northern cities to track and register speed-limit information that could first be used passively to warn drivers when they are exceeding the speed limit and then actively to reduce the speed of the vehicle through throttle or engine speed limiting techniques. Other European nations are contemplating such legislation that would allow a greater amount of state control over people's lives.

The ongoing test in the United Kingdom uses intelligent speed adaptation (ISA) technology developed by Leeds University's Institute for Transport Studies and vehicle research and testing organization.[8] Driving patterns are logged by computer. When activated, the ISA system tells the driver when he is in a speed-limited zone. The throttle is automatically restricted so the limit cannot be exceeded, though there is an override.

There exists no lack of technology for delivering such systems. Digital mapping companies like Navigation Technologies are now upgrading their databases to include the marking of boundaries between open-road and urban areas for future applications such as adaptive headlight systems as well as speed control and tolls collecting.

Once in place, such solutions can be employed in polyvalent ways, being applied to anything including leisure time taxes — starting with road tolls. As a recent article in *The Economist* stated, higher taxes might merely mean an abandonment of overtaxed work in favor of untaxed leisure.[9] But reality online solutions, like the successful implementation by the Swiss Customs Authority (see Section 4) and the British project, might track and tax even leisure activities. We shall see.

6.7 NOTES

1. Several of the applications examples in this chapter, as well as some of the basic concepts, have been contributed by Stanton J. Taylor, partner, Accenture Technology Labs.
2. Virtual doubles, and their usefulness, are further discussed in Chapter 8 in connection with the virtual customer concept.
3. Monte Carlo Forum, March 2000.
4. D.N. Chorafas, *Modelling the Survival of Financial and Industrial Enterprises. Advantages, Challenges, and Problems with the Internal Rating-Based (IRB) Method,* Palgrave/Macmillan, London, 2002.
5. *GPS World,* June 2003.
6. *International Herald Tribune,* February, 20, 2004.
7. D.N. Chorafas, *Management Risk. The Bottleneck Is at the Top of the Bottle,* Macmillan/Palgrace, London, 2004.
8. *European Automotive Design,* June 20, 2003.
9. *The Economist,* November 22, 2003.

7

EXECUTIVE INFORMATION SYSTEMS

7.1 INTRODUCTION

Chief executive officers worth their salt appreciate that when they have missed their timing it is very difficult to throttle back. Therefore, they need a mechanism to supply answers to crucial questions in the most timely way. For example, what have we planned to do? Are we doing it? Is the last policy working? What's our exposure? Do we have the financial resources to confront our challenges? CEOs need to answer these and other queries relating to competition, market penetration, pricing, cost structure, and profitability.

François Mitterand, the former president of France, used to say that the chief has to have only a few simple ideas. He should not explain, elaborate, or excuse. Complexities belong to the middle-management levels; if they reach the top, they paralyze. The CEO cannot be exposed to a hundred different sides of any issue, nor should he feel that he alone has solved a problem, even if all his immediate assistants accept his decision. Many decisions are phrased in a way that is ambiguous, and some are put in the time closet, ignored by those who should be looking after them.

The objective of an executive information system (EIS) is to support management's decisions and actions and to control activities with accurate, actual, and comprehensive information. An EIS must work in real-time, because management decisions and actions must be timely, focused, clear, and directionable. *If a decision can be misunderstood, it will be.* If a decision is misunderstood:

- The CEO will get the most of what he wants the least
- His people will be overcome by trivialities
- His company will lack direction and will drift

Why focus on an executive information system and not on a management information system (MIS)? Although either term might do, EIS is better because it clearly addresses itself to the organization's top level. The executive is a policy maker, which is not true of every manager. The manager's activities are largely internal to the firm; those of an executive are both internal and external. Typically, the members of the board of directors are executives. Some are also managers.

The target of EIS is decisions. Making a clear decision requires skill, practice, and daring. It also calls for timely and accurate information and therefore systems support in prognosticating developments, analyzing alternatives, formulating plans, and assuring these are properly implemented. *Focus* is the keyword. Focusing on an issue is more important than always being right. By not focusing on the subject(s) of a decision, the CEO and board members take risks that could eventually destroy the firm.

Well-managed companies are not adverse in taking risks, but they know how to keep them under control. George Moore, a former president of Citibank, said,"If we do not have troubles, we would not have any high priced people around to solve them." To Walter Wriston, Moore's hand-picked successor as Citibank CEO, Moore is rumored to have said, "Be brave to scare Chase (Manhattan), but not so brave to scare me."

Processes supported through EIS and MIS are briefly explained in Figure 7.1. Feedback is emphasized because controlling the efficiency of execution of decisions and plans is as important as making them. It is vital to effectively upkeep the plan as conditions change. These conditions may be internal: managerial, organizational, or financial. But they may also be:

- Induced by market changes
- Propelled by competition
- Promoted by clients who have a vision of their future needs

"If you know yourself and know your enemy, you don't have to be afraid of the outcome of 100 battles," advises Sun Tzu, the Chinese general and philosopher who lived 25 centuries ago. A critical function of an EIS is to help the company executives know themselves and their competitors.

Whereas an executive information system will primarily address the company's decision-making information requirement, bringing into perspective salient issues, a client information system (CIS, see Chapter 8) will focus on the business partners of the firm — their current and future requirements as well as the patterns that can be developed from past relationships through database mining. Also, the inference we can obtain from such patterns is valuable to the company's product design, relationship handling, and other decisions.

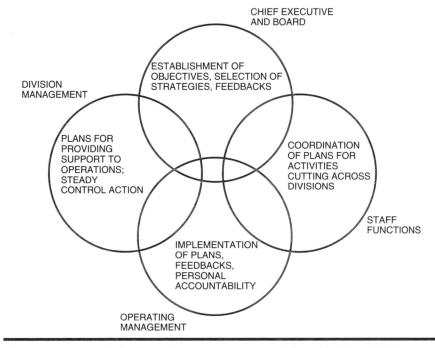

CHIEF EXECUTIVE
AND BOARD

ESTABLISHMENT OF
OBJECTIVES, SELECTION OF
STRATEGIES, FEEDBACKS

DIVISION
MANAGEMENT

PLANS FOR
PROVIDING
SUPPORT TO
OPERATIONS;
STEADY
CONTROL ACTION

COORDINATION
OF PLANS FOR
ACTIVITIES
CUTTING ACROSS
DIVISIONS

STAFF
FUNCTIONS

IMPLEMENTATION
OF PLANS,
FEEDBACKS,
PERSONAL
ACCOUNTABILITY

OPERATING
MANAGEMENT

Figure 7.1   General Outline of Processes Supported through EIS and MIS

7.2 CONCEPTS UNDERPINNING EXECUTIVE INFORMATION SYSTEMS

The concept of information systems at the service of management first appeared in the 1970s, followed in a few years by another notion, that of decision support systems (DSS). In several ways, DSS can be seen as a successor to operations research (OR),[1] which flourished in the immediate post-World War II years, and of digital simulation studies, which were the novelty of the mid-1960s.[2]

In their way, MIS extended the OR-simulation-DSS experience by creating a system in which information could be found and used effectively for management planning and control reasons. This technology-based decision support has been further promoted through the development of a corporate memory facility (CMF, see Section 4).

On the other hand, after the early excitement and euphoria over DSS and MIS, it became clear that any worthwhile application would need a great deal of database mining. That is exactly where the MIS effort of the 1970s has failed, because computer vendors could not provide timely and accurate information because real-life operational data was locked up in mainframes that were updated only through batch. What computer vendors offered with their batch data extract and data warehouses was too little, too late, and too erroneous.

What management, particularly senior management, needed was quite different than what the vendors offered. The sought-out pattern is best described in Figure 7.2. Interactive management information solutions were required both to answer the decision-oriented needs outlined in the Introduction and to enlarge the span of control in order to increase management efficiency. A large span of control is at the root of an well-oiled organization. A narrow span of control leads to an inefficient structure, where costs are high and performance is rock bottom.

Executive information systems providing executives and managers with accurate, real-time information make it feasible to cut organizational fat without losing overall control. The concepts underpinning good and poor structural solutions are shown in Figure 7.3.

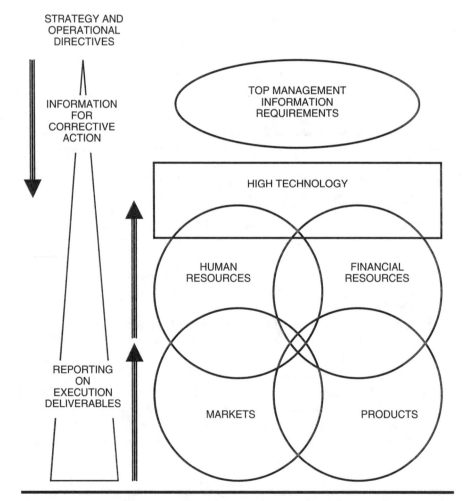

Figure 7.2 Top to Bottom and Bottom Up Approach to the Development of a Strategic Plan

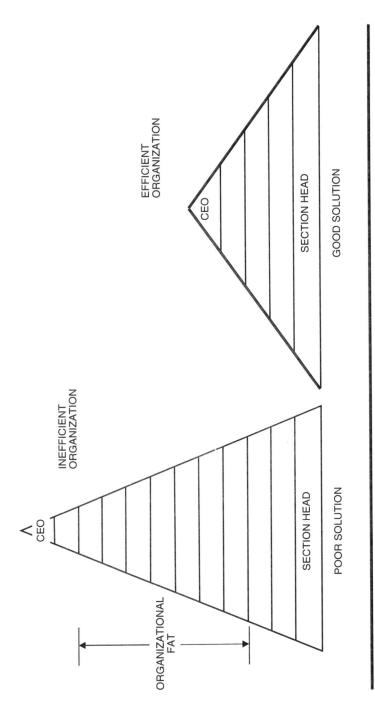

Figure 7.3   A Large Span of Control Leads to a Flat and Cost-Effective Organization

Well-managed companies did not take long to find out that the idea of online access to up-to-date information has merits because business and industry are characterized by an increasing need for rapid information access, not so much for internal purposes as for external. In fact, it was not yesterday but back in mid-1960s to mid-1970s that economic, technological, and social changes placed increased emphasis on the need for well-rounded managerial information that must be synthetic and for a backup of detail that, when necessary, can be used for analytical purposes.

In the ensuing decades, through an able answer to managerial information requirements, top-tier companies helped in structuring the branch of information systems engineering for executive decision and internal control reasons. This has been made possible by taking information technology from the state of artisans to that of high tech. Table 7.1 presents, in a nutshell, a contrast between managerial and operational information requirements.

The key variables are content, volume, type of application, and means of communication. As both managerial and operational requirements evolve, both columns in Table 7.1 must be subject to reexamination and restructuring. The careful reader should notice that new organizational structures demand new approaches to management decisions and typically require a greater sharing of knowledge. A major issue for executives is getting the right information, at the right time, and in the right place — real-time data collection. This is where reality online comes into the picture (see Chapter 6). Best practices in EIS pose other questions:

Table 7.1 Managerial versus Operational Information Requirements

	Managerial	*Operational*
1. Content	Synthetic Graphical Historical trend Reporting by exception Multidimensional models	Detailed Numeric Mainly positional • Massive Usually along one dimension
2. Volume	Relatively low	High to very high
3. Type of Application	One shot Ad hoc Heuristic *What if* experimentation Unstructured Modular Plenty of visualization	Repetitive Predefined Algorithmic Computational Structured Data stream oriented Voucher based
4. Type of interaction	More communicate than compute	More compute than communicate

■ What should senior management know about the promise of specific new technologies and emerging IT trends?
■ What is the critical path to exploiting new IT capabilities and improved ways of working in the human dimension?
■ How should management anticipate the direct impact of IT innovations and their contribution to management on a business?

The management of change, as Figure 7.4 suggests, rests on three pillars, one of which is real-time information pertaining to a chosen domain. In this connection, we will see a few practical examples from business and industry in Section 3. On the other hand, there are no flat answers to these questions because each organization has its own problems and its own culture. But there exist certain fairly general rules. Executive information systems should be designed so as to permit decision makers to easily respond to events. Working online with computers, they must in a position to experiment by:

■ Asking *what if* questions
■ Introducing hypothetical events
■ Projecting the effects of certain hypotheses on product and market variables
■ Tracking sales performance
■ Analyzing expected profitability
■ Monitoring the use of resources
■ Exercising real-time management (see Chapter 11)

An EIS worth its salt is one that effectively aids in management planning and controlling; in training personnel through simulation, making it possible to manage by objectives (see Chapter 2); in improving efficiency; and in meeting the market's demand for acting at the pace of Internet time (more on this in Chapter 16).

One way to appreciate Internet time is to think that the half-life of technology is growing shorter all the time. For many firms today, time is a prime source of competitive advantage. However, make no mistake about it, it is the people with momentum, know-how, and imagination who are working hard to make Internet time tick.

Executive information systems should therefore be designed for *people*, not for technology's sake. Their interfaces should be personalized for the *end user* and changed as the end user's requirements evolve (see Section 6).

The careful reader will appreciate the sea of difference that exists between these real-life implementation references and other traditional or legacy IT approaches to satisfying management's quest for data. Classical

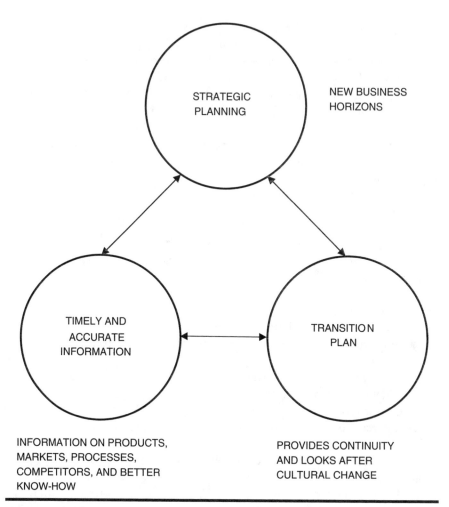

Figure 7.4 The Management of Change Rests on Three Pillars. Functional Dependence Is Crucial to Sound Management

approaches are top heavy in legacy software. This is shown in Table 7.2, which contrasts legacy programming to sophisticated software solutions that are able to leverage technology.

Expert systems and agents[3] can be instrumental in the personalization of interfaces. For instance, by means of full customization through the use of knowledge engineering, when an article of interest arrives, it is selected and instantly sent to the workstation of the officer(s) most immediately concerned. An alert icon or sound warns the end user that vital information is waiting.

Customization is most important. It is a means if distilling information so that managers and other professionals can avoid being overwhelmed by news items, financial data streams, and other data channeled into the

Table 7.2   The Contrast between Legacy Programming and Competitive Software

Legacy	Knowledge-Enriched Software	
	Expert systems	Agents
General purpose	Special purpose	
Largely procedural	Knowledge intensive	
Large programs	C++, if . . . then, visual programming	
Years in development	Small or very small programs	
10 or more programmers	1 or 2 programmer(s) + end user	
in a team	Hours or days in development	
Documentation often missing	Job-specific	Function specific
Very old programs	User actuated	Autonomous, proactive
Difficult, tedious maintenance	Rather localized	Highly mobile
	With built-in	Learning on the job
	knowledge	

system. An executive information system will be filtering end-user-specific information, and the executive and the professional are offered significant flexibility in requesting specialized information elements concerning companies, products, or other objects. In one EIS implementation made along this reference frame:

■ The end-user-oriented application automatically accesses a wide range of in-house and outside databases, returning this information online neatly catalogued in a virtual folder.
■ A corporate memory facility stores past decisions regarding products, customers, contracts, projects, or other issues, available on line to all authorized users

For instance, using this type of service, a financial analyst can access quantitative and qualitative information on a company or group of companies from research sources. Such information is collected in any form but typically presented in graphic form or on a spreadsheet to facilitate analysis. What is important is assuring a high-quality customized presentation. Other examples included in the following sections help to enrich the references just made on what an EIS should accomplish.

7.3   EXECUTIVE INFORMATION SYSTEM EXAMPLES WITH BNP PARIBAS AND WAL-MART

Section 2 has outlined the concepts underpinning an EIS and provided a number of examples, but it has not given a crisp definition. The best definition is that an executive information system is an integrated, computer-based configuration of people, procedures, and equipment designed to satisfy needs for experimentation at senior management level and offering interactive, real-time reporting to *ad hoc* queries.

Within the perspective of this definition and provided that the outlined characteristic requirements are fulfilled, it matters little if the solution is called EIS, MIS, or something else. For instance, some companies prefer the term management support system. The functionality being sustained, not the name, is most important. This functionality is demonstrated by the deliverables of applications. For instance, at the dealing room of BNP Paribas, real-time sophisticated software alerts its users:

■ *If* the time taken for price distribution exceeds a predefined short threshold
■ *If* prices were not acknowledged by an internal office of the counterparty
■ *If* there has been no receipt of spot rates from a particular location, within a given timeframe
■ *If* erroneous or unmatched trades reached a predetermined level
■ *If* there was a performance problem with any portion of the network

BNP Paribas believes this interactive expert-systems-assisted solution has brought improved customer service, cost savings, and better control of operational risk. All three are worthy goals pursued by the executed information system that — it cannot be repeated too often — should be judged by its deliverables.

A second practical example addresses different objectives. This case is the proprietary management information system through which Wal-Mart gives its suppliers full and free access to real-time data on how their products are selling, store by store. By sharing management information that other retailers jealously guard, Wal-Mart allows its business partners to plan production runs earlier and, as a result, to offer better prices.

By all evidence, Wal-Mart's business partners appreciate this type of real-time support because they care about efficiency and performance. Procter & Gamble's $6 billion-a-year business with Wal-Mart is so important to the firm that it has a 150-people-strong office in Bentonville, Arkansas, dedicated to just that. Wal-Mart treats suppliers as an extension of its own operations. At the same time, Wal-Mart cracks down on whatever raises costs and rewards whatever lowers them.

Initiated by Sam Walton, the company's founder, this strategy has produced excellent results. In less than four decades, Wal-Mart has come to the level of accounting for 60 percent of America's retail sales and more than 70 percent of total consumer spending, excluding cars and white goods. The retailer's same-store sales growth is running at five times the industry average, and its pre-tax profits have grown by 15 percent a year over the past decade — well over an estimated $12 billion in 2003.

No other global retailer comes close to Wal-Mart when measured by sales. Growth is coming from aggressive new store openings, a move into food, the addition of banking services supported by Wal-Mart's Internet retailing (which has not been entirely successful, given the downturn in Internet business), and IT contributions that favorably affect business partners.

In other companies some of the characteristics of Wal-Mart's proprietary IT solution might have been supported by commodity software as a substitute to obsolete, batch-type legacy systems and processes, for instance, enterprise resource planning (ERP, see Chapter 5), customer relationship management (CRM, see Chapter 8), and supply chain management (SCM) — provided that the board of these entities took the leadership in revamping the company's IT in appreciation of the fact that modern management requires analytical thinking and faster reactions as well as ways and means to achieve them.

Wal-Mart chose a sophisticated proprietary solution because it gives it a competitive edge. This is synonymous with saying that Wal-Mart's board members, CEO, and senior executives appreciate that in the years to come more intellectual effort will be organized around the problem to be solved, rather than around traditional functions such as production, distribution, or marketing.

Because senior executives today are under fire much more than their predecessors were, it is necessary to think ahead of events and examine alternatives and options in detail. Globalization and the pace of competition see to it that today decisions that might have taken a year three decades ago now have to be made in less than a month. Because globalization is instrumental in bringing such transformation, this is known as the shortened time-span phenomenon.

A shortened time-space requires a different decision-making culture from the one we have known for so long. It also emphasizes the need for making a profound effort to achieve excellence in management. How do we achieve this excellence?

1. *We must set a human developmental climate in our organization.*

   To do so, the board and CEO should be committed to steady management development at all levels. This means that the board must be profoundly interested in the company's human assets and their lifelong training.

2. *Senior officers must be involved in EIS design and its further development.*

   With this, senior management will be demonstrating the desire of the organization to obtain a first-class technology which, apart from providing the advantages we have already seen, helps in delimiting authority by emphasizing responsibility and by defining personal accountability.

Personal accountability must be enhanced through concrete measurements supported by the EIS through cost accounting procedures, risk management processes, efficiency metrics, and so on. All this is part and parcel of improved management information.

3. *It should be appreciated that because management ability is a highly individual art, no two managers do their work in the same way.*

Therefore, the executive information system must be designed so that it is steadily personalized to the decision process and mode of operation of the executive it serves. Standard and inflexible EIS deliverables have no place in the company's competitive armory. They are good only for people who fall in love with the status quo.

4. *Because people learn by actually managing, the EIS should enhance this role of on-the-job training.*

This is done through support of experimentation. Also, visualization and graphical presentation are good ways to improve a manager's perception and performance, as Section 5 will document. A snapshot on what is meant by this reference is given in Figure 7.5, with two examples: a threshold applied to market volatility and tolerances on exposures by specific activity.

7.4 A CORPORATE MEMORY FACILITY: CASE STUDY WITH MAGELLAN

The use of high technology should also be seen as a means for developing a documented and factual dissention, therefore permitting more focused decisions at the corporate level. As chairman of the Board of General Motors, Alfred P. Sloan always advised other board members and his immediate assistants to never accept an important proposal without having dissention, critical discussion about merits and demerits of the issue at hand.

For his part, Dr. Robert McNamara, former U.S. Defense Secretary and President of the World Bank, advises to never go ahead with a major project unless one has examined all the alternatives. "In a multimillion dollar project you should never be satisfied with vanilla ice cream only. You should have many flavors," says McNamara. This dictum applies nicely to all business plans and the way we screen them.

- Real-time information is interpreted differently by different people. Therefore, it can assist in developing dissention.
- A postmortem walkthrough of past decisions, with obtained results under perspective, is the best possible way to become aware of the possible aftermath in risk and reward.

1. THRESHOLDS APPLIED TO VOLATILITY

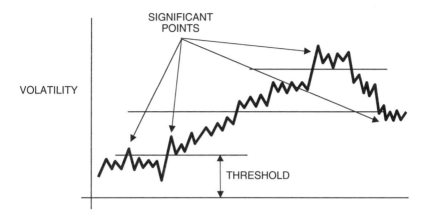

2. TOLERANCES ON EXPOSURE BY TYPE OF ACTIVITY

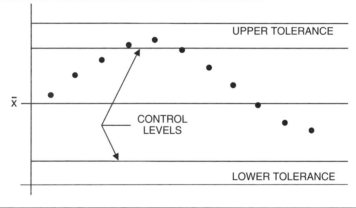

Figure 7.5 The Visualization of Financial Data Flows and of Computational Results Should Assist Comprehension in Real-Time

A corporate memory facility (CMF) is an integral and important part of an executive information system. Its development dates back to the late 1980s, when budget overruns with weapons systems led the U.S. military to demand a very special database in which all decisions regarding a weapons contract and its specifications, as well as all requests or initiations for changes (which led to the overruns) would be recorded.

Contractors working for the Department of Defense (DOD) were the first to implement a CMF, but the benefits were soon evident. Top-tier companies not only followed up with its implementation but also used it to execute postmortems on past decisions. The results obtained in relation to a decision's original goal are not self-evident without factual and documented postmortem walkthroughs.

Over the years, the technology of a corporate memory facility has significantly improved. In many applications, agents are now doing most of the servicing, and such systems operate in any place the company is present, at any time, for any person authorized to use it. One of the earliest and best examples of a sophisticated CMF, dating back to the early 1990s, is Magellan by Bankers Trust (BT).

Designed for senior bankers, Magellan is a fully automated decision support environment originally implemented in the Corporate Finance and Capital Markets areas of BT. Using technology to leverage financial expertise, it has provided professionals with the ability to access right on the desktop all the information they need, both external to the bank and generated within the institution. By integrating not only decisions but also other relevant data streams, the network has allowed professionals across distant physical locations to work on pertinent information cooperatively, to create new products and services and to market them effectively to clients.

The design principle has been that anyone on the network should be able to instantly send to anyone else multimedia information: text, graphs, tables, images, or spreadsheets. Through Magellan, new product terms, proposals, customer contracts, and master agreements have been made instantaneously available throughout the financial institution.

This system has facilitated communications, especially across geographic boundaries, and assured that the immediate handling of each new financial product and/or client proposal does not require total reinvention of systems and procedures. Voice annotation has allowed product specialists to pitch their latest ideas to the multimedia document or explain intricate issues of its rationale and of its marketing target.

Alert icons can flash at the corner of each one of its interconnected workstations. Smart filters go through huge amounts of news and financial data brought into the financial institution each day. These special, individually tailored filters scan the stories for items important to each bank officer. When an article of interest arrives, it is selected and instantly sent to his workstation. The icon alerts the officer to what data is waiting.

Along the principles explained in Section 2, a major part of the attraction of Magellan has been that real-time news wires from more than 16 services, and market data channeled into Bankers Trust every day, are filtered and individually tailored for the executive concerned by it. This way relevant information is always at the banker's reach. Also, when a banking professional requests information on a particular company or topic, knowledge-enriched software automatically accesses a wide range of global research databases on a particular company or topic.

Magellan has also made product term sheets, proposals, customer contracts, and master agreements instantaneously available throughout the bank.

This has significantly facilitated communications across time zones. As noted, voice annotation allows product specialists to pitch their latest concepts about a new product or proposal, providing advice on a global client base. The system works in real-time, as any and every EIS should, and it is subject to steady upgrade so that the latest technological development may be incorporated to enhance supported services and add new ones, without loss of time, money, or effort.

In the background of these references lies the fact that the executive information system is an integral part of the company's business architecture (see Chapter 13). A well-chosen and properly implemented business architecture must support distributed, intelligence-enriched, and management-oriented IT structures. It should be able to integrate all of the facilities offered by information providers that contribute to better governance.

The chosen architecture should ensure migration paths to make EIS renewal feasible and oversee a process in transition to determine the best approach and to recognize that there is a need to preserve the integrity of management decisions through technology, which permits it to be ahead of the curve against competition.

7.5 THE IMPORTANT ROLE OF VISUALIZATION IN EXECUTIVE INFORMATION SYSTEMS

Visualization is one of the critical design characteristics of a modern executive information system; indeed, it is one of its marks of distinction. By definition, visualization is the turning of numbers into graphics. Approximately 80 percent of what the human mind remembers is derived from visual stimuli. One way of coping with the information explosion is by reducing the large volume of data and statistics through graphs, pictures, and patterns.

Senior executives appreciate that visualization can be of significant assistance to their work. As Bob Woodward has it, from his study of Einstein's theory, Federal Reserve chairman Dr. Alan Greenspan knows the importance of finding discrepancies: light bending, time slowing, light being both wave and particle. Based on this know-how, Greenspan searches for discrepancies through visualization.[4] Greenspan accesses 50 charts interactively by computer and sees to it that all the information he wants is only a click or two away.

On a calm day, Woodward says, Dr. Greenspan checks the key charts once every half hour or so, anticipating the unexpected and making sure that something is *not* happening. It is most likely that as market fever mounts, database access is more frequent and visualization is more focused.

The president of an American manufacturing company came to the same conclusion about the impact of turning numbers into graphics. As shown in Figure 7.6, he used visualization to reduce the company's 300-page report to the board to one single page. Of the 20 pigeonholes, only

Just note differences.

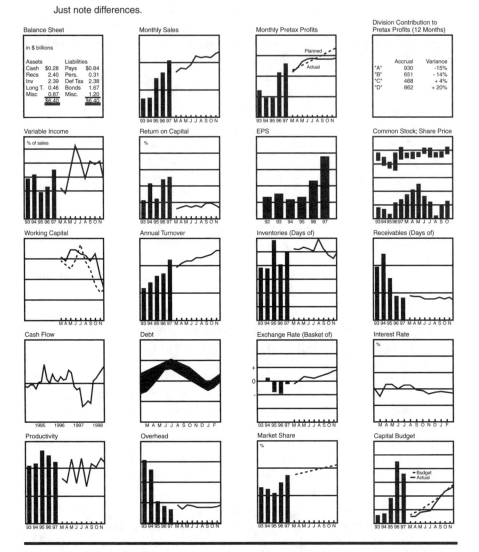

Figure 7.6   Patterning Management Information: A Bird's Eye View of Vital Statistics and Trends

two show numbers. The other 18 are graphical presentations of monthly sales, profits, income, return on capital, earnings per share (EPS), and so on.

The exact nature of pigeonholes in this figure is unimportant. What is crucial is the pattern they present, as well as the fact that visualization replaces long tables that are often tedious to read and comprehend in an effective way. Notice that even the two tables included in this presentation have been reduced to their essentials, an order of magnitude in billion of dollars. That is what is important to the members of the board.

The message the reader should retain from these examples is that controlling information flow is only half the battle. The other half is that of capitalizing on interactive visualization to enhance the services of managers and professionals, enabling them to comprehend information quickly and in a manner that allows immediate action. This process of visualization must be high quality and personalized, and it should answer each end user's preferences of how information should be presented.

Although many currently available approaches aim to help the user to correlate and gain insight into the available information, presentation need not be standard, as is the case with native query languages and old protocols on legacy systems. Three-dimensional figures, fractals, nonlinear mapping, and dynamic time series help the user to understand time-dependent processes. And because time is a most important parameter, the timeliness of visualization is also critical.

In fact, it is not only visualization that helps in making visible the form of a pattern's conceptual, operational, and experimental results. A growing number of practical examples help demonstrate that some of the current tools and projects go beyond visualization. As Figure 7.7 shows, user applications include sophisticated modes of presentation:

- Visibilization, the process of making visible very small and very large items or their measurements
- Visistraction, making visible those phenomena lacking a direct physical interpretation but having to do with concepts

These high-end implementations fit well with growing requirements concerning perception and conception of complex situations, and processing

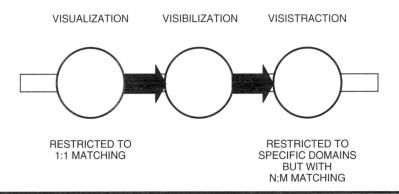

Figure 7.7 Making Visible Experimental, Operational, and Conceptual Results

power is offered at an affordable cost. Both visibilization and visistraction capitalize on the fact that not all computer information is numbers. We are always looking for a match between a problem and a solution; the crucial difference, for perceptual reasons, is in the way we implement the match.

In terms of human understanding, the processes of visistraction, visibilization, and visualization help to translate numerical computer output into figures, pictures, and moving images. Understanding this notion of translation and of 3-dimensional representation is important because much of the business and scientific data and their representations are spatial in concept.

To the executive who needs to comprehend a complex situation prior to reaching a decision, the visualization of real-time data streams offers a far better alternative than a tabular presentation. Many rules known from studies of perception can be applied to visualization to help in creative thinking.

For interactive presentation, we can take advantage of traditional metaphors or develop new ones to assist in the customization of presentation characteristics and, by extension, in perception. But before we do so, we should understand how the process of perception works and which factors are instrumental in finding insights that otherwise might go unobserved.

Figure 7.8 presents, as an example, a radar chart that maps deals in two derivative financial instruments "A" and "B" in terms of notional amount of over-the-counter (OTC) contracts and assumed risk estimated for the contract's lifecycle. The third dimension (not shown in this chart) is counterparty risk, which accounts for a significant part of the difference in the spread of the chart.

Another significant benefit offered by representation through figures over numbers is that statistics stand out as being wrong because they are surprisingly precise and because they are improbably pertinent.

This sees to it that statistics-based statements may collapse under a second look. Also present are the tendencies to boast and to understate, which contradict each other but do not cancel each other out. Also, often at fault is the sampling method, which is found at the heart of many false statistics. Samples may be too small, biased, or plainly irrelevant. Fundamentally, the results of every statistical study are no better than the sample it is based on. This fact, too, is not generally appreciated.

7.6 A WELL-DESIGNED EIS IS ALWAYS USER CENTERED: A CASE STUDY

Time and again, experience with EIS and MIS demonstrates that a useful and valid solution is user centered. The end user should not only be consulted bu also collaborate on its design. The case study in this section comes from a personal experience with a major financial institution. The

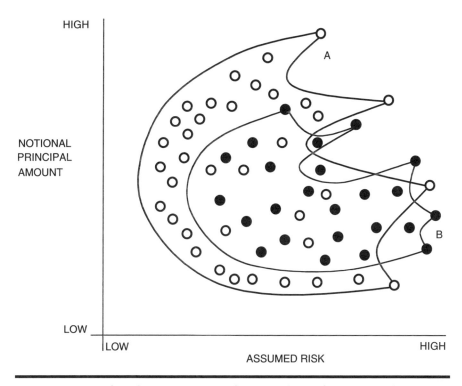

Figure 7.8 A Radar Chart May Be Used to Visualize Information Relationships between Off Balance Sheet Instruments

subject addressed by the project has been a significant improvement in quality of presentation.

The company in reference had in operation for several years an MIS. However, as its functionality expanded, new end-user requests came onstream and several modifications were made to its design. Evidently, the time came for a thorough revamp. As a start, a statistically significant sample was taken of end users receiving the support to be redesigned. The overriding considerations that were brought forward in the course of two end-user conferences were those of improving quality in the realm of financial services. Other specific goals were:

- The real-time usage of new information, including visualization
- Productivity-type improvements, all the way to investment decisions
- The ability to cut costs in information searches and other trivia

Examples of value differentiation discussed during the end-user meetings included not just presentation issues but also better-documented information, for instance, ways and means of improving the consistency of credit ratings of counterparties, more analytical investment recommendations to customers, and the creation of a necessary foundation, in management information terms, for new product development opportunities.

One of the senior people participating in the EIS study, a personal banking executive, particularly pressed the issue of what he needs to know after a week-long absence from his office. The sense of his request was that while he is physically away, he should keep in intraday contact not just through phone but also by means of the bank's EIS, with ad hoc queries and tools available to analyze alternatives and to improve customer contact.

"Such goals," stated one of the senior executives participating in the meetings, "are behind the fact that the need for new management-oriented applications steadily arises and better approaches are required to handle them. We have to go back to reengineering our approaches." As the planning meetings progressed, this reference was made with increasing frequency.

The magnitude of the needed effort in projecting a new, more sophisticated EIS solution was exemplified by the pace of the introduction of new financial products, their impact on the banking business, and the risks these instruments bring with them. The management information requirements posed by derivatives were dramatized in the course of this project by internal studies that documented an international explosion in issuing and trading derivative products such as futures, forwards, options, swaps, index trading, mortgage-backed securities, credit derivatives, weather derivatives, and a growing horde of exotics.

One of the board members requested a solution that brings collective intelligence to bear, in real-time, on a difficult problem. He projected the case of having unexpected questions in an online meeting with clients, peers, and other advisers located in widely separated financial centers. He also demanded a CMF, associated with the EIS to be consulted by lawyers and negotiators.

This is by no means a one-tantum request by a senior executive. It is a message I received on several occasions in my consulting practice and in my seminars as well as in interviews with money managers, securities traders, and chief financial officers of major corporations and financial institutions in the United States and Europe. In the background lies the fact that global loans, trading, and investment patterns are changing. Trading activity in traditional investments such as stocks, bonds, and currencies increases only slightly year to year. In contrast, the use of derivative financial instruments soars and is expected to continue as far as the experts can see.

Here are some statistics. More than 85 percent of financial institutions use derivative instruments, up from 63 percent in the mid-1990s. More than 70 percent are investing in stock indexes and baskets of stocks, up from 44 percent ten years ago, and more than 75 percent are dealing with securitized products such as bonds backed by mortgages, credit cards, auto loans, and corporates.

As the board member in the aforementioned EIS end-user conferences mentioned, the growing use of derivative instruments means an increasing amount of risk, and risk has to be managed in an able manner — in real-time. Other participants emphasized that a similar requirement is posed by cross-border trades. In general, more than a quarter of the trading volume involves foreign securities, up from 14 percent in the mid-1990s. In this specific bank, the percentage was in excess of 50 percent.

Moreover, the increase in the number of international money managers dealing in derivative securities who were clients of the institution in reference was in itself an indication of the attention that should be paid to global risk management. It is therefore understandable that traditional tools of risk control are no longer effective.

7.7 NOTES

1. D.N. Chorafas, *Operations Research for Industrial Management*, Reinhold, New York, 1958.
2. D.N. Chorafas, *Systems and Simulation*, Academic Press, New York, 1965.
3. D.N. Chorafas, *Agent Technology Handbook*, McGraw-Hill, New York, 1998.
4. Bob Woodward, *Maestro*, Simon & Schuster, New York, 2000.

8

CLIENT INFORMATION
SYSTEMS

8.1 INTRODUCTION

Client focus is the ability to understand the client's needs and to answer them in the most effective way. This should be done in an environment of client intimacy and in a manner that best suits client requirements through high-quality service. The deliverables must be visible and appreciated by the person to whom they are addressed and by the client company at large.

A company needs more than just a client database with address, phone number, and other particulars to support itself in its effort to steadily improve relationship management. This is the mission assigned to a specifically designed client information system (CIS). The term appeared for the first time, to my knowledge, at the Dai-Ichi Kangyo Bank in the mid-1980s (see Section 2), but the concept behind CIS continued to evolve over the last two decades.

Client information systems should include everything we need to know about the client; for instance, what makes him tick and how a company should structure efforts to meet and to continue to meet customer requirements through steady innovation and price improvement in products and services. Innovation is the ability to create business ideas that enable the core product lines of a firm to be differentiated from those of its competitors in a way that the customer would return time and again for more products and services.

This is an aspect of relationship management not always understood by financial and industrial entities, mainly because of failures in perception. In the 1960s and early 1970s, when IBM had reached its high water mark, more than 75 percent of its fast-growing annual business was coming from its existing client base. But the then-management of the company was slow to adapt to the minis and maxis and became devoted to its mainframes.

IBM paid dearly for such a serious oversight. By the 1980s, the customers had drifted away, IBM faced a sorry future. This is by no means an exceptional happening. For many decades the legendary watchmakers of Switzerland were so good at their craft and so widely admired that they owned a remarkable 65 percent of the world market for all types of timepieces. The drift started in the late 1960s. By 1980 the Swiss share of the market plunged below 10 percent. The Japanese watchmakers were taking over the world's watch market. Seiko, for example, became synonymous with a quality timepiece.

A similar case of loss of contact with the client base took place with German cameras. Zeiss and Leica were the world's quality standards, but they failed to move with their time and to lead the market into new areas. Nikon, Olympus, Pentax, and Konica, the Japanese camera makers, became masters of innovation, offering products at an affordable cost and taking the world's camera market away from the traditional German makers.

The Swiss did not suddenly forget how to produce excellent watches, nor did the Germans lose the skill of manufacturing first-class cameras. What they were guilty of was failing to keep in close contact with their clients, which would have allowed them to sense the turns and switches in the market. As a result, they failed to see the future.

In Switzerland's case, when an inventor suggested that quartz movement replace the mainspring of a watch, the Swiss watch producers scoffed. But the Japanese listened, and their companies seized the market. There are many such examples, all of which demonstrate that in business failures of vision and lack of courage to act forcibly are unpardonable sins.

The railroads were not developed as a pioneering departure from nineteenth-century leaders of the coach transport industry. The automobile industry was not a start-up financed by the mighty railroad companies. The airplane industry was not promoted by the motor vehicle companies as a way of reinventing itself through a new means of transportion. Thomas Watson, Sr., the otherwise brilliant entrepreneur who built IBM, foresaw that up to 10 computers could be sold worldwide, mainly to universities.

All of these examples are talking of the decay that follows top management's inability to keep in close contact with the customer base. Close contact is necessary to any company for positioning itself against market forces, before being overrun by events beyond its control. The goal of client information systems is that of helping management keep in close contact with customers and with the market, both for short-term purposes, essentially sales, and for the long-term survival of the firm.

8.2 THE NEW AGE OF RETAIL

Sometime in the 1990s, to a substantial extent thanks to the Internet (see Chapters 15 and 16), we entered *the new age of retail*. I define this new age as retail business models that are so enhanced by market sensitivity, cost effectiveness, *and* on-line relationship management that newcomers can leave the traditional competitors way behind, as happened with watches.

Examples of start-ups that became sizeable companies by capitalizing on the online medium are Amazon.com, eBay, and Yahoo!, the latter being a pure service company that invented a market. An example of huge cost-effectiveness advantage, by reinventing the retail marketing chain, is provided by Wal-Mart (see Chapter 7).

Owing to new and better shopping experiences provided by Internet retailers, consumers have been changing their buying habits and embracing the online buying practice faster than anyone could have predicted. According to some of the experts, we are in the very early stages of a retail revolution that will ultimately change the shopping landscape and make old retail models irrelevant.

As with any revolution, there will be moments when over-optimism rules and moments when over-pessimism holds sway. However, one thing we can say with certainty is that the revolution will create tremendous opportunities for some companies and will be a terrible threat to others that insist on the status quo. When the dust settles, few large online retail winners will, by all likelihood, have joined the ranks of the premier retailers of the world.

Wal-Mart offers a good example on how upstarts can overtake companies that are long established and, by so doing, usher a new age of retail. The company's 2002 sales of $244.5 billion were larger than the sales of Sears, Target, JC Penny, Kmart, Safeway, and Kroger combined.[1]

Sam Walton had many brilliant ideas that he put into practice, but *if* I were to choose the best one, *then* it would be the way he focused on clients and prospects. In the mid-1980s, when I was consultant to the board of the Union Bank of Switzerland, I did an international study with a significant sample of correspondent banks, aimed to define the profile of the most profitable customers of a financial institution and the types of services they were after[2] as well as the type of high technology a bank must provide in order to serve its clients in the most effective manner. As this study has documented:

- About 20 percent of the bank's clients contribute 80 percent of its profits
- The top 1 percent of the bank's clients contributes 30 percent to 35 percent of the profits, depending on the institution

Figure 8.1 presents the pertinent statistics. One of Japan's top city banks, Dai Ichi Kangyo, had reached the same conclusion. It had therefore developed, with the greatest possible care, the 1 percent database, which included 20,000 of its clients (largely businesses). This constituted the kernel

POPULATION OF CLIENTS
IN %

SUM OF PROFITS
IN %

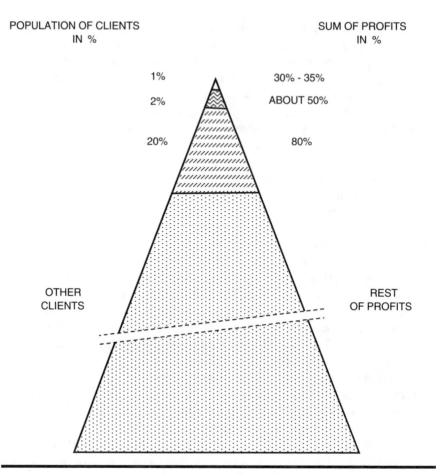

1% 30% - 35%

2% ABOUT 50%

20% 80%

OTHER CLIENTS

REST OF PROFITS

Figure 8.1 Pareto's Law Fully Applies with the Bank, Its Clients, and Its Profits

of Dai Ichi's new information technology and is at the origin of client information systems as a term.

Companies with experience in CIS design suggest that the timely and accurate follow-up on client requirements and drives should be one of the major inputs in defining the business architecture (see Chapter 13) because the contents are instrumental in shaping the way relationship management should work. As the reader is already aware from discussion on this issue, relationship management is no abstract notion. It is a core activity that closely relates to a company's cash flow and, eventually, to its survival.

Because handholding and sales orders correlate, an effective relationship management structure calls for giving full profit-and-loss (P&L) responsibility to the responsible business unit, down to the individual salesman, which can be done most effectively through an entrepreneurial approach. In this sense, the business architecture must enrich the CIS activity with:

- Knowledge-enriched artifacts for online assistance to the relationship manager
- An online capability to seamless system able to access all of the company's products and services, to enable cross-sales
- Client mirror services to evaluate what a customer costs and what a company gains, including customer history (see Section 5)
- Databases that are self-contained and self-sufficient for management accounting by salesman, profit center, business unit, counterparty, and product or service

Effective client-relationship management requires real-time solutions enriched through knowledge artifacts that, among other duties, keep track of customers and target them with new product and/or price offers to stop them from defecting. Self-service software solutions can reduce costs by helping customers do things for themselves. Different customers and markets have different requirements. Therefore, solutions have to be customized in order to be effective. Personalization can well be an add-on on off-the-shelf software (see Section 6 on CRM).

For example, instead of setting up a digital subscriber line (DSL) connection by sending an engineer to the customer's site, the telephone company uses software to do the same job more effectively and at lower cost. This is relatively easily accomplished by putting appropriate equipment in the central office and using expert systems to install it automatically.

Moreover, network operators are investing in Web sites to automate the configuration of new offerings, provide technical support, and make it possible for businesses to both order and configure new network services. The engineering for achieving such service goals in an efficient manner uses hybrid solutions, combining the support provided by existing systems and components through sophisticated software.

The implementors of a customer information system can learn a lesson from maintenance engineering, which uses knowledge-enriched software and databases to lower costs while making the work more effective. This happens, for instance, when the analysis of postproduction in-service information is valuable to people who maintain industrial equipment or durable consumer goods. Through databased information, they can track:

- How the objects are used
- When and how they break down
- What they need for restart and recovery, and so on

At the design end, with this information engineers can design products better suited to the way customers actually use them, spot opportunities for upgrades, and provide features to help in sales and in servicing. As the reader will appreciate, the new age of retail and associated market advantage is propelled not by one but a whole aggregate of contributions, and a good deal of the information elements belonging to this aggregate revolve around the CIS.

8.3 PREREQUISITES TO THE DESIGN OF A CLIENT INFORMATION SYSTEM

Much of what has been explained in Chapter 7 in connection to the design of forward-looking executive information systems is applicable to client information systems, as well. Top-tier companies, however, add other factors, such as the location of their factories from which they will expedite goods as well as of warehouses and sales outlets. An example has been provided in Chapter 6 in connection to the implementation of a virtual double strategy by a Mexican cement manufacturer.

Through analogical thinking, a bank would integrate into the CIS aggregate information on its customers, products, branches, and geographic distribution of skills, so that front desks and back offices can serve online client requests — from retail banking to lending, investments, trading, and treasury operations (see Chapter 10). Such an approach can serve multiple goals.

One of the objectives is to promote client self-service for bread-and-butter operations. This is the trend, but there are prerequisites, one of them being the use of high technology because without agents and object-oriented programming the quality of services being offered online may bend. As a result, a bank becomes uncompetitive and fails to retain high-value clients. CIS solutions cannot prosper by using legacy systems and obsolete tools.

Other prerequisites include cost reduction, greater accuracy through fully online data collection, and market research that addresses both manifested issues by the client and, whenever possible, background factors (see Figure 8.2). Identifying background factors can be instrumental in cross-sales, and cross-sales should be a basic objective assigned to client information systems.

A study done in 1999 in the United Kingdom provided evidence that British banks that two years earlier had disinvested themselves from their investment-banking subsidiaries fared badly in their private banking operations. Never before, to my knowledge, were retail and investment banking shown to be correlated. This study has demonstrated that by decoupling the investment banking arm, the bank's ability to innovative has been reduced and the institution loses some of its more sophisticated personal-banking clients.

Moreover, if the solution we adopt does not stress online delivery of what are now considered to be classical services through fully online solutions, the bank's cost structure will skyrocket. At the same time, failure to implement high tech will make the institution less able to motivate and

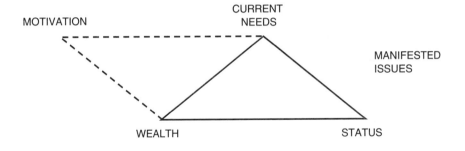

MOTIVATION · CURRENT NEEDS · MANIFESTED ISSUES · WEALTH · STATUS

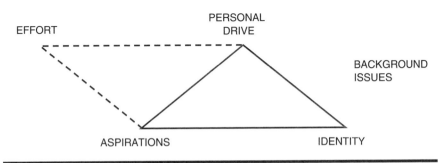

EFFORT · PERSONAL DRIVE · BACKGROUND ISSUES · ASPIRATIONS · IDENTITY

Figure 8.2 Market Research Associated with Relationship Management Must Address Both Manifested and Background Issues

service its most important clients. At the delivery end, able CIS solutions must take into account both the profile of clients and the service channels the bank is promoting.

The reader should notice that an analytical study based on these factors is in no way done once and then put in the time closet. Mergers, acquisitions, product changes, evolving client relations, and other factors oblige us to rethink and (most often) revamp our standing solution. As shown in Table 8.1, the merger of Citibank and Travelers into Citigroup presented both overlaps and complementarity in terms of channels; the overlaps had to be sorted out.

Beyond this, all of the channels that we support must be served through appropriate client interfaces, with an increasing amount of computer-based assistance being customized to leverage the services we offer. All online support must be fully automated and integrated with sales and service. These prerequisites typically mean that we will have to reengineer our IT to respond to requirements for customer profiles and product refinement, with the aim of improving the quality and sophistication of services and their effectiveness in terms of customer appeal and cost.

We should not only target a given client population but also analyze each of our important customers' behavior and profile. Both the present

Table 8.1   Channels and Customers in a Universal Bank. An Example from Citigroup

Channels	Customers	Origin
Retail Banking	Consumers, Small Business	Citibank
Personal Banking	High Net Worth Individuals	Citibank
Business Portfolio	Medium Size Firms	Citibank
Bank Guarantees	All Clients	Citibank
Wholesale Banking	Corporates	Citibank, Travelers
Portfolio Management	Individuals, Funds	Citibank, Travelers
Brokerage	All Clients	Travelers
Custody	Funds, Other Banks	Citibank, Travelers
Trading	Forex, Interest Rates	Citibank, Travelers
Securitization	All Clients	Travelers
Derivatives	Companies, Corr. Banks, Others	Travelers
M&A	Companies	Citibank, Travelers
Insurance	All Clients	Travelers

and the projected client base counts. We should carefully study types of customers, customer balances, transactions being made, and relationships with the bank as well as present fee income, costs, profits, and projected changes.

Studies done along this line are within the CIS realm. They provide an insight into which types of customers and customer relations are profitable and should be retained. They are also instrumental in helping us in selecting the pricing method most appropriate to meet our objectives.

For evident commercial purposes, we should keep the pricing method simple, remembering that the trend now is to unbundle service prices while integrating the service structure. Indeed, service pricing should be easy to not only understand and explain but also to administer. Customers resent a pricing method they do not understand or whose advantages to them are not evident.

In many cases, it is pricing simplicity that makes unbundling advisable. In the past, when spreads were high, banks often found it convenient and profitable to bundle their prices. Today, as interest margins shrink, competitors offer a growing pallet of unbundling services that can be purchased together at cost savings to the client.

Because product and service pricing, internal and external costs, and end profitability correlate, both analytical management accounting and account consolidation are musts. Preferably, they should be done in a way that makes feasible peer-to-peer comparison, study of the nature of a relationship, examination of onsite/offsite preferences in delivery, service targeting, cross-selling, and other factors. The CIS must make it possible for bank executives to data mine:

- Changes in deposits, lending, investing, and trading
- Policy followed by clients and correspondent banks in balances
- Workloads/costs associated with the different classes of transaction, the latter being handled through STP (see Chapter 5)

All this must be done by market segment and by instruments, with the findings being factual and documented. To do so effectively, we must have a plan that makes it possible to evolve the client information system while it remains operational at all times. In other terms, we must design the CIS for technology changes — a principle that is equally valid with EIS as well as with the risk management system (see Chapter 11).

Such design is possible. In one of the rare success stories in conversion procedures in the banking industry, in the late 1990s Barclays Bank restructured its risks archives. Then, when the new database was tested and proved operational, it shut down its main customer system for a weekend to move over to the updated structure accommodating 25 million customer accounts.

This new system seamlessly replaced three incompatible legacy procedures as well as their databases and programming support. In London, knowing people have said that Barclays spent at least £100 million ($165 million) on the upgrade but that it has derived from it enough benefits to cover the expense and leave a profit in the first two years of its operation. We must always think of return on investment in connection to IT at large and, most particularly, in regard to client information systems.

8.4 MIT'S VIRTUAL CUSTOMER AND ACCENTURE'S VIRTUAL DOUBLE

Since Chapter 1, the reference has been made that what we have available today in terms of information technology support is only a forerunner of things to come. The organizational studies we are undertaking should account for the fact that computation will become more or less freely available, entering many aspects of the everyday real world at home and in business. As studies at MIT suggest, by all likelihood the input/output to computer devices will be revolutionized through the ability to communicate naturally:

- Using speech, vision, and phrases to express intent
- Leaving it up to the computer to locate resources and carry out our intent[3]

One of the interesting projects at MIT is the Virtual Customer (VC) Initiative, a multidisciplinary approach targeting significant improvements in speed, accuracy, and usability of customer-oriented input to a supplier's product-planning and product-design processes. This concept fits well with the themes that have dominated Part Two: STP, ERP, reality online, EIS, and CIS.

The development of virtual customer solutions is expected to create enormous opportunities for effective client-handling processes as well as seamless insourcing and outsourcing. We are still not there, but this is the direction in which high technology currently moves. For a client information system to be effective, or even merely adequate, it must be explicit, systematic, and comprehensive. VC/VD approaches help in this process. Most particularly, they serve the aim to make the CIS self-generating to some degree. Data mining apart, solutions should be using algorithms and heuristics to increase the store of information regarding the client relationship. They should also ensure that as the VC (or VD) practice grows, tools are available to exploit it.

A virtual double project has both generic aspects, of interest to all applications, and specific missions it should fulfill in a specific implementation, following careful study and definition. For instance, the virtual double of a customer can gather vital information over the life of the relationship, increasing a company's:

1. *Sensitivity and response to customer wishes.* A significantly increased customer-oriented sensitivity leads some experts to the belief that reality online, sensors, and VDs will revolutionize product offerings. An example is dynamic insurance policies. Smart dust (see Chapter 3) embedded into cars may be tracking the driver and the vehicle in regard to speed threshold and other safety variables. But as with all technology, it may also be used for control purposes, transmitting, for instance, to a traffic police center that a driver goes too fast, talks on the cell phone, or does not respect pedestrian crossings.

2. *Effective handholding,* increasing by so much the entry price of competitors. As it has been brought to the reader's attention, handholding is effective when it provides rapid response. General Electric Capital uses Six Sigma[4] to control how the agents of its insurance subsidiary respond to client queries. There is no place for static, fixed, or rigid approaches, but there is a need for client-centered information elements that can develop knowledge and facts that will change perceptions of client relationships as well as evolve to reflect product and market requirements and feedback from the field.

3. *Ability to steadily enrich the client's personal data with new insight,* leading to more accurate perceptions of the business relationship. Indeed, the customer's virtual double can play a role similar to that of an executive information system but oriented to each business partnership. In this sense, virtual customer and VD solutions are

nearly synonymous, leading to a big step forward from present-day ERP and CRM applications. This, however, is true only if the company is willing and able to revolutionize its current marketing policies.

Personal data on any business partner may include background profile, contact preferences, ordering policies, and other habits that help to focus on the business relation. Beyond this come statistical analysis, modeling, and logic patterns that simulate reasoning and address questions that astute industrial leaders will ask while making decisions.

Dell Computer, for example, is a company that has revolutionized its former system, elaborating and implementing a new solution backed up by knowledge-enriched software, the result of which is a gain of 25-percent higher productivity from its existing facilities. A back-to-basics approach promoted by superior organization and high tech does not come easily, but its results are highly profitable. Dell Computer gained significant advantages by:

■ Renegotiating deals with suppliers
■ Redesigning inventory management
■ Installing new software that made it possible to increase by a quarter the capacity of its plants

The Economist states, "The new discovery is that the information technology in which so much was invested can really make a difference. As always, too much was expected in the short run and not enough in the long term."[5] Effective handling of business partners requires a sweeping overhaul of business processes to make the most of the system.

Once it comes into the mainstream, the culture of developing, updating in real-time, and exploiting virtual doubles will always be available and up to date, providing a logical focal point for organizing information in context and using that information as needed. It can also be made to provide a degree of consistency and vigilance that more manual approaches seldom, if ever, attain.

In order to obtain tangible benefits, virtual customer and virtual double solutions must be holistic. Partial approaches do not produce results. Data streaming from sensors requires registration, integration, filtering, and analysis for insight. Each of these steps can lead to messaging with agents being in charge of message exchanges.

An example of low-level messaging exploiting VD capabilities is the message itself presented on video about the printer. This VD of the printer has qualities the printer may not even have — therefore helping the operator to manage complexity. Stan Taylor mentioned that Asea Brown Boveri uses a virtual double concept in industrial IT, every machine having its VD that can provide information about the physical world, not available till now.

A major contribution of the virtual double is that it is focused. Whereas businesses usually complain about lack of data, very few know how to extract value out of information in their databases. This, however, becomes a must in a highly competitive environment, and a wealth of information is readily available with sensor technology working online in the physical world. For instance:

- Business-process data gives companies the ability to see the total picture, including where a product stands in its lifecycle.
- Observational data is available for any object, at any location, telling where it is, what it is doing, and how it is being processed.

The South African railway, for example, has a system with container intelligence tags. *If* a container is not tagged, *then* the system takes a photo of it and signals its existence. Marks & Spencer refitted all containers with sensors and seems to have obtained payback in 12 months. These sensors are tracking everything, everywhere and, hence, are increasing accuracy and reducing time spent.

Genscape, Inc., a U.S. company, planted sensors near the electricity distribution network coast to coast. The virtual double created a pattern of electrical distribution that no other electricity company has. The information producer sells this information at a high price, capitalizing on the fact that although technology is available to everybody, very few companies know how to use it effectively.

8.5 IMPLEMENTING THE CUSTOMER MIRROR

The *customer mirror* is one of the most important applications of a client-oriented implementation of high tech. It is a profitability report reflecting the P&L of the single client from the company's perspective. The concept is not of the twenty-first century. The first application that I did of the customer mirror dates back to 1973 with Commerzbank, Germany's third-largest credit institution, followed by implementations with Italy's Banca Provinciale Lombarda and Istituto Bancario Italiano. In all these cases, the objective has been to inform management whether the bank is making or losing money.

The concept behind this evaluation of customer profitability is shown in Figure 8.3. Solutions should be online, fully integrative, making full use of executive information systems capabilities (see Chapter 7).

The difference between the mid-1970s and today in customer mirror implementation is that, whereas then computation was expensive and customer mirror applications were restricted to the top 1 percent or 2 percent

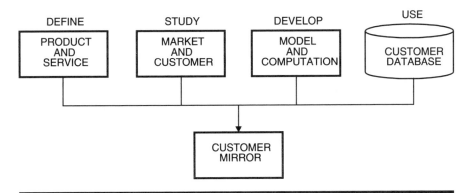

Figure 8.3 Using the Customer Mirror for Evaluation of Individual Customer Profitability: A CIS Application

of clients, and they were not interactive, today the top 20 percent of clients can handled through their virtual models, at an affordable cost. Building a mirror of each important customer's P&L toward the institution is a process that can be applied to every client relationship, whether in retail investment banking or not. The principles are the same in all three areas of activity. The customer mirror should be organized by:

■ Single customer on a consolidated account basis but with detail available for further analysis
■ Origin of individual account, analyzed by product line used by the client
■ Type of client relationship on a distributed basis by branch and by channel and also integrated at corporate level

The concept behind this practice is not alien to credit institutions. Many have been following innovative ways in establishing and communicating customer profitability information. In the late 1980s, for instance, First Union coded its credit card customers with tiny colored squares that flashed a color when service reps called up an account: green meant the person was a profitable customer, red was the tag of a money loser, and yellow indicated an in-between discretionary class.

This type of information helps not only in customer handling but also in making decisions on fees and rates. One of the banks participating in the research that led to this book suggested that the top 20 percent of bank customers generate up to six times as much revenue as they cost. By contrast, the bottom 20 percent cost three to four times more than they make.

Precisely because these and similar statistics are fairly well known in the banking industry, for more than two decades credit institutions have been increasingly segmenting their customers into profitability classes. But tiering has also drawbacks, particularly for marketing. Most classical sales programs fail to measure the potential value of a customer. Institutions typically measure only past transactions, and that contributes very little insight as to future business.

What someone spends today is not always a good predictor of what he will spend tomorrow, as employment patterns, family life, and spending habits change. The customer mirror does away with such permanent and semipermanent segmentations because it is a tool that can be restructured online and organized in different ways to fit ad hoc end user requirements, for instance, by:

- Type of customer account
- Industry origin of an account
- Type of financial instrument preferred by account holder
- Main branch from which high/low profitability accounts depend, and so on

One of the credit institutions that pioneered the client mirror has been Danish Handelsbanken. This bank's approach was that of a *customer analysis* procedure that computed, per client, average credit balance on a yearly and monthly basis, number of transactions per year (and month), possible interest income basis per time period, actual interest expense basis per time period, total interest result, transaction costs at standard cost rate, and contribution to indirect costs and overhead. The Handelsbanken objective has been that of summing up for any given client the costs incurred by the bank by doing customer-induced operations and revenues derived by the credit institutions as a result of the fees that it charged or other income sources.

To reach goals such as those given in the preceding paragraphs, both individually and collectively, customer mirrors should reflect *all* transactions by type, size, time of execution, handling cost, assumed risk (by client and by the bank), income to the bank, profit margin, and realized profit to the bank. The component parts of a customer mirror shown in Table 8.2 come from a real-life project.

The careful reader would appreciate the polyvalence of support provided by the client mirror when it reflects products or service we offer and the client buys, cross-product references we promote, branch or network through which our products are offered, type of operation that is executed in production and distribution, and number and value of operations by product identification. This list can be extended to cover other requirements, as well.

Among the important contributions of customer mirror that I have found in my practice are identification of cost involved in transactions based on standard costing, unit price of each product and deviations because of favors to the client, analysis of variation in fees and commissions we charge,

Table 8.2 Component Parts of a Customer Mirror

What the customer mirror does is to display periodically *and* **ad hoc:**

1. All transactions done with the customer, by channel
2. Cost of these transactions to the bank
3. Risk assumed by type of instrument and transaction
4. Monetization of risk the bank has taken with these transactions
5. Customer collateral and unsecured loans
6. Fees the bank charged for these transactions
7. Other fees pro rata, like portfolio management and safekeeping
8. Volume and amount of cross-sales in relationship banking
9. Milestones in the historical customer relationship (strengths and weaknesses)
10. P&L with this customer, seen as a profit center

and resulting profit margin. Figure 8.4 presents, in a nutshell, some of the benefits. These benefits will be much greater if the customer mirror design accounts for the need to plan and control operations in more than one dimension by:

■ Individualizing the bank's P&L by client relationship
■ Identifying the client's own P&L from an account-management perspective
■ Reflecting and integrating the cumulative risk the bank takes by client

Mapping in a comprehensive client-oriented manner the information necessary to produce such results has evident prerequisites. The most important are *costing*, that is, establishing standard cost of each banking operation; *pricing*, defining revenue by banking activity (product line and single product); and *risk focus*, by instrument, client, industry segment, topology, and other criteria.

A basic prerequisite in IT terms is that of a rich client information system and associated database(s). Another is *modeling* by developing comprehensive simulators of the product/customer/market interaction. A third is the development of sophisticated software, assisted by agents for exception reporting. All these component parts are necessary in visualizing relationship pricing and costing by chief activity and by client to build an effective CIS system.

8.6 USING CUSTOMER RELATIONSHIP MANAGEMENT SOFTWARE

Precisely for the same reasons that underpin a client information system; virtual double, and client mirror — improving customer service and assuring better profitability — business and industry have invested in customer

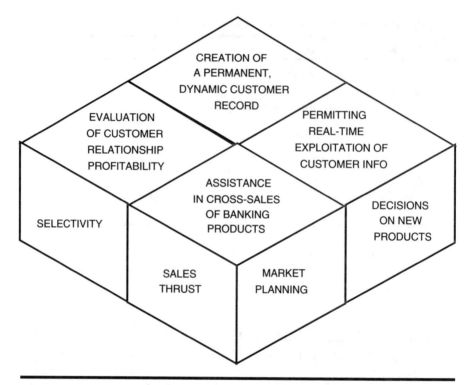

Figure 8.4   A Real-Time Customer Mirror Can Give Polyvalent Assistance to the Banker

relationship management (CRM) systems. CRM software can be bought as a commodity from different reputable houses. The challenge is in its implementation. One research project after another has indicated that only 30 percent rated such implementation as very effective. Major issues with CRM have been:

■ Lack of preparation to promote its functionality
■ Feeding into the system inaccurate information
■ Failure to pay attention to interoperability issues
■ Heterogeneity of platforms without a consistent effort to obtain seamless passthrough

The careful reader will recall that reference has already been made to off-the-shelf software for customer relationship management and supply chain management (SCM). It has also been stated that companies use commodity programs like CRM, SCM, and ERP to solve problems created by the limitations of their legacy systems and processes but very often fail to take care in eliminating the implementation roadblocks.

It needs no explaining that companies must use the best available enterprise solutions that, when properly implemented, can play the role of driver of organizational change. However, it should be understood that software alone will be providing a state-of-the-art integrated environment with seamless access to a global database. The prerequisite of thorough organizational work is unavoidable, no matter what the vendor says of the user company's management hopes.

Organizational prerequisites aside, another good precautionary measure is careful screening of off-the-shelf offers. Many vendors sell CRM and other software as part of the supply chain product line, but different routines within this realm do not necessarily work together in an efficient way.

The need for a study focused on integration is always present because it makes feasible working in a seamless manner. It also makes it easier to assure that contingency plans are in place. Without a long hard look at integration, major disconnects can surface at any time, in any place, leading to the inefficient application of technology, the inability to optimize customer relationship requirements, and other limitations.

The user organization should therefore do a lot of homework to assure the software it has available and the new one it acquires work in synergy. The appropriate study should take place not only within the user company's own premises but also up and down its supply chain, due to the fact that with CRM the sought-out goal is:

■ Understanding the customer
■ Increasing supply chain collaboration
■ Integrating business processes and data streams and effectively exploiting such information

In a significant number of cases, customer relationship management procedures are inseparable from those targeted by enterprise resource planning. For example, in a credit institution that I will identify as "W," CRM addressed itself to the task of efficiently managing front and back office operational processes associated with the customer, including marketing, sales, and steady handholding. As added value, this particular bank aimed at producing customer intelligence that could be used effectively in targeted marketing and improving the analytics behind decisions made in connection to new IT acquisition.

Given the goals that have been outlined, a legitimate question arises: Was this effort successful? The chief information officer (CIO) of a major bank responded to the query that CRM is only a label. It is the organizational work and other preparatory activities that the credit insitution did prior to its introduction that produced the deliverables.

Among these deliverables from executing the prerequisite organization streamlining and from CRM software, the CIO mentioned better sales campaign management, the use of customer intelligence to personalize marketing efforts, ability to efficiently disseminate customer information to all people that needed it, and so on. A value-added development provided management-defined criteria of performance in the customer relationship (see Section 5 on client mirror).

Another credit institution said that CRM software should track both incoming and outgoing customer communications, flash out types of client-initiated events, as well as register direct and indirect responses to business communication. This must be done in a way that can be effectively exploited. It should also provide a selective approach to business channel integration from the client's perspective.

Essentially what is sought through a CRM solution is the ability to incrementally increase customer account visibility, linking front desk transactions with back office ERP and legacy transaction processing in a way that gets the most out of the supply chain. *If,* and only if, it is properly executed, *then* this can be instrumental in:

- Closing the intelligence gap that exists today in most firms
- Effectively using evolving technologies to improve business operations

The reason behind my suggestion to pay significant attention to analytical business processes is the need for studying and integrating data streams to understand business partner activity and behavior over time and to evaluate the effectiveness of operational processes such as marketing and service support. Such information will enable a company to move toward personalizing products and sales while promoting customer value and loyalty.

Borrowing a leaf from the book of Bank "W," CIOs will be well advised to pay attention to interfaces. Integration with ERP software and other routines presents problems of heterogeneity. Even more difficulties are present when trying to integrate CRM with legacy systems. Among the problems typically encountered are:

- Data quality issues
- Multiple incompatible sources for the same data
- Complexities of misaligned windows of data availability
- Lack of a methodology for a common approach to design for all data feeds and data formats

Such incompatibilities do not permit the achievment of a single customer view; hence, it is wise to use the client mirror approach outlined in Section 5. One solution is that of establishing an *information portal,* making it feasible to subscribe, access, publish, and understand business information (which is, in principle, heterogeneous). There is significant merit in seamless access to incompatible data structures coming from, and going to, business partners.

8.7 NOTES

1. EIR (Executive Information Research), November 28, 2003.
2. D.N. Chorafas and H. Steinmann, *High Technology at UBS, for Excellence in Client Service,*" UBS, Zurich, 1988.
3. MIT, *"Innovation in the New Millennium,"* a conference program, Cambridge, MA, March 2002.
4. D.N. Chorafas, *Integrating ERP, CRM, Supply Chain Management and Smart Materials,* Auerbach, New York, 2001.
5. *The Economist,* November 15, 2003.

III

CASE STUDIES WITH
REAL-TIME ENTERPRISES

9

REAL-TIME APPLICATIONS
IN THE BANKING INDUSTRY

9.1 INTRODUCTION

This and the following chapters are case studies on the implementation of real-time systems. The banking industry provides the background. The text respects the principle that a case study must be a representative project able to retain the attention of committed learners. These four chapters cover some of the most important issues in modern banking: the general systems perspective (Chapter 9), treasury (Chapter 10), risk management (Chapter 11), and back office (Chapter 12). Viewing four different sides of the same industry is consistent with the fact that a case study must be worked out from different perspectives.

Another principle connected to case studies is that they must be fairly well documented in their presentation. In many cases, it is not possible to reveal the name of the bank behind the specific case being examined; therefore, the institutions in reference have been identified as "A," "B," "C," and so on. Moreover, a good case study must come up with a solution leaving a clear message. As the reader will see, this message varies from one case to the next, but they all share common elements in the quest for greater efficiency.

To explain the deliverables to be expected from *greater efficiency*, let me use a military case as an example. Ottoman armor of the fifteenth and sixteenth centuries was made with interlocking rings of flattened metal, reinforced at front and back with long rectangular steel plates. From the seventh century on, however, the armor was made entirely of chain. This proved to be more practical than its European counterpart because it permitted wider range of motion and its open structure allowed air to circulate freely, keeping the wearer cooler and more comfortable.[1]

In a quite similar manner, real-time information systems equipped with sensors for point-of-origin data capture (see Chapter 3) make feasible a

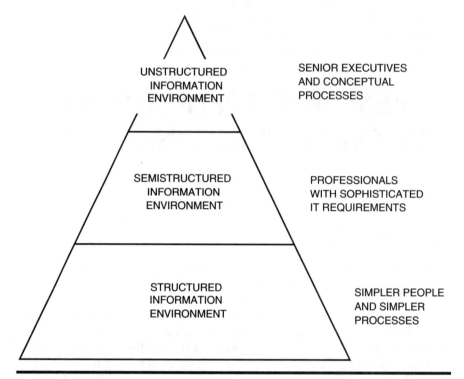

Figure 9.1   The Structure of an Information Environment Correlates to Its Intended Usage, and Is Served through Technology

wider coverage of operations, allow timely and accurate information to circulate freely from one unit to another, and make possible provision of IT support within semistructured and unstructured information environment. As Figure 9.1 shows, the structure of an information environment relates to and derives from its intended usage.

An information environment is structured either because of legal definition of what is and is not acceptable in reporting requirements, as is the case with general accounting, or following the establishment of specific supervisory rules. An example is the daily report by credit institutions on value at risk (VAR), in the aftermath of the 1996 Market Risk Amendment by the Basel Committee on Banking Supervision.[2]

An information environment is semistructured when it is subject to internal rules and regulations in terms of processing and reporting. Management accounting is a case in point. It must be accurate and timely, but it is typically less precise than general accounting, emphasizing order of magnitude rather than detail. Also, each company tends to have its own reporting format, which may change over time.

Lack of governmental or corporate rules on what must be regularly done in information handling and reporting leads to an unstructured environment that is typical of information needs at the top of the organizational pyramid. The most sophisticated and most important people in the organization want to have answers to ad hoc queries, and they want to have them immediately.

Relationship banking is a semistructured information environment. Its rules contribute to making clients more comfortable in their relation to our institution. The elaboration of such rules accounts for the fact that, as the global financial industry evolves, clients play a proactive role in specifying:

- What sort of banking services they want
- Where they want them delivered
- How they look at service quality
- How much such services should cost

Globalization has promoted price transparency, and it has increased client demands for service quality as well as for the sophistication of financial products. In the banking industry and other sectors of the economy, this trend is known as the rise of the *prosumer.*

To answer prosumer requirements in an able manner, banks increasingly depend on knowledge-enriched system solutions that are seamless and integrated, support flexible supply chains, and are increasingly easier to access. Technology evidently plays a key role in this evolution, with the leaders of the banking industry depending on advanced, real-time information systems for their market edge. This is the general background of the case study in the following section.

9.2 A 21st-CENTURY IT SOLUTION FOR A COMMERCIAL BANK

Bank "A" is a medium-sized, regional credit institution, whose management has followed a rather conservative policy for several decades. It steered clear of gambling with derivatives, adopted a prudent approach with credit risk, and kept a well-balanced investment portfolio, but it also has been satisfied with legacy IT, even if, informationwise, its deliverables were substandard. This past attitude toward IT came up for a thorough review when a new CEO took over. First, the new chief executive fixed the objectives and then asked an independent consultancy to audit all aspects of ongoing IT operations. Subsequently, he requested a new solution reflecting a modern real-time, knowledge-enriched approach, with none of the baggage carried at the grass-roots level by the old approach to IT.

This has been the second fundamental study done by Bank "A" under its new management. The first aimed to reposition the institution within the evolving landscape of financial services, which is shown in Figure 9.2. The chosen strategy was to keep the bulk of bank operations within the

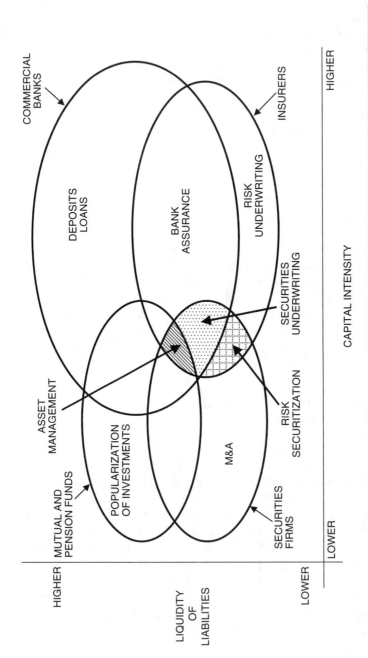

Figure 9.2   The Overlapping Worlds of Financial Institutions. A modified version of a figure in *Swiss Re, Sigma, No. 7,* 2001.

deposits and loans domain but also extend toward popularization of ancillary services. Included in this category were personal banking addressed to mid-net–worth individuals and a private assurance product line.

Another goal of new management at Bank "A" has been to make loans officers, traders, investment advisors, and customer relationship agents more sophisticated in their daily work. This brought into perspective the need for intensive training of human resources and the development of expert systems to support the bank's professionals. The same effort emphasized:

■ Online data capture
■ Database mining
■ Data analysis

The new CEO explicitly asked the bank's revamped IT team to build on the investments the company made in data-mining technology to capture and quiz information about customers. He also demanded tailored software that would allow the institution to manage its work more intelligently and efficiently.

These top-management requests put a premium on models that assist in mapping the market into the computer as well as on simulation routines and knowledge-engineering programs, permitting the whole portfolio be turned around for factual *risk and return* evaluations and for risk management purposes (see Chapter 11), including the ability to:

■ Track positions
■ Pinpoint opportunities
■ Analyze exposure
■ Develop hedging strategies

As these requirements developed, it became evident that current organizational solutions must be improved through extensive upgrades. The IT auditing by the consultancy also documented that particular emphasis must be placed on a continuously trained workforce able to proactively collaborate in gathering, categorizing, and interactively retrieving information. Every effort should be made to greatly reduce the manual component of this work. The advice has been to develop a family of knowledge artifacts that help the bank's managers and professionals in making better-documented business decisions, steadily improving customer services, and significantly increasing efficiency.

In banking, as in any other industry, success comes to companies that have the best information and/or use it most effectively, said Bank "A"s' CEO, adding that sound management requires substantial research and ruthless examination of our goals, culture, problems, opportunities, and processes. The board made the decision that a basic step in creating competitive advantages is the amplification of the bank's intellectual capital. Here is a sample of queries posed by board members:

- What types of knowledge are necessary for the bank's survivability?
- What information provides a competitive edge?
- Who uses this information and what does he derive from it?
- Is the knowledge used by the bank's professionals primarily explicit, tacit, or both?

The consultancy and Bank "A"s' new IT team were asked to consider both the types of knowledge used by the institution, including its context, and the pattern of information support required for short-term and longer-

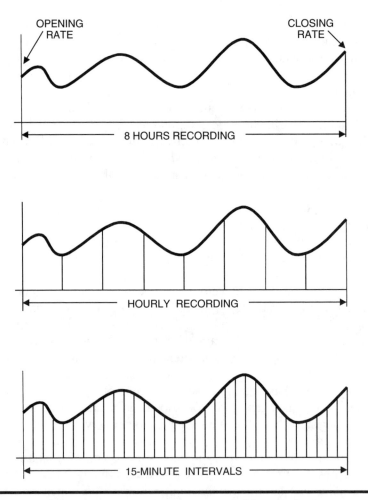

Figure 9.3 **Higher-Frequency Financial Data Provides Much Better Decision Support than Lower-Frequency**

term decisions by senior executive job. This is what was previously called an unstructured information environment. This study involved an examination of personality and functionality of each executive position recipient of new, sophisticated IT services, including the structure of the decision-making process.

At the CEO's request, the bank's information technologists examined the frequency of data capture necessary to create a database that helps the bank's professionals in gaining better insight into their work. The frequency of data streams was part of this issue; an example is given in Figure 9.3. As the reader will easily appreciate, the amount of information provided by increasing frequency of financial data is striking, even if between the first and third graphs in this figure the difference is only little more than order of magnitude.

The way Bank "A"s' CEO looked at this issue of high frequency data capture is that greater frequency is necessary not only for exploring business opportunities but even more so for elaborating risk control measures that make it easy to assess traders, loan officers, salesmen, and portfolio managers versus events. High-frequency data capture is a crucial step in risk management.[3]

Last but not least, one of the important board decisions at Bank "A" has been that the bank needs an information technology working in real-time, across the markets in which it is active. All of its officers and professionals must have direct access to the information they need, when they need it, so as to be on top of market movements and ahead of the competition.

The new IT project at Bank "A" has demonstrated that reaching such goals requires a communications, computer, and software system tailored to the market to which the bank appeals. Moreover, the chosen solution should be subject to steady technological innovation and it should sustain the institution's return-on-investment (ROI) principles.

9.3 REAL-TIME AND REALSPACE APPLICATIONS BY TOP-TIER INSTITUTIONS

The critical decision that led to thorough restructuring of information technology at Bank "A" was reached after the board appreciated that the any-to-any, enterprise-wide real-time connection is one of the key elements in differentiating a credit institution from its competitors. The consultancy explained to the members of the board that real-time is not a new development but one of the early- to mid-1960s. It took several decades to be effectively used in banking for complex financial services, but by year 2000, with its Cobol programs (legacy software), mainframes, and other backward technology, it was antiquated.

Bank "A" was left in the dust. Etymologically, the term *real-time* was coined to indicate practically zero response time. Over the years, however, it has been used to differentiate between batch operations, whose output took ages to reach the enduser, and the possibility to access online computer-based information stored in the machine, which is updated with minimal delay. The consultancy explained the reasons why the classical 24-hour cycle of information update is a disaster to the bank, even if it is still widely practiced. It creates a division of bankers and technologists and separates them by a thick wall.

As Figure 9.4 suggests, this irrational division in the culture of bankers and information technologists particularly characterizes poorly managed institutions. By contrast, the consultancy said, best results are obtained by exploiting in real-time the common frontier among different professions, which rests on *real-time connectivity*.

THE TYPICAL CASE IS:

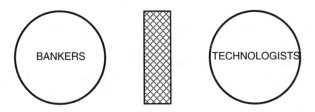

BUT OPPORTUNITIES LIE IN EXPLOITING IN REAL-TIME
THE COMMON FRONTIER

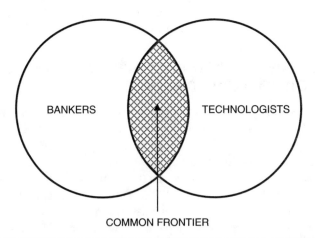

Figure 9.4 The Best Results Are Obtained in Cases In Which Banking and Technology Have Merged

It is appropriate to add that the now-classical real-time terminology refers to computer systems or programs that perform calculations during the actual time that a related physical process transpires. Real-time should not be confused with *timesharing* a central resource. The latter provides online service to many users by working on each one's task part of the time. In essence, with timesharing, each user steals computer cycles from the other user.

Definitions, however, evolve. With increasingly intelligent communicating workstations available today under every desk, the 1960s' image of real-time is no longer high tech. In order to survive in a highly competitive and sophisticated financial environment, a global bank like "A" needed not just to compress time but also to compress space. This is the concept behind *realspace*, which high technology makes feasible. Realspace virtually centralizes in an ad hoc manner distributed information elements, intelligent artifacts, and computing engines.

The information elements may be client accounts, balance sheet entries, risk of exposure, and so on. The consultants explained to board members and executive directors of Bank "A" that intelligent artifacts are interactive expert systems (agents, knowledge robots),[4] which two decades ago were peak technology but today are staple elements among top tier banks.[5] In their way, realspace solutions enriched with knowledge artifacts are the most versatile *personal* executive tools ever invented. The point was further made that:

■ Realspace solutions are particularly suitable for *conceptual* executives and professionals, who are able to perceive and integrate an holistic picture.
■ This holistic picture may be global or specialized to one domain such as business opportunity analysis or risk control.

The CEO of Bank "A," who was present at these high-level training meetings, pointed out that the references just made are a quantum shift in the way we look at technology's role and impact in the life of a credit institution. Although financial enterprises in general and banks in particular have for decades spent princely sums on computing and data management, such expenditures have typically been in two areas: general accounting and general ledger systems to comply with regulation, and consumer banking, as reflected by the retail-oriented approach such as call centers, web sites, and ATM networks.

The CEO explained that neither of these provides the basis for data analysis and risk management required to support economic decision-making. Credit decisions, for example, largely remained an art form divorced from analytics, because clean, historical time series did not yet exist at a significant level at Bank "A."

The CEO used a paradigm to dramatize his point. He said that banks that are not able to develop and use realspace technology are living in candlelight time. As a visitor at the huge reception hall at Dolmabace Palace, Istanbul, he learned that in the late-nineteenth and early-twentieth centuries, the large chandelier illuminating the hall had 175 candles that were renewed and lit manually every day. When electricity was introduced, these 175 candles were replaced with electrical bulbs and it took only a flip of a switch to light them. To the modern financial institution, real-time, realspace, and agents are the equivalent of electricity. To the contrary, information technology based on legacy procedures is no better than the manual lighting of 175 candles.

Let me elaborate a little more on this issue. In the case of Bank "A" and of practically any other major credit institution, realspace solutions could answer in an effective manner the demand by Basel II (the new capital adequacy regulation) to record and maintain obligor risk ratings. Because, however, such demand arose only recently, most institutions do not have in place systems to measure recovery rates from nonperforming obligors or to support credit analysts in quantitative and qualitative studies.

Basel II is a change in culture,[6] and banks should understand the real economics of investing in rigorous management of exposure associated with corporate credit, as well as, if not most importantly, in rigorous management of exposure associated with derivative financial instruments. A change in culture and technology is not an academic exercise. With the new regulations, it is synonymous to sound corporate governance.

An evident result of the old culture has been that the large majority of banks underutilized the technology at their disposal, for which they have paid dearly. Another outcome is that banks are on the brink of substantial spending to upgrade their data-management systems to comply with the risk-management requirements of the new capital adequacy framework by the Basel Committee on Banking Supervision (Basel II).

Moreover, data to comply with what is now required by regulators falls short of the need imposed by diversification management. Added to this is the fact that the cost of compliance itself is like a tax; there is no return on investment. In contrast, sophisticated decision support, unlike compliance, holds the promise of materially improving the economic fortunes of banks and their shareholders.

One of the most interesting areas of realspace applications is real-time access to the balance sheet. The State Street Bank, for instance, is able to compute worldwide its virtual balance sheet and, therefore, its exposure in less than 30 minutes. This gives it a most significant leverage over its competitors and in terms of risk control.

This has been one of the crucial missions given to realspace implementation at Bank "A," given that a major institution is a 24/7 operation. From New York to London, Zurich, Paris, Frankfurt, or Tokyo, the sun never sets on the international financial entity. When the markets open in Europe, they have not yet closed in Japan. When the exchanges open in New York, it is midday in Europe. Dealers, traders, and managers in different financial centers need to communicate among themselves as if they were in the same place. They are after zero lag time, and current technology can offer it to them at an affordable cost.

9.4 BANKERS TRUST: REPOSITIONING TO THE RIGHT SIDE OF THE BALANCE SHEET

A good example of the contribution of global networking and real-time technology to the management of exposure is provided by a 1990 event. On August 2, 1990, at 1:00 a.m., Kelly Doherty, Bankers Trust's (BT's) worldwide trading manager got a call from his No. 2 person in Tokyo: Iraq was invading Kuwait. Still at home, Doherty dialed into the bank's high-tech foreign exchange trading support, the resources management online system (REMOS), gaining real-time access to Bankers Trust trading positions worldwide.

Sizing up the situation and helped by the institution's powerful models, Doherty phoned Charles Sanford, Jr., the bank's chairman, and Eugene Shanks, Jr., its president, to alert them to potential problems. What worried top management was the firm's credit risk and market risk associated with the financial aftermath of the Iraqi invasion. There were reasons for such worry.

Carefully crafted for a peaceful environment, the institution's positions looked bad in the aftermath of the events that had just taken place. The Iraqi invasion had turned the tables, and the bank found itself on the wrong side of the balance sheet. Bankers Trust was:

- *Short* on sterling because the U.K. was in recession
- *Short* in dollars for the differential to Deutsche marks
- *Long* in bonds because rates were expected to decline

Under the new circumstances, Bankers Trust had one good position: the long yen yield curve. But this was not enough to compensate the wrong positions. The way it was reported at the time, senior management called up on the screen what Middle East counterparties owed the bank and when those payments were due; then it put them on credit alert.

With technology supplying all the information necessary for a factual evaluation of position risk, in an early morning conference Doherty, Shanks, and Sanford reviewed the bank's exposure and the finding about BT's exposure. Using the bank's sophisticated models, they were able to experiment on how to reposition the institution to the right side of the balance sheet.

Experimentation of the switches necessary for repositioning was done at a rapid pace. Through the bank's London subsidiary used as agent, within a mere two hours senior management had completely reversed the negative impact of some of the instruments in the portfolio. Such speedy action allowed Bankers Trust to avoid losses and even to make a tidy profit.

Its competitors may have enjoyed a sound sleep that fateful night, but they then had to labor long into the next days to sort out and correct their Middle East exposures. In fact, from what became later known, one of Bankers Trust's main competitors took 24 hours to do the repositioning, another took 48 hours, and still another took more than a week.

This is a telling example of advantages provided by real-time solutions, particularly when they are enriched by knowledge engineering and facilities for online experimentation. Notice that analysis and experimentation on changing the bank's repositions were done directly by the CEO and his immediate assistants, not by IT specialists. This is a good reference of how a user-friendly system design makes possible direct improvement by top management. In contrast, if the design is awkward or esoteric, the result will be delays, stress, and possibly major financial losses.

The Bankers Trust case study helps to bring into perspective that return on investment (ROI) associated with information technology and banking operations at large can be significantly improved through advanced system solutions. As Figure 9.5 demonstrates, since the mid-1990s, in the majority of institutions the curves of cost and market returns have crossed. High tech is the only way to bend down the costs curve and turn up the market returns curve.

Whether we talk of physical goods or financial accounts, rapid access to appropriate information, such as the examples we have seen in Chapter 6 and in Chapter 8 on the virtual double, can provide ingenious assistance. This is particularly true at a time of personalization of products and services. Personalization means relative lack of standardization, because components are individually altered and maintained and are, therefore, harder to describe in advance and to service.

Compliance is another major challenge facing banks, where sophisticated technology can contribute a great deal. The law has always required credit institutions and other entities to report and keep records on any suspicious transactions, such as frequent wire deposits that are immediately withdrawn or use of multiple accounts for no apparent purpose.

To help the authorities in controlling the washing of money and the financing of terrorist groups, for example, all cash transactions of at least $10,000 have to be reported. The same is true of all bank drafts, money

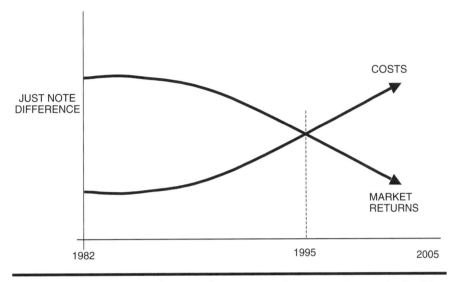

Figure 9.5 Since the Mid-1990s the Costs and Returns Curves in Banking Operations Have Crossed

orders, and traveler's checks of $3,000 or more. Financial companies file millions of these suspicious-activities reports and cash transactions with the U.S. Treasury every year.

Moreover, the U.S. Patriot Act brought thousands of new players, including casinos and car dealerships, into the reporting net. The result has been that suspicious-activity reports jumped 35 percent in the first year of the Act's implementation. Low-technology companies spending big money to comply with the law seem to be at a loss. Few firms have figured out a way to install a centralized customer-identification system for the entire organization, let alone to integrate regulatory compliance with internal control and risk management.

The message the reader should retain is that not only should each individual entity be keen to restructure its information systems and procedures but also the financial industry as a whole should collaborate in bringing about the necessary cultural change (see Section 3).

A similar reference is valid in terms of Basel II compliance by all credit institutions of the Group of Ten. No single bank's individual experience can provide a statistically significant credit experiment upon which to vet either default frequencies or recovery rates, says J. A. McQuown of Moody's KMV; therefore, banks need to commingle their experiences (i.e., data) to reach sufficient sample densities.[7] This is one of the most immediate requirements for sound corporate governance.

9.5 USE OF EXPERT SYSTEMS BY THE DEUTSCHE BUNDESBANK

A reference frequently made in the preceding chapters and sections concerns the contribution of knowledge engineering. The best way to explain its contribution is through a brief review of background provided through formal education, on-the-job training, and years of experience because this helps to explain what expert systems can offer.

Banking employees acquire their knowledge through many years of training and experience but also by trial and error, inspiration, and hard work. Typically, they begin with a formalized classroom education and then they apply that structured information to real-world financial problems.

After several years of experience, bankers learn what works and what does not, as well as why. Often, they also incorporate knowledge of organizational policies, practices, and goals into the work they do. This is the classical method, which uses the knowledge that can take a newcomer months or years to acquire. Can there be a better way?

The challenge is how to store and exploit knowledge from years of trial and error that teach a banker how to differentiate a good loan file from a bad one. For instance, a computer model that has already embedded such expertise can help the banker, and the bank, to save money and time by automating the process by which loan selection is accomplished.

This is precisely what the Deutsche Bundesbank has done. German law dictates that every loan by a credit institution of DM 3 million (about Euro 1.5 million, or $1.5 million) or more has to be declared to the central bank. Subsequently, the commercial bank can discount such loan at the reserve institution through a repo agreement. (The average amount of repo is Euro 5 million). However, the Bundesbank reserves the right to accept or reject such discounting, depending on the loan's credit risk.

An estimated 600,000 or more loan files are presented annually by commercial banks to the Bundesbank for repos. Classically this process of sorting the bank files into acceptable and unacceptable has been done through trained employees with some computer support. As in similar cases, this presents two risks: accepting a bad loan and rejecting a good loan

To improve upon the obtained results, in the late 1990s the Bundesbank designed and implemented an expert system for evaluation of loan files that significantly improved the quality of deliverables. With the old computer-based method, the risk of *accepting a bad loan* was 18 percent. This was reduced to 8 percent with the new expert system — a significant difference.[8] The exact placement of this knowledge artifact in the loan-screening procedure is shown in Figure 9.6.

Similarly, with the help of the expert system, the risk of *rejecting a good loan* has also been reduced by more than 50 percent. To gauge the economic impact of knowledge engineering, we should remember that:

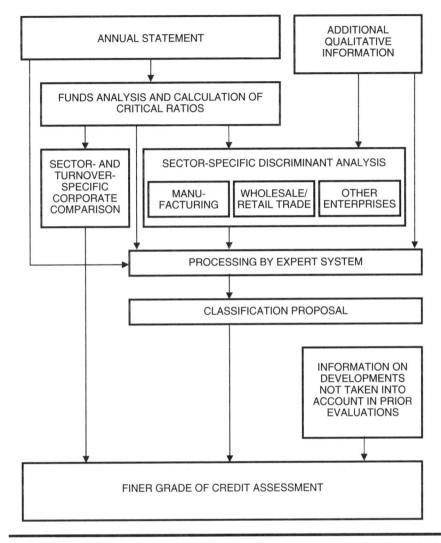

Figure 9.6   Improved Credit Assessment Procedure by the Bundesbank as of July 1, 1998

- The risk of accepting a bad loan has been reduced from 18 percent to 8 percent
- The average amount of a loan in a repo agreement is about Euro 5 million
- There are 600,000 or more loans discounted per year

Even if only 10 percent of the bad loans end in total loss because of bankruptcy, then the wake of returns in money terms is:

$$(10\%) \times (5 \times 10^6) \times (6 \times 10^5) \times (10\%) = \frac{30 \times 10^{11}}{10^2} = \text{Euro 30 billion}$$

Take as another example the case of an insurance company that has established corporate policies dictating all underwriting decisions. Some employees, through years of experience, are familiar with the details of such policies; others, by virtue of a variety of reasons, are not. Consider the savings, again in both time and money, if it were possible to significantly improve all underwriting decisions by means of:

■ A database that incorporates all past underwritings, their characteristics, and statistical results, mined online through agents.
■ An expert system featuring in its knowledge bank the corporate policies but also permitting the underwriter to add his own criteria within the realm of these policies.
■ Agents who follow up each individual policy and update the database about events and nonevents that impact on P&L and permit further refinement of underwriting decisions.

An underwriting system more complex than that was written in the early 1990s by the Mitsubishi Research Institute (MRI) for Mitsubishi Finance. Its deliverables for more than a decade have paid many times its development cost and left a hefty profit. (Mitsubishi Finance is the Zurich-based investment-banking arm of Tokyo-Mitsubishi Bank.)

These examples lead our discussion toward identification of value of knowledge assets. Deliverables like those we have seen make it possible to estimate the monetary significance of real-time, knowledge-enriched solutions. In a nutshell, the foregoing examples question the reason(s) why the majority of financial institutions still find it difficult to capitalize on their knowledge assets by means of expert systems — and suggest that something is wrong with their management.

9.6 TAKING AN INTEGRATED VIEW OF EIS AND CIS

As the real-life examples we have seen in this chapter document, the goal of our company's information system, including EIS and CIS, should be to provide tangible competitive advantages. For this reason, it must be established by the board and the CEO, though IT design and implementation are the responsibilities of technologists. Objectives can be much better focused if a number of questions receive an accurate answer:

■ How can we get ahead of the curve in competition?
■ How can we use high technology to serve the corporate strategy?

- What is understood by EIS and CIS strategy?
- What should be the precise EIS and CIS mission at corporate level?

The spelling out of objectives makes it possible to apply the MBO method discussed in Chapter 2. Other questions, too, are crucial: What is the impact of organization and methodology on our business architecture (see Chapter 13)? On real-time solutions? On knowledge-engineering implementation? On EIS/CIS design? How do we connect the chosen strategy to the evolving business environment and corporate structure? How do we establish an EIS/CIS coordination process?

Still other, more detailed questions stand out for valid answers: Which key elements should be included in the EIS? The CIS? Which knowledge artifacts? How do we establish follow-up procedures and milestones promoting business strategy? Since the introduction of new systems, products, and services requires significant investments, how can we cope with the rate of change in system solutions? (See in Chapter 8 the example on Dell Computer.)

The question of return on investment (ROI) is critical to every business. Dynamic pricing provides a good example of benefits. Consider the very simple case of a retailer who offers discounts to its clients. The store might sell 10,000 items, but within the perspective of the supply chain, any given customer might buy only 100, and among these the truly price sensitive might buy only 10.

The traditional approach is to offer all customers the same fixed discount on certain popular products. But by combining demographic data with newly abundant purchasing data typically available from checkout systems and other sensors, it is feasible to create a virtual double of each customer and his purchasing patterns. With this, the retailer can individually tailor discounts targeting customer populations and families down to the single client level.

A pricing effort will be more dynamic, and successful, if management is instrumental in regulating the price of products and services in a way able to create an incentive to use them but, at the same time assure a comfortable profit margin. Another important element to consider, particularly in connection with financial instruments, is the risk the product or service may present. This is a domain at the junction of MIS and CIS.

As we will see in Chapter 13 on risk management, able answers to the query of risk and return will not come as a matter of course. They require rigorous research and study, because such answers are, to a large extent, situational, though they also abide by general principles. A basic argument in a recent study I was involved in was how to redraw the dichotomy between analytical (or managerial) accounting and general accounting, given that a newly designed system of internal control had to ensure the accuracy of profitability analysis by transaction and position.

The result of the study was that managerial accounting should isolate *every* cost element and document how it is distributed among the range of products. Risk, for instance, is a cost. Analytical accounts are an integral part of executive information systems, but they also have to do with CIS. Real costs and standard costs must be chosen in function of their usage as aids to:

- Strategic planning
- Commercial activities
- Cost reduction by channel
- The swamping of overhead expenses

Data for analytical accounting is derived from general accounting, with emphasis on accuracy rather than precision. The virtual balance sheet, covering global operations and made available in no more than 30 minutes, is part of analytical accounting (see Section 5). By contrast, the balance sheet to be submitted to supervisors, which must be absolutely precise, is a general accounting financial report.

I have previously made reference to structured and unstructured information environments. General accounting norms are fixed by laws and regulations, but those of managerial accounting are not. They are the means to follow up on short-term and long-term objectives, chosen to make a company a leading institution in its domain of activity. As we have already seen, strategic objectives correlate with organizational and IT requirements. Both EIS and CIS find themselves at the pivotal point of the semistructured and unstructured information environment definition.

The overall strategic plan, the management of change, and the transition plan are EIS domains. Any executive information system worth its salt should bring timely and accurate qualitative and quantitative information to all three domains and the control of functions associated with them. The CEO and his immediate assistants must see to it that their positions are backed by a solid body of evidence that is consistent to their functions and can be effectively used to obtain results.

9.7 NOTES

1. The reference comes from the Topkapi Museum, Istanbul.
2. D.N. Chorafas, *The 1996 Market Risk Amendment. Understanding the Marking-to-Model and Value-at-Risk*, McGraw-Hill, Burr Ridge, IL, 1998.
3. D.N. Chorafas, *How to Understand and Use Mathematics for Derivatives, Volume 1—Understanding the Behaviour of Markets*, Euromoney Books, London, 1995; and D.N. Chorafas, *How to Understand and Use Mathematics for Derivatives, Volume 2—Advanced Modelling Methods*, Euromoney Books, London, 1995.
4. D.N. Chorafas, *Agent Technology Handbook*, McGraw-Hill, New York, 1998.

5. D.N. Chorafas and Heinrich Steinmann, *Expert Systems in Banking,* Macmillan, London, 1991.
6. D.N. Chorafas, *Economic Capital Allocation with Basel II. Cost and Benefit Analysis,* Butterworths-Heinemann, London and Boston, 2004.
7. J.A. McQuown, "Managing Corporate Credit Risk at Banks: Catalytic Effects of the Basel II Accord," Moody's KMV, San Francisco, June 2003.
8. D.N. Chorafas. *Managing Credit Risk, Volume 1: Analyzing, Rating and Pricing the Probability of Default,* Euromoney Books, London, 2000.

10

REAL-TIME TREASURY OPERATIONS

10.1 INTRODUCTION

In the post-World War II years, even two decades ago, the primary mission of the treasury was to ensure that the company had enough money to face its immediate and medium-term obligations toward its employees, its suppliers, and other business partners. This now-classical treasury notion gradually changed, starting in the 1960s with the conglomerates and their financial needs. Then, the change in mission given to the treasury accelerated because of globalization.

Not only has the number of functions assigned to the treasury significantly expanded, but many of them are also interlocking, for example, monitoring cash flows and bank accounts in many currencies; managing foreign exchange risk; holding investment accounts on a global scale; doing cash management, also on a global scale; and exercising control over transactions, payments, and settlements.

Clearly, the treasury needs sophisticated technology to face up to these expanding responsibilities, cross-reference accounts in different currencies, handhold with a growing number of business partners, and work in many other dimensions, as Figure 10.1 suggests. Take Italy's formerly high-flying Parmalat, the dairy products firm, as an example. Its liquidity crisis was triggered in December 2003, when it:

- Admitted to a Euro 496 million ($496 million) investment in an offshore mutual fund
- Nearly defaulted on a bond repayment and saw its credit rating slashed to junk status
- Falsely reported having an Euro 5 billion credit at Bank of America
- Ended having a gaping hole in its treasury of more than Euro 12 billion and was nicknamed Europe's Enron

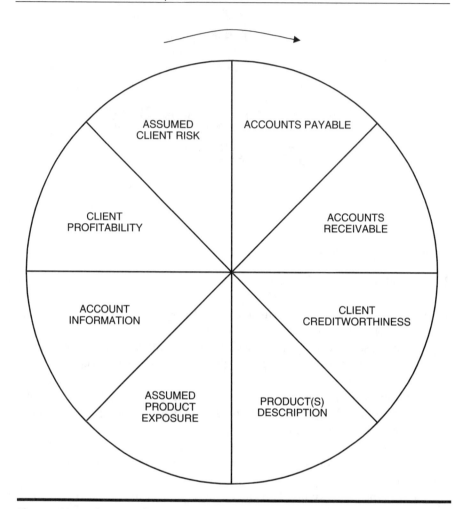

Figure 10.1 Cross-Referencing Accounts and Business Clients Has Become Cornerstone to the Analysis of Financing Patterns

Even well-managed companies face a geometrically increasing complexity in running their treasury operations. Citigroup has more than 36 counterparties doing 100 transactions each, every day. Only high-tech, real-time solutions can serve in keeping counterparty risk under control. Instantaneous cross-referencing is very important. For instance, one desk may be short with a given counterparty, whereas another desk may be long with this same party. Management control requires a system that works 24/7 anywhere in the world.

Nothing short of instant knowledge of exposure can keep treasury operations under control. This is much more urgent than it might seem because foreign exchange risk, interest rate risk, event risk, and a number of other exposures assumed during operations have led the treasury to hedging activities — and, with this, they have changed its culture.

The growing use of derivative financial instruments initially for hedging and then for for-profit operations has engineered such cultural change and brought along a rapid evolution in requirements for more rigorous IT support. With derivatives, risks have increased most significantly. One of the greatest challenges treasurers now face is that they cannot plan for tomorrow by studying what happened yesterday, as they used to do.

Sometime during the last three decades of the twentieth century, one of the longer periods of continuity in economic history came to an end and the economy at large — and therefore also treasury operations — moved into turbulence. Such turbulence culminated in the 2000–2003 market meltdown. In practically every company the treasurer was in the frontline of its aftermath.

In the early years of the twenty-first century, one of the first priorities of the treasury function has been the need to repair the company's ravaged balance sheet. Wise treasurers grabbed their chance to move quickly and in a determined way before interest rates moved north. Swift action always has to be done under steady risk assessment, and it cannot be accomplished without analytics and experimentation, or, hence, without top-of-the-line IT.

Critics say that treasurers contributed to the damaging of their companies' balance sheets because of running their operations for profits through complex derivatives and synthetic instruments. These helped to build personalized products that, bankers suggested to them, could meet any financial need. Both institution investors and corporate treasurers were attracted by them, often with little understanding of assumed risk.

While such criticism is not unfounded, the fact remains that treasurers must be able to simultaneously plan ahead and do damage control. They have to watch out for economic and monetary developments, exchange rate and interest rate changes, spreads, labor market requirements, liquidity conditions, the company's solvency, and crisis resolution. This is a very complex job that cannot be accomplished without significant skill and high-technology support.

10.2 PILLARS OF TREASURY CONTROL: A CASE STUDY

As previously stated, there was a time when the main, if not the only one, function of the corporate treasury, was to ensure the cash flow necessary to finance the company's operations. This consisted of managing cash coming from the market through the sale of products and services, looking after internal cash flow originating in depreciation and amortization, and negotiating loans with banks to finance expansion and other operations. Good corporate governance mandated that sound treasury control rested on several pillars:

- Cash balances
- Bank acounts
- Assets & liabilities (A&L) management
- Payment systems
- Control over transactions
- Reliable accounting

This has been the orthodox view. But, as already discussed, in the last three decades of the twentieth-century treasury, functions have been changing because of globalization, and this was accelerated in the 1990s through the trend of running the treasury for profit. Complex derivative financial instruments have been used quite extensively, although the dangers derivative instruments involve have not always been appreciated.

"It has not yet reached epidemic proportions, but it is a growing problem," said Robert Studer, then-president of the Union Bank of Switzerland.[1] His reference was to the tendency for banks' corporate customers to run their treasuries for profit rather than for cash management and pure exposure control. Most evidently, the more complex and more risky treasury operations become, the greater the need for a real-time system and for sophisticated software.

In appreciation of the fact that to enhance his understanding of assumed risk the treasurer requires plenty of real-time information as well as of knowledge-engineering support, Bank "B" did a thorough study to define what is precisely needed to improve its treasury operations. The answer was all information pertaining to instruments, counterparties, and transactions, whether these regard loan(s), trading, investment(s), position-keeping, risk management, or regulatory reporting.

Because counterparty is one of the three axes in the framework, this essentially means real-time access to all information pertaining to a relationship with a business partner, conducting commitments with this party, managing the relationship, and, if necessary, exiting the relationship. A similar statement is valid in terms of instruments and transactions. The treasurer of Bank "B" identified three areas where real-time support is most essential to him:

- Cash management
- Assets and liabilities management
- Effective risk control

The treasurer stated that in today's business environment, all three activities constitute the top functions in the responsibilities column of his job.

In addition, effectiveness was demonstrated by the quality of execution; for instance, accuracy in cash flow forecasts and availability of sources of financing.

For greater effectiveness, he asked for additional data such as access to both credit risk and market risk by transaction in loans, trading, and other activities. As Figure 10.2 suggests, loans do not only have credit risk and trading does not only have market risk. Other data required by the treasurer was analytical, to be used for research and for management accounting purposes — such as intraday prices, or ticks — and some was historical

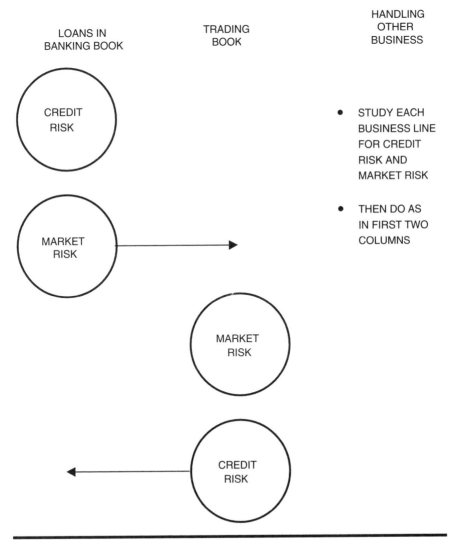

Figure 10.2 Swapping Credit Risk and Market Risk in Banking Book and Trading Book

information. *Efficiency,* found in the significant cost reduction in performing the treasury function, was assisted through new, advanced IT solutions.

Due to the dynamics of the market, the treasurer felt that his operations must benefit from full real-time support, thereby making it possible to rise to market challenges rather than falling victim to them. He stated that to see ahead, the global treasury needs instruments like the virtual balance sheet (see Chapter 9), permitting mapping global assets and liabilities in a matter of minutes after a request. This calls for high-tech capability that is able to collect and filter a great deal of information:

- Existing in the institution's distributed databases
- Connected to new transactions taking place with clients and suppliers
- Reflected in the company's books through marking-to-market and marking-to-model

The treasurer also stated that he wanted the organization department to develop a global standard of cost efficiency, valid throughout the corporation but assuring real-time information sharing anywhere in the world. This required not only high technology but also ways and means for better client account management, so that the bank could benefit from an effective use of its resources.

In his request for more accurate and timely client account management, the treasurer was joined by the bank's commercial director. Since the late 1990s, the latter has been worried by the fact that wholesale clients were doing financial account repositioning. The direct result of such concentration in banking relationships has been that Bank "B" has lost some of its major client accounts to competitors.

Statistics help to better explain this reference. The challenge in account management in Bank "B" is privy, but a good example that is already in the public domain is the concentration of banking accounts for better management and cost control by Hewlett-Packard.[2] As the HP experience demonstrates, it is possible to integrate 90 percent of all treasury operations in just one year; the results that were obtained are summarized in Table 10.1. In this table, "World Class" indicates the best reference found anywhere. Notice the difference that exists between average results in bank account management and the most cost-efficient solution, which should be every company's goal.

A&L (assets and liabilities) management provides an example of targeted effectiveness in treasury operations at Bank "B." The case has been that of risk-based pricing of portfolio positions. Typically, this is accomplished by gauging each position through comparison of its riskiness with a practically riskless investment, such as U.S. Treasury bonds. (See also in Section 4 the discussion on divergence of bondholder and stockholder views.)

Table 10.1 Criteria for Greater Efficiency in Corporate Banking, Outlined by Hewlett Packard

	Average	World Class	Achieved by HP in 1 Year
Banks per $1 billion of revenue	17	3	10
Bank accounts per $1 billion of revenue	127	7.5	30
Average number of accounts per bank	7.5	2.5	3

For example, with equities this extra riskiness is captured through the equity-risk premium, known as the *beta* of an individual share. Beta is the volatility of a certain equity compared to that of an index, for instance, the S&P 500. Other things equal, a factual and documented risk-based pricing sees to it that an equity that offers higher returns than the risk investors are willing to take is cheaper. By contrast, one with lower returns is more expensive, and it should be avoided or at least priced in a way reflecting its embedded exposure.

The distinction made here has been adopted in Bank "B" as a policy and reflected in its new treasury project. Such definition is consistent with establishing cost of equity as risk-free rate plus the share's beta multiplied by the projected equity risk premium. The Capital Asset Pricing Model (CAPM) works along these lines. The problem, however, is that CAPM and similar artifacts are static. They also mainly look toward past performance, or backwards, whereas, as the treasurer of Bank "B" often stated, the past is no predictor of the future.

Moreover, the treasurer said, models such as CAPM do not properly account for market volatility, which is a negative. Bank "B" wanted its risk-based pricing solution to be dynamic, with volatility being part of the equation. Dynamic solutions are challenging, requiring on the treasurer's behalf both insight and foresight, enhanced through rigorous analysis, conceptualization of results, and ability to make predictions at a given level of confidence. The treasurer demanded that the new IT solution pay great attention to analytics, including:

■ Past data
■ Current data
■ Projections
■ Business context
■ Qualitative information

The Bank "B" treasurer said that he would judge the new project's deliverable by the support it would provide him in deciding what to do now and in estimating how his current decisions affect the institution's

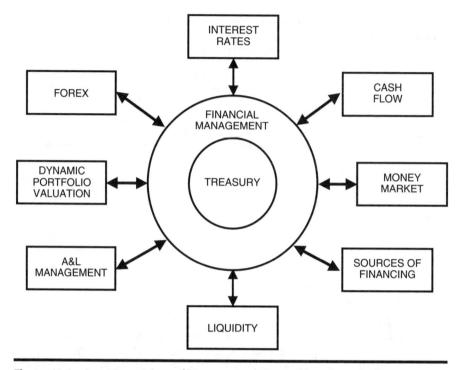

Figure 10.3 Long-Term View of Treasury and Financial Management

future. Insight is *not* just looking at last year's data to discover trends, the treasurer stated, the challenge is that of establishing a business process that is articulate and actionable, with people accountable for it. This is a matter of effectiveness, particularly in connection to the longer-term view of treasury operations and financial management presented in Figure 10.3.

10.3 A CLOSER LOOK INTO ASSETS AND LIABILITIES MANAGEMENT

Sound assets & liabilities management is, to a significant extent, a matter of definition. Many companies define short term for cash in a way distinct from short term for other investments. Cash and cash equivalents include cash on hand, amounts due from banks, money-market instruments, commercial paper, and other investments having maturities of three months or less at date of acquisition and reflected as such for purpose of reporting cash flows.

Cash equivalents are stated at cost that approximates fair value. By contrast, short-term investments include certificate of deposits, commercial paper, and other issues having maturities longer than three months at date of acquisition. For reporting purposes some companies state such investments at cost that approximates fair value; others mark them to market, a policy usually followed with mid-term and longer-term investments.

The letter of the law concerning definitions varies from one country to the next. Therefore, for compliance purposes, a global enterprise must not only be very careful with these definitions but also endow its treasury with sophisticated IT for common analysis across countries of operation and business units while observing companywide standards set by the board. Critical streams of assets and liabilities must be identified and prioritized to minimize risk and reduce parochial dependencies.

Time-consuming data cleanup should be performed after using an appropriate classification (see Chapter 2) with corresponding identifiers and filters. This is the policy that was adopted by Bank "B" for the redesign of its treasury technology, and it produced commendable results.

Given the nature of its operations, Bank "B" found significant potential in expert systems that provided rule-based cleansing and consolidation of data streams connected to assets and liabilities. The overall solution used flexible extraction and mapping tools, data capture at point of origin, and a customizable data model. Expert systems support was extended to several applications, examples being foreign exchange risk and interest rate risk in different currencies.

The principle applied in connection to the second point is that balance sheet interest rate risk must be monitored and managed primarily based on marking to market. At the treasurer's request, this approach became more sophisticated by involving tests on the hypothesis of rising and falling interest rates.

Research among correspondent banks provided further insight. First, it showed that for asset and liability management purposes, value at risk (VAR) is calculated based on the 99-percent confidence level and a twenty-day holding period — which is about what Bank "B" had done. Then, however, it demonstrated that the majority of correspondent banks were unhappy with such coarse metrics as VAR could offer. As a result, Bank "B" went further in its new treasury project, with specifically designed eigen-models and the filtering of five years of underlying data used to derive market movements for this calculation.

Moreover, because large portions of the retail portfolio of a commercial bank consist of nonmaturing accounts such as variable-rate mortgages and savings products, the treasurer asked for modeling sensitivities on the basis of effective repricing behavior of nonmaturing accounts.

Contingent liabilities and irrevocable commitments have evidently been given the attention they deserve. Contingent liabilities include credit guarantees in the form of avals, guarantees, and indemnity liabilities; bid bonds and delivery and performance bonds; letters of indemnity; irrevocable commitments in respect of documentary credits; and other performance-related guarantees.

The treasurer requested that a system of multithreshold evaluations be studied and implemented, able to combine the more classical aspects of A&L management and the results of rigorous analytical processes and the board's framework of strategic guidelines. Its framework is shown in Figure 10.4. This has been implemented by major business units as a means of holding, permitting to detect, and to act on local patterns of A&L management, on a consolidated group basis.

The treasurer also explained to the project team that among the most important elements of a sound corporate financial planning and control system is the linkage between long-range planning and short-term financial planning and budgeting. Objectives were outlined in the following terms:

■ Long-term planning is the development of a companywide plan of action within established objectives and policies.

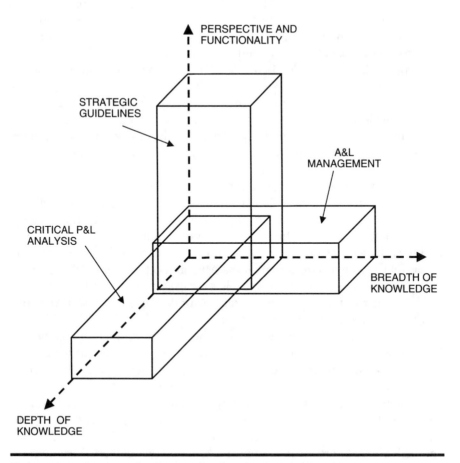

Figure 10.4 Framework of an Evaluation System Linking A&L Management to Strategy and Profit and Loss

- Financial planning targets a shorter-term plan for maintaining adequate capital, and it includes financial goals.
- Budgeting is financial planning, a guiding instrument for projected expenditures aimed to facilitate controls over money being spend.

As the treasurer saw it: If budgetary analysis permits short-term continuing review of costs and of deliverables to ensure a realization of profit objectives, then assets and liabilities management takes the longer view of compliance to asset preservation targets with timely reporting on status issues reflected in this reference. Both require steady accumulation, analysis, interpretation, and reporting of fairly detailed information that should be accessible online at request and preferably through visualization (see Chapter 7).

There is nothing really radical about these concepts. The problem, however, has been that the old treasury IT, which was programmed in the 1970s, did not provide supports needed to meet such requirements, in spite of all its patches. Essentially, what the treasurer wanted to obtain interactively were the answers to four basic questions crucial to any good manager:

- Do I know myself?
- Do I know my direction?
- Do I have a plan?
- Do I get results commensurate with my efforts?

He asked that basic data elements needed to respond in a documented manner to these and similar queries be incorporated into the new financial planning and control system and its analytics. There were also other refinements over current practices that had to be considered and adopted.

One of these refinements has been knowledge management, in the belief that sustainable competitive advantages come from mining stored knowledge and from postmortems that permit fine-tuning of the decision process (see Chapter 7 on CMF). The treasurer insisted that innovation really goes beyond creativity in the sense that, for business reasons, both the bank and its customers should find real benefit from analytics. This has never been a characteristic of legacy, old-generation operational support, but Bank "B" made it a basic goal of its new IT solution.

10.4 CRISIS OF FUND MANAGEMENT: A CASE STUDY

The Fund Forum Conference that took place in Nice in the last week of June 2003 revealed that trust between fund managers and their clients is at crisis point. Somehow, the effectiveness of fund managers has been put into question by investors entrusting them with their assets. Such feeling has become rather widespread, and it was reinforced by a survey conducted by KPMG and Create, a U.K. think tank.

Chief investment officers and other practitioners participating in this survey said their industry was suffering from a leadership vacuum as well as from inflated egos. The effectiveness of fund managers has also been challenged by an increasing amount of funds under their wings, often at the expense of attention paid to customer needs and earnings. Other comments revealed by the KPMG/Create study were that fund managers are putting too many products in the market for which they have scant risk control and that they are using a relatively old technology to assist them in their job, unable to satisfy their customers' increasingly sophisticated requirements.

These are valuable references for treasurers because, for all practical purposes, they are entrapreneur fund managers for the companies with which they work. "In my 35 years in the industry, I have never seen such a low level of trust between intermediaries and investors," said John Towers, vice-chairman of State Street Bank, at the Fund Forum Conference. Towers added, "It will take years for that trust to be rebuilt."[3]

Other speakers contributed what they believe to be the salient problems facing the fund management industry. Both effectiveness and efficiency challenges (see Section 2) were raised. In the opinion of several practitioners, beyond a long list of management reasons was the fact that the extended bear market of 2000–2003 not only hit the fund management industry in its bottomline but also:

■ Punished its clients with trillions of dollars in losses
■ Exposed the whole sector's track record of poor business management

With the loss of confidence in the fund management industry's ability to deliver has surfaced the fact that many asset managers run their businesses like a cottage industry — contrary to the sophisticated real-time reporting requirements we have seen in Sections 2 and 3. Through most of the decade of the 1990s, over-rapid growth concealed structural weaknesses in fund management activities such as:

■ Poor asset allocation
■ Nonexistent cost control
■ Poor risk management practices (see Chapter 11)

The vast majority of fund managers lack the sophisticated technology necessary to present them with factual measures of exposure. However, they are increasingly assuming greater risks as a result of their partnership with hedge funds and of alternative investments.[4] Based on a real-life implementation of rigorous risk control, Figure 10.5 shows the radar chart that

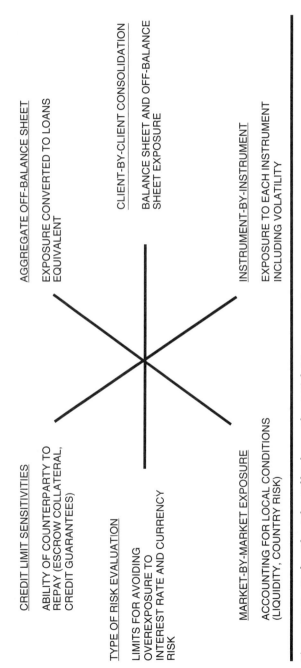

CREDIT LIMIT SENSITIVITIES

ABILITY OF COUNTERPARTY TO
REPAY (ESCROW COLLATERAL,
CREDIT GUARANTEES)

TYPE OF RISK EVALUATION

LIMITS FOR AVOIDING
OVEREXPOSURE TO
INTEREST RATE AND CURRENCY
RISK

MARKET-BY-MARKET EXPOSURE

ACCOUNTING FOR LOCAL CONDITIONS
(LIQUIDITY, COUNTRY RISK)

AGGREGATE OFF-BALANCE SHEET

EXPOSURE CONVERTED TO LOANS
EQUIVALENT

CLIENT-BY-CLIENT CONSOLIDATION

BALANCE SHEET AND OFF-BALANCE
SHEET EXPOSURE

INSTRUMENT-BY-INSTRUMENT

EXPOSURE TO EACH INSTRUMENT
INCLUDING VOLATILITY

Figure 10.5   Radar Chart for Off-Balance Sheet Risk Management

should be in place to provide ad hoc, at a moment's notice, information on exposure resulting from off-balance sheet instruments.

These severe flaws in management control were both hidden and (ironically) sustainable as long as the markets were powering ahead, but they became visible and damaging when the bubble burst. The implications of such ineffectiveness are far reaching, because they impact on the fund management landscape, bringing to the foreground the fact that effective governance of entrusted assets is a question of first class risk control (see Chapter 11). This is a quality that few asset management outfits really possess, thereby damaging their reputations.

Few would argue that for fund managers, a steady long-term upward trend in financial markets provides an ideal business framework, whereas a market crash brings several perils. Even when the bottom seems to be near, clients back away in fear of another slump. Top-tier fund management, however, is not only seen in good times. The real test is in bad times and, as cannot be repeated too often, costs matter.

Beyond the control of expected and unexpected risks, effective management of the client's assets must account for the fact that the portfolio will (most likely) include both stocks and bonds, and, down to basics, there exists a difference in viewpoints of equity analysts and debt analysts. The difference can be expressed by the way shareholders and bondholders look at return on equity (ROE), a focal issue in A&L management and in the treasurer's mission. Taking the shareholders' perspective, equity analysts concentrate on the word *return* (R). By contrast, to protect bondholder interest, debt analysts concentrate on *dependability of equity.*

This is additional evidence that bondholder and shareholder interests are not necessarily convergent, but few fund managers truly account for this dual perspective. The same is true of company treasurers. Next to the control of risks comes the control of expense ratios, which often go wild.

A June 2003 report from Standard & Poor's has pointed out that U.S. mutual funds with above-average expense ratios have consistently underperformed competitors with below-average expense ratios. Typically, the difference is on the order of 100 to 200 basis points a year. That is not what chief executives with margin problems want to be told.

Beyond an uncontrolled overhead, fund managers remain under heavy pressure from squeezed profits and demoralized clients who want to know what value the investment management industry has delivered. And as the aforementioned Fund Forum Conference confirmed, fund managers are not finding it easy to define their industry's value position in the future. Instead, they seem to have adopted a default strategy by promoting whatever it seems clients are keen to buy or whatever they are being told to buy by *their* advisers, to whom they have outsourced some of their responsibilities.

Because investors seem to be increasingly dissatisfied with the governance of the funds to which they entrust their wealth, experts at the Fund Forum Conference predicted a wave of consolidation in the industry, with a number of larger banking and insurance groups abandoning certain product lines or even selling their entire fund management operations. Cost and benefit are behind this repositioning because, after the global stock market bubble burst, many fund managers have seen their revenues and profitability decline sharply.

Neither are private-banking operations of commercial banks free of the inadequacies to which the previous paragraphs have made reference. In June 2003, a study by the consultancy Booz Allen Hamilton and the Reuters information group concluded that private bankers spend too much time on internal administration and not enough time on clients. Their survey found that, on the average, private bankers spend just five to ten hours a year with each client.

These results are based on interviews with 60 advisers from 27 private banks in the United Kingdom, Germany, and Switzerland, plus 60 clients of private banks from the same countries, with an average wealth of Euro 4.7 million. The message delivered by these research results has been that:

■ Private clients are not satisfied with the service they are receiving
■ They are beginning to reconsider their options

It is appropriate to note that not every negative response is due to defective handholding. In ways similar to those of other fund management outfits whose level of client dissatisfaction was reviewed in earlier paragraphs, the banks' private clients have suggested several areas for improvement. These include a competent and reliable point of contact; 100 percent correct transactions, which means overcoming operational risks; and easily understandable financial reports. All three are elements of good governance.

10.5 BENEFITS FROM AN A&L ACID TEST

As new kinds of securities come into the market and the financial industry as a whole becomes increasingly dynamic, well-managed financial institutions base their estimate of equity value on the market value of a firm. Moreover, they are valuing assets and liabilities on a daily basis and intraday. Through this approach, financial statements are improved, and they become more transparent both to management and to stakeholders. With the reflection of market values, balance sheets become more accurate. Several kinds of abuses of book-value accounting become evident and, therefore, are corrected.

Among the often-used tricks with book value is that companies tend to sell assets that have market values above book while retaining assets for which the market value is below book. This is a practice that works to the detriment of the firm. But marking to market has its own challenges, a major one being that for many instruments — for instance, over-the-counter (OTC) derivatives — there is no market. Instead, marking to model is used, which sometimes degenerates into marking to myth.

Because not all models are reliable and, furthermore, there is a shortage of applicable historical data, new problems are confronting regulators, bankers, treasurers, and investors. Some lie in the fact that the current accounting system fails to provide the necessary information for a knowledgeable evaluation of assets and liabilities, over and above the issue of finding the correct market value.

For instance, wheras the market values of publicly traded stocks and bonds are on information providers' networks every day, this is not true for private placements and commercial mortgages. Still, values can be arrived at for some assets using some estimating. This estimating process becomes rather unstable when it comes to liabilities.

The regulators need to know the fair value to better assess a company's financial strength. Financial Accounting Standard (FAS) 115, by the Financial Accounting Standards Board (FASB), allows companies discretion to classify assets into several buckets, so that all changes in market value pass directly through the earnings. By contrast, liabilities are not dealt with in such manner. However, without a methodology for the fair valuation of liabilities, it is not clear what a financial statement may mean.

Part of the difficulty of attacking the liabilities side is that although a market for liabilities exists, it is often very narrow. There are only a few declared liabilities transactions a year, as most are confused with assets transactions. Financial analysts suggest to use fair value for liabilities in a way consistent with the market value of heavily traded assets of similar characteristics. An acid test that covers both sides of the A&L balance sheet is of interest to many industries. For example, in the insurance business, *if* it is possible to calculate the fair value of life insurance liabilities, *then* it is also possible to use the same technique for the calculation of premiums.

The principle is that if we understand the fair value of liabilities, we can assess the worth of company stock. With that knowledge the balance sheet, income statement, and complementary statement of recognized gains and losses take on greater value and meaning. The last few years have seen a hybrid approach by central banks and financial analysts that includes in the numerator the market value of assets and in the denominator the book value of liabilities. As proxy for the market value of assets is taken its capitalization.[5]

$$\frac{\text{Assets}}{\text{Liabilities}} = \frac{\text{Market Value of Assets}}{\text{Book Value of Liabilities}}$$

This is an acid test of a company's solvency. There is also the benefit of estimating liquidity based on a virtual balance sheet. High-tech institutions are able to prepare this in a matter of a few minutes (see Chapter 10), albeit at order of magnitude level, which is acceptable because the virtual balance sheet is a management accounting tool.

The acid test provides information that helps in both solvency and liquidity evaluations. Treasurers of well-managed companies appreciate that although liquidity and solvency are different concepts, sometime they tend to merge. At the height of the October 1987 stock market crisis, Gerald E. Corrigan, then-president of New York Federal Reserve, argued that "there was no way to tell the difference between just short-term liquidity problems and outright insolvency."[6]

For its part, the Financial Services Authority (FSA) defines *liquidity risk* as the risk "that a firm, though solvent, either does not have sufficient financial resources available to it to enable it to meet its obligations as they fall due, or can secure them only at excessive cost." This, FSA says, is a basic business risk faced to some degree by most financial services firms.[7] The treasurer is well advised to do stress tests to keep him ahead of the liquidity–solvency curve.

A good way to look into these statements and the text in this section, is that to effectively manage risk one should not be basing decisions on the slow-moving, annual consolidated balance sheet or even a quarterly balance sheet. We must be proactive in our approach, breaking down exposure at each post to its basic elements and paying attention to risk tolerance. This should be done not only at bank level with virtual financial statements but also all the way down to the desk and the trader. (See Chapter 11 for more on risk management.)

10.6 CHALLENGES WITH HOME–HOST FINANCIAL REPORTING

Beyond the factors discussed in the first five sections of this chapter that significantly affect the treasurer's job, there are two other major background problems facing the treasurer and the institution's financial reporting policies and practices. Both have to do with the globalization and regulation of financial business — to be managed in an able manner — and both require real-time reporting, including differences in legal mandates and authority kept in national jurisdiction.

Among themselves, these problems create the so-called *home–host* issue which goes beyond Pillar 1, capital adequacy, and has a great deal to do with the internationalization of banking and finance. Global credit institutions will, in principle, be under supervisory control at home, but they also have to follow the regulations of each country in which they operate. National regulatory discretion sees to it that, unavoidably, there will be differences in rules and regulations regarding reporting requirements.[8] Theoretically, these are taken care of by the first and second Memorandum of Understanding (MOU) among banking supervisors. Practically, existing differences are not likely to soon be ironed out, even if there are regular meetings between banks and supervisors of the Group of Ten (G-10) and other countries.

Among possible hurdles are materiality issues, often interpreted differently in the home country and in the host countries. There is also the fact that in most emerging markets local regulators are unprepared for the new capital adequacy framework by the Basel Committee on Banking Supervision (Basel II), which impacts Pillar 2, regulatory oversight, though the Bank for International Settlements (BIS) does its best to train emerging markets' regulators.

In a globalized economy, regulatory unpreparedness coupled with accounting system differences can have disastrous effects. One of the major victims is the consolidation of balance sheets, which becomes difficult because of incompatibilities in different legislations and regulations. And as far as Basel II is concerned, differences characterizing the jurisdictions certainly impact market discipline (Pillar 3) as well as transparency of financial statements.

In addition to these references is the fact that the rules and regulations of Basel II, which concentrate on capital adequacy, best fit home supervision requirements. Host supervisors are more interesting from the viewpoint of depositors' protection and capital needs associated with deposit insurance.

Furthermore, *prescriptiveness* accentuates sovereignty issues because regulatory prescriptions differ from one country to the next, in spite of what is usually said about the effects of globalization. This has a heavy material impact on transborder operations and the way the treasurers do their job. For example,

- Citibank operates in 101 countries
- Royal Bank of Scotland operates in 80 countries
- ABN Amro operates in 60 countries and has three hosts: Holland, the United States, and Brazil
- Crédit Suisse operates in nearly 100 countries and has 3 hosts: Switzerland, the United States, and the United Kingdom

Theoretically, there should not be much of a problem connected to home and host countries. According to Basel Committee Publication No. 100 of August 2003, the Supervisors of the Group of Ten recognize that the

new capital accord will require more cooperation and coordination between *home* country and *host* country authorities because the new rules
will be applied at each level of the banking group. This poses significant
technical requirements in providing capital adequacy (Pillar 1) and regulatory assessment (Pillar 2).

Practically, the home–host problem is a major one, because of the different versions of financial statements that have to be produced for local
authorities, although some sort of reasonable consolidation of incompatible regulation should always be present. This is indeed difficult and increases the importance of a real-time solution that permits evaluation of
the different home–host reporting versions and provides a factual and documented discussion with home and host country supervisors.

One of the commercial bankers who contributed to the research leading to my book *Economic Capital Allocation under Basel II*[9] pointed out
that the commercial banking sector has made constructive proposals on
ways and means for resolving home–host problems. These include the
establishment of a college of supervisors per international bank and the
naming of a lead supervisor to coordinate, preferably the home country
supervisor.

However, the regulatory authorities did not embrace this proposal, most
likely because of problems with responsibilities from the national legal
mandate at the host supervisor side. In the aftermath, credit institutions
believe that the ball is in the court of supervisors; they are the parties that
must now come up with constructive solutions. Leaving things as they now
stand generates:

■ Huge uncertainty
■ Risk of divergence
■ Burden for both banks and supervisors

There is a need for global coordination regarding Pillar 3, which also
impacts the work treasurers. The principle of consolidated supervision sees
to it that a banking group that has operations in a country other than its
home base may need to obtain approval for its use of certain approaches
to financial reporting from both host country and home country regulators.
Although the 1996 Market Risk Amendment involved similar requirements,
Basel II:

■ Creates several new implementation challenges
■ Significantly extends the scope of multiple approvals, with an evident aftermath on the transborder credit institution

The Basel Committee correctly wants to promote the ability of all host
regulatory authorities to exercise effective supervision over foreign institu-

tions operating in their jurisdictions and to strengthen the coordination between host and home country supervisors of these institutions. The problem, however, is that to comply with different versions and interpretations of Basel II rules leads to an inordinate amount of costs, which should not be the case.

Sovereignty, legislation, and differences in interpretation of rules create severe challenges for all multinational commercial and investment banks as well as other commercial and industrial entities. Multiple, incompatible regulations is no more globalization, but fragmentation, of the global market. Several regulators look at this as an implementation issue, but in reality it is one of streamlining legal mandates.

In conclusion, as far as the home–host challenge is concerned, the overarching question is: Are we really moving to more international standards and convergence with inevitable compromises, mutual recognition, and alignment to prevent international crises—or divergence because of national interests and other reasons that create a nonlevel playing field? These are critical questions that currently receive imprecise answers. To face them in an able manner, the treasurer needs the best state-of-the-art technology and the ability to implement it in a sophisticated way.

10.7 NOTES

1. *The Economist*, London, June 4, 1994.
2. Trema Forum, June 4–5, 2003, Monte Carlo.
3. *Financial Times*, July 26, 2003.
4. D.N. Chorafas, *Alternative Investments and the Mismanagement of Risk*, Macmillan/Palgrave, London, 2003.
5. D.N. Chorafas, *Economic Capital Allocation with Basel II. Cost and Benefit Analysis*, Butterworths-Heinemann, London and Boston, 2004.
6. Bob Woodward, *Maestro,* Simon & Schuster, New York, 2000.
7. FSA/PN/115/2003, "Improving Liquidity Handling to Head Off Financial Failures," Financial Services Authority, London, 2003.
8. D.N. Chorafas, *Economic Capital Allocation with Basel II. Cost and Benefit Analysis*, Butterworths-Heinemann, London and Boston, 2004.
9. D.N. Chorafas, *Economic Capital Allocation with Basel II. Cost and Benefit Analysis*, Butterworths-Heinemann, London and Boston, 2004.

11

REAL-TIME
RISK MANAGEMENT

11.1 INTRODUCTION

Etymologically, risk is the chance of injury, damage, or loss, i.e., a hazard. In banking and in insurance, risk is expressed quantitatively as the degree or *probability of loss*. The doors of risk and of return are adjacent and identical. The concept underpinning risk management is based on controlling assumed exposure: identifying risks, updating them steadily, and evaluating financial staying power to confront and take charge of them. The nature of risk, its extent, and, aftermath change over time. It may even reverse some of its characteristics. This makes the management of exposure much more difficult. Down to basics, risk is a *cost*, but the criteria we use to judge it are not statistics. Thinking by analogy, an excellent paradigm of risk being assumed is people's weight. As stated in *The Economist*, "When the world was a simpler place, the rich were fat, the poor were thin, and right-thinking people worried about how to feed the hungry. Now, in much of the world, the rich are thin, the poor are fat, and right-thinking people are worrying about obesity."[1]

Obesity is a risk, though most of the people who are underweight have not yet seen it under this prism. In 2000, the World Health Organization labeled obesity an epidemic and also said that it is heavily implicated in diabetes, cancer, and other diseases. Obesity has a great deal to do with risk and its monetization. It is a major problem to insurance-financed healthcare systems, and it is turning some of the traditional insurance-coverage principles on their head.

Because obesity is a risk, it has been suggested that insurance companies should be able to charge overweight people higher rates. As documented by statistics, overweight people cost more in terms of healthcare. Alternatively, insurance companies could give discounts to people in fitness programs. The principle is to charge overwieght people and bad drivers what they really cost.

This same principle, of charging what it costs plus a margin of profit, should be applied with every transaction. The risk of obesity does not need real-time tracking, but risks taken with financial operations do. This chapter addresses itself to real-time applications for effective control of risk associated with financial instruments. A *financial instrument* is cash, evidence of ownership in equity or debt, or a contract that meets obligations and rights. Financial instruments are subject to *credit risk* and *market risk*. Like obesity, both types of risk denote the presence of accounting loss.

Credit risk is the possibility that a loss may occur from failure of another party to perform according to terms of a contract. *Market risk* concerns the chance that future changes in market prices may make a financial instrument less valuable or more onerous. Both credit and market risk are often defined in terms of changes in values between two dates. This fits well with market risk and can be extended into credit risk with default as the trigger, but it is not fully applicable with operational risk.

Operational risk is the risk of loss from inadequate internal processes or failed internal control. These processes may regard people, tools, methods, procedures, or systems. Operational risk also stems from external events that are not always under the control of the organization. We will not be concerned with operational risk in this chapter.

A major difference between risk in finance and in other domains like engineering or the military is that exposure is related to the variability of the future value of a position due to market changes and other events of an *uncertain* nature. Risk and uncertainty correlate, as shown in Figure 11.1. To overcome uncertainty and measure risk, we must make assumptions. The challenge with assumptions is that they are usually subjective, and their aftermath cannot be easily measured.

A real-time system is of significant help because the timely and accurate data streams it makes available permit us to test early enough our assumptions about exposure and reject them if they prove to be wrong. Uncertainty is somewhat reduced, but risks remain. What changes is the way to control them. That is what dynamic risk management is all about, as the following case study documents.

11.2 ORGANIZATION, TECHNOLOGY, AND ENTERPRISE RISK MANAGEMENT

Over the years, the board of directors of Bank "C" has been increasingly preoccupied with the institution's ability to control the credit risks and market risks it has been assuming. In the opinion of the majority of directors, the bank's exposure has significantly increased as the institution expanded its operations internationally and adopted a product innovation

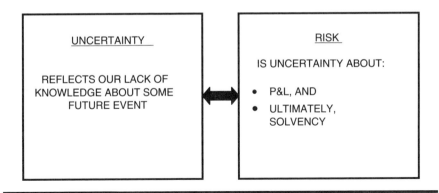

Figure 11.1 Uncertainty Always Underpins the Notion of Risk

policy with increasing dependence on derivative financial instruments. There have been essentially two major challenges connected to risk control: organization and information technology.

The origin of the organizational challenge is one of responsibility and personal accountability for the control of exposure. Bank "C" had a split between its traditional Credit Risk department and its Market Risk Control, a newer unit. In the 1990s, with the Market Risk Amendment by the Basel Committee,[2] the latter was set up. The people working for these two risk control units had different cultures, and their collaboration was not as effective as it should have been.

However, in the experience of some of the board members, credit risks can morph into market risks and vice versa. Therefore, the board of Bank "C" decided that an *integrated* Risk Management entity was necessary. It was to be equipped for addressing credit risk, market risk, and operational risk in compliance with Basel II, and it was also to be able to exercise specific risk-control directives by the supervisory authorities of the home country and of all of the host countries where Bank "C" was active (see Chapter 10 on the host–host issue).

The board noted in its decision that because financial entities are in the business of taking risk, they have to pay attention to managing their exposure in a timely and accurate manner and strike a desired balance between risk and reward. The board added that although this concept has been intrinsic to the business of financial institutions, in the last decade the discipline of *risk management* has become more explicit and formalized but, at the same time, subject to steady evolution of:

- Concepts
- Methods
- Tools
- Challenges

A study requested by the board and done by a consultancy among peer financial institutions documented that there is no best approach to risk management, but there are principles. These include clear and comprehensive board decision, the choice of a rigorous risk-control method, and right economic incentives and real-time information technology solutions for better risk management. The evidence provided by this study pointed to the fact that effective enterprise risk management must be a structured, disciplined approach, aligning:

- Strategy
- Policies
- Systems
- Processes
- People

The goal was the evaluation of new risks being assumed and those inventoried in Bank "C"s' portfolio. The consultancy also pointed out that the credit institution's IT was in need of thorough revamping. Indeed, the consultancy said, this must be felt by many other companies, too, because today between 60 percent and 80 percent of new technology implementation is in system integration. At Bank "C" system integration should be aiming to:

- Provide a sound platform for further product- and account management functions
- Identify and size risk with any instrument and any counterparty, anywhere in the world
- Become core to the bank's economic capital allocation process, which should be based on risk and return[3]

A second study commissioned by the board of Bank "C" focused on the level of sophistication and complexity of an effective risk management solution. Based on research findings, the answer to this query was that the methods that we choose should be characterized by overall simplicity so that both principles and control structures are understood by everybody. The consultancy suggested that if they are not generally understood and appreciated, they will not be effective.

Some of the directors were concerned about the reduction of uncertainty. (See the reference made in the Introduction.) One of the board members answered that, in his opinion, a valid answer in this connection is the risk management concept outlined by Robert F. Rubin, the former U.S. Treasury Secretary and former CEO of Goldman Sachs. Rubin believed that nothing can be known for sure — everything is probabilistic.[4] No matter how good one's information or judgment, it can always turn out to be wrong. There is nothing that cannot go wrong, and one has to be prepared for the consequences.

The chairman of Bank "C" agreed to this concept, adding from his experience, that even the best looking deals can go wrong on the basis of things we did not anticipate. The corollary to this, the chairman said, is that although it is necessary to take risks, it is also important to recognize our fallibility, because economic forecasting is an imprecise science that does not approach mathematical certainty, and, to a point, the same is true of prognosticating the outcome of:

■ Loans
■ Trades
■ Investments

In answer to a query posed by the board, the consultancy advised Bank "C" that both real-time information systems and a whole family of eigenmodels and expert systems would be needed to map the institution's market into the computer. This is a necessary condition for taking the whole portfolio and turning it around with acceptable accuracy and without inordinate personnel costs. Moreover, organizational prerequisites had to be fulfilled; the block diagram shown in Figure 11.2 maps some aspects of this process.

In collaboration with Bank "C"s' own IT experts, the consultancy suggested to the board the necessary extent of information technology restructuring for *global risk management.* It also explained that *if* the objective is to provide the institution with the ability to track positions, pinpoint opportunities, evaluate risks, develop hedging strategies, and do cross-market arbitrage, *then* very significant departures from the current, rather centralized IT policies had to take place.

In the background of the proposed new IT approach has been the fact that risk management is a combination of judgment and analytics. Expert systems can help in amplifying the decision maker's judgment, and algorithms are of significant assistance in analytics. Moreover, setting risk management's goals by the board must account for both:

■ *Probable* evolution of credit risk and market risk by instrument, counterparty, and area of operations
■ *Improbable* outcome due to unexpected risks, credit deterioration, market volatility, liquidity squeeze, event risk, and other factors.

The consultancy also raised the point that cultural clashes are not inevitable because risk managers have different opinions than traders, loan officers, and investment advisers due to differences in outlook and in objectives. Such differences are concerning types of risks being taken, horizon

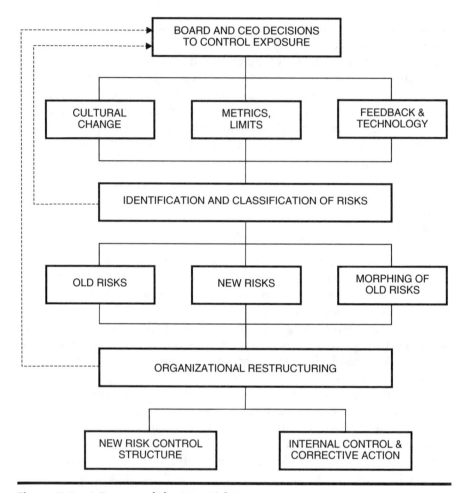

Figure 11.2 A Framework for New Risk Management

of these risks, resulting core exposures, sustainability of returns, and available economic capital to face assumed risks. Following the evidence provided by the consultancy, the chairman of Bank "C" said that the board would pay particular attention to the likelihood of cultural clashes.

11.3 UNCERTAINTIES CONNECTED TO CREDIT RISK

The Introduction has given a brief but comprehensive definition of credit risk. It has also stated that because nothing can be known rationally and with total certainty, the risk manager must be an extreme doubter and skeptic. To perform his functions in an able manner, he must be a person at ease in living with uncertainty in:

- Inputs
- Outcomes
- Probabilities

If the risk manager and his assistants cannot do that, they should not be in risk control in the first place. The job of the chief risk management officer is *not* that of conveying, or even endeavoring to convey, the impression of a triumphal march in risk containment through bombastic and hollow statements as Napoleon's bulletins sent back home from his campaign in Russia. The job of people responsible for risk management is to be:

- Inquisitive
- Analytical
- Pragmatic
- Objective

All four qualities are necessary to be in charge of assumed exposure. They are also the pillars on which risk-based pricing rests. Price competitiveness is assessed through cost and price relationships, with assumed risk being one of major costs. The best indicators of real price competitiveness are those that capture risk and return in every chapter as comprehensively as possible. Cost information is instrumental in indicating not only a company's but also an economy's international competitiveness. Return is influenced by variables such as:

- Market acceptance
- Product quality
- Customer satisfaction
- Capacity for innovation
- Flexibility in customer relationship

All five bullets outline qualitative features that are difficult to capture in their totality. They are also greatly influenced by the level of technology being used. Technology and innovation are *forward-looking* indicators whereas up to a point, market share is a *backward-looking* indicator that tends to reflect past strengths and weaknesses rather than future ones.

What is noteworthy in this context is that risk analysis provides both a backward-looking indicator in the sense of reflecting past mistakes and a forward-looking one because of the message that it gives both on the entity's survivability in the longer term and on its competitiveness in the short term, as perceived by its counterparties. In turn, this translates into possible gains in market share.

Moreover, although risk-based pricing reflects assumed credit risk and market risk, it also maps into itself factors affecting an entity's business risk. Joseph Wieleman of ABN Amro Bank defines *business risk* as risk caused by uncertainty in profits due to changes in the competitive environment that damage the franchise of operational economics of an enterprise. As such, business risk:

■ Relates to the volatility of the operational earnings of a bank, driven by changes in revenues, and
■ Reflects changes in operational earnings as a consequence of changes in volume, prevailing margin, and structure of the cost base.

Notice that all three factors — cost base, margin, and volume — constitute the company's *operational leverage*, which is influenced by both internal decisions and external events. In that sense, business risk represents uncertainty of future volumes and margins due to macro economic conditions as well as by the level of operational gearing caused by fixed costs.

The fact that financial and industrial entities wake up very slowly to business risk, and might do something about it only at the final hour, is a talking example of lag in management action, which adds to the uncertainties surrounding a company's exposure. Risk managers must appreciate that the uncertainties and probabilities to which frequent reference has a priori been made are around people, money, instruments, transactions, other parties, and the markets at large. Such uncertainties underpin questions to which nobody really has the answer. This is precisely the challenge of the risk manager's job. *If* risk managers had complete capability to look into the future, *then* their jobs would be simple and straightforward

Indeed, these concepts are a summary of what the consultancy said to the board of Bank "C," including the fact that to effectively integrate credit risk, market risk, and operational risk under one head, it is necessary to develop a common culture based on two pillars: management control system, paying full attention to the notion of uncertainty, and crisp metrics. With the new capital adequacy by the Basel Committee (Basel II), the crisp metrics consist of expected losses (EL) and unexpected losses (UL).

Due to failure on the part of any customer, correspondent bank, or other counterparty to fulfill obligations assumed toward *our* bank. Major credit risk uncertainties include:

■ Probability of default (PD)
■ Default point (DP) of the counterparty
■ Value of collateral and recovery rate
■ Loss given default (LGD)
■ Exposure at default (EAD)
■ Correlation among defaults
■ Synergy of defaults and credit cycles

- Inadequate accounting of expected losses
- Frequency and impact of unexpected losses

Based on the principles of capital allocation under Basel II, Figure 11.3 outlines the place in the distribution of expected losses and unexpected losses, and their relation, respectively, to regulatory capital and economic capital. Expected losses are typically at the body of the loss distribution. Unexpected losses are at the tail, manifested through spikes and rare but very costly risk events.

This presentation is consistent with the fact that well-managed banks now classify credit provisions into 2 or 3 major classes. The first is that of expected loss, which essentially represents an *expected value* in a normal or lognormal distribution, computed annually as part of the cost of doing business. The second class is that of an unexpected loss, typically computed at 99 percent of confidence, or at the 99.97-percent level. The latter is chosen by banks targeting the "AA" creditworthiness grade.

Another extreme of this unexpected loss class, or taken on its own as a distinct category, is a *super-cat risk*. Super-cat stands for a very major catastrophe. This is the other 1 percent, 1 permille, or 3 per ten thousand percentile which cannot be effectively met by the bank's capital. As such, it needs extraordinary reserves to be found in capital markets and/or a lender of last resort.

The reference to "AA" rating needs explaining. Standard & Poor's (S&P), Moody's Investors Service, Fitch Ratings, and other agencies classify entities, their securitized loans, and their bonds along a 20-grade scale. For presentation purposes, in Table 11.1 this is compressed into 8 grades. Notice that the ratings change from year to year. Table 11.1 is essentially a transition matrix from one grade level to the next. Banks need AA rating for several reasons:

- To attract deposits
- To be sought after trading partners
- To appeal to the capital market
- To have a good standing with correspondent banks

Credit ratings, however, are no exact science. They are based on evaluations and they involve uncertainty. No independent rating agency can have a holistic idea of a credit institution — or of a borrower — without having seen the financial figures, the internal controls, the top people, and evidence of actions. Sometimes these transactions are hidden, as evidenced in the major scandals that shook the financial industry in 2001 to 2003. Essentially, the "AA" or any other grade is a proxy of creditworthiness.

In conclusion, Figure 11.4 presents, in a nutshell, component parts of effective credit risk management. As the careful reader will appreciate,

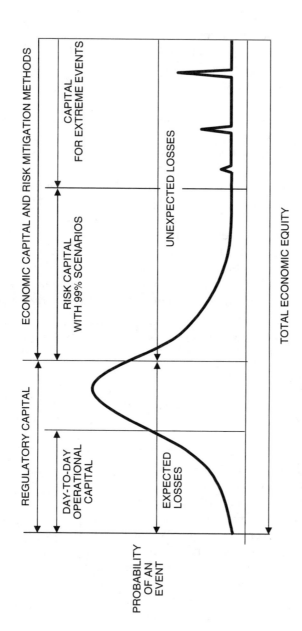

Figure 11.3 Classification of a Bank's Capital Requirements According to the Newest Management Methodology for Risk Control

Table 11.1   A Transition Matrix Based on Average One-Year Transition Rates

Courtesy Standard and Poor's

Initial Rating	AAA	AA	A	BBB	BB	B	CCC	D
AAA	88.72	8.14	0.66	0.06	0.12	0.00	0.00	0.00
AA	0.68	88.31	7.59	0.62	0.06	0.14	0.02	0.00
A	0.09	2.19	87.74	5.32	0.71	0.25	0.01	0.06
BBB	0.02	0.31	5.61	81.95	5.00	1.10	0.11	0.18
BB	0.03	0.13	0.61	7.03	73.27	8.04	0.91	1.06
B	0.00	0.10	0.21	0.38	5.66	72.91	3.56	5.20
CCC	0.18	0.00	0.18	1.07	1.96	9.27	53.48	19.79

what is required is much more than simply knowing counterparty risk. Data mining for all component parts of this integrative picture must be done online. The information elements themselves must be accurate and steadily updated, and presentation should be done in a comprehensive and comprehensible way. All these are characteristics of real-time systems, — the only way to effectively face credit risk.

11.4   UNCERTAINTIES RESULTING FROM MARKET RISK

Section 3 made the reference that the risk manager must be analytical, pragmatic, and objective. Implicit in this statement is the fact that he should

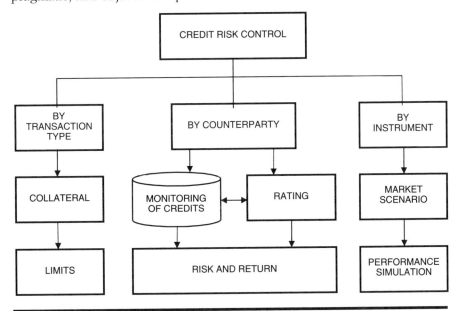

Figure 11.4   The Interactive Management of Credit Exposure Requires Much More than Knowing Counterparty Risk

leave his emotions at the door: emotions are the enemy of analytics. Another characteristic of a good risk manager is the ability to appreciate the importance of independence of opinion and, therefore, of vigorous dissent.

Dissent should be invited because challenging the obvious is vital in an environment of risk control. Dissent, however, has the nasty aftermath of increasing the amount of uncertainty. This is another reason why, as we have seen, risk managers should learn to live with *constructive ambiguity.*

Risk management is like building a mosaic — the bull's eye comes at the end, and this is true of both credit risk and market risk. Market risk uncertainties are mainly due to unexpected price changes in stocks, bonds, interest rates, currencies, and other commodities, causing capital losses or lower income in the future.

With simple financial instruments as well as availability of rich databases and analytics, market risks are relatively well understood. But constraints remain. These include macroeconomic impact, short-term volatilities, nonlinearity between P&L and risk factors, instability in correlations, market risk aftermath of defaults and credit cycles, and other factors like yield curve changes and spreads.

Because so many risk factors are at play, market risk controllers and the institution's management at large must understand that exposure feeds on itself. Markets are psychological animals that cannot be reduced to mathematics. Because analytics are essential to unearthing market risk trends, people whose job it is to track exposure should use Einstein's method as their model for discovery: careful, scrupulous observation and picking apart of measurements to determine what is changing and where the turning points are.

The search for changing market risk patterns and conditions and turning points explains why analytical concepts can provide bankers and other company executives with insight into nascent market risk in evolution. This is something that most market players failed to detect in time in 1994, as the Federal Reserve raised interest rates in six consecutive steps. The bond market's bottom fell in the aftermath.

Experience in market risk control demonstrates that of the many advantages analytics offer to the risk manager, perhaps the most important is that it furnishes a perspective of the evolving situation in terms of exposure, provided that all the fundamental assumptions are explicitly formulated and objectively examined.

However, even when these conditions are satisfied, it does not automatically follow that one can arrive at a satisfactory solution merely because he uses algorithmic and heuristic models. Whether or not analytics and modeling will be useful must be learned from experience resulting from experimentation and by testing or comparing the model's output with real-world time series.

Figure 11.5 presents an example of tracking over a four-month period the market exposure assumed in the trading portfolio of a credit institution

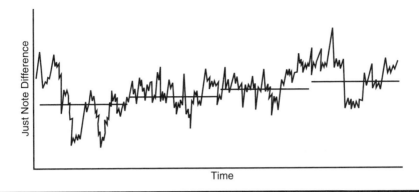

Figure 11.5 Daily Value at Risk and Monthly Average at a Major Financial Institution

through value at risk (VAR). The careful reader will appreciate that volatility of exposure changes from one month to the next while, at the same time, the mean value of exposure increases. This is an excellent example of creeping-up market risk.

In their efforts to keep risk under lock and key, risk managers are assisted by rocket scientists who use powerful metaphors for model-making, and are mapping real-world situations into a model. The idea of a road to be traveled in the control of exposure culminates in the method. Theory is nothing but a technical product. So is truth. We cannot make even the simplest model unless we have previously made a small theory about it and have set a course to discover the truth or, at least, its elemental ideas.

To a substantial extent, this explains some of the conceptual qualities a risk manager needs, beyond those that are analytical. Perception and conception should not fight the ambiguity embedded in credit and market risk. Instead, they should use it as raw material to develop and test alternative hypotheses about assumed exposure as well as ways and means to keep it within established limits.

Moreover, risk managers and their assistants should use all the support high technology can provide to help themselves, in finding out both how much risk is enough and how they can effectively control the limits. In doing so, however, they should always appreciate that all tools are imprecise. As it cannot be repeated too often:

■ Nothing can be known for certain
■ Everything is stochastic, and "sure" deals can turn sour

Both analytically and subjectively, market risk managers should calculate how much is needed in tightening limits and reduce probability of loss below a properly established point of tolerance. This is partly a subjective exercise, because the point-of-risk tolerance is not only that of their company but also their own. That is the level they can live with. For its part, senior management should always be keen to establish limits and be prepare to follow up on them.

This is just as true of market risk as it is of credit risk and of their synergy. The notion of a probabilistic behavior of exposure, as well as the computation of capital at risk that the bank writes in its books because of irrevocable commitments, converge through credit risk and market risk limits — and their timely control. Every instrument counterparty, desk, and trader should have associated exposure limits that are steadily supervised in real-time and updated through board and CEO decisions when necessary. The bank as a whole should have a holistic approach to limits. One of the underlying concepts is visually explained in Figure 11.6 through a coordinate system. Risk behavior, within this frame of reference, should be controlled in real-time, which talks volumes of the sophistication of information technology required to be in charge of short-term and longer-term risks.

11.5 THE REAL-TIME EVALUATION OF GAINS AND LOSSES

After the Barings bankruptcy in early 1995, a Barclays executive was quoted by *Business Week* as saying, "You cannot stop someone from going berserk.

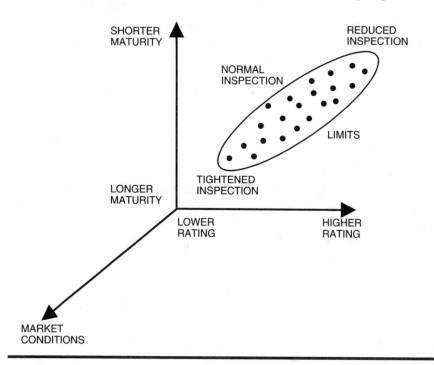

Figure 11.6 Limits Are Usually Set in a 3-Dimensional Space

But you can have a system to catch it in 24 hours." One of the prerequisites for reaching this goal is having a CEO who is computers- and model-literate as well as willing and able to take immediate corrective action. Another prerequisite is an information system that works in realspace (see Chapter 9) and catches exposure *tick-by-tick* at subsecond level.

The usual management reporting cycle, a 24-hour delay, is a long time, but in some circumstances a one-hour delay can be fatal. Delays in management reporting are known in the organization; therefore, they are an invitation to major disasters — loss of the bank, in fact. This is what has happened with Barings (more on Barings in Chapter 12).

From the front desk to the back office, accounting must capture, record, and report changes of the large and small scale. An example of a major change occurred in March–April 2000, when an 18% drop in the Nasdaq Composite Index wiped $1 trillion from investors' portfolios. Although that major correction was the result of an overvalued technology sector that suddenly confronted reality, there was a clear connection to creative accounting and flaws in financial reporting.

Small-scale changes are the tick-by-tick changes affecting a company's fortunes, its risk exposure, and its future. Here the problem is that the backward-looking financial statements used today in many cases do not capture the minute changes taking place in the market. However, when there is a trend, minute market changes can pile up, becoming a tsunami. Classical accounting presents its figures long after the facts, and these figures lack transparency in a management-oriented, decision-making sense.

The result is that of flying blind, condemned to do so through the use obsolete information, with the aftermath of suffering wild market mood swings. While first-class accounting cannot cure the market's volatility, it can provide senior executives with a better picture of their company's risk and return.

The need for improving speed of information as well as transparency highlights the fact that the current accounting treatment of complex financial products, like derivative financial instruments, is behind the curve. Effectiveness can, however, be improved through real-time data capture, data mining, analytical presentation, evaluation, and reporting on risks and their effects as well as flashing out events that overrun established limits (see Section 4).

Beyond this, the financial industry faces challenges with the quality of its internal control system, which is often of questionable dependability, if it exists at all. The more a bank is exposed in derivative financial instruments and in alternative investments,[5] the more it is in need of real-time reporting as well as a real-enough time verification of its exposure. This definitely impacts on systems, procedures, the accounting system, available tools, and management principles.

As Dr. Gordon Bell, a senior scientist at Microsoft, suggested, technology for risk management is not a computing problem. The overriding requirement is to be able to answer in real-time. This is a database mining problem: "Who got what." Quite evidently, it is also a matter of organization, of models, of knowledge engineering, and of visualization (see Chapter 7).

Existing software can help for tracking purposes, even if it has been developed for other reasons that have similar data-mining, transaction-handling, and presentation requirements. For instance, *cybercash* was developed for small amounts, but it can track practically everything, including the $17 billion J.P. Morgan Chase loaned to Worldcom before the company went bankrupt.

The crucial issue is instantaneous response. On paper, given where we are with computers, we can do nearly everything currently required, such as establishing a real-time basis for tracking transactions and risks. Real-time tracking is very important because thus far most institutions do a miserable job knowing where their cash goes. In reality, however, what is lacking is the analytical spirit and the ability to challenge the obvious.

This is not the first time that I am emphasizing that these points are crucial in the management of risk. As Dr. Peter Drucker, one of the fixtures of modern management theory, aptly argues, every agency, every policy, every program, and every activity should be controlled through a number of critical, focused questions:

- What is your mission?
- Is it still the right mission?
- Is it still worth doing it?
- If we were not doing this, would we go into it now?

Pinching pennies here and there may be all well and good, but top management's main problem is not only that of spending too much money. Indeed, there may be things on which it should be spending more, not less. The larger trouble is that it spends almost randomly, trying to do everything imaginable without critically sorting out its priorities. The same is true with the control of exposure.

Alert management is aware that it needs risk metrics that work in real-time. Nothing less than that is satisfactory. A dozen years ago, a once-per-day estimate of recognized but not realized gains and losses might have been sufficient. That's how value at risk (VAR) was born. In the early 1990s, the then-CEO of J.P. Morgan asked for a 4:15 p.m. report on estimated exposure.

At that time, the parametric VAR developed to answer this request was state of the art. Today, VAR is more or less an aberration. Beyond this, there is a big difference between answering the requirements of just one bank and becoming the market risk measurement standard of the banking industry worldwide, let alone employing VAR not just for market risk but also for credit risk. Both in terms of obsolescence and misuse, banks fail to appreciate that models have locality of usage and that they become irrelevant, if not outright dangerous, outside their domain.

It is therefore sad to see that in the early twenty-first century several banks look favorably to the so-called "99.97 percent VAR" as a way out of their difficulties is estimating unexpected losses. This is a very poor way of managing credit risk. First and foremost, VAR is:

- An unsophisticated model
- Of limited perspective
- Carried into credit risk from market risk

Each one of these bullets would have been enough reason *not* to use a VAR approach with credit risk, this model or any other. There are, however, more reasons, the most important being that VAR 99.97 is not even a shadow of what Basel requires for credit risk control. Moreover, VAR 99.97 is *not* a proxy for unexpected losses (UL) in the way it has been used. A sound solution should permit management to steer the bank while responding to regulatory requirements.

Only focused, reliable, real-time information can serve the company's internal control and its risk management system. Senior executives urgently need dependable information on loans, creditworthiness, investments, volatility, liquidity, notional amounts, market values, and unrealized gains and losses. Solutions should be provided in full appreciation of the fact there is no valid one-size-fits-all approach. Solutions must be targeted. This is the message the omega curve in Figure 11.7 brings into perspective.

11.6   ISAAC NEWTON'S POLICY FOR EFFECTIVE CONTROL

Newton's contribution to the British Treasury proved invaluable — thanks to the conceptual and analytical skills he demonstrated through his work in mathematics and physics. As a schoolboy he was able to design and build working models for which he gained something of a reputation. As a mathematician, he improved upon this art, and as the Warden, then Master, of the Mint he used his inquisitive mind in a domain he confronted for the first time but that he wanted to control.

It would be difficult to find a better example of the complex personality required by the person who would be in charge of enterprise risk management than that of Isaac Newton. His cross-disciplinary background steadily encouraged him to watch others at work and to ask penetrating questions. This permitted him to focus on a subject and to draw together the many threads that led him from his work in physics to leadership in economics and finance.

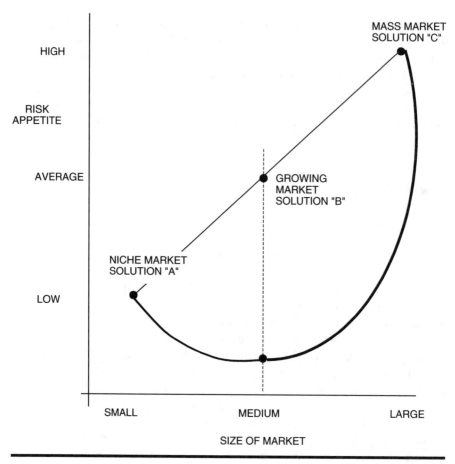

Figure 11.7 Omega Curve and Three Totally Different Risk Control Solutions

Another trait found in Newton was that he stepped away from what he was taught, what he saw as routine, and what, by all likelihood, seemed to be "obvious." His investigation into the natural sciences led to new departures. He focused on the subject he was investigating rather than spreading himself thin over different issues. He had the ability to ask penetrating questions that led to the heart of the matter he was investigating. Newton was an analytical scientist who primarily worked on his own, and for his own satisfaction. His conceptual abilities permitted him to draw together the many facts that led from ancient times to modern science.

Newton's study involved both mathematical analysis and thoroughly documented experimental evidence. He had an acute appreciation of the fact that lack of focus, and of analysis, produce an opaque picture of reality. These are fundamental ingredients into the work of every risk manager and of every researcher. An investigative spirit helps in deciding how successful will be the rules and tools put into place for control of exposure as well as what might be expected in regard to quality of results.

To better understand what motivated Newton's great mind, we must keep in perspective that the late seventeenth and early eighteenth centuries were (like today) of a rapidly changing environment. Conceptual persons understood that what was conceived at the time as "tomorrow's" demands were not the same as those of "today" or "yesterday."

Subconsciously at least, the physicist's queries had a deeper financial background influenced by his association with Charles Montagu, which, by all evidence, was prompted by Newton's leadership in mathematics and physics. How important is assets and liabilities management to the finances of the kingdom? How could the Mint best manage money supply? What is the influence of money supply on interest rate risk? Is there something that should be done to strengthen the unofficial regulatory system and the supervisory activities befalling the Master of the Mint office?

If we translate these and similar issues to modern time, this will given an equally exciting set of challenging queries: Should the IMF act as the reinsurer of bad risks by international investors and inept governments? Should the IMF be the world's lender of last resort? What is the most likely development of the economic situation in the aftermath of high leverage? Who would pay the huge liabilities of derivatives exposure? What challenges do new asset classes present?

Superficially, it may not seem that way, but experimentation is cornerstone to factual and documented answers to queries such as: What is the implication of lower/higher interest rates on structured products with guarantees? Where does the focus on shareholder value lead us? Experimentation can also help us in deciding what *our alternatives* are, how much each will cost us, and what benefits we are likely to derive.

As the Introduction brought to the reader's attention, risk is a cost. Together with risk management, cost control at large is an important issue often overlooked in terms of supervision by senior executives. However, costs, particularly runaway and unjustifiable costs, can bring an organization to its knees. To be in control, costs must remain within the standard cost chain. (See more on the cost-control issue in Chapter 17.)

The failure of cost control is, for all practical purposes, an *operational risk,* based on the way it has been defined in the Introduction.[6] In a manner similar to what happens with other risks, some organizations are absolutely unable to keep their overhead and their operating costs under lock and key. The runaway budget of the European Commission's (E.C.) building in Brussels provides an example in which cost control has taken a leave and has gone it went personal accountability.

Belaymont, the E.C.'s 13-story home building in Brussels, had to be renovated because of asbestos and other defects. The original budget was $149 million, which was already too high. The timeplan was 1990 to 1992.

Work started in 1995, with 5 years' delay. In 2001, six years down the line, this job was far from being complete, but a new estimate of costs put the renovation price at $1.03 billion, a 691 percent budget overrun. That's how things get out of control.

I bring the Belaymont example into perspective because substandard risk management is not the only weakness of banks, hedge funds, and other financial institutions. Another major weakness is disregard for costs. As with the E.C. building, they spend an inordinate amount of money on overhead and other unnecessary expenses. The cost-to-income ratio (known as the overhead of the institution) can run from about 44 percent to over 75 percent.

- An overhead of 44 percent is enviable
- An overhead of 75 percent shows galloping mismanagement

Both the control of risk and the control of costs are signs of good management. After being appointed Warden at the Royal Mint (and before becoming Master), Isaac Newton concerned himself with how to increase the efficiency of the minting process. He carefully watched each step and carried out a time-and-motion study more than two centuries before Frederick Winslow Taylor (see Chapter 1):

- Newton calculated where and how improvements could be made
- He analyzed the process of minting in every detail, step by step

Newton also applied his mathematical skills to *cost analysis,* and this led him to clashes with greedy government contractors. Says Michael White, "Long years of study and practical work at a quite different furnace had enabled Newton to calculate that one troy ounce of alloy for the production of coins could be produced at a cost of 7½ d. So when the financiers . . . submitted tender of 12½ d. per pound, Newton called their bluff and forced them down."[7] Risk managers should look at this as a first-class lesson for their jobs.

11.7 NOTES

1. *The Economist,* December 13, 2003.
2. D.N. Chorafas, *The 1996 Market Risk Amendment. Understanding the Marking-to-Model and Value-at-Risk,* McGraw-Hill, Burr Ridge, IL, 1998.
3. D.N. Chorafas, *Economic Capital Allocation with Basel II. Cost and Benefit Analysis,* Butterworths-Heinemann, London, 2004.
4. Bob Woodward, *"Maestro,"* Simon & Schuster, New York, 2000.
5. D.N. Chorafas, *Alternative Investments and the Mismanagement of Risk,* Macmillan/Palgrave, London, 2003.
6. D.N. Chorafas, *Operational Risk Control with Basel II. Basic Principles and Capital Requirements,* Butterworths-Heinemann, London, 2004.
7. Michael White, *Isaac Newton,* Fourth Estate, London, 1998.

12

IMPLEMENTING REALSPACE
SOLUTIONS TO REPLACE
OFFICE AUTOMATION

12.1 INTRODUCTION

"The life of the law is not logic, but experience," Justice Oliver Wendell Holmes once said. Systems experience documents that this dictum applies hand-in-glove to advanced technology projects. Both in legal matters and in system design, a great deal can be learned from successes and failures of the past, taking into account not only what needs to be done and when but also the current and projected state of the art and how far it is possible to spearhead into the future.

The past may not be a prognosticator of future events, but it helps by providing guidance. Insight and foresight are gained by analyzing the reasons for successes and failures as well as structural strengths and weaknesses. When past evidence is properly used, one avoids repeating the same mistakes. Whether we talk of finance, commerce, or technology, there is no glory in rediscovering the wheel.

Take the bankruptcy of Barings, the venerable British bank, as an example. At the end of the nineteenth century, when Barings was going down the drain because U.S. municipalities defaulted on loans issued, the Bank of England came to the rescue — an act at the origin of the term "lender of last resort." However, in February 1995, the Bank of England brought Barings to bankruptcy after a derivatives speculation involving a collision between front desk and back office. Barings' gambles with derivative financial instruments at the Osaka stock exchange:

- Hit the level of $27 billion in derivatives contracts engineered by Barings' Singapore office
- Ended in a cool $1.5 billion loss, wiping out the bank's $900 million in capital.

On the surface, the mistake was one of taking an inordinate amount of market risk by purchasing, in a few weeks' time, 20,000 index contracts. This error was compounded when the trader who committed it sold puts and calls to cover his position. There were other flaws, as well, of interest to the *dos* and *don'ts* in banking, but in brief, the aftermath of two weeks of derivatives trades resulted in the destruction of two centuries of banking tradition.

Three months after the collapse of the venerable institution, the Bank for International Settlements (BIS) issued a report on Barings. This report said that its bankruptcy did not affect futures and options trades, which rose to a record 304.5 million contracts. But BIS added that Barings' bankruptcy did reveal gaping holes in *regulatory armory* and the institution's own *internal control*. As BIS pointed out that among the ingredients of the failure were:

- Regulatory arbitrage between competing exchanges
- Defective information sharing and coordination between supervisors
- Substandard internal risk management policies and support systems in Barings
- Lack of differentiation between Barings' own account and customer trading
- Failure to separate authority and responsibility between front desk and back office

The BIS report emphasized that at Barings management controls were practically nonexistent and senior management particularly failed to separate front-desk responsibilities from those connected to the back-office routines. On the surface, this has nothing to do with office automation (OA), but a closer look reveals many links. Since the late 1970s, when OA passed the level of secretarial word processing, office automation provided the missing connectivity between management and the back office.

Since then, management information and office automation have been two issues that correlate among themselves and with the technology being used. The link OA provided has been vital to keeping the feedback channels open, therefore assuring better internal control. Just as important, however, is management's determination to trust in different hands front-desk and back-office responsibilities. This, too, had failed at Barings.

Nick Leeson, Barings' trader in Singapore and on whose shoulders fell all of the blame for the bank's collapse, ran the back office—which is against both good sense and sound management principles. He also kept double books. But even if this were not the case, unless Barings' Singapore branch was connected in real-time with headquarters in London and timely internal control was exercised, the bank would have gone under. Its huge exposure would not have allowed a moment's delay in exercising rigorous risk control.

12.2 OFFICE AUTOMATION MUST BE UPGRADED WITH REAL-TIME TECHNOLOGY

Readers old enough to have worked on office automation projects in the 1980s will remember that the purpose of any good OA solution is four-fold: first, to offer market advantages; second, to provide support to managers and professionals, not just to secretarial staff; third, to support a better basis for management control than was so far available; and fourth, to make feasible the steady addition of back-office-type value-added services to the clients.

In this sense, a valid office automation approach and a first-class Internet time solution (see Chapter 15) have a good deal in common, at least in regard to the first, second, and fourth of the aforementioned goals. This cannot be said of those of current office automation implementations that have limited themselves to secretarial chores and therefore look at information technology through the rearview mirror. In these cases, the problem has been with the organization, the policies, and the practices being followed with OA.

Traditional thinking and failure to challenge the obvious are the core issues that are defective. Throwing money at office automation problems will not solve a company's IT challenges, but it may make matters worse while giving false hopes that there will be (through some miracle) significant improvement. However, throwing money at the problem is the most widespread practice I have found in my 50 years of professional experience.

What is meant by "traditional thinking" in the preceding paragraph is the use of OA hardware and software to reinvent the typewriter. In data processing, this finds its counterpart in using computers as glorified (and expensive) punch card accounting machines, which, for the majority of companies, has lasted for more than 50 years and is still found in several firms.

This punch card thinking dates back to 1910; it is not yet a century old, but almost. As for the typewriter tradition, Remington introduced its typewriter in 1876, and in 1882 came the portable typewriter, which has been somewhat equivalent to the portable PC of the late twentieth century. Sometimes, like old soldiers, old traditions never die.

The point the reader should retain from these references is the urgency for thoroughly rethinking and renewing back-office systems — getting away from these 130-year-old "traditional" concepts of how technology should be used. (See the case study in Section 3.) Aside from the obscenity of typewriter-type thinking, many back offices today are served by Paleolithic, legacy, or mainframe-based accounting systems. Moreover, they still depend on historically slow software development cycles and feature end-of-day batch routines.

In the typical case, the situation is made worse by multiple platforms implemented at different locations of the same entity, with different principles and approaches. Rapid reaction to events, which might have saved Barings, and with it a focused management control attitude are handicapped by limited interoperability between systems and by the maze of different OA multiple dependencies.

If office automation solutions are worked out in a way that adds complexity to the services supporting the back office and the company retains typewriter thinking, mainframes, Cobol software, and end-of-day reporting, *then* it is better to forget about management control or gains to be obtained from OA and its modern-day evolution. Senior management should also appreciate that the rate of obsolescence of information technology projects, evidently including office automation, is staggering.

Well-managed companies have been aware of this effect of obsolescence since nearly 20 years ago, and they are eager to take countermeasures. In the late 1980s, a critical evaluation of IT at Bankers Trust found that for 80 percent of going information systems projects, the usefulness simply was not there because:

- Competitors had leaped ahead
- The market needs had changed
- Delays in deliverables made certain projects unnecessary or plainly irrelevant

It is one of the major weaknesses of information technology that to the judgment of those responsible for new programming products, business opportunities have to wait for software to be developed at a leisurely pace. In OA's case, this magnifies the defects of typewriter-type thinking. One of the background reasons for such an irrational attitude is that:

- Projects are not rigorously managed
- Paperwork still calls the tune
- A sense of personal accountability is not in place

Of course, the counterargument may be that paper world has not been significantly affected by OA or by computerization. Among major financial institutions, 90 percent of all information necessary for office work is still on paper. A leading computer manufacturer commented that:

- 75 percent of information produced in the office is for internal consumption only

■ 60 percent of all information produced throughout the organization stays at headquarters

A sound way to interpret these statistics is that office automation and other computer projects have failed because they are attacking pseudo-problems while the paperwork hydra continues to grow its heads. These projects have failed because they have not had the benefit of fully rethinking the objectives nor of using real-time solutions with online data mining, rather than typewriter thinking and paper supports.

Another common impediment relates to the back end of the software life cycle. Precisely, the maintenance burden that consumes significant staff time and money is usually late and sometimes introduces new errors into the program. An IBM study has found that every one instruction changed affects seven other instructions. Furthermore, about three-quarters of a company's development staff are focused on maintenance, not new developments.

Reinventing the wheel is still another reason for failures and for substandard results. This might sound like an awkward statement in connection to OA, because office automation has historically been the major domain where off-the-shelf packages were adopted. But it should not be forgotten that an important OA project cannot work stand-alone. It needs connectivity to other IT routines. That's precisely where real-time solutions can add value.

Real-time OA solutions and interactive data mining can be greatly assisted through straight through processing (see Chapter 5) and reality online (see Chapter 6). This evidently requires steady interoperability, which is one more major challenge. In most environments, a hodgepodge of hardware and software platforms impedes the work flow all the way to making users uncomfortable at their desktops. Both end users and computer professionals are also frustrated by the rapid pace of technology change and the difficulty of integrating new systems and applications with existing ones.

These problems were not born yesterday. To a considerable measure, they are as old as computers themselves, which means middle-aged. But as long as information systems worked stand-alone as discrete islands, the challenges in reference were not visible. What made them visible is the integration of applications, of which the early 1980s version of office automation is one of the best examples.

This is why in this chapter I am starting with what has been learned from office automation and proceed with the most modern applications of *realspace*. The careful reader will remember that the concept of realspace has been explained in Chapter 5. We will talk much more about it in the next sections.

One of the useful lessons learned from office automation, as well as from other IT studies, is that able solutions to problems of productivity and competitiveness call for a strategic look at information systems projects, critically evaluating them against new policies established by the board and CEO.

Time and again, the results of the acid test I have administered to a number of companies as consultant to the board have documented that business strategy, computers, and communications systems have been considered as belonging to two different worlds, yet they are highly dependent on one another. Because they are very closely related, they should be handled as an integrated subject. That's the policy every well-managed company should apply. The case of Bank "D" is an example.

12.3 CASE STUDY ON THE REVAMPING OF OFFICE AUTOMATION

Because of problems associated with data integration, Bank "D" wasted money. The CEO was of the opinion his IT people did not drive for a fundamental solution, and he was not pleased with their deliverables. Therefore, the board of Bank "D" asked a consultancy to challenge the current IT practices and, most particularly, to look into the process of data collection, online data access, system integration, and system integrity. Another mission given to the consultancy was that of rethinking the bank's office automation processes and solutions.

In the opening meeting with the consultancy, the CEO emphasized his decision that as a modern credit institution Bank "D" needed an integrated front-desk–back-office system, able to provide real-time support to managers and professionals as well as online subsecond response to their ad hoc queries. He asked the consultancy to pay particular attention in seamlessly integrating in real-time:

■ Front-desk dealing
■ Back-office support

The mission specified that this had to be done without breaking the firewalls previously put into place for separating authority and responsibility between front desk and back office. Not only did existing security measures have to be observed, but they also had to be strengthened with the new solution.

The CEO explained to the consultancy, and to his own people participating to this project, that high technology had to be used to strengthen the implementation of a decision by the board separating front desk and back office everywhere Bank "D" operated. He said that although policy decisions are very important, all by themselves they do not suffice for effective separation of responsibilities. Classical IT solutions, the CEO added, are acceptable only when risks are small and operations are very simple.

Therefore, in his judgment, an able approach required full online integration of management controls, real-time supervision of limits, automatic alerts for limits violations, and estimates of exposure that can be provided at a moment's notice. The CEO wanted rapid feedback for corrective action, emphasizing that all these deliverables had to be done at an affordable cost.

Given the size of Bank "D" and its geographically dispersed activities, the CEO wanted assurances that multiple, locally developed product- and region-specific approaches would be aggregated into one system. Also, because corporate actions tend to become complex, he wanted this aggregate to be flexible and open to an evolutionary process. The CEO felt that inability to integrate new sophisticated services would inhibit the bank's advantages in providing innovative, customer-centric services and in controlling assumed risks.

The chief executive further added that he did not need to remind the consultancy that many processing chores are still manually intensive, not only in Bank "D" but also throughout the industry. Therefore, he wanted knowledge engineering approaches to bend the curve of increasingly having to employ highly qualified and expensive people for trivia and administrative duties.

To press his point, the CEO made reference to a previous study that demonstrated that about 35 percent of the time of medium-level managers was productive while the balance was spend on trivia and administrative duties. There was a unanimous decision of the board that one of the top goals of IT and office automation revamping must be to reverse these ratios.

Figure 12.1 presents these statistics on productive and wasted managerial time. The consultancy, according to the CEO, had the responsibility to provide evidence on how to go from here to there. Other Bank "D" executives, participating in the kick-off meeting, stressed the fact that in a highly competitive environment like the one in which they were working, quite often a single missed corporate action may result in liabilities of millions of dollars and even in reputation risk.

Bank "D"s' chief operating officer (COO) noted that as trading volumes increase, processing costs tend to rise more than proportionately. He also brought to the consultancy's attention the fact that the added complexity of cross-border activities compounds this problem and, moreover, it contributes to the institution's operational risk (see Chapter 11 for definition).

The COO added that with Basel II, Bank "D" had to be very careful with operational risk in all of its channels. He wanted the new office automation project to be capable of data collection and data analysis for operational risk in order to support the *loss distribution* approach the bank had adopted among the alternatives offered by the Basel Committee.[1]

Topping the list of the COO's requirements was the fact that, in the past, difficulties associated with data integration had led many of his assistants to believe a large volume of information is lost in the organization while, at

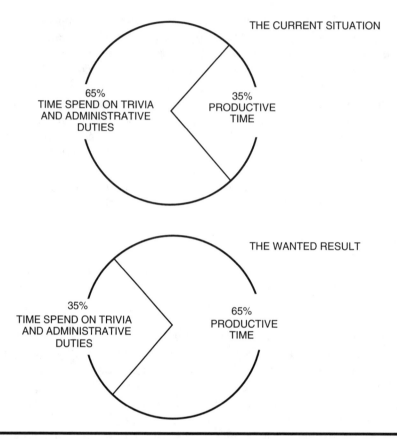

THE CURRENT SITUATION

65%
TIME SPEND ON TRIVIA
AND ADMINISTRATIVE
DUTIES

35%
PRODUCTIVE
TIME

THE WANTED RESULT

35%
TIME SPEND ON TRIVIA
AND ADMINISTRATIVE
DUTIES

65%
PRODUCTIVE
TIME

Figure 12.1   A Major Goal Set by the Board at Bank "D" Was to Reverse the Ratios of Productive and Wasted Managerial Time

the same time, unproductive redundancies of information elements were rampant. The consultancy stated that this was not unusual. Time and again it had found in its studies that:

- 70 percent of data and applications are duplicates
- In many cases, error rates in management-oriented databases are as high as 35 percent.

Let me add a personal note to this statement. My personal experience is no different from these statistics indicated. On several occasions I found myself in office automation/information center projects that were suffering from similar defaults. Although over the years such error-prone results have improved, the challenge has not disappeared. Whereas some of the data-related problems have been solved, others have come up to take their place.

In retrospect, the reason why office automation had hoped to some-how solve outstanding data integration issues, which haunt information systems specialists up to this day, is that it was the first conscious effort in opening up a new frontier in the battle for office productivity. The hypothesis that did not pass the test of time was that OA projects will be doing things in a different way:

- With less paper
- More machine intelligence
- Greater integration

Actually, the results have been quite uneven, both between countries and among companies. A *Business Week* study states that, from 1995 to 2000 in the United States, output per hour grew considerably faster than in Europe: 1.97 percent versus 1.42 percent — and the gap has widened in the 2002 to 2003 timeframe.[2] (See also the discussion on needed cultural change in Section 4.)

The kick-off meeting at Bank "D" did not benefit from these statistics, which are more recent, but a couple of the institution's executives did notice in looking up their old notes taken in the course of past office automation projects, although at a project's start OA was characterized as a powerful tool for the preservation of company resources, including men and money, these goals were not necessarily reached, at least not to their satisfaction. Therefore, they expected that the technologists would be more successful with their deliverables.

The COO insisted that he wanted assurances the new project would not only implement high technology in line with the bank's strategic planning but also meet productivity targets. Moreover, because costs matter, this had to be done in the most cost-effective way. Short of this, the COO said, he would be skeptical about the new integrative office automation study and its projected impressive payoffs.

At this point, the CEO of Bank "D" intervened to save the day with the statement that OA, information technology at large, and productivity issues are both a technological solution and a state of mind. The consultancy added that this is just as valid with real-time and realspace applications. The key issue is the management of change, which requires a transition plan for adaptation and continuity.

The CEO had the last word, stating to his immediate assistants, those who are not decided about the management of change in compliance to the bank's strategic plan better keep out of the project. Then he quoted Harry Truman, who once said, "If you can't stand the heat, stay out of the kitchen."

12.4 CULTURAL CHANGE IS INEVITABLE, NO MATTER WHAT THE NEW SYSTEM IS

Back in 1953, Willis Ware, my professor of computer design at UCLA, taught his students that every time something changes by order of magnitude, our whole decision-making process must change. This order-of-magnitude paradigm is valid in more than one way, from the pace of innovation to globalization and to technology. But perhaps the more dramatic reference is that of leaders who are ahead of the curve in cultural change and of followers who stay way behind.

With the cultural change of the early 1980s, office automation established itself as the solution, and it did so again in the early 1990s when an integrative office environment was studied and implemented. It is helpful, as well, to recall that prior to these events we had stand-alone word processors (WP) that were at the core of the first-generation OA of the 1970s. The integrative perspective of the 1980s and 1990s set for itself the goals of:

- Communicating online between workstations
- Sharing office data on a larger landscape
- Controlling the quality of information used by the company

Some of the more far-sighted office automation projects of the early 1980s, like Citibank's Project Paradise, set for themselves management productivity objectives. Project Paradise aimed, among other goals, to increase Citibank's span of control from about five to eight. (Span of control refers to the number of managers reporting to the same boss.) This would have been instrumental in eliminating intermediate management layers.

With support from Walter Wriston, who was then Citibank's CEO, Project Paradise nearly reached its objectives, but other OA projects did not. This is not necessarily a criticism, because 20 years ago, in the early 1980s, such office technology was still in the formative stage. Today we master it to a considerable degree, but our goals have also changed, moving at a higher integrative level with plenty of knowledge artifacts embedded into it. Still, we should take note of the fact that well-designed OA systems must be flexible and dynamic, sensitive to changes in:

- Office procedures
- Personnel qualifications
- End user requirements

Although there is still no comprehensive theory about office information systems, we know that the office of the future will lean heavily on modeling. Ten years ago this was a hypothesis. Today it is a certainty. Moreover, goals such as the quantification of productivity requirements by Bank "D" (see Section 3) and the wider span-of-control goal by Citibank can be expected to spread in terms of requests for deliverables.

Apart from the span of control, the careful reader will also notice other similarities between the early 1980s and the early part of the twenty-first century, such as the goal of providing a platform for, and window to, background applications that assure connectivity to other computers and communications and software resources of the firm. A more recent aim is to integrate online, and in an interactive manner, all supported services, providing *one* flexible, user-friendly environment.

Then as now, self-respecting information technologists appreciate that OA has to be an open environment, permitting polyvalent access to multimedia information as well as making feasible the industrialization of knowledge. Attaining such objectives presupposes and requires a steadily upgraded infrastructure involving architectured solutions (see Chapter 13), distributed deductive databases[3] including seamless access and data mining (see Chapter 14), intelligent networks[4] and the Internet ecosystem (see Chapters 15 and 16), and agile intelligent workstations with interactive visualization (see Chapter 7).

I have found that companies would pay for technology if they could obtain productivity improvements. As Section 3 has shown through statistics, this goal is better reached in the United States than in Europe. On one hand, as Figure 12.2 demonstrates, technological investments lead productivity results by a considerable margin. On the other hand, there is nothing like a stable return on investment through an increase in productivity. Some companies, the leaders, are able to gain major benefits, but other companies, the laggards, just throw money at the problem and misrepresent the statistics.

The difference between these two groups largely rests on the fact that the leaders know that nothing can be achieved without cultural change. As evidence accumulates that the able use of technology leads to significant return on investment, companies become interested in renewing their information technology infrastructure, but many fail in changing their culture. A recent study found that over the next two years between 40 percent and 60 percent of fund managers in Europe will be changing their IT and will reengineer some of their backbone operations.

But this study made no comment on cultural change that should accompany the new investments in case the company wants to have return on its investment. Still, even if ROI is wanting, it is good to take notice about the money to be spent on new IT and on infrastructure.

One of the basic reasons why fund managers have fallen behind in technology is that during the boom years of the 1990s they distributed their huge profits to partners and shareholders, but they did not reinvest in their IT. This had the aftermath of customer dissatisfaction with the fund managers' deliverables, which always comes from falling behind. Now assets managers are beginning to see that they can no longer afford to fall behind in technology.

An important issue to explain to senior management is that one of the lessons office automation studies have taught is the need of innovative thinking rather than continuing with old habits. *Step-by-step mechanization*

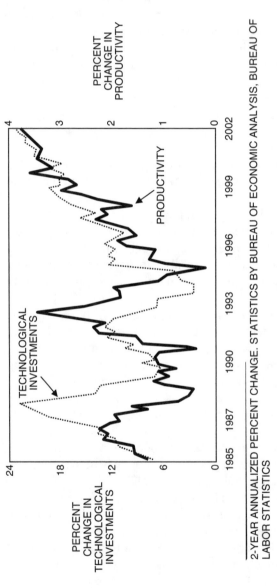

2-YEAR ANNUALIZED PERCENT CHANGE. STATISTICS BY BUREAU OF ECONOMIC ANALYSIS, BUREAU OF LABOR STATISTICS

Figure 12.2 Non-Farm Labor Productivity versus Technological Investments in the United States

has been the old way of implementing technology, which just scratched the surface of the problem and proved to be inefficient. The basic system remained unaltered. It just got more deadwood and an accumulation of costs. To the contrary an efficient solution requires radical system renovation, with on-line access to the company's text and databases and reengineering the whole system, basing it on an intelligent network and knowledge-enriched processing.

Under current technology, the preferred solution is one that provides windows to background applications, seamless connectivity through networks, and increasingly more intelligent software resources. Typically, this approach integrates all online supported services, providing *one* flexible, user-friendly environment. This is an open environment that permits polyvalent access to multimedia information as well as makes feasible the industrialization of knowledge.

But today's current technology is tomorrow's backwater. Therefore, advanced solutions presuppose and require a steadily upgraded infrastructure. Reengineering must see to it that the business architecture becomes pivot the point of renovation (see Chapter 13). This evidently implies costs. In fact, the main costs an advanced IT project is faced with are, in order of importance:

- Reengineering of procedures
- Rebuilding of systems and procedures
- Contingency planning for business continuity (see Chapter 17)

Management planning and control are essential to success. Figure 12.3 presents, as an IT example, business modeling for a new application environment. Among the costs, one should take into account the fact that not all office automation tasks or other IT projects reach a happy ending. Many fall by the wayside because of poor management. An order-of-magnitude classification of reasons for breakdown is given in Figure 12.4. Those projects that reach their goal, however, open new perspectives on how to conduct system studies to get commendable results.

12.5 ADVANCED SOLUTIONS REST ON REENGINEERED REAL-TIME APPLICATIONS

Among companies that know how to use technology to gain competitive advantage, office automation solutions have had three main goals: to keep them ahead of the curve in the market place, to provide more efficient secretarial support to managers and professionals, and to stimulate thoughts for value-added services to the clients. The best OA solutions achieved these goals to a significant degree, but this is not true of the much more general, average-type approaches and their results.

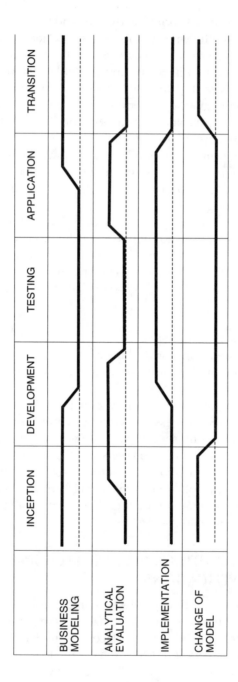

Figure 12.3 Business Modeling Is a Never-Ending Process of Inception, Test, and Transition to a New Version

The most persistent problem with substandard outcomes has been on the side of organizational studies, uncertain management policies, and wanting practice associated to Paleolithic data processing, such as the use of 3270 protocol and mainframe-based OA. Not only has confusing OA with obsolete DP practices been wrong, but throwing money at office problems also did not solve existing challenges; it only made matters worse.

Companies that risk-sized their office automation challenges went straight for online solutions with distributed information systems. They appreciated the fact that real-time technology was in their reach, because technically speaking, *real-time* has been a development of the early to mid-1960s. In one of the major projects that I was personally involved with in the early 1980s, we implemented front-desk to back-office automation for corporate events processing, weeding out a major amount of paperwork. The aim was that of transforming the organization through an office automation solution spanning:

■ Products
■ Business functions
■ Office chores
■ Geographic dispersion

This project targeted infrastructural issues, and it was one of the first to apply the principle of *one entry, many uses* of each information element, which is doable provided that information elements are normalized and data collection is done online, in real-time, and at point of origin.

One of the key advantages of the approach I just outlined is that online interactive access is practically compressed to a few seconds, increasing the efficiency (and satisfaction) of end users. Moreover, as alert information technologists appreciate, without *value-added* characteristics of the more classical OA and DP chores, the user of a computer-based system is not able to operate in actual time, for instance, as market action is taking place and as events occur.

When using network resources among many attached devices and tasks, subsecond-level *response time* is of essence. This makes the timesharing ideas of the 1960s (which still widely prevail in industry) a backward-looking extension of the notions associated with batch processing. The point I wish to press with these references is that those companies still using old concepts of timesharing and real-time, let alone batch, are unfit for any role in the Internet world (see Chapters 15 and 16).

In addition, the man–machine interfaces of these companies are not worth their salt, which works against the foundations of the concept of self-service, one of the goals of modern IT implementation. Self-service is necessary both for efficiency and for applications in Internet time, but without high tech in man–machine interfaces, the quality of deliverables

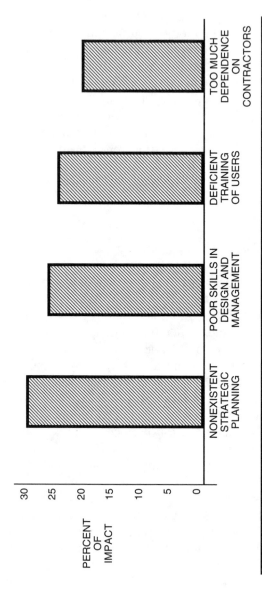

Figure 12.4 Reasons for Breakdown in Office Automation Development Projects

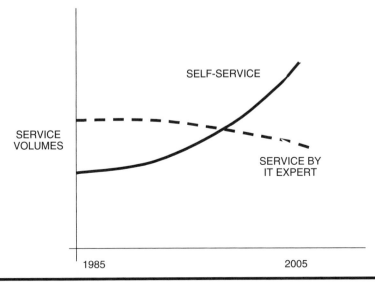

Figure 12.5 The Growth of Self-Service Should Not be Done at the Expense of Quality. But Without High-Tech Man–Machine Interfaces Quality May Bend.

may bend, as Figure 12.5 suggests. After all, Internet time is the aftermath of a distributed high-tech information system with any-to-any connectivity and a large and growing number of users of diverse background.

Distributed real-time system design raises application challenges that go beyond those that have been traditionally posed by mainframes and, more generally, with centralized systems. People who have been accustomed to address centralized processing problems and have not bothered to retrain themselves find it difficult to switch to working at Internet times. The culture is greatly different because, in distributed systems, scheduling decisions must be made by a number of nodes with incomplete information.

- From the perspective of a particular node, some resource requests could be delayed.
- Other resource requests may even not be seen, depending on the relative position of the node in the system.
- The challenge is to achieve predictability in network resource allocation, under these circumstances.

Able scheduling of traffic is essential. In real-time applications, computational correctness depends not only on inputs, processing algorithms, and expected type of deliverables but also on when the intermediate outputs are generated. A measure of merit in a real-time system is predictably fast response to urgent events as well as accurate scheduling. Whether we talk of process control, air traffic control, or business solutions, proper scheduling constitutes a measure of the number of transactions timely executed per unit of time and defines the degree of resource utilization at which proper timing requirements of tasks can be assured.

Another critical characteristic is stability under transient overload. Even if events overload the system and all deadlines cannot be met, the design we have adopted must still guarantee the deadlines of selected critical tasks. This, too, impacts scheduling, all the way from the conceptual framework supporting the adopted solution to the resources being incorporated, to algorithms and heuristics. We will return to this issue in Chapter 13 in connection with the business architecture.

12.6 OFFSHORING THE BACK OFFICE AND REAL-TIME CONNECTIVITY

The thesis presented by this chapter would have been incomplete without reference to the most recent trend of *offshoring*[5] back-office procedures. It matters little whether this outsourcing of office work is done for cost reasons, as is mainly the case in the United States, or because of both costs and a demographic crunch, which characterizes European countries. What is important, in connection with the thesis of this book, is that only real-time solutions can provide effective connectivity between:

- The enterprise in the *home* country, and
- Its office work executed offshore in a *host* country or countries

A 2002 study by Forrester Research claimed that a decade down the line, by 2015, 3.3 million white-collar U.S. jobs — more than 15 percent of them in information technology — would shift offshore to host countries such as India. India has three significant advantages in offshoring:

- English speaking
- First-rate technologists
- Low-cost labor

The fact that India is largely English speaking has made it a prime center for offshoring services. By contrast, China's primary focus is in the low-cost manufacturing industry, where, ironically, India subcontracts manufacturing jobs. The other two of India's advantages may, however, erode. A great number of Indian engineers and scientists have immigrated, and are immigrating, to the United States, Germany, and the United Kingdom, to the extent that India imports engineers from Vietnam. And, with shortages of qualified personnel, wages are rising.

Another study, this time by the McKinsey Global Institute, suggests that this process of offshoring benefits both the outsourcers and the countries involved in insourcing. That offshoring countries are beneficiaries is, up to a point, evident. But this is not a one-way street. Benefiting from low-cost real-time links, French companies outsource office work to Mauritius Island in the Indian Ocean. For the first time, this brought employment and wealth to Mauritius. Then, overspending developed into a lending boom and a banking crisis.

Contrarians to the idea that offshoring benefits the outsourcers say this is by no means a win–win formula. Stephen Roach, chief economist at Morgan Stanley, talks about a new and powerful *labor arbitrage*[6] that has led to an accelerating transfer of high-wage jobs to the detriment of employment opportunities in the outsourcers' home countries, adding to the bias toward jobless recoveries in Group of Ten economics.

By all evidence, offshoring has played a role in the fact that, with the 2003 U.S. business cycle upswing, it has taken longer than before for signs of a turnaround on the labor markets to accumulate. This means that *the employment threshold* — the growth rate from which employment rises — is now higher than it used to be. On the other hand, a study by the Federal Reserve Bank of New York describes the 2003 recovery as a new type of economic fact driven more by productivity growth than by increased employment.[7]

Ironically, the authorities seem at a loss on what to do next. Several U.S. states have moved faster than the federal government in trying to halt labor arbitrage. For instance, lawmakers in New Jersey proposed a bill to stop firms using foreign workers from fulfilling state contracts. The federal government, however, seems to have moved the other way, tightening up on the granting of visas that allow foreign workers to enter the United States for temporary employment.

- In October 2003, the annual quota for H-1B visas used by itinerant Indian software programmers fell to 65,000 from 195,000 a year earlier.
- The aftermath has been mixed signals. According to some accounts, this tightening has fed the trend to offshoring because of needed skills.

Office work outsourcing has not yet been a wave, but nobody can guarantee that it will not become so in the future. Today fewer than 5 percent of western companies are involved in offshoring, but among those who do outsource, between a third and a half of their information technology goes to insourcers. In essence, home-country IT experts are asked to establish real-time connectivity between their company acting as outsourcer and its chosen insourcer(s) of office work in order to practically eliminate their own jobs.

If the aforementioned 5 percent of U.S. companies is the bleeding edge of white-collar jobs, there is behind it another 10 percent believed to be committed to offshoring of office work, for which real-time links to insourcer(s) are (or would be) a must. As these references suggest, it is not that real-time connectivity is going to replace office automation sometime in the future; it is doing so right *now*.

Not only IT but also aeronautical engineering work goes offshore. Boeing, for example, is said to be outsourcing some design engineering work to a new center in Moscow, and this is causing layoffs in the Unitd States that are allegedly cutting deeply into Boeing's talent pool. Critics say that such offshoring practice may impact the safety and quality of Boeing airplanes.

The objective of this book is not to make value judgments about offshoring but, rather, to bring the reader's attention to the fact that real-time connectivity solutions are an inescapable step from this new trend, a different way of implementing office automation. This is true not only for technical reasons but also because that is the way society as a whole is moving.

What happens in the United States in terms of offshoring actions and reaction can become a trend setter because, according to some estimates, the United States today accounts for 70 percent or more of offshoring business. A distant second is the United Kingdom, where big companies regularly announce that they are moving office work and other white-collar service jobs abroad.

In late October 2003, London- and Hong Kong-based Hong Kong and Shanghai Banking Corporation (HSBC) announced that it was taking 4,000 jobs from Britain to India. In early December 2003, Aviva, the Norwich Union insurance group, said it was transferring 2,350 jobs, also to India.

How far can this go? Logically, there must be service-type limits to the shifting of service jobs overseas. For instance, jobs in hotels, restaurants, and health clubs are not easy to outsource abroad. But there is news of British patients going to hospitals in India for treatment, because the U.K.'s National Health Service is such a mess.

On the other hand, there are alternative pools of labor at home that could be exploited at a lower-than-going-wages level. For example, Citigroup has hired about 100 U.S. college students to do programming for $17 an hour. The bank reckons that, taking greater productivity and tighter super-vision into account, this is about half what it would have to pay compa-rable programmers abroad if every cost were counted.

The example I have just given is a different way of looking at the aftermath of implementing real-time solutions at home. High technology and the use of real-time to substitute old office automation approaches can see to it that several of the jobs currently going to low-cost centers offshore may eventually return. The likelihood that this would happen is propor-tional to an evolution in underlying technology, in a way that makes eco-nomic sense of putting off-shored jobs back into their country of origin.

There is the likelihood that because supply-and-demand costs at the offshore centers will rise as they, too, compete for skills in the local labor market. Information that has recently become available indicates that this is indeed happening with some offshore back-office functions.

The careful reader will remember that back in the late 1980s and early 1990s, companies such as American Express, British Airways, and General Electric were among the first to set up their own captive outsourcing operations offshore. According to certain accounts, however, some of these captives are now finding that their costs are up to 50 percent higher than those of independent third parties. This puts squarely on the table the choice between bringing these office jobs back to the home country or keeping them in a host country fully outsourced. The use of high technology can tilt the balance to the first of these alternatives.

The careful reader will also notice that outsourcing engenders, as well, major risks. The way the Basel Committee on Banking Supervision details them, these are: Strategic, reputational, and of compliance type, relating to counterparty, country, type of contract, other outsourcing agreements, exit from the outsourcing relationship, and lack of control over systematic risk in the industry the outsourcer belongs.[8]

12.7 NOTES

1. D.N. Chorafas, *Operational Risk Control with Basel II. Basic Principles and Capital Requirements*, Butterworths-Heinemann, London and Boston, 2004.
2. *Business Week*, December 1, 2003.
3. D.N. Chorafas, *Intelligent Multimedia Databases*, Prentice-Hall, Englewood Cliffs, NJ, 1994.
4. D.N. Chorafas and Heinrich Steinmann, *Intelligent Networks. Telecommunications Solutions for the 1990s*, CRC Press, Boca Raton, FL, 1990.
5. Offshoring is not synonymous with outsourcing, because several companies have captive entities offshore. On the other hand, several of these captives are profit centers on their own, independent of the mother firm.
6. *The Economist*, December 13, 2003.
7. E.L. Groshen and S. Potter, "Has Structural Change Contributed to a Jobless Recovery?", *Federal Reserve Bank of New York, Current Issues in Economics and Finance*, vol. 9, August 2003.
8. Basel Committee "The Joint Forum. Outsourcing in Financial Services," BIS, Basel, August 2004.

IV

PREREQUISITES FOR REAL-TIME SOLUTIONS

13

BUSINESS ARCHITECTURE
FOR A REAL-TIME
ENTERPRISE

13.1 INTRODUCTION

A modern business architecture is a functional description of an any-to-any communication system, designed to provide specific services to its users. This functional description is accomplished through a set of rules regarding connectivity and other conventions multiple products must utilize in order to:

■ Interchange communications
■ Be subject to system control

A holistic business architecture can be divided into smaller architectural units. These are the building blocks of the larger, more complex system. Compliance to architectural standards by such building blocks is very helpful because without such compliance it is difficult to draw a line around an application and say that we control everything connected to its performance.

For instance, business partners' value chains extend beyond supplier and IT solutions systems designed within the confines of a single system support, yet the seamless, efficient work of this value chain is to each partner's interest. Moreover, in many applications domains, data is distributed over a multitude of heterogeneous, often autonomous, information systems, yet the exchange of data among these systems must be effectively done and in a way friendly to end users. This requires an architectural approach characterized by:

■ A holistic concept leading to appropriate specifications
■ Interoperability, so that component parts and subsystems can talk to each other

- Linking the major applications areas together as necessary to meet objectives
- Solutions able to provide intelligence and reconnaissance for command and control
- A layered approach promoting flexibility and adaptability in reaching specific missions

The upper layer of a business architecture is oriented to end user application, including visual interfaces. This brings into perspective the need to define internal and external data mining and processing requirements of the business concepts characterizing the real-time enterprise. Its rules must link to the technical solutions outlined in the mid-, technology-oriented layer of the architecture that addresses general characteristics of applications, including workflows for business processes. To a significant extent, this is a conceptual level expressed in terms meaningful to both users of application systems and the technological supports: platforms, links, nodes, servers, and their software.

Platforms, links, nodes, servers, and their basic software constitute the lower layer of the business architecture. Some of them will be new devices. Others will have been there for some time. They are most likely heterogeneous. It is part of the mission of the midlayer to provide seamless connectivity.

Within this layered approach, solutions regarding the effective integration of supply chains and other intercompany and intracompany processes will have to be addressed in the most able manner, accounting for the fact that each business partner's information system is highly autonomous. No doubt, this is making the integration process a very challenging task indeed. An integrative approach to the three layers is presented in Figure 13.1.

For information, computation, and communication reasons, none of these three layers can be treated in isolation of the others or of the business processes served by the aggregate. Concurrent real-time action is required to support all business processes while, at the same time, business process reengineering aims at steadily improving the supports as well as to address new requirements that are continuously added.

But although a holistic approach to the business architecture is recommended, each one of these three layers has its design criteria that should reinforce one another. This is a demanding task. If we have just one design criterion per layer we have a relatively easy time finding a good solution. A business architecture, by contrast, can have more than 100 important criteria to meet at the same time. Therefore, optimization has to be multiparametric. The design challenge is most significant, both in functional and in technological terms.

Inevitably, part of the design challenge is that of taking care of incompatible and backward-looking legacy systems, which are more often than

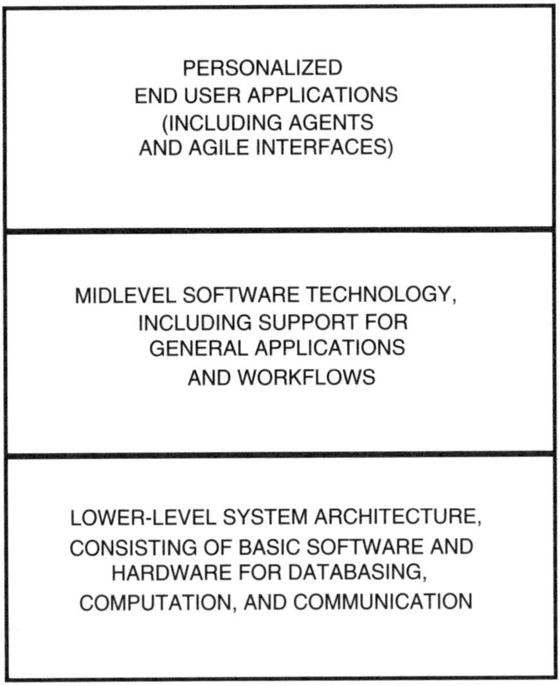

```
┌─────────────────────────────────────────┐
│  ┌─────────────────────────────────────┐ │
│  │          PERSONALIZED               │ │
│  │        END USER APPLICATIONS        │ │
│  │        (INCLUDING AGENTS            │ │
│  │        AND AGILE INTERFACES)        │ │
│  │                                     │ │
│  ├─────────────────────────────────────┤ │
│  │                                     │ │
│  │    MIDLEVEL SOFTWARE TECHNOLOGY,    │ │
│  │        INCLUDING SUPPORT FOR        │ │
│  │         GENERAL APPLICATIONS        │ │
│  │            AND WORKFLOWS            │ │
│  │                                     │ │
│  ├─────────────────────────────────────┤ │
│  │                                     │ │
│  │   LOWER-LEVEL SYSTEM ARCHITECTURE,  │ │
│  │  CONSISTING OF BASIC SOFTWARE AND   │ │
│  │    HARDWARE FOR DATABASING,         │ │
│  │  COMPUTATION, AND COMMUNICATION     │ │
│  │                                     │ │
│  └─────────────────────────────────────┘ │
└─────────────────────────────────────────┘
```

Figure 13.1   The Layered Structure of a Business Architecture

not the result of monolithic designs of the 1960, 1970s, and early 1980s. Today we know that modular hardware and software should be chosen in a way that speeds up the introduction of new services and features. This, however, was not appropriately appreciated in the past.

13.2   DESIGNING A BUSINESS ARCHITECTURE TO PROMOTE CLIENT FOCUS AND INNOVATION

Client focus is the ability to understand the client's needs and answer them in the most able manner. This should be done in an environment of intimacy in client relations, in a way that best suits the client's requirements at reasonable cost of execution. A company's policy should be one of high-quality services and of deliverables that are visible and appreciated both by the persons and by the companies to whom they are addressed. In finance, client focus is expressed through relationship banking.

- Online interoperability helps in making handholding much more effective.
- The analysis of client inputs also assists in reengineering products and services, promoting the drive for innovation.

A frame of reference that helps in sustaining a competitive edge is shown in Figure 13.2. Next to effective handholding, the effort to meet customer requirements in a consistent manner centers on steady innovation of products and services, supported through online interaction. *Innovation* is the ability to create business ideas that permit a company's core business to differentiate itself from that of its competitors, doing so in a way the customer can comprehend and appreciate.

Today, through agents and networks we can accomplish a great number of things that were simply not possible at an earlier time. An example from manufacturing is toolkits linked to the design department that can expand the client's ability to design what he wants and that can serve as valuable input to the firm — from R&D to sales. Car manufacturers follow this strategy by making it feasible for their client to design a custom-made car and to take delivery of that car within a few days.

Other notable applications include Web-based market research techniques that enable to reduce by almost an order of magnitude the time it takes to incorporate customer input into product design. This can be instrumental in influencing the pace and direction of technological changes across a product line and in delivering market value at practically every stage of product development.

A company's business architecture should support its business strategy by enhancing communication and collaboration among members of project teams and the clients for whom its products are intended. This is a basic reason why well-managed companies refuse to adopt a vendor architecture, choosing instead to develop their own.

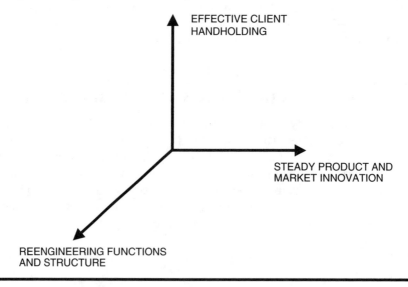

Figure 13.2 A Frame of Reference for Solutions Able to Sustain a Competitive Edge

Top-tier global financial institutions were among the first to learn how to face the increased challenges of being responsive to client requirements, including distant market signals. They focused on this issue because they understood that, to attract AAA- and AA-rated clients, they must have in place interactive handholding systems beyond a strong balance sheet and top credit rating. Because transactions done by important clients can be large and of a much longer duration than typical cash-type operations, relationship banking has taken on new aspects such as:

- The ability to assess market liquidity in real-time
- The tools to put into place a rigorous risk control solution (see also Chapter 11 and Section 4 in this chapter)

The skills necessary for effective client relationship management include not only product knowledge and proficiency in rocket science but also familiarity with tax laws and regulations. This is very important to specific segments of the client base and/or geographic regions of operations. To be worth its salt (and its costs), the business architecture should provide such services in real-time.

In the manufacturing industry, too, whereas production workflow focuses on internal processes, considerable management attention is paid to *relationship management* as an ongoing process, all the way to back-office routines that address through technology what used to be the paperwork of customer service requests. (See Chapter 12 on office automation.) Networked computers, intelligent software, and database mining see to it that a new style of workflow is reaching across organizational boundaries.

The business architecture should benefit from integration of Web application server technology with business process automation (sometimes called an *e-process*; see Chapters 15 and 16). This is still an emerging segment of customer-focused workflow technology. The core value is that of improving customer service through better visibility and management of customer-related processes across divisional boundaries. Another plus is the ability to integrate personalized customer experiences:

- Evaluating the effectiveness of touch points by means of alternative criteria
- Clustering customer communities to which a type of already personalized product might appeal

For instance, technologically advanced telecoms use service-call percentage tracking. One of the reasons is to track in real-time what happens and what *does not happen* but should have been happening. Another is to develop a means of gauging the cost of a system's *corrective maintenance* requirements. Also known as demand maintenance, corrective maintenance is a response to problems resulting in the dispatch of a service technician to a subscriber's home or a network component requiring attention.

On the average, cable systems have service-call percentages of 3 percent per month, but well-maintained systems feature 1 percent or less. On the contrary, for poorly maintained systems service calls reach 10 percent or more. Both reliability and cost should therefore be followed online in an accurate manner, using facilities provided by business architecture.

The careful reader will appreciate that what I am saying has more to do with top-tier organization than with technology at large. But, as it has been emphasized since Chapter 1, by all evidence *superior organization* is what will differentiate winners from losers in the next ten years. The technology is available to everybody, but not everybody uses it in the best possible way.

Here is a positive example. MAN Trucks, a German global manufacturer, has implemented an accident investigation system that sees all reported accidents being added to a database, routing them via workflow software to experts for immediate analysis. With 55,000 trucks in operation around the world, each valued at $130,000, the company has much to gain from:

■ Analyzing causes of failure
■ Avoiding accident recurrence
■ Keeping its trucks on the road

Aircraft manufacturers and airlines employ the generic term *datalink* to identify communications between air-traffic control and the airplane. There is a good deal of information being exchanged between the ground and the airplane, and for several years companies have used datalink diagnostic information.

On the ground, a maintenance system collects all of the faults on an airplane. Diagnostics work in real-time to separate cause from effect and reach a conclusion as to exactly what has failed and why it did so, consolidating this information into a report available before a plan's arrival at its next destination. This way, mechanics get ready to proceed with the repairs precisely when the plane arrives at the gate.

In the background of these references lies the fact that the type, amount, and quality of available information should be dependent on the sort of company we are and on the way we depend on analytics. Figure 13.3 conveys this message through four quadrants that identify types of companies according to their culture and the approach taken by their management in reaching critical decisions.

As another example, this time from the financial industry, at Deutsche Bank more than 100,000 staff members have access to its NetFicient content publishing solution. This system collects local knowledge such as legal and regulatory information, market updates, and advice on selling new products, making it available worldwide, internally to the credit institution, and to every corner where it operates. (See also in Chapter 7 the reference to Magellan.)

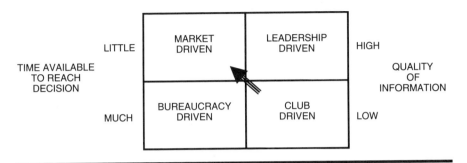

AMOUNT OF AVAILABLE INFORMATION

| | | MARKET DRIVEN | LEADERSHIP DRIVEN | HIGH |
| | LITTLE | | | |

(diagram: quadrants labeled — top-left MARKET DRIVEN, top-right LEADERSHIP DRIVEN, bottom-left BUREAUCRACY DRIVEN, bottom-right CLUB DRIVEN; left axis TIME AVAILABLE TO REACH DECISION with LITTLE / MUCH; right axis QUALITY OF INFORMATION with HIGH / LOW; top axis AMOUNT OF AVAILABLE INFORMATION)

Figure 13.3   The Type and Amount of Information a Company Requires Depends on Its Culture and the Approach Taken by Management in Reaching Decisions

13.3   CHALLENGES A BUSINESS ARCHITECTURE MUST OVERCOME

There is a long list of challenges business architecture must overcome to enable a company to break ranks with the majority of its competitors and to put itself in the forefront of new developments. Take investment banking as an example. Two of the key terms heard in the investment banking industry are *placement power* and *distribution network*. How should technology help?

If we are in the business of originating loans, underwriting or placing securities, and performing other investment-banking activities, we must have a distribution network that makes possible the turnover of assets at competitive pace by selling them to investors wherever they might be located. The business architecture under which such distribution network is developed must be characterized by several attributes, key among them being:

- *Globality*, accounting not only for topology but also for fluidity and shifting patterns of worldwide political and economic situations
- *Capillarity*, reaching every corner of operations and every potential client, to deliver investment financial services
- *Instantaniety*, the reality is that if one is a market operator or investor, one risks major losses if the reaction time is too slow — after the fact

Among the deliverables of a revamped IT technology, within the perspectives established by a modern business architecture, are event triggering, automatic calculation of position risk, automatic recalculation of entitlements on a cancel/amend basis, aftermath of the portfolio of transactions for long and short position redemptions, and so on. All this must be agent assisted to be cost-effective.

The online system should be able to automatically distinguish unsettled trades and open repos, withholding rates, local tax rates and their implications, and depot account rates. It should also be in charge of settlement and custodian information, integrating such data with notification and claims management. These functions are not new, but they have been classically supported 50–50 manually and by old batch processing — which make no more sense — because it is not a competitive practice.

The careful reader will remember from Chapter 10 the factual and documented evidence that there is a crisis in fund management. This has come about because technology budgets have been weak, the fat years in asset management were thought to last forever, and, above all, there was significant resistance to change in the investment-banking industry.

There have always been exceptional individuals and companies capable of moving faster and, through their policies, seeing further than others, without allowing slacks to develop. After salvaging Turkey from disintegration, Mustafa Kemal Atatürk favored replacing Arabic with Latin script. Once he made up his mind, there was no letting go. Steady pressure was exercised not only at the top but also at the bottom. Mustafa Kemal went to towns and villages and talked to the common man. Then, once engaged, reform was carried through within 6 months.[1]

This, however, is not the way the average executive operates. Organizations are made up of people, and people are often slow in making decisions and even more so in putting them into effect. Therefore, the metalayer of a business architecture should act as catalyst to rapid motion, providing management with the ability to spot opportunities instantly while always keeping in mind that business opportunities are often a by-product of mismatched conditions that are very short-lived.

Senior management can much better exploit such transitory conditions if the business architecture is flexible and knowledge enriched, able to handle online not only vital information from information providers, customer connectivity, and transaction execution but also counterparty claims, real-time position reports, and other event management activities.

The business architecture we adopt should assure that the company has a fast reaction time because, as already mentioned, mismatched conditions that create opportunities tend to reach equilibrium quickly and disappear. The architecture we put into place must enable our company, its managers and financial department. All three elements are to:

- Test new products on a trial basis
- Modify them as the market requires
- Be ready to transform them into a volume operation, to keep up with expanding demand when these products succeed

At the same time, as Alfred Sloan, the legendary chairman of General Motors, once suggested, we should have at our disposal accurate and timely information: marketwise, productwise, and financial. All three elements are vital because we must always be prepared to change if our product does not meet with market acceptance, or risk and return turns on its head. We must also be able to cope with the multiplicity of financial risks characterizing modern business (see Chapter 11). The design of our architecture must account for the market's rapid pace and global nature, which requires constant attention to:

- Position risks
- Credit risks
- Liquidity risks

The reader is by now aware of the fact that highly competitive solutions have many prerequisites. One of them is *open communications*. All executives, including the most secretive, should openly discuss their policies and problems through conference calls that contribute to *global oversight*.

Components of the business architecture should enable top management to police compliance and disclosure practices by business units as well as to accurately assess the risks they are taking. Members of the board and the CEO must have information at their fingertips to head off speculative movements in any unit of the firm that essentially attack the company's financial fabric.

The reason why I insist on these points is that, in my experience, in the majority of financial institutions this is far from being a present-day practice. To the contrary, reference data is often characterized by opacity, though practically all operational areas are impacted by risk events. Legacy software is not the only reason. Most off-the-shelf packages typically have their own models for reference data that are incompatible with the next application and could be governed by different naming conventions and incompatible data formats.

This makes much more difficult, if not outright impossible, significant analysis of events, particularly so if the response is needed in real-time. As we will see in Chapter 14, changing reference data upstream of trading and settlement systems leads to problems that may even disrupt the core business of the bank. This is often viewed as an IT problem only, but in reality it is an organizational issue. Systems and procedures failed to deliver an internally homogeneous solution.

On its own, a business architecture will not solve the problem I have just outlined, but the technological solution should be flexible enough to facilitate streamlining operations. A similar statement is valid in regard to retrofitting. Quite often, introducing new technology becomes problematic because of the *retrofit* issue. That is why smart architectural solutions divide explorations into two domains: new technology the company continues to look at and to phase in and existing technology that is being examined all over again in new and different ways.

Aircraft manufacturers provide an example. When they introduce something into production, they consider what they are going to do downstream with the airplanes currently in the field. Is it a retrofittable solution? If it is not, then the airlines wind up with split fleets. This means that the new airplane they received last month differs from the one arriving this month, which causes them pain and, in the longer run, works to the disadvantage of the aircraft manufacturer.

Another challenge to be addressed by a business architecture is that of close coordination between the business domain and the technology support area. Table 13.1 brings this issue into perspective. A sophisticated approach to the online exploitation of information elements can bring significant benefits, but is the architecture we have adopted able to accommodate new applications in an efficient manner?

- The business architecture must see to it that IT is aligned to the strategic plan.
- The strategic plan must incorporate a steady increase in significant IT deliverables, a process enabled through the business architecture.

Up to a point, challenges faced by a business architecture are eased by the fact that day in and day out the majority of corporate actions follow relatively predictable scenarios that, to a significant degree, can be automated. The key lies in the ability to distill from process experience a valid model that permits realization of significant savings and operational efficiency gains while remaining open to innovation. Last but not least, the business architecture should keep and exploit detailed audit trails, designed to improve management's capability of being in charge of operations.

13.4 THE INTERIM BUSINESS ARCHITECTURE OF A MONEY CENTER BANK: A CASE STUDY

Following a major acquisition, Bank "E" found itself obliged to integrate the IT resources of the two institutions. Incompatibility of platforms

Table 13.1 Synergy between Business Domain and Technology Support Area

Business Domain	Technology Support
Strategic Plan on products, markets, clients, line of business, financial resources	IT-enhanced opportunities for new products and markets and increased support to existing clients/products
↓	↓
Organization: business units and functions needed to realize strategic plan(s)	Information systems from backbone to direct end user services

and of applications software as well as major procedural differences made it impossible to extend to either of the two formerly independent banks the other institution's system solution. Though the board wanted the integration of the two systems to be done as soon as possible, this could not be done too fast — a reason that led to the concept of a *core switch*.

The object of the core switch was to provide seamless access from one to the other of the two system architectures, at the lower level of the adopted organizationwide integrated procedures. In a way similar to the concept described in Section 2, the system designers decided to project the midlayer as an aggregate of interoperating applications services supporting the overall business functionality of a virtual system.

In brief, the core switch was projected to provide a number of midlevel supports generally of a hybrid applications and technical nature. It was conceived as a scaleable means able to invoke technical features of either and both of the two incompatible information systems in a secure and manageable fashion, including the ability to:

■ Evolve over time in response to changing business needs
■ Take advantage of ongoing developments in technology during the period this interim business architecture will be in operation

The developers were conscious of the fact that this is far from being an optimal architectural solution. It was an approach with two technological leads, like the Byzantine eagle, but the sheer volume of an applications library of 35 million Cobol statements, plus the decision to start a new fully homogeneous IT project based on a modern business architecture, made unwise any extensive rework on either or both of the information systems of the banks prior to their merger.

In this sense, the core switch was conceived as a cooperating collection of *kernel services,* each of which provided a defined subset of overall system functionality spanning various hardware and software platforms. One of the main challenges was marshalling data between them to byte-swap between machines and to perform code conversion between ASCII-based and EBCDIC-based equipment. Data representation service was developed to support operations involved in this marshalling.

One of the challenges at the lower architectural layer (see Figure 13.1) was the fact that the acquired bank still had a Paleolithic centralized IT, whereas the surviving bank had long ago adopted a distributed information systems solution. These distributed resources had done away with the inefficiency resulting from a multitude of formerly centralized operations. They had also been instrumental in simplifying part of the processing complexity and eliminating a good number of incompatible IT resources formerly parked at the central location.

The designers of the core switch appreciated the aftermath of failure to fully exploit the synergies between computers and communications technologies of the formerly two distinct entities, but they did not underrate the challenge involved in effectively blending them to provide an integrative solution. Part of the mission of the core switch was to lay down rules defining what an application must do in order to be considered *conforming* and therefore able to interoperate with other applications supported by the system. With the adopted interim architecture:

■ Every application had to register its services with the core switch and then wait for requests for those services
■ Security routines were given the mission to verify that an application is authorized to make its services available to the aggregate

The designers paid particular attention to the fact that, by all likelihood, legacy applications would exist for at least several years and the system must be able to bridge the differences that existed between legacy, new internal developments, and purchased third-party products. The chosen approach was that responsibility for integration of new routines was shared between cooperating subsystems of the overall organization.

Adjunct to the lower layer of the interim business architecture, systems management routines controlled all types of resources to ensure that they were run with a cohesive view in this complex environment. The reference just made encompasses the entire IT infrastructure, including platforms, networks, databases, and applications.

Within this overperspective, one of the projects undertaken under the interim business architecture aimed to do away with overnight batch, converting operations to real-time positions and trades for several procedures including loan positions, client/book positions, and actual positions and claims generated in real-time (a new application). Another project focused on issues such as decisions for unallocated holdings subject to optional corporate action events. Advisories and a corporate action notification were sent to traders and clients.

One of the technical challenges was the seamless roll-in of new applications and roll-out of those replaced to enhance the existing functionality. Whether custom-developed by the bank or third-party products, new applications were provided with an interface conforming to core switch standards in order to assure ongoing co-existence between the old and new software within the adopted interim solution.

On an explicit request by the chief executive officer, particular attention was paid to real-time support for applications addressing credit risk, market risk, and corporate governance, for instance,

■ Default calculation date and value date

- The control of limits
- Exposure to foreign exchange rates and interest rates
- Effect of equity prices on the bank's portfolio
- Internal control, corporate audits, compliance, and legal issues

In principle, the new risk management and corporate governance projects were part of the new business architecture, but until its implementation they had to operate within the framework of the interim solution. This meant that they had to be designed with a dual objective, satisfying the new applications perspectives and compliance to the rules characterizing the proper functioning of the core switch.

The designers proposed and senior management accepted that this duality was a reasonable price to pay to do away with a long list of current ills. The latter included multiple records on legacy systems; a variety of incompatible client communication mechanisms; many entries for one use, as client instructions often require multiple rekeying; limited ability to track claims; and little integration between front-desk, risk management, and settlement systems.

In the background of the decision that led to the interim solution and core switch has also been the fact that corporate action processing frequently employed many highly qualified and expensive human resources. In the case of Bank "E," more than 900 staff members were involved in corporate action processing globally. The goal was to reduce this by at least 40 to 45 percent.

Moreover, as trading volume was projected to increase, the added complexity and tax implications of corporate actions on cross-border activity compounded this problem, leading in some cases to operational risk and reputational risk. A missed corporate action could result in major liabilities for the institution as well as loss of confidence among its clients. At the same time, delaying major upgrade to the combined IT resources of the merged banks made it difficult to provide value-added services to the clients. This essentially amounted to a competitive disadvantage that most definitely had to be corrected.

13.5 CONVERGING TOWARD IMPLEMENTATION OF A REALSPACE ENVIRONMENT: A CASE STUDY

The concept of realspace is not alien to the reader; we spoke about it in Part Two. The point has also been made that any-to-any interactivity brings into the picture important technical requirements, including the fact that it is not enough to operate in real-time location by location; it is also necessary to connect in real-time these distributed systems among themselves. This results in a realspace solution, which was the goal of the new business architecture designed by Bank "E."

Since the start of the project, the designers carefully laid down rules for seamless transition between the interim core switch and the bank's new business architecture. The realspace solution was projected as a high-performance market- and customer-oriented technological infrastructure and applications environment (see Section 2), whose services and products support all business lines and which may also be made available to business partners to provide competitive advantages and leverage fixed costs.

In this new business architecture, structures, processes, data mining, and processing were focused in the needs of the bank to strengthen client retention and commitment through market-driven quality service standards. The relationships with customers was +projected on service-level agreements with dynamic pricing for deliverables, to be made transparent based on individually costed services.

In the background of the client-oriented solution chosen lies the fact that Bank "E" is a global institution. Space should be no constraint to the modern enterprise. This fact had to be fully reflected in the bank's IT. Basically, a realspace implementation *is* the best example of Internet time (see Chapter 15), though the two terms are not necessarily synonymous. Bank "E" decided to use intelligence-enriched approaches for interconnecting its global marketplace,

- Making both time and distance seamlessly availabe to the system's end users
- Supporting experimentation to unearth trading opportunities at any time and in any place
- Providing to all authorized people database-mining opportunities for prognostication, pricing, and other reasons

These aims brought into perspective the need for dependability in system functions. Not only should a realspace system be reliable, but it should also be predictable. It must provide for a global synchronization of operations.

The new information system of Bank "E" was designed to operate around the clock in business time, in appreciation of the fact that a money center bank operates 24 hours a day. From New York to London and Tokyo, the sun never sets on the global company. When the financial markets open in Europe, they have not yet closed in Japan. When the exchanges open in New York, it is afternoon in Europe.

The role played by realspace is evidenced by the fact that dealers, traders, managers, and risk controllers in different financial centers need to communicate among themselves *as if* they were in the same place. As far as real-time information is concerned, it is a *zero space* alert IT users are after, and current technology can offer it to them. Designwise, the new system architecture differentiated between basic- and advanced banking services. According to the Bank "E" definitions:

■ A *basic service* is a simple standardized offering characterized by high degree of reusability in various applications.
■ An *advanced service* is built through the basic services enriched by means of add-ons, usually based on knowledge engineering.

Turning back to Figure 13.1 once more, basic services are part of the midlayer of the architecture presented in this three-layered structure. In contrast, the value-differentiated advanced services are an integral part of the top layer, which is end user oriented — whether the end user is the bank's manager or professional, a client, or any other business partner.

All basic and advanced services were designed to operate in real-time. Realspace characteristics were necessary because of the fact, a leading financial institution has to operate at any time, in any market, on behalf of any major customer. It has to trade in all major currencies, in all key financial centers and therefore be able to see global, regional, and local market patterns, mapping them in real-time into its system.

As the concept of the new business architecture evolved, the existence of realspace facilities led to *value differentiation* in financial services and provided the basis of a competitive edge to Bank "E." Although real-time and realspace access to databases is not the only factor promoting leadership in banking or in any other highly competitive industry sector, its role in this connection is vital. This is particularly true when the use of networks is enriched with knowledge-engineering artifacts.[2]

The principle is that high-capacity networks, distributed databases, supercomputing, algorithmic solutions, heuristics, and knowledge engineering permit *mapping the market into the system*. This is a necessary condition for many advanced technology applications as, for instance, taking the whole portfolio and turning it around. It is also a basic requirement for *global risk management*, including the ability to:

■ Track positions
■ Pinpoint risks associated to opportunities
■ Evaluate exposure
■ Develop hedging strategies
■ Do cross-market arbitrage

Presented with these five points, the board of Bank "E" decided that all of them are fundamental to satisfying the needs of a growing range of modern financial instruments and of addressing themselves to markets separated through tens of thousands of miles. The board, however, asked the system specialists to confirm in writing not only that realspace is feasible but also that it can:

■ Be achieved in a highly functional manner
■ Provide a realistic appreciation of the bank's exposure
■ Be implemented *within* the authorized level of expenditures

Chapter 15 will present additional background to the evaluation that took place at Bank "E" prior to settling on the design parameters of the new business architecture, particularly some of the issues relating to the critical review of the support to be given by the Internet. Chapter 16 will elaborate on benefits to be obtained through Internet time, identified as being a major cultural advantage for Bank "E."

In hindsight, one of the gains from the research that preceded decisions relating to the new business architecture was the fact that some of the best applications made along the real-time/realspace line of reference by leading financial institutions tended to suggest that there is a developing affinity between advanced business solutions and the way biological systems work.

One of the characteristics found to be common to top-tier information technology design and biological systems is that they are both pulsating. Another interesting finding has shown that by including some major ineffi-ciencies into an integrated system, the whole process may break down. As in the convoys of World War II, the slower ship sets the pace for all others, but few IT designers have the experience to appreciate that no chain is more reliable than its weakest link.

One more important reference is the fact that, because of the level of sophistication they involve, realspace solutions address themselves to differ-ent types of executives and professionals than the more classical applications. This is true both of the personality and of the functionality of the recipient of the online service.

Realspace solutions address themselves particularly to people of induc-tive reasoning who live and thrive in an environment characterized by ambiguity and uncertainty. (See Chapter 11 on risk management.) Such reasoning is *conceptual* in nature. For these people realspace is much more important than real-time because it permits the bringing together of diverse cultural environments, each with its own information and knowl-edge requirements.

13.6 NOTES

1. Andrew Mango, *Atatürk*, The Overlook Press, New York, 2000.
2. D.N. Chorafas, *Agent Technology Handbook*, McGraw-Hill, New York, 1998.

14

DATA MINING ANYWHERE,
AT ANY TIME,
ON ANY SUBJECT

14.1 INTRODUCTION

The proverbial long, hard look is the only acceptable answer to databasing and data-mining problems, including the dependability of storage media and survivability of the enterprise in case adversity hits its store of information and knowledge. Historical precedence provides an example. Consider the simplest form of storage on papyrus. In 391 A.D., the frailty of single-copy texts became apparent when fire destroyed the Library of Alexandria and its original manuscripts.

Centuries later, moveable type and the printing press would not only revolutionize the impact of the written word but also ensure its legacy through multiple copies. But though the printing press solved the single copy risk, the proliferation of paper-based records made much more complex the

- Updating of information elements
- Instantaneous retrieval of sought-out references

Delays in updates, retrieval difficulties, and costs associated with information element searches are highly counterproductive to the competitiveness of a modern enterprise. (See also in Chapters 7 and 8 the discussion on EIS and CIS.) The same is true of inefficient processing due to database reasons, particularly a fragmented and overlapping database infrastructure, heterogeneous forms and codes, and the slow-going process of exploiting this database. This results in high costs and in poor, undocumented decisions made by managers and professionals.

This backward-looking information environment is made worse by inability to automate processes due to legacy-type requirements for manual data entry. Non-real-time storage, update, and access to databases amount to a lack of leverage of internal and external data sources. There is, as well, further economic loss due to errors in the database and/or difficulties with online access. An example is management's inability to understand the credit risk of trading across multiple linked accounts because cross-references are nonexistent, defective, or possible only through batch processing.

It is not a secret that many companies not only manage their operating databases in an inefficient way but also continue to spend time and money on obsolete data warehouses. Also, they do not appreciate that such sort of service not only provides a very limited platform for cross-functional controls and standards but also is of very little (if any) support to:

- Business opportunity analysis
- Factual risk management action

As Figure 14.1 shows, knowledge navigation through an architecture that supports any-to-any databasing and data mining plays a crucial role to the business success of a modern enterprise. Knowledge navigation is an executive information system level, whereas the midlayer of straight through processing contributes to data storage (also requiring online database access) and reality online steadily enriches in real-time database contents.

The sense of the pattern in Figure 14.1 is that of an integrated data pattern. By contrast, a fragmented data infrastructure is a very poor reference in the context of market leadership, because it makes it harder to react to market change. It also inhibits a common view of the client base. Poor data quality and significant manual intervention correlate among themselves and to increases in head count. Furthermore, poor internal data structures are now exposed to clients by Internet commerce initiatives (see Chapters 15 and 16), and this definitely impacts the company's reputation.

All these reasons converge to emphasize the fact that organizations have a vested interest in developing, implementing, and maintaining a top-tier database that works in real-time. Management should be satisfied with nothing but the best solution — one that provides the company with online interactive database updates and data mining, enhancing the all-important flexibility in reacting to change, including cultural change.

14.2 END USERS AND THE NEED FOR REAL-TIME DATABASES

Quite recently, two major financial institutions looked at missing links in their technology and uncovered several interesting statistics. For instance, 80 percent of the work one of them did in directly supported foreign exchange operations was not addressed by the installed technology. At the same time, the bank's IT had placed emphasis on work that was rarely done by end users or considered to be rather unimportant by them. Among

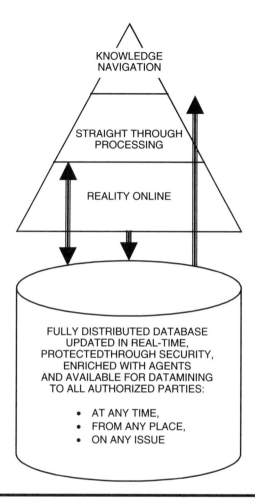

KNOWLEDGE
NAVIGATION

STRAIGHT THROUGH
PROCESSING

REALITY ONLINE

FULLY DISTRIBUTED DATABASE
UPDATED IN REAL-TIME,
PROTECTEDTHROUGH SECURITY,
ENRICHED WITH AGENTS
AND AVAILABLE FOR DATAMINING
TO ALL AUTHORIZED PARTIES:

- AT ANY TIME,
- FROM ANY PLACE,
- ON ANY ISSUE

Figure 14.1   The Critical Role of Databasing to the Real-Time Enterprise

the most important issues the IT auditing in the second bank unearthed
were that:

■ There has been no practical research on information held in its databases on customers and their trading practices
■ Research on turning points in the market's behavior was an alien
topic to its IT specialist culture (see also Chapter 7)
■ Data was still displayed in tabular form. There was no visualization
(see Chapter 7) to help traders, loan officers, and investment advisers quickly orient themselves, decide, and act.

The findings of IT audits in the two credit institutions were very similar
in the sense that they both presented serious database design and

implementation failures. Another similitude revealed by these audits was in terms of management's handling of whatever meager data became available. Both institutions filed this information in a time closet and took no corrective action. What was different was the postmortem to the IT audit report.

One of the two banks did nothing to improve its antiquated policies of database handling. If anything, its senior management became angry when presented with the evidence. To the contrary, the other financial institution immediately acted upon it.

The CEO of the second bank understood that data is an important company resource whose content should be exploited in a timely fashion. The CEO also realized that the whole of the bank's database should be mined in real-time. Having understood this issue, the CEO posed the right questions to the consultancy he hired to do the IT audit, including: What are the prerequisites? The answer was provided through a couple of examples. One focused on information elements relevant to selected end users. The other made the point that otherwise relevant information may be too little or too much.

Both are legitimate concerns for database design. For instance, due to information overload, too many companies are building ever-larger warehouses for raw data that they already have elsewhere. As a result, data keeps accumulating without critical analysis of the company's information requirements.

This is a widespread practice, and it is most unfortunate for the companies that find themselves in this situation. Some firms believe that bigger and bigger data warehouses are a problem created by advances in technology. They also think that there is one technology that can solve the problem single-handedly. Both statements are wrong.

The oversupply of irrelevant and obsolete information accumulating in data warehouses is not the result of technology but of inappropriate management decisions in regard to IT choices. Although it is true that agents can help sort out data requiring our attention for:

- Operational
- Legal/compliance
- Decision-making
- Management control reasons

The most critical issue is the establishment of appropriate management policies. For instance, the careful reader would remember from Chapter 6 the discussion on reality online. But is senior management ready to implement it?

In the background of this query lies the fact that as sensors become more sophisticated, they are also becoming capable of judging information content, forming ad hoc networks and communicating with databases and computer applications. But it is useless to talk of a knowledge-enriched technological world where objects around us take care of themselves if the company still has the old DP culture, with its mainframes, legacy Cobol programs, 3270 protocols, and other IT obscenities.

Any valid statement in connection to pruning existing databases and warehouses has in its background a radical change in IT culture. Agents may well be more careful than other people in assuring that good data is not lost, but old methodology would never allow the implementation of such service. A similar reference is valid in regard to data feeds and data mining, using agents to identify data feeds that:

- Are paid for but are not downloaded
- Are downloaded but not utilized
- Have to be filtered by specific criteria before loading to the database
- Have specific needs for identification, authentication, protection, or encryption
- Are available through better or cheaper sources, and so on

One of the financial institutions participating in the research that led to this book has set for itself a dual goal in regard to restructuring its databases: (1) provide real-time data mining capabilities to all of its people and to most of its business partners (on a "need-to-know" basis) and (2) target 50 percent reduction in data management costs through appropriate filtering, data compression, and, above all, emphasis on:

- Data quality
- Avoidance of duplications
- Order of magnitude reduction in errors

Filtering plays a significant role in the new economy. Collaborative filtering and recommendation engines on the Web have helped Internet commerce practitioners improve online sales. Other benefits have been derived by incorporating algorithms that create sophisticated customer profiles from analysis of customer buying patterns, price sensitivity, and other data. In advanced applications, algorithms embedded in such applications are used to adjust prices and focus on product lines.[1]

Several companies have also said that they are targeting an important reduction in IT resources required to support what has so far been duplicate data repositories. Some look at straight through processing (STP; see Chapter 5) as a means that will help in avoiding cost associated with increased data volumes required. Not only data storage, but also data maintenance requirements have to be optimized.

Top-tier financial institutions and industrial companies consider real-time databasing and data mining, with end user orientation, as part of their enabling strategic initiatives in the coming three years. Particularly banks look at this direction for support in fulfilling Basel II requirements.[2] My research has also revealed that a growing number of credit institutions have adopted a policy that new applications must use the choice of an integrative data model natively. In several cases, the remaining legacy applications employ adapters to translate to required format, preferably the new model.

Among well-managed companies, senior management keeps a close eye on return on investment. Time and again, ROI considerations have proven that companies tend to be processing rich and data poor. Whether we talk of database design or overall system solutions, one of the major errors lies in the junctions of three weaknesses related to information technology:

- Big IT budgets
- Long timetables for deliverables
- Trivial attention paid to ROI

Because of asymmetric approaches to cost and return, organizations end up by being "processing rich," for instance, 30 million Cobol statements, but "data poor," with databases thin in urgently necessary content and with lots of obsolete data. Moreover, Paleolithic IT concepts fail to provide operating executives and professionals with cross-database capabilities; data mining services seamless to the user; real-time updates of operational results; and responses to ad hoc online queries on assets, liabilities, P&L, balance sheet, and other financial information that help in improving corporate governance.

14.2.1 Storage Area Networks and Cost-Effectiveness

Costs matter, and companies should not shy away from using the principles of cost-effectiveness in every possible way. This has been at the core of meetings with major financial institutions that I conducted during a research project based in London at the end of March 2004. One of the subjects discussed during these meetings was storage area networks.

During the last decade companies have been confronted with fast-growing storage requirements, that put the issue of costs on the table. Since the late 1980s redundant arrays of independent disks (RAID) have challenged the dominance of mainframes, and their top-heavy database management systems (DBMS), because they present a significant cost-effectiveness. This accelerated in the late 1990s with network attached storage (NAS)[3] and storage area networks (SAN)[4] — both have the advantage of offering more sophisticated solutions than mainframes can provide.

According to their promotors, and many of their users, storage area networks can boost the utilization rate of hardware to as much as 80 percent, from about 20 percent in the one-array-per-computer world of directly attached storage (DAS). It is therefore not surprising that a number of competitors have joined EMC in the SAN arena — IBM, Hitachi, Hewlett-Packard, and Veritas.

Experts believe that SAN and NAS solutions already account for more than 60 percent of the $15 billion global storage market, and continue gaining market share. They are also featuring new design advances. For instance, EMC has introduced a solution known as Information Lifecycle Management (ILM), which is the intelligent version of SAN. Servers are attached not only to one cluster of arrays, but to several different classes of storage devices; some are high tech and, more expensive, while others are cheaper, but more dated.

Knowledge-enriched software moves data between these devices — a concept originally developed by EMC. Real-time information ends up in the high tech engine, while slow moving records and less vital numbers get moved down a tier. More valuable data deserves top technology. Sorting information elements by importance and priority, sees to it that the IT operations do not overcharge — this will happen if they store all information elements at equal costs.

As the London meetings revealed, many advanced projects favor the growth of SAN and NAS applications. In a computer storage market expected to be between $18 billion and $20 billion by 2008, by all likelihood the share of SAN alone will stand at 60 percent; that of NAS at about 22 percent, with the balance still staying with DAS. Senior management should realize that old technology, like DAS, is much more expensive than new technology, but at the same time, it is much less efficient.

14.3 INCREASING RETURN ON IT INVESTMENTS THROUGH DATA MINING

The primary interests of a financial institution are cashflow and profits. The pillars on which profitability rests are business opportunity analysis, risk management (see Chapter 11), and cost control. The latter is implemented through lean production and distribution services and an integrative approach to the evaluation of actual versus budgeted expenses.

All of these goals are reachable, provided the solution ensures the necessary means for analytical, continuous, and interactive assessment of all business opportunities, risks, and costs associated with each counterparty. It must also address an aggregate of clients, a market, cross-markets, and each financial product in a cross-product sense. Through the use of information and knowledge, risk spreads can be ascertained to keep a bank both productive and profitable. The typical problem, however, is that information needed to secure the future of a financial institution:

- Is locked in various heterogeneous databases
- The system as a whole is too slow to respond to queries, or too complex to access by end users

Some years prior to its merger with Verizon, General Telephone and Electronics (GTE) sought to correct both slow access and complexity in accessing its heterogeneous databases through an ingenious expert system known as IDA (Idea Database Assistant). Its first implementation was in California for billing and online answers to billing queries posed by clients, whose information is usually spread between incompatible databases.

Known as CALIDA, for California Implementation of IDA, this application was one of the first and most successful intelligent artifacts designed for database mining. The most impressive results in terms of response time obtained with CALIDA in connection of 31 types of ad hoc queries usually posed by GTE's professionals and the company's clients are shown in Figure 14.2.

Seamless, consistent, and easy-to-use approaches to database access are so important because data mining has the potential to effectively exploit information and knowledge stored in electronic, magnetic, and optical media to the greatest extent possible. The term defines the process of interactively exploiting the data resources that come from data streams, transactions, internal processing, and other sources, available either quite recently or accumulated over time.

The goal is to enrich the information available to managers, professionals, and business partners, for instance, to help them in business opportunity analysis, client handling, risk management, and cost control or to prepare

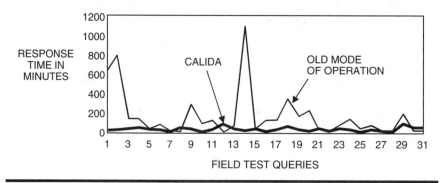

Figure 14.2 The Impressive Calida Field Test Results

for worst-case scenarios. Intelligent artifacts must be available to assist in the proper analysis and evaluation of a given situation, avoiding surprises through proper preparation. There are many domains where data mining is important, but time and again bankers tend to think that the following areas top the list:

- Marketing
- Relationship banking
- Better exploitation of business opportunities
- Risk management
- Design of new financial instruments
- Profit and loss by customer, product, and area of operations
- Cost control
- Repositioning the bank's balance sheet in case of crisis

Combined with algorithmic and heuristic approaches, data mining helps to improve the reach of marketing campaigns. Several banks and brokerage houses already actively manage money using data mining and advice generated by computers to help test hypotheses and to provide a significant level of confidence in decision making. But not all computer-based approaches offer commendable results. Banks with experience in data mining long ago came to appreciate that legacy software run on mainframes hides reality from its users. Quite often, little attention is paid to client needs because the search for information is imperfectly done.

Databases that can be interactively and simultaneously mined by several authorized parties provide important services, because in banking, as well as in engineering, product development is a collaborative process whereby professionals from diverse disciplines cooperate to specify, design, test, market, and maintain a product. The ability of any financial institution to compete in the global marketplace depends on how effectively its managers and professionals coordinate with one another.

Computers and simulation play a significant role in facilitating this collaboration, allowing professionals working on distributed workstations to share information and to interact closely and dynamically with one another and with the client base. But the technology chosen to reach this goal must be able to access widely scattered heterogeneous databases.

Giving people who are separated, sometimes by several thousand miles, the ability to collaborate on the same product and communicate via databases and networks is a definite advantage. Through the knowledge-engineering principle of *inheritance*, information held in different heterogeneous databases can be operated on by means of unique definitions made at corporate level. This makes efficient data-mining operations possible.

Efficient data mining is closely connected to the tools available for seamless access to the distributed information elements, either in a taxonomical way, following a tree and its branches, or directly through idea database principles. The following example gives a quick glimpse of both methods.

In a location-independent computing environment, users on the move like to be given at least two database-access capabilities: *fuzzy inquiry* and *quick inquiry*. An inexperienced person can readily retrieve the information through fuzzy inquiry. This means that the exact data element is retrievable simply by entering a few items that are approximate, i.e., some sort of description or general designation. The system should propose alternatives, helping the end user find what he is after.

Quick inquiry, by contrast, requires exact identification, which sees to it that information can be rapidly retrieved with precision and in a priority manner, e.g., via keywords. This will not be the typical way of handling customer requests for Internet commerce but, for competitive reasons, it has to be interactively available.

The provision of alternatives to data mining to suit the specific needs of different end users increases productivity and therefore contributes to return on investment. Another factor that impacts ROI is close watch over expenditures. This can be done in two ways:

- Efficient choices of database platforms and their DBMS software. Arrays in inexpensive disks are much more cost effective than mainframes for similar storage capacity. The purchase price of server-based DBMS is no more than a few months of, say, DB2 rental.
- Appropriate planning and control of storage capacity expansion rates through truly efficient utilization of available resources. One of the interesting aspects of the rapid growth of storage requirements during the last six years is that it leads companies to outsourcing part of their database in an effort to keep costs under control. Today, in the United States, database bandwidth requirements increase by about 40 percent per year (on average) and much more than that among new economy companies.

As should be expected, this rapid growth in databasing has created major problems to data centers, and a new industry of *storage on demand* has been born. Customers outsourcing part of their database look for savings not only in storage cost but also in salaries of system engineers, who command $100,000 per year. They also take this step in the expectation that during the coming years the demand for storage will further increase as advances in Internet infrastructure leads to greater databasing requirements. (See also in Chapter 4 the discussion on the virtual company and risks of outsourcing.)

In the background of this preference lies the fact that advances in Internet infrastructure and data mining are connected. They share the challenge of communications and storage bandwidth. How much bandwidth will be required during the coming years depends on:

- Applications
- Protocols
- The physical layer (links)

It is also dependent on design criteria such as efficiency, flexibility, scalability, and quality of service. In terms of network design, there is significant difference between *raw bandwidth* and *useful bandwidth*. In communications we now plan for terabit/second (TPS) capacity. In databasing terabyte storage capacity has become a reference unit: the greater the capacity, the more pronounced is the need for planning and control.

14.4 IMPROVING THE SOPHISTICATION OF INTERACTIVE DATABASE ACCESS

In the early 1980s, when the personal computer entered the daily practices of managers and professionals at desktop level, computer literacy consisted of knowing how to work with the (then) new engine, from feeding data into it to running a chosen program and getting an output. Though still necessary, this level of know-how is no longer enough. Competition demands more, including literacy in:

- Sophisticated applications
- Global datamining
- Potent analytical models

In a way, through the able use of technology, professionals become innovators and managers become aware of changes that are necessary in organizational structure. For managerial and professional purposes, the exploitation of database contents requires the end user's appreciation of on-line mechanisms for access to heterogeneous databases and the ability to use appropriate algorithmic and heuristic tools to exploit corporate resources.

As cannot be repeated too often, everything should work in real-time, and a system needs to be developed that addresses new database structures while accommodating legacy databases — those which have been developed over time and which contain important information but are not any more technologically advanced. Chapters 7 and 8 brought to the reader's attention that computers, communications, and software specialists must:

- Provide end users with visual tools able to solve complex problems
- Ensure higher-quality, reliable, and accessible information elements

■ Significantly reduce development time and effort to meet online a growing list of demands

Systems, procedures, and tools falling under these three bullets must steadily become more and more sophisticated, same is true of the end user's culture. Full exploitation of database contents requires not just remote access and flexible search but also insight and foresight by the end user.

With legacy systems, batch interfaces were written to exchange information between distributed resources and mainframes. Now the foremost organizations develop and implement knowledge-enriched interfaces that can better exploit facilities provided by intelligent networks, high-performance computers, and large distributed databases. This is the role assigned to knowledge-engineering artifacts entrusted with effective visualization, visibilization, and visistraction.

An integral part of this effort, particularly in regard to sophistication of applications, is an effective change in the way systems and procedures work, from the classical accounting orientation characterizing the majority of applications routines to a *customer orientation* with effective relationship management as the goal. In steering themselves through this changing environment, well-managed companies pay appropriate attention to competitors' moves and their meaning as they develop, in terms of potential loss of business.

To reach the objectives identified in the preceding paragraphs, the database contents themselves must be classified, identified, and organized in a logical, easily managed manner. Classification, identification, and organization are three general areas on which every entity should focus re-engineering of systems and procedures.

Classification of information elements is ordering. This covers everything from a client relationship, an account, a service, an existing product, or a market segment to assets, liabilities, and beyond. Everything in the database must be in its proper place and only in that place.

Once this principle is established, for every information element there should be a unique name or number, weeding out synonyms and homonyms that act as "noise." The purpose of identification is easy access by the end user in accessing all information related to a given query without loss of time for the user from superfluous machine cycles and data storage resources.

The third step, organization, is also ordering but on a different scale. The proper organizational work is a prerequisite to any activity, for instance, the aforementioned transition from an accounts and accounting-oriented database to one in which the pivotal point is the client relationship, known as a *client-oriented database*. This transition requires a significant amount of organizational work.

Contrary to what might seem to be the case when examined in a superficial sense, classification, identification, and rational organization are not that difficult. Successful work depends on proper skill and can be significantly assisted through knowledge engineering in the developmental phase and object orientation in subsequent implementation.

There is also the challenge of the transition from the old file-oriented data-processing procedures, the legacy system, to the new streamlined and reliable distributed databases. Figure 14.3 provides a snapshot of this transition from an application with Osram, the lamp manufacturer. The necessary approach has been explained in detail in a previous book, with practical examples from implementation in banking and in manufacturing.[5]

In my seminars, several executives ask why this orderly database restructuring is necessary. The answer is simple: because of the environment in which companies now operate and the competitive pressures that go with it. Let's face it: what we ask today from information technology is a great deal more than we did in 1990.

For instance, diversification and innovation in financial products and services, as well as in specific market segments, call not only for skills but also for a significant amount of information. Much of this information is in the bank's database, but management has to be organized to ingeniously exploit it, to bring into perspective both the occurrence and nonoccurrence of events.

As I have already mentioned, the nonoccurrence of events, such as transactions normally expected to result from customer relations but that do not, has become significant for financial experts. This is particularly true due to the fact that much of the power once wielded by banks has gone to institutional investors, the financial holdings of which are large and growing. But the identification and classification of nonevents are not that easy.

Absence, as such, can be quite clearly specified in a laboratory setting. In a market context, however, it is not always simple to conceptualize it in a meaningful way. Advanced tools for database mining allow professionals and managers to better understand the meaning and impact of nonevents. Through classification, identification, and sophisticated tools, comprehending nonevents and using obtained results in an able manner become much easier.

In other words, a sensitivity analysis becomes possible through identification and classification. The concept underpinning the use of sensitivity analysis is not just one of awareness to events and their impact. It is also a reflection of the fact that most decision makers get frustrated when confronted with ambiguous data, blurred pictures, or fuzzy events. Unclear meaning destabilizes them, although through greater sensitivity they can again be in charge.

Of course, by itself the effective mining and exploitation of databases are not going to change human nature. But the operations I am describing

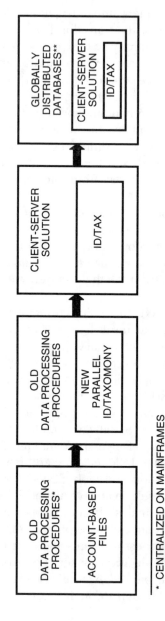

* CENTRALIZED ON MAINFRAMES
** INTERCONNECTED THROUGH A BROADBAND INTELLIGENT NETWORK

Figure 14.3 Phase-by-Phase Conversion from Fractioned Account-Based Files to an Interpreted Customer Information System

can help to focus attention on what is important, such as market situations and customer relations that may be atypical. Seen in a different way, sensitivity analysis is a technique for dealing with uncertainty in a decision-making process — from loans to trading investments.

If the value of a parameter is not known, then the analysis is repeated with alternative values that themselves are objects retrieved through data mining. A common form of sensitivity analysis is the worst-case scenario, which shows, for instance, what would happen to the borrower's ability to repay a loan under the most pessimistic hypotheses or conditions.

The message to retain from this discussion is that success in sensitivity analysis largely rests on data mining and modeling. The database contains information on historical relationships, management assumptions and projections, sales forecasts, pricing and cost data, and other factors needed in experimentation. A sensitivity analysis combines all of this information and allows for easier perception of customer behavior or other variables targeted through analytics.

Like sensitivity analyses, profiling is a multifaceted process that may be developed in different ways, since the objectives can also differ. Again, the foundations and documentation are found in database contents. The goals, however, range from being alert to underlying characteristics of a counterparty to a better-focused appreciation of market drives and the ability to profile client desires in order to customize banking services.

Profiling enables service providers to identify latent or evolving characteristics and to pinpoint important variations. Profiles in marketing efforts, relationship banking, cash flow, and profitability are among the most valuable references management can get out of mining database contents in an able manner.

14.5 DATABASE SOLUTIONS AND QUALITY OF SERVICE

No matter what the theoreticians may be saying, in practical terms the primary criterion for quality of services (QoS) is end user satisfaction. But neither quality and innovation nor customization of products always satisfies this rule. However, quality of service is instrumental in propelling one entity ahead of another.

Alert management uses service quality as the basis upon which to transform the culture of the organization. The challenge is to understand the end user's requirements, not only currently but for the coming years. The challenge is to do right now what is needed to be ahead of the curve in QoS.

Take banking as an example. Since financial products are designed ultimately to service clients, their design and their merchandizing have to meet not only client needs and profiles but also service quality expected from them. The more competitive the financial environment is, the greater the likelihood is that a service will have to be frequently enough redesigned to fit specific client demands, based on an obtained profile and QoS reference level. This process is an integral part of personalization or customization.

Data mining provides the raw material for analyzing the client base, making it possible to study customer information in order to identify customer characteristics that, combined with current market trends, would provide the specifications for redesign. Enriched with scoring techniques and market segmentation, this process:

■ Leads beyond the evaluation of a product's lifetime value
■ Makes it feasible to identify the interest that prospects, new customers, and mature customers have in the bank's products

Some financial institutions use this information for quantification purposes, such as the calculation of allowable customer acquisition cost for, say, the top 20 percent and bottom 20 percent of the customer base. Other banks rely on the same references to devise marketing campaigns, with different communication tracks depending on the segment to which the customer belongs (see Chapter 8).

One of the important quality-of-service characteristics in relation to data mining is the ability to test online, interactive hypotheses about extreme events. Usually market risk management models such as value at risk (VAR) work within the confines of a confidence interval, such as 99 percent. Extreme events, however:

■ Happen at the far-end tail of a distribution, at 10 or 15 standard deviations from the mean
■ Their detection requires stress tests that must data mine a golden horde of the entity's information elements, distributed in different databases (see Figure 14.4).

Quality of service, in the sense the term is used here, underpins quality of business planning, of administration, and of control; in other words, it is cornerstone to total quality management (TQM). Financial institutions experienced in TQM suggest that there exist three elements crucial to a service quality program, and these can be implemented only with explicit top management support. They are:

■ Motivation, through incentives, formal recognition, merits, and demerits affecting promotion and salary
■ Training, including both individual formal training and group interaction and role playing

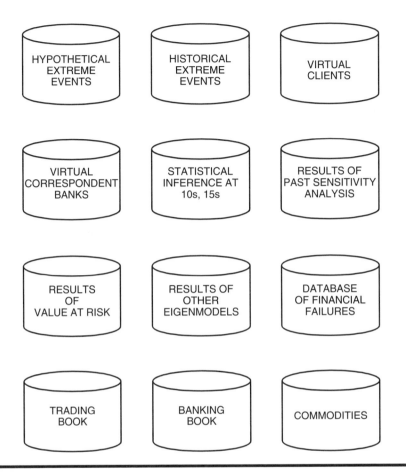

Figure 14.4   Hypotheses about Extreme Events and Database Mining Are Integral Parts of Quality of Service

- Measurement, through the tracking of deliverables, surveys, focus groups (quality circles), and other studies based on preestablished metrics

After such an MTM policy has been established and is policed in a consistent manner through data mining, there must be a follow-up on evolution of quality criteria to meet higher competitive standards. As this reference suggests, comprehensive quality management aims to make the best use of a company's customer base, products and services, and its human capital and technology potential.

Contrarians may well ask: If so much can be gained by using quality criteria relating to technology and its deliverables to answer marketing and other requirements as well as provide efficient support for relationship banking, why has this not been done by every financial organization? The simplest and most frequent answer to such query is because of resistance to change.

The forces against innovation are often stronger than those favoring it. Thus, any transition in technology, including quality of service, requires that top management fully understands the need for, and means of, ensuring cultural transformation among staff members. This is often the most serious hindrance to the effective adoption of new technology and the implementation of higher quality standards.

Most people who fear change harbor the impression that their positions will be threatened. Their resistance to change has a very negative aftermath on system solutions. As we have seen through practical examples, new technology has made it imperative that institutions streamline their systems, moving them all the way to real-time applications. Without the management of change, it is not possible to relieve technology-related pressures, which include requirements that:

- The architecture should definitely be open, permitting the integration of heterogeneous databases
- Solutions should not be limited by the location and size of the database
- At all times, every authorized person should have open access to all information elements
- Approaches being adopted must be both secure and reliable
- Resources attached to the network should be scalable to serve both local conditions and the global scheme

Moreover, to be competitive, effective approaches should feature minimal hardware, software, and personnel costs. There is also the requirement that, with 24-hour banking and fully networked resources, there should be no single point of failure. All can be effectively done if technological change is seen as a friend, not as a foe, with transition to more and more sophisticated system solutions implemented without upheaval in ongoing operations.

The members of the board, CEO, and IT management should appreciate that to innovate is to compete. But it is neither feasible nor wise to replace software wholesale every time new information technology emerges. (See in Chapter 13 the case study on bank "E".) The better way is to plan for change by achieving a balance between stability and innovation, which is instrumental in making change work. In terms of system solutions, such approach requires the ability to create and sustain a framework for change, envisaging the components that enter into the new solution and carefully defining the relationships as well as interfaces between the new components and the old.

This is particularly important in large organizations whose computer systems were built piecemeal over 50 years. Such legacy applications simply cannot be dismantled and replaced wholesale, no matter how much a higher quality of service is wanted. Hence, the transition in business architecture and the interim solution explained in Chapter 13 come into play.

An integral part of this reference to the need of integrating diverse and often-incompatible systems is the fact that, as far as information providers are concerned, specific attributes may only be available from certain vendors, though all vendors have proprietary data streams. Also, there exist many internal sources of database heterogeneity affecting quality of service. Quite often, front-desk description of a customer entity is quite different from that of the legal entity used for settlement by the back office. However, there is no excuse for such discrepancy, because while elements of partner data may be sourced externally, the majority typically remains internal. Streamlining is therefore both feasible and necessary, and it is part of the job of database reorganization outlined in Section 4.

Within the broader perspective of an effective holistic database solution, taxonomical classification and identification of information elements are most crucial. A rigorous data platform organization is a key business enabler, though it is also a major implementation challenge. A modern company must have the skills and experience to overcome the obstacles and see the benefits realized from such streamlining.

It would be superfluous to point out that commendable results require consistent understanding of key reference data entities, such as definition of a client and of an instrument, as well as multiple ways of referring to the same entity within the established taxonomical context. Another prerequisite is standards enhancing the ability to share data across applications, at any time, anywhere in the world, for any purpose. Still another prerequisite is end user training in the tools and practices necessary for effective data mining.

14.6 NOTES

1. The MIT Report, February 2001.
2. D.N. Chorafas, *Economic Capital Allocation with Basel II. Cost and Benefit Analysis*, Butterworths-Heinemann, London and Boston, 2004.
3. Promoted by the Network Appliance firm, NAS uses Internet standards to connect processing unites to storage arrays.
4. A concept developed by EMC.
5. D.N. Chorafas, *Integrating ERP, CRM, Supply Chain Management and Smart Materials*, Auerbach, New York, 2001.

15

CASE STUDIES ON INTERNET-INTRINSIC MODELS

15.1 INTRODUCTION

Because, as a result of globalization, the world has become one big market, the adage is that no bank, industrial organization, or merchandising firm can stay out of global networking and still survive. This may be an exaggeration, but at the same time it describes a trend that dominated the last decade and shows no sign of abating. Globality and connectivity are the driving forces behind the Internet. Web access is today what the telephone was in the post-World War II years.

To be a player in Internet commerce, a company must fulfill a number of prerequisites, one of them ironically being the freedom to fail. At least 210 Internet companies shut down in just one year (March 2000 to March 2001), and nearly 60 percent of them failed in the fourth quarter of 2000, amidst the great Internet shakedown. About 75 percent of the dot.coms that have closed, 157 companies, targeted a consumer audience.[1]

The subject of this chapter is not the dot.coms but what Internet technology can provide as well as how fast the Internet's contribution is changing and why. Whether positive or negative, the practical examples contained in this chapter are a prerequisite to the broader discussion on Internet time and the Internet ecosystem in Chapter 16, the latter subject having been introduced in Chapter 3. Notice that by 2004 barebone references to i-commerce have faded from the headlines. This is in part because Internet commerce is largely taken for granted and because the emphasis on what can be done with the Internet is moving from consumers to business-to-business (B2B) connectivity.

The sort of computer-based wireline commerce that was high tech in the late 1990s is now usually referred to as *traditional i-commerce*, whereas innovation involves wireless, image/voice, and other emerging technologies.

More developments are on the horizon. At the same time, in the wake of dot.com crashes, i-commerce as a concept also brings an amount of useful skepticism.

■ Was the potential of i-commerce oversold?
■ Could it really have delivered all of its promises?

It is more rational to answer such queries through practical applications examples and their deliverables before talking about the Internet's impact and most-likely evolution, which is the theme of Chapter 16. The subject chosen as general background in this chapter is financial markets and financial services with the Internet and, more generally, networks. This discussion brings up several questions:

■ Have networks enabled new services that are up and running?
■ Are these services continuing to revolve? In which way?
■ What has been offered by online access to businesses that has changed the way we seek out information and services?
■ How bad is the situation in connection to Internet security and cybercrime?

In November 2003, an article in *The Economist* described cybercrime as "not a technological problem, but an economic problem." It then went on to say that security has to be built into software from the beginning; patches are just what their name suggests.[2] Security is a priority issue related to Internet governance. (See chapter 16 for additional issues.) A valid approach to the problems of Internet, including insecurity, is to focus both on accountability of software vendors and on the Internet's users (more on Internet security in Chapter 16). The time has come for legal rules of universal reach to discourage bad behavior and to ensure that criminals can be traced and brought to justice. This and other issues are fundamental to the banking industry and the banking public. Therefore, it is under this perspective that this chapter should be interpreted.

15.2 INTERNET TECHNOLOGY TOWARD 2010

A discussion of technology's applications will be nearly meaningless if it limits itself to what has happened in the past. Perspective can only be gained by looking into the most-likely future, albeit based on some of the past developments and capitalizing on ongoing trends. This dual approach helps to provide insight. For instance, current projections are that *prior to 2010* almost everything will be Internet connected. The computer, big or small, as we know it today may well disappear as a self-standing entity.

Computing devices will integrate by the millions into other machines and *connectivity* will be the overriding competitive advantage.

Hence, our notion of a computer and what we do with it has to change. The way to bet is that pervasive networks — the so-called *object Internet* — will dominate; nanotechnology devices will play a top role; and sensor technology, based on smart devices able to sense almost anything, will come of age at low price (see Chapter 3 and Chapter 6).

Moreover, practically all content technologies will be digital, models will become an integral part of the infrastructure, and knowledge engineering applications will be seamlessly integrated into almost every device, product, and system. In terms of design and implementation, emphasis will be placed on:

- Close customer–supplier integration
- Lower and lower costs at device level
- Increasing efficiency in operations
- Compliance to regulations, which will become automatically monitored

Practically all of these bullets are positive news regarding the Internet and its evolving characteristics. Delivery of customer services through the Web and online collaboration between businesses necessitate networks that are able to deliver on the promise of greater efficiency across the value chain.

Effective, and hopefully secure, B2B solutions can revolutionize the way organizations do business. Through online procurement, the cost of processing a purchase order is expected to fall dramatically (see Chapter 5 on STP). Agent assistance to self-service access will lower the entry point-of-service providers while increasing end user satisfaction.

Figure 15.1 outlines the successive layers of end user interface midware, and basic support services in an Internet connection, taking an i-banking application as an example. (See Sections 3 to 6 for more detail.) The weakest link to these nine layers is security. Practically every month there is a glorious announcement about having solved the security challenge, and then hackers and other intruders see to it we are back again at point zero.

One of the reasons for this fallback on security is that it is not easy to implement radical solutions, as these contradict some of the principles of free speech and human rights. For instance, proposal no. 4 for Cisco System's shareholder meeting of 2003 was the recommendation that the board prepare a report to stockowners on Cisco's hardware and software products that can allow monitoring, interception, keyword searches, and/or recording of the Internet, or act as a firewall:

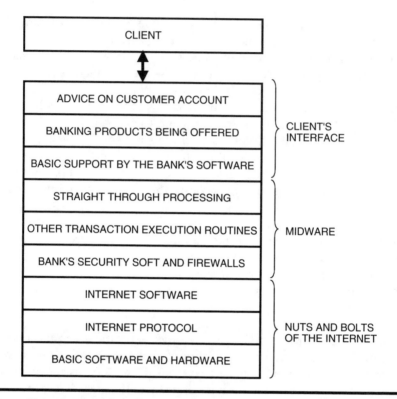

Figure 15.1 Support for All Internet Products and Services Follows a Layered Architecture, with Security the Weakest Link

- By which selected Internet traffic can be prevented from reaching its addressee outside the country of origin
- Or by which downloading of information from selected sites outside the country of origin is prevented

Cisco's board reacted against this proposal, mainly for reasons of freedom of speech. Similar action has been fielded by other high-technology firms, and this is only one example of existing constraints. On the other hand, because of insecurity, entitlement, and resistance to change, it is no less true that i-commerce has not yet achieved its full potential.

Another reason that Internet commerce has not gone higher is what I call "reinventing the past." The focus of i-commerce at the outset was on automating tasks that could be done while the customer was sitting at a computer. This involved only some of possible aspects of i-commerce. Such concept, which largely continues, has put to i-commerce a self-imposed limit.

As long as Internet-based transactions continue to be limited by the above constraint, there will be a relatively low ceiling to the way business gets done and costs are carried. Moreover, one of the major missing links is the automatic connection between sales orders and, on one hand, their execution through STP (see Chapter 5), and, on the other hand, their physical materials handling. This is now approached through smart materials,[3] which, by all likelihood, will be one of the pillars of the Internet ecosystem (see Chapter 16).

It is projected that the use of powerful, very low-cost microsensors and antennas will make it possible for essentially any object to be smart and interactive, altering the current concept of Internet commerce. This is a very important development (though somewhat behind schedule) because, even in an i-commerce world, businesses incur a large portion of their costs managing physical assets.

Toward the end of this decade, the truly new-generation Internet will be that which can digitally handle physical objects, moving them around and managing them at significantly reduced costs. Such a solution will evidently increase yield and drive efficiency, provided several milestones are crossed in an able way.

For instance, at Accenture Technology Labs, the Sensor Aggregation Model is an application that receives data from tiny sensors through a wireless connection; transforms millions of discrete sensor snapshots into a cohesive, integrated view of the environment; and then builds visual models of the data. The latter reflects the current real-world situation.

The company believes that, in practical terms, this would be useful anywhere management control action must span tens or hundreds of miles across varied and often inaccessible terrain. An example is provided by oil pipelines, which are vulnerable to different threats at any point along the way. Delivery of goods through a wide geographic area in the aftermath of Internet commerce is another example. Figure 15.2 provides the pattern of this Internet ecosystem (see Chapter 3 and 16), which rests on:

■ Broadband telecommunications, fixed wire and mobile
■ Virtual company concepts (see Chapter 4)
■ A range of possibilities for virtual office implementation offered by mobile telecom links

The aftermath will be seen not only in the world of services, which has been the Internet's first target, but also in the movement of physical goods from plants and warehouses to a final destination. That's the landscape in which reality online (see Chapter 6) and microminiaturization of sensors will make most of their impact felt.

Stanton J. Taylor believes the combination of tiny smart sensors and Sensor Aggregation Models could offer important advantages in handling any physical asset: equipment, plant, or far-flung facility that is difficult to monitor continuously but cannot be allowed to fail. The physical delivery

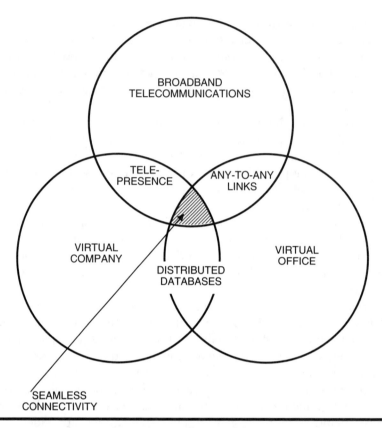

Figure 15.2   An Internet Ecosystem Is All Around the Virtual Company, Capitalizing on Cost Effectiveness of Global Telecommunications

of goods ordered through i-commerce could be seen as a giant delivery plant, in which smart-sensor technology will be instrumental in providing a major upgrade.

Another prototype at Accenture Technology Labs is that of Sentiment Monitoring Services. It helps in using Internet information sources to gauge public perceptions of various features, products, brands, or supplier organizations. Combining a search agent and a perception engine, this prototype:

■ Searches preferred web sites or newsgroups for opinions
■ Reads electronic content in multiple languages
■ Interprets the sentiment of the text being read toward the product or service
■ Analyzes the results quickly and continuously, providing vital information to its user

This process of providing up-to-the-minute market behavior information and rapid feedback on any timely development like new product launch is the alter ego of full automation in physical handling. It is a marketing tool that might eventually change the type and perception of services provided by the Internet. Let us, however, always keep in mind that the great challenge of security has not yet been addressed in a rigorous way, and if this continues, it may well become the stumbling block of i-commerce and i-banking.

15.3 INTERNET-INTRINSIC BUSINESS MODELS

As far as developments in this decade are concerned, what the reader should retain from the discussion on Internet-assisted marketing in Section 2 is that today research laboratories, industrial companies, and financial institutions are actively working on solutions that are breaking new ground. The possible evolution of new services should be seen in conjunction with online database mining and real-time analysis of incoming data streams for marketing reasons.

Well-managed companies realize that daily ongoing operations bring into their database a wealth of market and sales information as well as of client behavior patterns. This serves well marketing, which is a strategy of seduction and therefore requires:

- Customer profiling
- Sensitivity analyses
- Affirmative policies

All three bullets identify processes vital in banking and merchandising as well as in many other industry sectors. The foremost objective of marketing is repositioning. The crux of a repositioning program is undercutting an existing product, concept, or service, whether this is a company's own or a competitor's. Repositioning is done by offering a better alternative than what the competitor can offer.

Long years of experience in marketing demonstrate that the winning product is not necessarily the ideal one. It all depends on the functionality and appeal of other products and services that are in the race, on their costs, on the competitors' marketing strategies, and on the ingenuity embedded into the sales effort, which can make or break a product and eventually a company.

In 1954, the only outfit with a commercial computer that could be installed and run on customer premises was Remington Rand. I refer to the famed Univac story. Competitor IBM had no comparable computer to offer, commercial or scientific, since Thomas Watson, Sr., had decreed that computers are toys that only university professors like to play with.

But Watson was no one-track mind. He saw his mistake early enough, set up an efficient marketing force, endowed it with applied science specialists, and started selling computers well before it had one that was deliverable. The strategy was that the vendor could not and should not deliver a computer before the customer was ready for it. Applied science specialists were there to help the client in getting ready. IBM's marketing strategy worked to perfection.

This was a masterly reconnaissance of the direction the American business environment was moving. In general, an accurate reconnaissance is very difficult because marketing largely deals with ideas, concepts, and beliefs. The reader should also keep in mind that marketing battles are not usually fought in an open landscape; they are fought inside the minds of product designers, traders, salespeople, and prospects — current customers and new ones. And, at the end of the day, it is customers who count.

As a connectivity medium, the Internet may be the proper landscape to fight future marketing battles. Every industry today finds itself confronted with competition, both from traditional players and from emerging ones. Coupled with this is a more discerning, and less loyal, customer base. Thus, the key to survival is:

■ Connectivity to head off marketing headwinds
■ Quality at affordable cost
■ Real-enough time information about customer wishes and trends

In regard to the first and third bullets, able use of the Internet should be instrumental in ensuring that the client base is fenced and enlarged (see Chapter 8 on CIS). The customer should be not only pleased enough to maintain an ongoing relationship with a bank but also willing to refer friends and family. This is why it is so important to become familiar with the Internet's new hues and capabilities — these may present advantages.

Some U.S. experts advise that Internet-intrinsic business models are needed to capture the estimated $300 billion opportunity in i-commerce and its more than $500 billion latent global potential. This, however, requires a growing amount of customer contact, including confidence in the relationship, and building up business confidence calls for:

■ Reality online in data capture (see Chapter 6)
■ Rapid identification of customer needs
■ Merchant-specific information
■ Product evaluation and brokering
■ Counterparty verification prior to a transaction
■ Negotiation and confirmation
■ Straight through processing of the transaction (see Chapter 5)
■ Payment and delivery
■ Dependable security and privacy services

Each of these bulleted phrases poses a challenge, but their fulfillment can help the emergence of new dynamic marketing procedures and markets with interactive supply chains and distribution channels beyond what we have known so far. Any solution should account for the fact that there can be aftereffects.

A positive one, for instance, is that because of any-to-any networking provided by the Internet, the financial market will most likely become more liquid. Experts think that, within a broader i-business perspective, trading volumes will increase as wholesalers and retailers intensify their sales of services and wares and markets are open all the time.

From a different viewpoint, however, intermediaries may become the losers. For example, from a financial instruments perspective, auction markets for initial public offerings and other traditional investment banking products will be recast as customers buy directly from issuers. At the same time, both risk taking and the need for risk management will increase, a process that is underlying the need to develop and market sophisticated opportunity analysis and risk control tools.

This is a likely scenario. The *ifs* connected to it are largely based on whether or not customers will become increasingly knowledgeable to deal online and to feel more comfortable in migrating toward the Internet for transactions. For instance, in finance, although computer programs may provide good money-management guidance, business is based on confidence and building up confidence will be the determining factor.

Another one of the *ifs* concerns the financial industry's ability to capture market potential at low cost. To do so, institutions will need, to a significant degree, to dismantle current, expensive sales, marketing, and product promotion infrastructures. Instead, they will have to:

■ Gain the customers' confidence that online solutions are dependable, secure, and fair in financial terms
■ Build a reliable, direct pipeline to customers, concentrating on distributing current financial products while creating new ones

Still another factor critical to the acceptance of Internet-based financial transactions is that governments establish rules and regulations to make financial institutions and their operations more open and transparent than ever before and to severely punish computer crime. Transparency is much more important than in the past, as it is expected that financial institutions, individual investors, and the governments themselves will make a lot of mistakes in the new world of Internet finance as they move up a learning curve. These mistakes are of an operational risk type and must be identified and corrected in a way that helps to increase business confidence in the online system.[4]

If, and only if, all goes well, a net result of this scenario is that more liquid and open markets will give investors the power to drive change. They will reduce costs, add value, break down bureaucratic barriers, drive to restructure workforces, and oblige firms to build an information infrastructure with focus on competitiveness. Notice, however, that cornerstone to this transformation is the existence of an ethical code for cyberspace by which everybody should abide and on which everyone can depend.

15.4 CASE STUDIES ON INTERNET USE IN RETAIL BANKING

Internet banking is generally tuned to the profile of the average Web user who is college educated, male rather than female, and earning a relatively high income. These demographics account for the prevalence of online technology in the banking industry and are the motor behind financial services advertising focused on a market thought to be the more promising.

To give a realistic appreciation on how financial institutions joined the Internet, let me start with a couple of examples from early electronic banking history. At the middle of the 1990s decade, Internet page www.bankerstrust.com, set up by Bankers Trust (BT), had an audience not only in the United States but also in Europe, Australia, and Asia. This Internet page usually carried:

- Internal news
- Financials
- Press releases
- Department sites
- A phone directory

It also supported internal discussion groups. Other services included BT client to external client connectivity, deal entry, gateways, and an authentication server programmed to increase the user's perception of site dependability. There was a template-driven Web page for publishing purposes.

In about the same timeframe, the Internet site of the Bank of New York included fact sheets, marketing, and stock transfer services. Another implementation by a major institution application addressed human resources, banking professionals, institutional investment management, mortgage banking, and personal banking. Practically every institution had its own approach to contacting clients and potential clients online.

In these Internet-based applications, the Bank of New York distinguished itself from other financial institutions by the fact that it had set in motion a project-approval process. This included *project justification*, with emphasis on cost reduction, revenue generation, and relief from competitive pressures. Impact analysis of Internet servers included hits, data transfer rates, data transfer volume, communications lines occupancy, and so on. Because costs matter, cost evaluation of Internet moves went all the way from development to implementation, upkeep, and other maintenance chores.

There was a security review, with approval depending on project scope and associated privacy/security considerations, a public relations and investor relations review, and a legal review. Other reviews and authorizations focused on technical issues, assuring consistency of interfaces, evaluating contents, examining navigation coordinates, migrating new pages to production, and monitoring utilization of servers and communications lines.

Another example from the early i-banking applications comes from the Bank of Nova Scotia, in Canada, which established its Internet site in January 1996. This seemed to be rather successful when measured in hits per day, according to then-prevailing standards. Services included financial results concerning the bank, production information, location of branches, and location of ATMs as well as:

- Interactive models for budgeting by clients
- Models for saving and investing by clients
- Support for "what-if" calculations by clients

A discount brokerage subsidiary of the Bank of Nova Scotia posted pages on stock charting and portfolio monitoring. The retail-banking operations supported pages for student loan application, mortgage qualification, and Visa card application. Because of security reasons, like so many other institutions, the Bank of Nova Scotia did not feature transactions on the Internet.

Contrary to brokers, the policy of commercial banks and retail banks has been to tune their approach to i-banking mainly to information provision and advertising. There are, however, exceptions, some of which have been successful whereas others have not. An example of an unsuccessful Internet banking offer has been Wingspan, by BankOne, which is rumored to have cost $500 million. A successful example is that by the Imperial Canadian Bank of Commerce (CIBC).

Contrarians say that even if Canadian Imperial Bank of Commerce is one of the leaders in Internet banking, about 90 percent of the credit institution's sales still come from the branch office network, whereas the Web is used mainly for client access and lower-level operations. However, 10 percent of a big bank's business is a respectable number.

This figure of 90 percent to 10 percent should be kept in mind when planning Web sites, because it identifies the fact that Internet banking competes with brick and mortar as well as with telephone-based banking, even if it tends to address the lower base of the client pyramid. Particularly targeted through the Web is the retail mass market. By contrast, business lines for institutional clients are handled through branches and special representatives because they require a high-grade skill and handholding and are heavy in technology investments, including specialized bank-to-client links.

This being said, the use of Web sites at Canadian Imperial Bank of Commerce seems to have been fairly successful, particularly because senior management decided that it would not go for a "me, too" approach. Correctly, the credit institution decided that the Internet-based solutions had to be focused. CIBC's client-oriented Web applications are:

■ Transaction engines
■ Content management
■ Personalization
■ Customer support
■ Site analysis
■ Campaign management

The infrastructure taken into account in postmortems and return-on-investment (ROI) studies includes marketing campaign, software development, carrier, hosting center, routers, Web server, application server, database server, and support services. CIBC has found that digital message and transaction volume expands at a fast pace. The bank can do 200 to 300 phone calls per day, but it can handle 200,000 to 300,000 electronic messages per day. This means three orders of magnitude upgrade in message exchange potential.

Sometimes, a success story in one country turns on its head in another, frequently downgraded by local culture. In early 2002 Britain's spunky Egg PLC, promoted by Prudential, a major insurer, was winning hurrahs after it emerged as one of Europe's rare profitable online banks. Egg attracted a lot of customers with:

■ Relatively high interest on deposits
■ Cheap rates on mortgages
■ Offers of 0 percent interest for six months for new credit card customers

From a standing start in 1998, Egg's British customer base grew rapidly, to 1.35 million in 2000 and 3 million at the end of 2003. It earned an estimated $120 million in its home market in just one year, 2003. But the strategy that has shown Egg the way to success in Britain apparently did not speak French. In January 2002, Egg's chief executive Paul Gatton announced he was buying a small online bank across the channel that he would use to hatch an Egg clone. Since then, everything that could go wrong has gone wrong.

The French did not like Egg's credit cards and rejected its banking fees, which they regarded as too high. Even Egg's advertising campaign backfired. After a year of hard sell, Egg had attracted only 140,000 French customers. Its Paris-based operation lost $118 million in the nine months through September 30, 2003, raising questions about the British bank's ability to follow through on plans to expand elsewhere in Europe.[5] Internet-intrinsic solutions are by no means a sure thing.

15.5 RETHINKING THE HORIZON OF INTERNET RETAIL BANKING SERVICES

In corporate America today, the use of the Internet is not an event but a process. Like manufacturers and merchandisers, many bankers have been restructuring their computers and communications solutions to make the best use of facilities provided online, with the majority appreciating that time is of essence because networking has become so popular.

Contrary to transactions concerning other wares, however, Internet financial services must account for the fact that in a way similar to the supply with foodstuffs of a major city like New York or London, the Internet is owned and managed by nobody and by everybody. Moreover, Internet banking is still a model with which few credit institutions are truly comfortable. It is a process that might be misleading in regard to benefits and risks, as Section 4 has shown.

Leaving aside the issue of security, briefly discussed in the Introduction and in Section 2 (which is a major subject but does not enter the scope of this book), financial professionals, computers, and communications specialists must appreciate that although content is important, it is only one of the salient problems. Technology is an enabling mechanism to do something else. It is not an end in itself. The crucial question is: What does the bank aim to accomplish on the Internet?

To a substantial extent, today the financial industry is pretty clear what the emerging technology is going to be. What is still a puzzle is how one should use this technology to make profits. This evidently calls for strategic guidelines that must be established at board level and clarified by the chief executive officer. The board and the CEO — *not* the CIO alone — should answer the queries:

- What do we wish to reach online?
- What we want to be as an Internet bank?
- Where in cyberspace we want to compete?
- What are the services on which we can be strong?
- How are we going to produce and deliver these services to remain a low-cost producer and distributor of added value?

There are no linear answers. First, a bank must clearly define its product, market, and profit goals. Second, it must focus on which road will taken to that destination. The Internet is a generic term; it is not a precise answer, nor is it a drug that can cure other organizational deficiencies. This is true, incidentally, of real-time applications as a whole.

Well-managed companies appreciate that generic terms come and go, but a precise cost–benefit analysis of products and processes requires specific evidence. Chances are that in generic terms the patterns characterizing quite different industry sectors would resemble one another. Over the years in one industry after another, some products have become so low cost that their business performance is trivial. Other products and services had the opportunity of potentially high performance, but entry and support costs were too high.

Between these two populations, there is a large area where business opportunity may be good and costs are reasonable. A bank must be very specific in its evaluation of its future course. Do we have an appealing model for i-banking? Or will our offering be another "me, too?" "Tomorrow's banking landscape today" is the failed description of many Internet services for retail banking marketed by several credit institutions at a loss; it has failed because it is not focused.

Also, some general statistics are not making much sense as far as management decisions about a course of action are concerned. An example of a general-type statement is that, on average, branches and their staff account for about half of the costs of a typical retail bank. And then what? What's the projected cost and benefit of *our* alternatives? What will *we* gain by moving onto the Internet?

Bankers at one stage hoped that they might be able to persuade their customers to do business through the Internet, allowing branches to be shut down. But over the years their customers have made it clear that although they want the convenience of Internet banking, they also insist on branches. A public-relations disaster hit Barclays Bank after it closed 171 British branches in a single day.[6] This experience has made other British banks very wary of trying something similar.

In addition, one should not discount the fact that the new i-banks that have succeeded in attracting customers have reached their goals at a high cost. Egg PLC, which opened in October 1998 (see Section 4), experienced a good public reception in its first year, but it also reported a loss of £155 million ($256 million) in 2000. "Customer acquisition costs were so high for Egg that there was hardly any margin," said Patricia Neuhaus, an analyst with Jupiter.[7] (These references shadow Egg's British results shown in the previous section.)

Some of the challenges facing i-banks have proved so daunting that many ambitious plans to start operations in Internet banking have been abandoned. One of several examples is the Swiss private banking firm Vontobel, which pulled the plug on its "y-o-u" Internet banking project after spending CHF 150 million ($125 million). Vontobel cited high costs and the length of time needed to reach profitability as reasons for shutting down i-banking.

Analysts say security fears and reluctance to go through the hassle of changing banks are among the main reasons that online banks, especially new i-banking ventures launched by companies outside the retail banking sector, have not taken off as expected. Some point out that customer attitudes are bound to change as technology develops, but they have not changed that much yet, at least in the general case.

New i-banking ventures by nonretail credit institutions suffer from the old maxim in the banking industry that "you are more likely to get a divorce than change your bank." Internet banks have been trying to change this with a combination of media campaigns, new technology, and a broad selection of services. But the results continue to be wanting.

Moreover, a major factor inhibiting online banking is that customers rely on a strong personal relationship with their local bank. This is particularly true in Southern Europe, although in Nordic countries banking is more of an impersonal affair. This cultural difference explains, in part, why online banking is more successful in northern European countries than in the more traditional southern Europe.

Brand recognition, too, is important, particularly for i-banks that want to operate across borders. Also critical is the content of i-banking services being offered, which in the majority of cases are carbon copies of what is done at brick-and-mortar branches — by no means exciting stuff.

Some experts think that part of the deception with i-banking, when there is such deception, has been the fact that most of the emphasis is on machines that are basically personal computers with special software routines added to them. This software is written by technical staff and suffers from the same ills as the bank's inventory of legacy applications. It is far removed from front-desk online customer contact.

Decisions about supported functions and equipment on which these will perform are made in an ivory tower. This is not what would put the imagination of consumers in motion. A successful project that exploits the impact of high technology to the maximum would take a banking job and turn it inside out. For example, look at what such a program could do for gross sales connected to lending.

The financial intermediary is now beyond matching depositors with surpluses with those who have shortages. This "beyond" is behind the developing trend in turning loans into securities, whether we talk of mortgages, consumer installment loans, auto loans, credit card receivables, or corporates.

A credit institution's business is no longer just lending. In the United States, home mortgages, home improvement loans, and car lending account for about 72 percent of consumer loans. Another 20 percent is represented by credit card payments. This 92 percent of all consumer loans is a vast pool that has been increasingly exploited through securitization.

Based on this background are two crucial questions generally confronting every bank: Do we know how to use i-banking to feed the securitization pool? Do we have a strategy and the skills to securitize the receivables — package them and market them online?

15.6 INTERNET AND THE SECURITIES INDUSTRY

"You can lose as much money in Internet stocks as in Indonesia. But in Indonesia you cannot make the wild gains you might do with Internet stocks," a Wall Street securities expert told me during a meeting in early 2000, prior to the meltdown. This was the time of the high-water mark of the Internet bubble, and some of the brokers were conducting sophisticated courtships of dot.com investors in cyberspace by arranging matches in split seconds and doing so without layers of floor middle men.

At the time, experts thought that cybermarkets would have a profound effect on every citizen interested in accumulating assets in equities as well as on every publicly traded company, every brokerage employee, and countless others. Some, the more foresighted, said one of the effects of the Internet on the securities industry would be to raise the question of global regulation and global investor protection.

One of the results that many experts believed to be a sure thing was that, with the advent of electronic trading systems, there would be more choice among trading methods, with exchanges integrated globally through high-speed data links — both terrestrial satellites. This has been a prophecy that will take a couple of miracles to materialize. By the late 1990s the most enthusiastic of the pros professed that many equities and debt markets will simply migrate to the Internet, and the question will be raised whether we really need exchanges in their current form.

Some of the experts even ventured to suggest that the Internet will put squarely on the table the wisdom that companies list their shares globally through the Internet and see them trading round the clock rather than in this or that stock exchange pit. Another of the opinions rejected by reality has been that the cost of raising capital could decline as the Internet makes it easier to distribute shares of initial public offerings and more investors pile into this new over-the-counter market.

All these have been proven to be assumptions whose time did not come. A likely reason is that, although the Internet helps stockbrokers, too many questions remain. Will Internet stock trading prove to be a dependable practice? A rewarding one? Will the risk of default be reduced by instantaneous settlement of trades instead of T-3 (three days)? Will it be as easy and cheap to buy Microsoft from Athens or Seoul as it is from New York?

Some of the stock exchanges argued that enabling solutions for T+0 clearing and settlement anywhere in the world, at any time, should *not* be grafted onto a process that involves many real people. Rather, clearing and settlement should be handled through the existing system, by means of rapid-fire switches based on the best technology can offer.

But 1998, 1999, and the first quarter of 2000 were the years when everybody, particularly the experts, thought that practically everything was possible. Then the market retreated, investors lost large amounts of money, mismanagement and scandals came to the fore,[8] and nearly all of the different rosy projections about the Internet's future and downgrading of the exchanges turned to dust. Little has remained of them that is worth reviewing.

The positive outcome is that the securities business got more mileage from the Internet than did retail banking. As a result, brokerage firms are working to devise innovative Web-based applications and practices. They continue to experiment with evolving Internet-related technologies, whereas as we saw in Section 5, some of the retail banks have given up.

One of the factors favoring online brokerage is that the forces of deregulation have reshaped the securities industry, and they have brought into the picture a higher level of competition. To survive, investment banks must be more proactive than their counterparts in commercial banking. Charles Schwab, for instance, has implemented a customizable alert system that helps to notify clients, in real-time via e-mail, of events specific to securities of interest. Investors may configure alerts based on different criteria like:

- Breaking news
- Price volatility
- Earnings releases
- Analyst recommendations

When one or more of these criteria are met, near-instantaneous notification is delivered. This is a customer-driven approach that outdistances traditional means in terms of timeliness and tailoring. It is also the sort of advantage Internet can offer.

On the marketing side, the process of mass customization permits brokerage firms to target marketing efforts to specific groups of investors. An example is that of patterning the trading activity of each client, enabling the securities firm to customize promotional offerings and capitalize on exclusive Web site features.

This being said, there is no general model among brokerages on how to handle the Internet connection. Some firms prefer to continue providing clients with traditional full-service offerings but add to that detailed account information on current positions, portfolio values, and other issues.

This approach does not have the ability to execute trades online but still provides value differentiation compared with traditional solutions. Other brokerages provide their customers with the possibility of choosing from different types of service options. The latter are ranging from online trading services to complete investment advice and financial management.

Some brokerage firms, particularly discounters who want to be both innovative with respect to technology-based services and cut costs with a sharp knife, have been developing and implementing their brand of customer services. Typically, these add online trading. Discounters, however, continue operating through brick and mortar and over the phone.

Then there is the click-only model and full Internet brokerage service associated with it. These approaches are designed for investors who wish to make decisions independently of their broker's investment advice but who are technology literate. The main target of i-brokers is active traders who are after the power to execute trades as quickly and economically as possible. In this sense, i-brokers compete on price rather than service and excel in the area of trade execution but rank lower than discounters in customer service.

In conclusion, in comparing Internet-based solutions by securities firms with those by commercial and retail bankers, we see that brokerages are richer in terms of supported alternatives. They have different views on how to reach and hold the investors' attention and a much better hold of the market to which they appeal through real-time services. As such, they are closer to the Internet ecosystem model that has been introduced in Chapter 3 and is discussed in greater detail in Chapter 16.

15.7 NOTES

1. Communications of the ACM, March 2001, Vol. 44, No. 3.
2. *The Economist,* November 29, 2003.
3. D.N. Chorafas, *Integrating ERP, CRM, Supply Chain Management and Smart Materials,* Auerbach, New York, 2001.
4. D.N. Chorafas, *Operational Risk Control with Basel II. Basic Principles and Capital Requirements,* Butterworths-Heinemann, London and Boston, 2004.
5. *Business Week,* December 1, 2003.
6. *The Economist,* March 24, 2001.
7. *International Herald Tribune,* April 2, 2001.
8. D.N. Chorafas, *Management Risk. The Bottleneck Is at the Top of the Bottle,* Macmillan/Palgrave, London, 2004.

16

END-TO-END DELIVERABLES THROUGH INTERNET ECOSYSTEMS

16.1 INTRODUCTION

Since Chapter 1 we have spoken of the great importance of any-to-any connectivity. Subsequently, Chapter 15 has presented strengths and weaknesses of this approach through case studies in Internet banking. These are not necessarily representative of commerce at large; industrial and merchandising activities have had their own success and failure stories. Accounts, however, vary as to which contributions are most appreciated by end users and their companies. One survey has found the following factors as foremost in the minds of user organizations (in order of importance):

- Improved customer relationship
- Better time to market
- Fast order processing
- Reduced processing cost
- Opening up of a new customer's base
- New markets
- Improved supplier relationship
- Greater possibility to build alliances

According to another survey, the topmost benefit from Internet commerce is fast order processing, with reduced order processing cost in second position and improved supplier relationship in third position. Still other surveys on perceived Internet commerce benefits end up with a different order of priorities and some more factors like more visionary and strategic approaches and demarcation against competitors.

Something like an overall agreement exists in regard to shortcomings associated with Internet commerce. The concerns include (in order of importance) data confidentiality, security, need for reliable payments solutions, difficult integration into business processes, acceptance by business partners, acceptance within one's own company, restrictive laws, conflict with traditional distribution channels, needed integration with legacy systems, lack of technical know-how to master the Web, and more.

Though it is true that confidentiality and security are a top concern for nearly all Internet commerce users, vendors, and clients, it is surprising that superior technical know-how to master the Web tends to be at the bottom of the list in terms of importance. At the origin of such oversight can be found common hype about Web sites. Here is a short list of my findings.

1. *Designing a Web site needs to be done only once.* That's absolutely not true. Web sites must be maintained all of the time. Therefore, they represent a steady concern.

2. *Web sites are inexpensive, and operating costs are trivial.* That, too, is false. There are both start-up costs and operational costs (internal and external) not to be recovered during usage.

3. *Web sites can be set up and dismantled quickly.* This is true only when one has plenty of experience on how to handle Web sites and the right skills in setting up and dismantling.

4. *Most customers' needs are served from a single Web site.* Such a statement is not sustained by facts. All business units must care for their market appeal. Therefore, they want their own Web site, as each has to look after its bottom line and is reluctant to share costs it does not control.

5. *Web sites are easily located and you don't need a business-specific portal choice.* The ease of locating is a myth, particularly when one uses different search engines and each business unit makes its own choices.

6. *You don't need architecture for Web sites.* That's a lie. You do need a good deal of architectural considerations (and you'd better stick to your business architecture) as well as tests to ensure i-commerce fits the company's strategic plans.

7. *Web sites can be scaled and changed rapidly.* Typically, scaling flexibility diminishes with greater security, increased complexity, and more design parameters. These are conflicting goals.

8. *If you set up a Web site, you are ahead of your competitors.* This is not so. You have to steadily watch what your competitors do; otherwise, you fall behind very fast in terms of Internet sex appeal.

9. *You can depend on customers to provide feedback leading to a new Web site design.* This is very rarely, if ever, true. To give your Web site a competitive edge, you must have an R&D budget and do your own homework in terms of development.

10. *There is no need to back up Web sites.* Reliable backup must always be provided; it is part of the responsibility of managing Web sites.

11. *There is no reason to audit Web sites.* This is patently false. Not only is there plenty of reason for doing Web site auditing, but also this must be executed from a number of different viewpoints, including fraud by the company's own employees.

Chapter 15 brought the reader's attention to the security issue. We will talk more about security concerns in Section 6, after having introduced the concept of end-to-end connectivity and broadened the perspectives of the Internet ecosystem.

16.2   END-TO-END ON THE INTERNET

Competitive improvements do not become available automatically simply because a company is doing business in cyberspace, nor is the effort to establish and maintain Web sites trivial business. As with any other business, a company must have a clear idea about what it wants to achieve and how best to go about it.

Challenges start with the Internet's nuts and bolts, such as the growing shortage of addresses and the need to scale them up to cope with faster connections. Another technical issue is that of implementing at global scale broadband Internet and of ensuring that coverage is universal. Industry sectors can be shaped by the way the chips fall in terms of Internet services.

On the surface it may not seem that way, but down the line regulatory issues, technical issues, expensive supports, and a difficult financial market are conspiring against the spread of the introduction of broadband fixed network access. On the other hand, pan-European broadband wireless operators are reshaping their business models to include digital access technologies and value-added offerings, from Web site design, hosting, and i-commerce applications to other services.

For instance, Internet traffic is increasingly expected to include content such as full-motion video on demand, high-definition video, multichannel high-quality audio, online videoconferencing, image transfer, online gaming, and other broadband applications. It is expected that their delivery will result in greater demand of available bandwidth.

The reason universal-coverage, broadband channels, and value differentiation are so important is that, unless they are taken care of, the universal *end-to-end* principle on which the power of the Internet rests could be under threat. This is clearly unwanted because any-to-any, end-to-end capability is one of the motivations of companies to be on the Internet, bringing more and more of their business to the Web. Among the value-added services from the last five years are straight through processing (STP) and enterprise resource planning (ERP) software.

As we have already seen in Chapter 5, ERP-supported facilities proved to be popular because they made feasible analytical queries regarding the status of orders, among other deliverables. This enabled clients to find a real-time answer to status questions, which was not available otherwise. Pass-through routines provided answers in a fast, accurate, and seamless manner, proving, through this process, that nothing short of real-time automatic status reports is a satisfactory solution.

Indeed, the cutting edge of competition sees to it that end-to-end is not just a better way, it is the only way for modern business. In turn, this requires that the network should be omnipresent, highly capillary, very reliable, and increasingly smart. The response to online queries must be without fault, with minimal delay, and without any discrimination in regard to transaction packets being handled. All packets must be treated equally, and their contents must not be tampered with.

According to the principles of packet switching implemented with the Internet, packets may arrive at their destination in a different order than that in which they were sent, but computers at the nodes at each end of the connection do not have to worry about how the packets are delivered. Their responsibility is to reconstitute messages and transactions in the order in which they should have been sent.

The Internet, intranets, and extranets relieve the company of some of the more basic technical chores associated with private networks, but other challenges remain. Foremost among them is to maintain the basic simplicity of the Internet's infrastructure while improving and innovating its environment. Every effort should be made to preserve the end-to-end nature, and this means avoiding short-term fixes that disregard the end-to-end principle and/or hinder future innovative approaches.

A systems study associated with end-to-end solutions must see to it that background factors are properly studied and foreground mechanics are simulated and experimented with, prior to being settled. Vitally important is the visibility of deliverables. If there is no factual and documented evidence of what we are going to get, we cannot talk of cost-effectiveness, no matter how sophisticated the end-to-end system is going to be. This requires forward-looking studies.

Moreover, as other types of information technology implementation have demonstrated, the greatest challenge is at each end of an online, interactive solution. The reason for this statement is that the most sophisticated element, the one that is the most highly fragile and complex as well as most likely to malfunction, is *the end-user*. From this derive two axioms:

1. To obtain the time functionality of a real-time solution on the Internet or any other network, the user must be appropriately trained.
2. Rather than spending precious time to reinvent the wheel (software), brainpower should be applied to rethink and reorganize a company's systems and procedures.

This is the concept underpinning Figure 16.1, with end user functions at the top of the pyramid and systems and procedures in the middle. Among the upper layers, the overriding emphasis is that of upgrading, qualitywise, the organization and its people. As has been discussed, this is an integral part of the degree and depth of preparatory work that has to be done for end-to-end solutions.

Project after project demonstrates that all in-depth preparatory work involves *strategic* considerations necessary to establish goals, describe deliverables, elaborate timetables, and set budgets. In brief, there must be a plan that defines the nature, extent, and outputs of end-to-end operations.

An integral part of an effective end-to-end approach is *adaptability* to the end user's requirements, making his job easier and more productive. A similar statement, in terms of expected benefits, is valid in connection with economic considerations to ensure return on investment from the end-to-

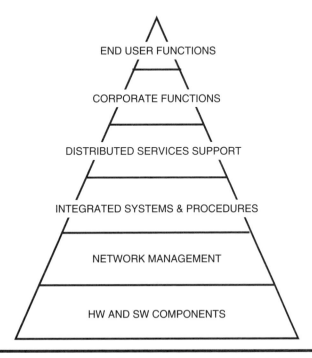

END USER FUNCTIONS

CORPORATE FUNCTIONS

DISTRIBUTED SERVICES SUPPORT

INTEGRATED SYSTEMS & PROCEDURES

NETWORK MANAGEMENT

HW AND SW COMPONENTS

Figure 16.1   Intranet Functionality Permits a More Holistic View of Network Functions than So Far Possible

end solution. Improvements in cost-effectiveness require *steady review* and reevaluation by senior management, to ensure the solution remains state-of-the-art and to eliminate dead wood, besides adding new functionality.

Among the deadwood is the support for past services, despite the fact that one of the top issues regarding the Internet is the steady increase in *demand* for access, products, bandwidth, sophistication in applications, greater market appeal, and increasingly more effective man–machine interfaces.

Last but not least is the correction of current woes and those foreseeable in the future. For instance, in terms of channel capacity, the Internet is getting bogged down at peak usage times, worries regarding security and freedom from viruses are on the increase, and more and more sophisticated applications are needed to keep up the Internet's appeal to its users. There is, however, a silver lining to all this trouble.

16.3 TIME AND ITS CHALLENGES

The Internet creates an interesting twist to the challenge of managing time, obliging its users to set priorities and to move quickly. This is not the first case in which our approach to the management of time has changed. It also happened in the nineteenth century with the introduction of the telegraph and the telephone. But the change now taking place in the aftermath of the Internet, is even more pronounced. Figure 16.2 shows the benefits from, and prerequisites of, the able use of Internet time.

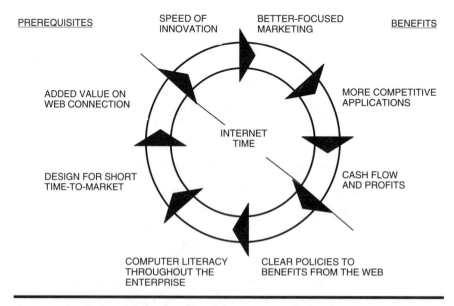

Figure 16.2 Prerequisites of and Benefits Connected to Internet Time

One of the reasons Internet time impacts business and industrial operations is that advanced applications involving communications and computers deal with minute fractions of time. The execution of each operation is affected by both rules and metarules. *Metarules* are rules about rules and stand in higher-up esteem in a control structure of space and time. Their presence implies the existence of layers of reference.

A metalayer control structure reflects that the concept of time, and of its control, have changed both "in the big" and "in the small." "In the big" means in connection to longer-term thinking. Nowhere in ancient literature do we read about the establishment of a policy, the founding of an industry, or the making of a colony *as events with a long-term perspective.* Babylonians, Egyptians, Chinese, Greeks, and Romans focused on the *moment.* There is no evidence that ancient peoples were after rewards in the next century, though many believed in the next life.

This lack of longer-term thinking inhibited the ancient world and leading cultures from planning far ahead and thereby being able to foresee the waves of change. The ancients felt the same about controlling their environment. In short, it was a static approach. When setting goals, they did not consider time in the longer run.

In a way, the ancient world associated motion and time and therefore, change with decay rather than with development. In Greek mythology, and before Babylonian, the god of gods Chronos ate his children, and Chronos in Greek means *time.* Stability was considered to be perfection. In contrast, our philosophy as well as our business age promotes change and an evolving perspective. A similar reference is valid about time "in the small." As we move to smaller and smaller fractions of time, change is accelerating. Nearly everyone in the Western world works by the clock. Most of the events regulating our life go by the clock.

This notion of smaller and smaller fractions of time is not an abstract concept but something pragmatic. We spoke of it in Chapter 1 in comparing business time to clock time as well as coarse time measurements done by the minute all the way to subsecond time fractions. Such fractions are today increasingly used in financial analysis and high-technology applications.

Though we may not realize it, computers and communications enhance this process of regulation by the clock. As a result, they change our prevailing views about the established physical and logical order, its timing and its landscape. In this process, it is not the single program but the holistic view that matters — the way every single program interacts with every other program in the system, the way it integrates within its intended environment, and the results it gives by way of providing solutions to the problems confronting us.

In the immediate post-World War II years, this holistic view was a local and relatively limited preoccupation. With the Internet it is now globalized. Although we are still very interested in those features prevailing in a particular place and a particular time, our attention is increasingly focused on the global domain. This has a much deeper impact on the way we look at real-time systems than we may think.

Notice that timing constraints encompass different granularities that, among the better-managed entities, tend to become finer and finer — in the sense that they tend to abide by an increasingly finer filter in measuring and managing time. In turn, this sees to it that a company will find itself obliged to rethink and reinvent its culture, its products, and its market position more and more frequently.

Within the constraints posed by fractions of time, realspace solutions are loaded with human, technological, and economic characteristics. Some address themselves to engineering design and manufacturing requirements, calling for very close coordination between faraway and, so far, distinct laboratories and production facilities (e.g., General Motors' operations in the United States, England, and Germany).

Because global coordination among engineering labs has optimization as a goal, with a view toward greater cost effectiveness, it is inevitable that supply chains are affected. In late 2003 the *Detroit Free Press* reported that General Motors had put its suppliers on notice that it can, with 30 days' warning, cancel a contract and give it to another supplier that charges less. The supplier would not be reimbursed for the cost of tooling, R&D, or other investments. GM says the new contract terms do not represent a radical change in the way it does business, but the opinion of the supply industry differs.

GM's suppliers are on the receiving end of the consequences of the Big Three's failure to deal with their own problems. Generations of union deals have left the big U.S. automakers with horrendous pension and health liabilities plus factory floor pay rates that make them uncompetitive. Moreover, they have to face up to the fact that buyers of top-of-the-range quality cars are favoring European and Japanese carmakers.

All this, however, is a reaction by looking at the surface. A much deeper examination would reveal that globalization has changed the contours of every supply chain, while technology has made it feasible to reach for lower-cost solutions to the four corners of the earth and Internet time has accelerated this switching process. No companies are immune from putting suppliers under price pressure, but it has taken a significant cultural change to turn this into a trend.

Another example in which cost awareness, time constraints, and realspace solutions work in synergy is marketing. Meeting the challenges imposed by Internet marketing and sales activities very much depends on a focused and coordinated effort. This requires not only Web sites supporting instantaneous telecommunications but also expertise on how to use available facilities to reach a broad spectrum of customers and other counterparties. This has a downside when virtue is wanting.

16.4 VIRTUE IS KNOWLEDGE THAT CANNOT BE TAUGHT

The world in which we live acts both as a catalyst and as an incubator of new ideas. We also know that, unlike what is taking place with genetically transmitted physical characteristics, neither the acquired know-how nor our logical assets seem to be hereditary. Hence, there is need for continuing research and implementation able to help in knowledge acquisition and in knowledge transfer.

The moral standards under which activities take place are an issue rarely raised, yet such standards are of primary importance. Ancient wisdom based virtue on a foundation of knowledge and morality but without properly outlining which ones of their eternal sources are the most dependable. If virtue, as Socrates said to Protagoras, is knowledge that cannot be taught, then there are neither teachers nor students of virtue. But there are teachers and students of knowledge.

There are also *virtuous people.* They enhance themselves and their social environment in response to societal goals. Since man became a self-conscious entity on this earth, he has labored to improve his physical environment and, in recent years, even his own molecular and genetic substructures. In contrast, people have done very little to better their ethical basis.

Every new advance, the Internet ecosystem being one, improves our capability to interconnect but also brings along aftereffects that tend to obey the law of unwanted consequences, for example, the risk of killing the goose that lays the golden egg. This is what has happened with the mutual funds scandal in 2003, among a myriad of other scams.[1]

Evidence accumulated during 2003 suggests that investors' trust has been misplaced. Some experts believe this is one of basic reasons behind the prolonged 2000–2003 bear market. Some of the problems that have come out of investigations by the authorities in New York State, the Securities and Exchange Commission, and findings through internal audits are as follows:

- *New York State and SEC:* Alliance Capital, market timing; Bank of America, market timing and late trading; Bank One, market timing; Federated Investors, market timing; Fred Alger & Company, market timing and late trading; Janus Capital, market timing; Morgan Stanley, directed brokerage; Prudential Securities, market timing; Putnam Investments, market timing; Strong Capital Management, market timing
- *New York State and internal audit:* Charles Schwab, questionable trades
- *Revealed through internal audits:* Citigroup, market timing and late trading; Pilgrim, Baxter & Associates, market timing; in addition, a client lawsuit was filed against Bear Sterns for market timing

As a result, scores of employees have been fired. At Allied Capital, two employees had booked a $190 million charge. At Bank of America, three employees had booked a $100 million charge. At Fred Alger & Company, the vice chairman was convicted of felony and fined $400,000. At Morgan Stanley, a $50 million settlement aimed to compensate investors.

Behind practically all of these scams is lust and greed indivisible from human nature; networks and 24-hour trading acted as catalysts and enablers. The global market and any-to-any networking tremendously expanded the trading domain of foreign exchange, securities, treasury operations, and derivative financial instruments. Significantly improved connectivity sees to it that money center banks operate simultaneously in New York, London, Zurich, Tokyo, and other financial centers as their main axes of doing business. This both provides business opportunities and aggravates the risks. Stock exchanges in these financial centers have common *time windows*, allowing traders to be not only in contact but also in synergy with one another. Interest rate and forex operations are executable in any exchange at any time, resulting in firm commitments. After-hour networks are increasingly able to do 24-hour business, which is the sense of globalization.

All this sounds positive, and it is, but there are also legal troubles, some of them an outgrowth of what has been considered competitive advantage. For instance, after-hours trading (or late trading) is an illegal practice when buying or selling mutual-fund shares at the trading day's price after the market has closed.

Another practice made possible through global networks that is today considered questionable is market timing. It consists of rapid trading of mutual-fund shares with the goal to take advantage of the gap between the price of a fund, which is set once a day, and the continuous changes in value of the underlying portfolio of securities.

One of the ambiguities relating to the virtues of the global financial environment is that, contrary to late trading, market timing is in several countries generally legal — but still allows to gain advantage at investors' expense. There are many other practices that have also come under scrutiny, finding themselves on the borderline between legal and illegal. This mainly happens because formerly crisp definitions of ethical and unethical practices have become fuzzy. Internet libel and slander provide an example.

Libel is a damaging statement in printed or written form. Slander is a damaging statement that is spoken. Both are a form of defamation, though not every form of damaging language is defamatory, since some statements are true. A question currently puzzling the legal community is whether some happenings in electronic communications are libel or slander. Since slander is more difficult to prove, defendants in defamation actions hold to this standard, whereas plaintiffs prefer bringing to court a libel suit.

The difference in viewpoints is far from being academic: Is communication over the Internet more like speech or print? Is something that shows up on the Web spoken or published? These and many more fundamental queries that have to do both with law and with virtue are part of the emerging concept of an Internet ecosystem as defined in Chapter 3: a new business model for Web-connected businesses to serve interconnected customers that is able to present many competitive advantages but also engenders a number of unknowns and risks.

The fact that the doors of risk and return are adjacent and identical does not make things any easier. The open nature of the Internet reflects the principles of our open society and encourages complementary business alliances that create a unique set of interwoven dependencies and relationships. But legal risk is also present. The fact that the Internet ecosystem is open encourages new members to participate. This helps to foster a collaborative relationship among members but also brings up new factors for which there is no jurisprudence.

Let me add that the Internet ecosystem should not be confused with virtual reality,[2] though the two have in common a number of important characteristics. Companies in the Internet ecosystem use the Web as a the medium through which to create value for their customers. Examples of how they expand their ecosystem include the creation of new business partnerships and the forming of different types of unique alliances.

Novel solutions to product development and market support are designed to accelerate business success in a fast, innovating, and very competitive landscape. But operational risks, too, have to be fully considered, including legal risk and its many unknowns, whose number increases exponentially as the global landscape expands.

16.5 LEARNING HOW TO DO INTERNET ECOSYSTEM STUDIES

The first lesson learned 20 years ago with what were at the time new departures in office automation (see Chapter 8) is that the number of cooperative users must be large enough to sustain and increase the attraction of available networked resources. For example, unchecked electronic mail boxes will soon discourage senders of important messages from trusting their mail to the system. Without messaging, other network uses grow at a much slower pace, and operational skills correspondingly degrade. In the aftermath, the employment of available resources quickly reduces to the hard core, and justification of investments made to provide a given solution is questioned.

These and similar past lessons can help a great deal in creating knowhow that serves in Internet ecosystem studies. Experience from the 1980s and 1990s teaches how and why integrated office systems were challenged to acquire critical mass. To the extent that they have failed, the chain reaction of new applications has been dampened. This is, to my judgment, one of the most significant lessons that can serve the case of broadband Internet.

Another important lesson is that management technology and the training of managers and professionals to effectively use that technology correlate. *Management technology* is defined as those tools and techniques that allow groups of people to work together, through a managerial viewpoint, toward a common goal. This is the sort of interaction through which we can effectively get increases in productivity.

For this to happen, the board and CEO have to articulate the vision of the company and to align all levels of management along that vision. Everyone should appreciate that management technology follows on the heels of technological innovation. Therefore, its able implementation must be planned; we must *not* just throw in the technology and wonder why it does not work. There has always been a gap between what the users want and need and what the systems people think that users need.

The best way of closing this end users–technologists gap is through both training *and* prototyping. Every new application targeting the Internet ecosystem should do so through prototyping, giving the end user a chance to comment on what he will be getting. Prototyping facilitates better communication of end user needs and serves to significantly reduce the time of deliverables.

Still another lesson from office automation that impacts on how well we will be using the Internet ecosystem is the need to investigate, in a rigorous way while the project is at the drafting board, from *where* the next problem will surface and when. If this principle had been applied to mobile communications, telecom companies would not have run themselves dry by spending a fortune on UMTS.[3]

These references point to the fact that the effective use of new technology requires discipline and strong foresight on the part of management. Whereas during the 1960s and 1970s technological capabilities evolved on a piecemeal basis, since the late 1980s integrative perspectives have replaced these discrete islands, making resources more widely attainable. With this, we came to appreciate that an efficient definition of IT investments, and their deliverables, consists of four key components that are most vital with the Internet ecosystem:

1. *The new frontier is the battle for productivity.* In terms of analysis, development, and implementation, a most vital role in all information technology applications, including those involving the Internet, is played by our *state of mind.* A key issue in terms of productivity is *the management of change*, which requires more planning, less paper, more machine intelligence, and greater integration.
2. *Technological solutions must provide the means to support and enhance the decision-making power of managers and professionals.*

Throughout the years, few highly qualified executives had the uncanny ability to see major trends before anyone else and to capitalize on them. New technology is by no means a clone of such high executive skills, but it can be made to assist *all* managers and professionals to see more clearly into the future and, most importantly, to experiment on the aftermath of their decisions (see Chapter 7 on EIS).

3. *Analysis and experimentation can provide powerful tools for preservation of company resources.* An organization must be results oriented. Results come from the able usage of resources, including client, relationships, personnel, financial staying power, market appeal, strategic products, and advanced system solutions. The goals to be reached should be clearly stated by top management by way of defining what the firm will look like in future years.

4. *The cost-effective implementation of high technology needs first-class skill. It will not happen by accident.* Technology should not be employed at any cost. Benefit studies are an important prerequisite. This involves innovative system analysis and design, projection of deliverables and identification of their worth, and increasingly more sophisticated software solutions. It also calls into play our ability to evaluate return on investment objectively, without distortion and prejudice that comes from false hopes.

In a project in which I was involved in the late 1990s that studied the operations of a leading company, I found that personnel costs increased steadily over 10 years (such costs being computed in steady 1988 money), in spite of a huge amount of money spend on IT. That money was poorly spent. There was an uncontrolled proliferation of diverse noncompatible equipment while the company's senior, middle, and junior management kept on doing trivial functions.

This happens quite frequently and will continue as long as the old technology culture retains the upper ground. How many companies really get a big benefit out of their technology? Cisco, Dell, Amazon.com, and a couple of dozen others are the exceptions. Thousands of firms are on the Web so as not to be left behind, but they are left behind when they do not get significant profits from being there.

16.6   DELIVERABLES FOR THE SMES AND THE VIRUS THREAT

Whether we talk of the Internet or any other services, the product is for the consumer. Therefore, an implementation study must be focused; averages would never give commendable results. This is not just the better way to do system studies; it is the only way. First, we must establish the perspective, and then we must make the choices. Take the managed services market and the role of small and medium enterprises (SMEs) as an example. Companies can be generally classified into:

- Very large
- Medium to large
- Medium size
- Small and medium
- Micro, or very small

The definition of SMEs is not cast in stone, but they are falling into the classes defined by the third and fourth bullets. SMEs typically employ from 10 to fewer than 250 employees, and they have a turnover of somewhat less than $50 million (Euro 50 million) per year. Forrester Research, for example, says that by the end of this decade in Europe, SMEs:

- Will be driving 48 percent of the managed services market
- Will be the most important outsourcers
- Will spend billions in services like Web hosting, virtual private networks, and security

Much of this activity will feed into the Internet ecosystem. Internet usage by SMEs is increasing, as a 2003 study by Provence-Côte d'Azur (in the southeast of France) has shown. The Regional Chamber of Commerce and Industry Provence-Côte d'Azur, together with the French National Council of Scientific Research (CNRS), conducted research among SMEs. Results showed that 61 percent of the companies were active on the Internet and 39.6 percent confirmed having found new clients through Internet contacts.

But many said that they lack experience in maximizing their Internet exploits. To answer this complaint, the Provence Côte d'Azur region established a budget of Euro 18 million to close the perceived gap. Applications being promoted emphasize five economic sectors: services, tourism, artisans, transport, and commerce.

Part of the money is earmarked for a response to supply-chain challenges, aimed to help small- and medium-size companies understand and manage the new ways of marketing and doing business in the digital economy. One of the goals is how to appreciate what Internet business is all about, how it works, and how to select a model that fits one's organization, including a matrix of change in systems and procedures.

A more distant aim is that of strategies for creating *trust-based* Web sites to enhance Internet marketing results and of ways and means for working at supply-chain clockspeed. Even if this requires cultural change and impacts on the SMEs procedures, in the overall this effort has received an excellent commentary, but response is mixed in the specific domains of trust-based Web sites and security at large.

Reaction in the United States is not too different, and statistics explain why. Some time prior to this research by Provence-Côte d'Azur and CNRS, *Communications of the ACM* published very interesting references on management concerns about fraud on the Internet, with the overriding concern being internal fraud. Statistics relating to these findings are shown in Figure 16.3.[4]

Indivisible from proper management of Web sites and of electronic commerce at large is the steady watch over multifaceted Internet crime and near-crime, from spam to viruses. Here is just one example. Beginning Saturday, January 25, 2003, at about 12:30 a.m. Eastern Standard Time, a distributed denial-of-service attack spread rapidly throughout the global Internet. Within ten minutes, most of the vulnerable hosts on the Internet were infected.

For instance, Bank of America customers could not withdraw money from 13,000 ATMs. The Web site of Continental Airlines was offline, forcing manual check-in. Normally heavy Internet trading in some stock markets

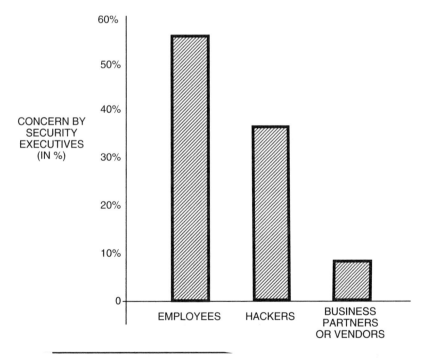

COMMUNICATIONS OF THE ACM, APRIL 2003, VOL. 46, NO. 4, BASED ON A CSO MAGAZINE
SURVEY OF 53 COMPUTER SECURITY OFFICERS AND SENIOR SECURITY EXECUTIVES

Figure 16.3   The Most Worrying Sources of Cyber Insecurity, According to a 2003 Survey

vanished, while many Web sites and associated Internet services were inaccessible. Responsible for the attack was the Sapphire, or Slammer, worm.[5]

Because viruses can hit the Internet ecosystem at any time, banks that respect their clients inform them about the risks being involved. Here is, as an example, the text of an e-mail received on April 3, 2002: "Internet communications are not secure and therefore Barclays Group does not accept legal responsibility for the contents of this message. Although Barclays Group operates antivirus programs, it does not accept responsibility for any damage whatsoever that is caused by viruses being passed."

As we will see in Chapter 17 (when we discuss business continuity), IT is not the only battleground in the fight to avoid business disruption, but it is where one of the major risks lies. There is no such thing as 100 percent security, nor is there a dependable fix to the security issue. Indeed, one of the main business disruption challenges today *is* the Internet, due to:

- System failure
- Execution errors
- Weak points in design
- Ill-studied access mechanisms
- Incompetence in maintenance
- Internal mismanagement, and other events

The more sophisticated the IT solution and the more integrated it is into the business fabric, the greater the resulting risk from disruption is, as Figure 16.4 suggests. Therefore, spending on IT security should be treated as a form of insurance, proportional to the impact of identified threats. Moreover, since both internal and external conditions change, IT security plans and systems must be reviewed regularly, and a sound policy should include a great deal of staff training as well as appropriate instrumentation.

Because SMEs are particularly vulnerable to business disruption, some of their managers have questioned the wisdom of going wholesale online and have been particularly concerned about the aftermath from lack of security. Another concern I found in my research revolves around the vexed issue of who controls the Internet.

This issue of Internet governance was supposed to be settled by the end of 2003, but it has been postponed until 2005. Currently, regulations and standards are decided by companies, and they are generally perceived as too closely aligned with their interests. Beyond this, rich and poor nations are squabbling over how to best run the Internet ecosystem — a debate that can be expected to intensify as broadband services expand globally and a great deal of attention is paid to content.

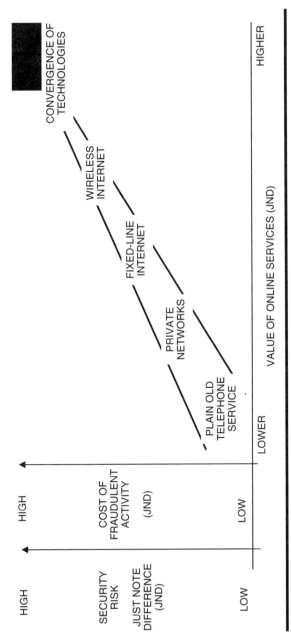

Figure 16.4 Security Concerns Increase with the Growth of Value-Added Services

16.7 WHO CAN MAKE MONEY ON THE INTERNET?

There is one more critical subject to be brought to the reader's attention. Many companies are concerned about how to make money on the Web, when fierce price competition, consolidation, dwindling product differentiation, and vanishing brand loyalty seem to be all but eliminating profits.

Contrarians to the idea of an all-out effort to promote Internet commerce would suggest that arguments such as "40 percent of our business will come from Internet-related service" are not factual. They look at them as part of a herd syndrome rather than of analysis, and they argue that there is no standard for measuring this 40 percent. Should it be:

- By volume of transactions?
- By revenue?
- By assets held?

One of the SME entrepreneurs suggested that to get 40 percent of revenue from the Internet, he needs to handle online much more than 40 percent of the volume he trades. Others were concerned that because of competition, revenue from Internet-related services are likely to be a lot less than from current channels.

These are legitimate concerns that exist all over the Internet landscape, and they cannot be brushed aside. They can only be answered through examples of what superior organization can provide, in full understanding of the fact that because of cultural and other reasons, a superior organization is not at every company's reach.

There exist, however, some first-class examples of what can be achieved through the Internet ecosystem. Among entities active and successful in Internet commerce, CISCO is years ahead of its competitors when it comes to using the Web to link itself to customers and suppliers. Statistics are startling:

- The company sells 80 percent to 85 percent of its equipment over the Net
- Through a leap in productivity, it produces $650,000 of revenue per employee per year

In comparison, rival Lucent Technologies sells only 30 percent of its equipment on the Web and brings in just $250,000 per employee per year. Aiming for profitability, not just for growth, Cisco has gained some $450 million annually by moving many of its supply-chain operations to the Net.

- Clients can configure products and place orders entirely on the Internet

■ Fifty-five percent of orders received are shipped without any human intervention

Most important in the context of this book is that business partners can tie in directly to Cisco's enterprise resource planning system (see also Chapter 5). This gives access to valuable information, available in real-time. In an environment where information is instantaneous, traditional retailing barriers are disappearing and buyers can immediately compare the offerings of sellers locally, nationally, and worldwide. The question then becomes: how do *we* differentiate ourselves from our competitors?

The most sound advice in this connection is that a company adapts to the Web's competitive realities, developing strategies to combat the risk of being left behind the curve. Very important is the ability to compare the pricing behavior of a set of products sold on the Internet and those sold via conventional channels, reaching appropriate conclusions about which way the marketing effort should go.

Another issue companies active on the Internet must look after is how the cost of Internet commerce differs from conventional sales and how price levels, price changes, and price dispersion are affected. Other crucial elements are how flexible pricing affects markets and competition, how to drive consumer focus away from pricing, and how successful Internet marketing strategies that focus on criteria other than pricing have been.

These queries are not typically asked in an Internet commerce study, yet they are crucial in getting ahead of competition in an age when price visibility has tremendously changed past sales standards. Moreover, because most companies have practically lost pricing power, management will be well advised to use Internet services not only for sales but also as a way to swamp internal costs. We will return to the issue of cost control in Chapter 17.

16.8 NOTES

1. D.N. Chorafas, *Management Risk. The Bottleneck Is at the Top of the Bottle*, Macmillan/Palgrave, London, 2004; D.N. Chorafas, *Corporate Accountability, with Case Studies in Finance*, Macmillan/Palgrave, London, 2004.
2. D.N. Chorafas and Heinrich Steinmann, *Virtual Reality—Practical Applications in Business and Industry*, Prentice-Hall, Englewood Cliffs, NJ, 1995.
3. D.N. Chorafas, *Enterprise Architecture and New Generation Information Systems*, St. Lucie Press/CRC, Boca Raton, FL, 2002.
4. Communications of the ACM, April 2003, Vol. 46, No. 4, based on a CSO magazine survey of 53 computer security officers and senior security executives.
5. Communications of the ACM, April 2003, Vol. 46, No. 4.

17

BUSINESS CONTINUITY AND CONTINGENCY PLANNING

17.1 INTRODUCTION

Criticality is an emerging term associated with vulnerabilities that are establishing themselves in sectors of the economy that are increasingly dependent on system reliability and business continuity. The concept of criticality, which is already well understood in engineering and physics, suggests that in extreme circumstances certain infrastructures or products may change their status and structure. This has significant aftereffects on individual performance and system failures.

In his investigation of the *Challenger* disaster, Dr. Richard Feynman, physicist, analyzed the space shuttle's computer system: 250,000 lines of code running on obsolete hardware. He also studied in detail the main engine of the shuttle and found serious defects, including a pattern of cracks in crucial turbine blades that paralleled similar problems with the solid rocket boosters. Feynman documented a history of ad hoc slippage in the standards used to certify an engine as safe and estimated that overall the engines and their parts were operating for less than one-tenth of their expected lifetimes.

This paradigm explains what underpins criticality. In typical bureaucratic fashion, as cracks were found earlier and earlier in a turbine's lifetime, the certification rules were repeatedly adjusted to allow engines to continue flying. Beyond this documentation of sloppy performance that significantly affected dependability, Dr. Feynman's most important contribution to the understanding of the *Challenger* disaster came in the area of risk and probability.

The physicist showed that a core function in a tough mission is that of weighing uncertainties. By contrast, NASA and its contractors had ignored statistical science altogether and had used a shockingly vague style of risk assessment. The tragic events of September 11, 2001, demonstrated that the majority of enterprises that were hit had shown a similar disregard for business continuity and contingency planning. Therefore, it is instructive to bring into perspective Richard Feynman's comment in the *Challenger's* case:

> A kind of Russian roulette. . . . The shuttle flies (with O-ring erosion) and nothing happens. Then it is suggested . . . that the risk is no longer so high for the next flights. We can lower our standards a little bit because we got away with it last time. . . . You got away with it, but it shouldn't be done over and over again like that.[1]

Science has tools for attacking such problems. NASA was not using them. Something similar happens quite often with business continuity and more generally with risk control. Risk is not always seen as the stochastic part of a complex situation that somewhere down the line ends in major disruption of economic activity, as the 1990 meltdown of the Japanese economy has shown. By analogy to Feynman's observation, certain conditions such as: significant illiquidity, excessive volatility, overleveraging, and gambling with derivatives[2] disrupt the efficient operation of the markets because they alter the players' behavior and/or weaken the financial fabric. Other factors have severe effects on the defenses built into structural solutions or technological systems. Hence, the importance of defining what constitutes critical infrastructures and services and what can be done to protect them is demonstrated. It is just as mandatory to establish countermeasures to cover threats and vulnerabilities associated with the modern economy.

17.2 MANAGEMENT OF BUSINESS CONTINUITY AND THE TERRORIST THREATS

Business continuity management (BCM) is the act of anticipating incidents that will affect mission-critical functions and processes, ensuring that an entity responds to any incident in a planned and rehearsed manner. For business continuity planning purposes, scenario analysis must target:

■ New and evolving risks
■ Different types of incidents
■ Sensitivities associated to innovation
■ Command and control centers and processes
■ Proximity and readiness of backup sites

Business continuity management is more effective when examined in coordination with supervisory authorities. For example, the Bank of England, Financial Services Authority (FSA), U.K. Treasury, and U.K.'s Turnbull Committee have been concerned with internal controls and the financial industry's resilience, including issues of:

- Corporate governance
- Auditing
- Liability and interoperability
- Insurance
- Outsourcing
- Supply chain
- Internet commerce

Chapters 15 and 16 have demonstrated that by acting as means of real-time linkage between business partners, the Internet plays a role akin to that of an intermediary. As shown in Figure 17.1, its services are characterized by layered functions, the outer one being business continuity.

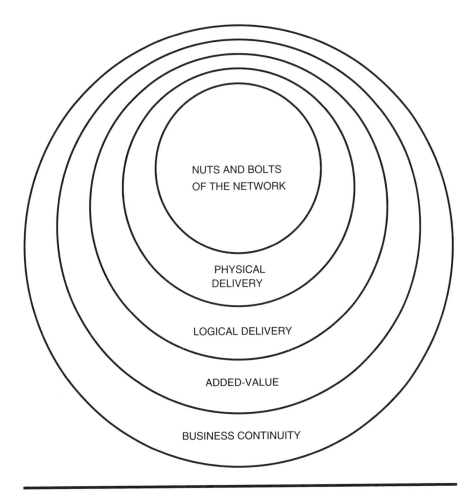

Figure 17.1 A System Acting as Intermediary Will Be Characterized by Many Layered Functions, the Outer Layer Being Business Continuity

A major business continuity preoccupation relates to the behavior, resilience, and criticality of an entity's technological infrastructure. When in the late 1990s the Year 2000 (Y2K) problem had caught practically everybody's attention, the Bank of Boston evaluated the aftermath of a Y2K failure. The tests that were done have shown that:

- A one-day disruption posed no major problems
- A two-day disruption required contingency planning
- A three-day disruption called for considerable damage control

Thereafter, the Bank of Boston said the situation was alarming. Its simulated business discontinuity documented that *if* the bank cannot recover in four days, *then* the fifth day and thereafter will be impossible to recover and to resume its usual business. A similar reference is valid about discontinuity that hits a company for any reason.

The September 11, 2001, terrorist attack in New York and Washington served as a dramatic reminder that in a global marketplace, disaster can strike at any time and anywhere, with repercussions far beyond domestic shores. A postmortem study by the U.K.-based Institute of Management revealed that fifty-eight percent of U.K. organizations were disrupted by the attacks, with one in eight severely affected. In New York the scale of the terrorist attack drove many companies from their offices, fully destroying records and forcing senior management to review emergency backup plans.

The silver lining in the tragedy has been that disaster recovery planning moved from a relatively low position on the must-do list to one of priority. But it did not always lead to corrective action. Even today, a large number of companies still have no disaster recovery plan or have one that is out of date under currently prevailing conditions.

A recent study has demonstrated that, when it comes to putting business continuity management solutions in place, retail organizations are often overlooking issues critical to their communications infrastructure. That was one of the messages coming from the inaugural Business Continuity Planning for Retailers conference in November 2003 in London.

"The most overlooked and underrated issue of (business continuity) is the comms infrastructure, possibly because people have got used to communications being more reliable than IT," said Tarlok Teji, head of Enterprise Risk Services at Deloitte. "Some well-known (U.K.) high street names have no contingency plans for a breakdrown in communications but have prioritized data. You can live without your accounts for a few days. But without communication between your stores, your warehouses, your suppliers and lorries, a company is paralyzed. A few days of empty shelves and you'll find you've lost a lot of customers permanently."[3] This lecture and others pressed the point that downtime is a critical threat to retail organizations and, moreover, the origins of potential threats are multiplying very fast.

Statistics concerning the aftermath of disasters are nevertheless appalling. A study by Gartner reveals that more than 40 percent of businesses that are hit by a disaster cease operations within two years. Other reports on business discontinuity suggest that even entities that have a disaster recovery plan do not test it at least annually to make sure it works.

Senior management should have the experience to appreciate that it is crucial to reevaluate and test the company's recovery plan periodically, doing so under stress conditions. Every critical system component should be subjected to stress tests: "What would happen *if.*" Historical experience provides a basis for scenarios. For instance, computer and software problems in the control room of besieged Ohio utility FirstEnergy were, by all evidence, a major cause of the record Northeast power blackout on August 14, 2003, according to congressional testimony and documents.[4]

Just for the record, at least two and one-half hours before the 4 p.m. blackout, FirstEnergy technicians who monitored the company's power lines got several telephone calls from power plant operators, warning of serious problems on the Midwestern electricity grid. In these alerts, power plant operators stated that they had seen:

- Odd surges of power
- Shutdowns of some power plants
- Transmission lines overloaded with electricity

Similar events can hit a telecommunications system. The Internet, for example, is overloaded in its current structure, particularly during certain hours of the day characterized by spikes in demand for bandwidth. A well-done business continuity plan should use stress tests to evaluate all types of likely and unlikely disruption at each of the critical components and the system as a whole, as Figure 17.2 suggests. Moreover, to be taken seriously, business continuity plans must be supervised by board members and implemented as an integrated part of the organization's policies and internal control structure.

Experts point to the fact that although some terrorist attacks act as wake-up calls, the message that they carry tends to attenuate very rapidly. The experience of the 1993 bombing of New York's World Trade Center, and the work that financial services firms did under the regulators' prodding, helped to prepare for control of the year 2000 technology bug. But only the better-managed firms benefited from these experiences in a significant way. Those who did benefit had a plan that functioned rather smoothly when adversity struck on September 11.

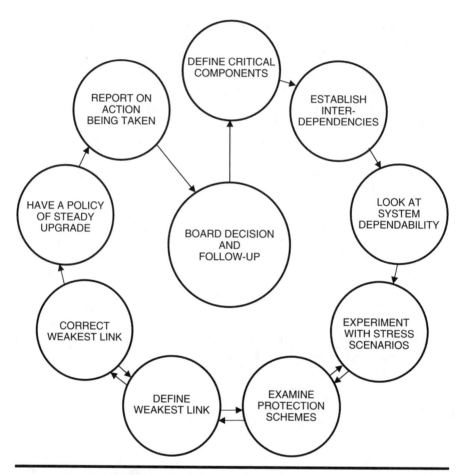

Figure 17.2 A Methodology for Business Continuity Planning to Be Supervised by the Board

Merrill Lynch, headquartered in the World Financial Center adjacent to the Twin Towers, was able to switch its critical management functions to a backup command center in New Jersey within minutes of the attacks. Other Wall Street companies, however, did not manage such a smooth transition. Postmortems connected the impact of September 11 on business continuity in the financial services industry and found several vulnerabilities. For instance:

■ Corporate backup plans did not include sites in different geographic areas

■ Some entities had failed to consider that land and air transport could be disrupted

■ Still others paid little attention to the energy and telecommunications infrastructures, particularly alternative networks that could be used quickly

Several companies discovered that although they had backup facilities outside Manhattan, their staff could not easily reach them because of the disruption to transportation. The lesson is that the selection of a recovery site and recovery plan must take account the people who will man it as well as of all the contingencies necessary to bypass bottlenecks.

As several postmortems indicated, financial and industrial entities as well as the markets were exposed to a few key hubs. Examples from the financial sector are exchanges, clearing houses, and interdealer brokerages. Many companies found out the hard way that disruptions at choke points trigger significant spillover effects for the rest of the financial services system and the markets as a whole.

17.3 LEARNING A LESSON FROM THE LAW OF UNEXPECTED CONSEQUENCES

The law of unexpected consequences is valid at all times, on any issue, in any place. An example is presented by the failure of the shuttle *Columbia* in 2003. The test at the Southwest Research Institute, whose results were announced on July 8, 2003, was the second in an advanced study using actual shuttle material. The objective was to establish the reasons for disintegration of *Columbia* in reentering the earth's atmosphere. The first test produced small cracks. The result of the second was a 40- × 40-cm² gaping hole.

This hole had been caused in the test by insulating foam. According to investigators it was a completely unexpected finding. Both the first and second tests intended to replicate damage caused to *Columbia* by insulating foam that broke loose on liftoff from an external fuel tank and, as experimental evidence has indicated, punched a large hole in the shuttle's wing panel.

The hole appeared to be closely emulating the range of the size of the one that led to the shuttle's fiery destruction when it reentered the earth's atmosphere the morning of February 1, 2003. This experimental result has several difficult implications for the space agency, including the fact that the investigation board had already recommended that the shuttle carry a patch kit. But whatever the possibility for patching a slit or a crack, a hole of about 1,600 square centimeters would appear to be very tough to repair in space. That foam will create a hole of 40 × 40 cm² sounds technically unreasonable, if not outright impossible. Speed made the difference, and this is an important finding in terms of the way the law of uninterrupted consequences works.

Though *Columbia's* disintegration was a dramatic and deadly event, the results of the second test were also quite powerful — proof that unexpected consequences always exist and, in many cases, they can be catastrophic. To confront major consequences originating with relatively small failures, we must properly plan ahead of time how to make systems more resilient and how to exercise damage control (more on this later).

In all likelihood, both tests set the two extremes of damage that the foam could have caused: from a relatively small crack to a big gaping hole. In the second test, researchers shot a chunk of foam toward the wing at more than 800 kilometers per hour, using a type of gun ordinarily employed to test airplane windshield resistance to bird strikes.

The goal was to hit one of the 22 wing panels in the way that would produce cracking or a small gap at the outboard edge. Notice that such test conditions were not worse case, because they used average values for estimates of the speed and mass of the foam and angle of impact. Still, the results revealed how system dependability can take a leave because control of vulnerabilities is very much wanting.

In the week of August 25, 2003, a panel of experts established that the shuttle *Columbia* was doomed in part because NASA relied too much on computer simulations and mathematical formulas that failed to accurately predict damage to the shuttle from flying pieces of foam. Nuclear and aviation industry safety experts said NASA officials were *wrong* to only rely on simulations to gauge risks. Let this be a lesson.

Notice that although some of these simulations were done before the launch, others took place during the mission. Too much was based on erroneous assumptions about the ability of the shuttle to withstand damage. Erroneous assumptions are by no means unheard of in business. When they are made in connection to business continuity, even the best laid-out plans for damage control will fail.

Through their investigation, the independent board's members also found that NASA's safety office was ineffective and underfunded. This compounded the other failures. The major findings of the investigation panel help, by analogy, in business continuity studies:

1. The shuttle's budget was decreased by 40 percent because the spaceship was considered to be a "mature product."

For the same reason, the shuttle's contractors were reduced to one and there was no oversight by NASA. This speaks volumes about the risks of outsourcing and has ominous implications on information systems. Moreover, when an organization decides that oversight is superfluous, it means that mismanagement holds the upper ground.

Constant readers would take good notice of this (pitiful) reference to "mature products." It is important because today many banks, insurance firms, and other companies consider their mainframes, Cobol programs, and other technological obscenities to be "mature products"and, therefore, "reliable." Precisely the opposite is true.

2. There has been life cycle uncertainty around the shuttle. Its replacement was originally projected for 2005–07, then slid to 1012–15, and finally fell to beyond 2020.

What the investigators particularly criticized was that while the shuttle's replacement was steadily postponed, there was no change on the stand that it was a mature product and therefore could do with less and less surveillance and maintenance. Does this sound like a familiar practice in IT?

3. The maintenance and test equipment used for NASA's shuttle fleet was 22 years old, far behind state of the art and beyond its lifecycle.

Such finding is most significant for business continuity because it documents that equipment that has fallen behind state of the art renders very bad service and is leading to disaster. If 22-year-old equipment is partly responsible for the shuttle's failure, what about the 40-year-old software still used by most banks and industrial firms?

4. Poor data quality has played a key role in the disaster because it kept the reasons for the oncoming failure opaque.

As the investigation panel revealed, during the last *Columbia* mission at least 75 shuttle experts with NASA and its contractors were so concerned about poor quality of data used for analyses they were preparing that they recommended taking photos of the shuttle in space. Those photos could have shown whether foam had damaged the left wing. Instead, NASA (mis)managers trusted the analysis that the experts said was so flawed.

Poor data is nothing new in business and that's why this book devoted Chapter 4 to the correlation between high-quality data mining and quality of service. Based on poor data, the analysts wrongly estimated where the foam hit and concluded that the shuttle had not sustained significant damage. Had NASA known the extent of the damage, it would have probably launched a rescue mission to save Columbia's crew. The use of poor data sets, augmented by flawed judgment, reinforced the issue of overdependence on simulations and vice versa. Although mathematical models are very useful tools, overdependence on them can be fatal.

To help in evaluating our hypotheses and assumptions, which is a must in experimentation, there is no substitute for real-life tests. Safety experts in high-risk industries say they have learned the hard way that mathematical formulas and computer simulations cannot fully emulate nature. The proof is that, in Columbia's case, the results by computer models and data analyses used to assess damage from foam strikes were fully inadequate and misleading.

As a matter of fact, several major aviation crashes and the Three-Mile Island nuclear accident were caused by poor analyses. Equally unreliable results have been produced by simulations done for option pricing and other derivative financial instruments because the hypotheses were flawed. That's precisely why Warren Buffett says that sometimes marking to model is marking to myth.

5. Mismanagement, too, played a major part in the disaster. Investigators found the space agency's managers *had no understanding of the work-*

ings of their organization and had been lulled into complacency by the shuttle's past success.[5]

This is the conclusion reached by the panel appointed by the U.S. government. As a consequence, the board of investigators has demanded an overhaul, not just of technical standards but also of the agency's "values, norms, beliefs, and practices." Board members essentially want NASA to break bad habits, including what it calls the agency's "culture of invincibility." This fits hand in glove with requirements connected to business continuity in the majority of companies.

"The old saying is 'technology is easy, people is hard,'" NASA board member Scott Hubbard said. If private and public entities think cultural change is tough, they should appreciate that it will be most difficult in an agency as proud as NASA, which has always thought of itself as can-do. Yet this was the same agency that the panel criticized for not having a plan to rescue *Columbia's* crew and that seemed uninterested in trying to determine how badly the shuttle was damaged after liftoff.

17.4 OPERATIONAL RISK CONTROL, CONTINGENCY PLANNING, AND DISASTER RECOVERY

Operational risk is embedded in practically every action we take. What is new about it is management's awareness, largely due to the fact that according to the new capital adequacy framework (Basel II, by the Basel Committee), banks must set aside adequate capital to cover operational risk. An operational risk control policy, says the Financial Services Authority (FSA), is all guidance on high level rules. The aim is to highlight issues for consideration, not just to be prescriptive. Therefore, policy developments must cover:

- Legal requirements, including internal and external events
- Management of people, including employee accountability
- Caliber of staff, including steady training
- Availability of staff, including what to do *if* unavoidability
- Management of processes and systems, including IT
- External changes, including effect on business continuity
- Outsourcing of services, including advantages and downside
- Capital requirements, including insurance coverage

As the careful reader will appreciate, an important consideration underpinning these eight bulleted items is preparedness. For instance, availability (and its opposite unavoidability) of skill and services primarily focuses on the company's own personnel and secondarily on dependability of supplies, which impacts upon business continuity.

In regard to outsourcing,[6] The Financial Services Authority (FSA) advises setting a minimum target of performance as well as making contingency arrangements. The FSA does not explicitly say so, but a recent European survey by the Gartner Group shows that as many as one in six outstanding contracts could be cut short because of unsatisfactory performance.[7]

Contingency planning is an integral part of an operational risk policy. In the United Kingdom, the Financial Services Authority underlines that operational risk disasters and contingency plans are, most definitely, senior management's concern. They represent a major challenge in day-to-day managerial responsibilities — while disaster planning is longer term, the availability of disaster recovery means must be instantaneous. A sound principle is that the longer-term policy reflects the fact that all firms are exposed to operational risk, and the breadth of operational risk impact can be wide.

Prominent among the factors driving this focus on operational risk are the new regulations, particularly in the financial industry. Reference has been made to the fact that the Basel Committee on Banking Supervision has revised and updated the 1988 Capital Accord (Basel I), and Basel II, the new accord, would be implemented, 2006. Basel II rules have strict requirements on operating risk management, and this is forcing a careful examination of disaster recovery at large and of data storage.

Take the annual growth in data storage and aftermath of decay in storage media as an example. The two issues are related, since the second increases at the heels of the first. In terms of cost-effectiveness, online data storage is significantly cheaper than paper or film. This, however, is not without challenges, which include the fast growth of online storage requirements and the skills and costs necessary for managing this storage.

In the United States, capital investment for databases stands at the level of 50 percent to 75 percent of IT expenditures for hardware. The cost of managing online storage is $300 per gigabyte per year, including tune-ups and backups. This is a significant expense, given that *petabyte* online memories are in the horizon.

The challenge associated with storage management, from both a business continuity and cost perspective, is increased by the fact that today over 56 percent of storage used in enterprises is networked rather than directly attached, according to Yankee Group.[8] Part of the reason is that the better-managed companies seek storage that can be accessed by more than one server — a positive note but with other consequences.

For obvious reasons, financial institutions and other companies want to break the physical link between an application server and its direct attached storage (DAS). This is a fundamental system design decision, and it represents a bid to wider sharing of data within the organization and with authorized external clients.

Such policy is a direct result of the growth in volume of information and the organizational dependency on it. Moreover, a flood of government regulations have been put into place since September 11. Compliance requirements for data retention, for example, have spurred a greater upsurge in storage activity than might otherwise have occurred.

An aftermath is that telephone companies have sensed an opportunity to offer managed storage solutions because connectivity is integral to taking data off site. But if the need to move corporate data away from a company's primary data center has coincided with the crash in bandwidth prices, it has also served to bring a greater amount of attention to risks connected to storage decay.

Digital media decay is a major operational risk that should attract full attention in contingency planning. It would be superfluous to explain why companies must make digital media preservation a priority when considering operational risks connected to computer systems. As Table 17.1 shows, statistics on storage decay are disquieting. Also arguments based on superior quality should not be taken at face value. These are estimates largely based on the assumption that media is accessed infrequently and stored under optimal conditions, whatever that means.

Whereas policies on operational risk control, contingency planning, and disaster recovery are in evolution, good lessons can be learned from other endeavors, like internal security in the United States and the role played by IT. The U.S. Congress has put some basic prerequisites to the approval of the new Department of Homeland Security. Three of these relate to state-of-the-art information technology:

■ Have up-to-date computers tied into a central intelligence network at every critical border crossing
■ Replace computer systems in the Treasury Department and Customs Service with up-to-date equipment

Table 17.1 Prevailing Statistics on Storage Decay

	Standard Quality	Superior Quality
Magnetic Tape Formats		
3480, 3490, 3490E	5 years	20 years
Optical Discs		
CD-ROM	5 years	50 years (?)
Magneto-Optical	2 years	30 years (?)
Microfilm		
Archival quality	50 years	100 years (?)

■ Effectively integrate the CIA, FBI, National Security Agency (NSA), and Drug Enforcement Administration (DEA) data that would go into the new department — a database challenge

Translated into a business perspective, this will mean stress tests to be conducted at all four pillars of a modern technological infrastructure and to the system as a whole. Figure 17.3 maps this process in visual form. Contingency plans must be developed for each of the main subsystems, and the same is true of policies and practices addressing damage control. Besides obtaining senior management's full support, to be effective any disaster recovery strategy has to ensure that:

■ The company's communications channels are always open
■ Recovery and damage control goals are explicitly stated
■ Disaster recovery training is an integral part of every manager's responsibilities

"Ultimately, what are we looking for?" asks Lisa Wild of FSA.[9] She answers her own query by saying that, in this domain, the British supervisory

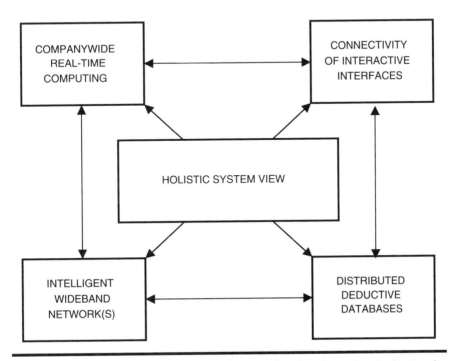

Figure 17.3   Solutions for Operational Risk Control and Business Continuity Require Stress Tests of All Major Subsystems and of the Whole Aggregate

authority's goals target senior management buy-in; emphasis on sound practices, not minimum compliance; firm understanding of operational risks and of the way to control them; and properly documented, fully updated damage-control processes. All this together makes a rigorous internal culture directed to operational risks.

Companies with experience in contingency planning and disaster recovery appreciate that many systems and procedures relative to operational risk control relate to the business architecture that has been chosen (see Chapter 13) and the infrastructure that has been implemented, for example, multiple mapping of information elements into arrays of independent disks used as servers, so that if one of them goes down, it does not mutilate the company's database.

Disaster recovery is also highly dependent on software for deal mirroring, which is internal to the application, directing an image of the transaction in different systems. As these references demonstrate, hardware and software requirements correlate. For instance, the level of mirroring is a function of both available disk space in independent units and sophisticated software support.

Ideally, disaster recovery must be parameterized. The best approach is through mirroring, the challenge being that not many institutions have a real-time mirror system. A large number still work through father–grandfather generations of data, a 50-year-old solution. This is an issue of technology leadership. In disaster recovery, as everywhere else, institutions pay a heavy price for maintaining medieval approaches.

For the record, a modern solution will not only focus on real-time mirroring but also see to it that everything is on an intranet or another private network, with backups in case a problem might occur. Some companies are concerned with whether being on the Internet is good enough. As we have already seen, there is security risk; because of this, for financial transactions private networks with 99.99 percent reliability are a better option, though a more expensive one.

17.5 CONTROLLING THE COMPANY'S COST STRUCTURE THROUGH TECHNOLOGY

Since Chapter 1, this book has pressed the point that costs matter. Chapters 13 and 14 made several references to the need for cost control. Chapter 16 brought to the reader's attention that with pricing power having taken a leave because of globalization, small- and medium-sized enterprises are particularly vulnerable if they are not in charge of their costs. Eventually, failure to control costs leads to the greatest business discontinuity of them all: bankruptcy.

But the assurance of business continuity also costs money. The same is true of operational risk control. Therefore, significant attention should be paid in swamping costs, not only in regard to issues that are the primary subject of this chapter but much more generally throughout the landscape of a company's activities, including IT.

Chapters 7 and 8, respectively, have stated that both the EIS and CIS should be responsive to the need of improving the quality of the company's information services while at the same time helping in bending the costs curve. Cost control are less of a problem as long as profit margins are fat, because fat profit margins are usually hiding many inefficiencies. However, without pricing power, wide profit margins are not possible and vigilance in cost cutting has become essential. The Internet, executive information systems, and client information systems can make a significant contribution in this effort.

Sometimes projects are undertaken without appropriately studying their consequences in terms of costs, deliverables, and return on investment (ROI). Data warehouses are an example of the failure of half-baked measures compared to the alternative of real-time solutions. Based on research findings, a recent estimate has been that two out of three data warehouse implementations have failed to produce promised results. Responsible for this shortfall is a wide range of reasons, including:

- Poorly defined goals
- Organizational hurdles
- Too little, too late in deliverables
- Technological inefficiencies
- Poor project management

Company politics and keeping data too close to one's chest also play a role in gaining only mediocre ROI, if any at all. Data warehousing brings out the same problems that have long existed with management information systems and decision support approaches: cultural, managerial, and the geriatric survival of old platforms.

Failure to capitalize on new technology is instrumental in keeping operational costs high. According to Merrill Lynch, the banking industry's average cost per transaction is 1 cent on the Internet versus $1.07 at a branch, 54 cents on the phone, and 27 cents at an automated teller machine (ATM). A Microsoft study estimates that switching the mortgage process to a full-service, Web-based activity could eliminate two of the three percentage points people currently pay in closing costs.

Apart from the lack of pricing power, the growing competition is a crucial reason why cost cutting has become a vital exercise. Internet business can be much more efficient because through connectivity lenders have easier access to data about borrowers. Another reason is that lenders may quickly bundle the loans together and sell them to investors in a fast-track securitization.

Such processes are available to every entity, and competitive pressure on financial institutions to bring down costs is tremendous. One likely innovation in the coming years is the emergence of Web-based aggregators of financial services. Using technology, these aggregators will automatically allow companies and individuals to simultaneously monitor all their financial relationships and to experiment on cost–benefit in order to optimize revenue and expenses.

Optimization for cost–benefit reasons is a fundamental process at the financial end of business continuity, and it is done by a growing number of industrial entities. If banks do not respond in kind, they will lose another chunk of their intermediation. Well-managed credit institutions understand this kind of risk and are using data collected through their client information systems to improve their ways and means to cut costs (see in Chapter 8 the discussion on the customer mirror). In the banking industry, for instance, being in control of one's costs means assurance that less than 50 percent of noninterest budget is for personnel expenditures, the so-called overhead.

To bring overhead below that benchmark, a bank has to have a standard costing system as well as senior management guidelines to target profitability on all income and expense items. An example of a profitability target is more than 20 percent return on investment on information technology.

A properly designed executive information system must capitalize on the fact that the ingenious use of Internet facilities can turn commercial costs on their head, including client acquisition, the act of selling, and maintenance of client relations. Rigorous cost studies must see to it that each cost chapter is thoroughly revised to cut off the fat.

The Internet and other IT tools are enablers. They are not a goal.

Another prerequisite is to put quotas (quantitative objectives) on cost performance and to control compliance. Not only must the productivity of every person working for an organization be steadily improved but also, because of the wider diffusion of information, some functions that have become deadwood should be chopped off. Their continuous existence in the organizational chart drains financial resources.

When in the late 1980s and early 1990, expert systems started to perform the "assistant to" and other middle-management chores, clear-eyed organizations did not miss the opportunity to flatten their structure by eliminating entire middle-management layers. In a meeting in London, the then-general manager of IBM said that expert systems were doing a good part of the job formerly performed by layers of middle management.

Only well-managed companies pay due attention to gains to be derived by high tech. For others, reengineering and cost control are pipe dreams. Many financial institutions, for instance, still fail to appreciate that the banking system, as we know it, was designed when information about markets and companies was costly to acquire — and secretive. But with the Internet, this has changed. *If* the cost of acquiring and disseminating information falls, *then* the advantage of the old model falls, too. Banks need a new paradigm.

Competitiveness is no longer based on old standards. Indeed, altering the way of doing business becomes a criterion for survival. For more than a decade, sophisticated software has added itself to global networking, and obtained results in competitiveness are one of the key reasons why the old model of banking is no longer rewarding. Still, there is resistance to change and this comes from different sources:

- Company politics
- Backward looking senior management
- Failure to define the exact nature of costs
- An obsolete methodology that continues to be employed

Some of the roles played in the past by investment advisers are an example of organizational deadwood. Knowledge engineering now provides programs that can continuously calculate an individual's net worth by keeping track of all of the investors' assets, liabilities, and their market value. Agents are able to search the universe of financial institutions and report on lowest-interest rate mortgages or highest-yield money-market rates. Why shouldn't a warning system exist when a desired asset allocation is out of balance?

Such examples are largely based on current accomplishments and document that knowledge-enriched Internet applications are changing the nature of financial services more rapidly than we have imagined. Only top-tier banks comprehend the depth of this change, which cuts to the bone of the intermediary's business.

In conclusion, i-commerce and i-banking have created a new landscape of competition in business. The good news is that they present a pallet of opportunities. The bad news, for backward-looking entities, is that they are squeezing per-unit profits further by providing an even more cost-efficient mode of production and distribution. In merchandising, many items that can be purchased at a traditional retail store are available on the Web. For cost-conscious consumers, the trend adds up to unparalleled leverage. For sellers, savings come via lower brick-and-mortar costs and other reduced outlays.

This has been true for several years, but it took time to slip into the organizational conscience. In mid-1999, a Lehman Brothers survey compared i-commerce prices of more than 100 retail items with those in moderately priced retail outlets in the New York City area. On average, they found that goods cost about 13 percent less on the Web. Such price disparity has increased over the years. No executive who rates the survival of his company seriously would forget such statistics. Exploring new opportunities offered to the real-time enterprise is a complex operation that necessitates well-trained personnel prepared for this role.

17.6 NOTES

1. James Gleick, *Genius. The Life and Science of Richard Feynman*, Pantheon Books, New York, 1992.
2. D.N. Chorafas, *Stress Testing. Risk Management Strategies for Extreme Events*, Euromoney Books, London, 2003.
3. *Total Telecom Magazine*, December 2003.
4. *USA Today*, September 5, 2003.
5. *USA Today*, August 27, 2003.
6. D.N. Chorafas, *Outsourcing, Insourcing and IT for Enterprise Management*, Macmillan/Palgrave, London, 2003.
7. *Total Telecom Magazine*, December 2003.
8. *Total Telecom Magazine*, July 2003.
9. As outlined in her lecture to the "Basel II Masterclass" by IIR, London, March 27–28, 2003.

V

INDEX

INDEX